Reshaping Welfare States and Activation Regimes in Europe

P.I.E. Peter Lang

Bruxelles · Bern · Berlin · Frankfurt am Main · New York · Oxford · Wien

SALTSA

A Joint Programme for Working Life Research in Europe

SALTSA is a programme of partnership in European working life research run by the Swedish National Institute for Working Life (NIWL/ALI) and the Swedish Confederations of Trade Unions (LO), Professional Employees (TCO) and Professional Associations (SACO).

The aim of SALTSA is to generate applicable research results of a high academic standard and relevance. Research is largely project-based.

Research is carried out in three areas:
* the labour market
* work organisation
* the work environment

The Work Environment and Health Programme

Research on work environment and health focuses instruments and methods for healthier working conditions, the effects of certain risks in current working life as well as the conditions of selected groups of workers. Projects are designed with the ambition to contribute to the political debate and decision-making, applied occupational health and work environment management as well as participatory processes involving social partners in European working life.

Chairman of the SALTSA Programme is Professor Lars Magnusson and programme secretary for this area is Charlotta Krafft.

website: www.niwl.se/saltsa

Amparo SERRANO PASCUAL & Lars MAGNUSSON (eds.)

Reshaping Welfare States and Activation Regimes in Europe

SALTSA — JOINT PROGRAMME
FOR WORKING LIFE RESEARCH IN EUROPE
The National Institute for Working Life and The Swedish Trade Unions in Co-operation

"Work & Society"
No.54

No part of this book may be reproduced in any form, by print, photocopy, microfilm or any other means, without prior written permission from the publisher. All rights reserved.

© P.I.E. PETER LANG S.A.
Éditions scientifiques internationales
Brussels, 2007
1 avenue Maurice, 1050 Brussels, Belgium
info@peterlang.com; www.peterlang.com

ISSN 1376-0955
ISBN 13 978-90-5201-048-9
US ISBN 978-0-8204-6693-4
D/2007/5678/10

Printed in Germany

Bibliographic information published by "Die Deutsche Bibliothek"
"Die Deutsche Bibliothek" lists this publication in the "Deutsche Nationalbibliografie"; detailed bibliographic data is available on the Internet at <http://dnb.ddb.de>.
CIP available from the British Library, GB and the Library of Congress, USA.

Table of Contents

Acknowledgments 9

Reshaping Welfare States: Activation Regimes in Europe 11
  Amparo SERRANO PASCUAL

**The United Kingdom's 'Work First' Welfare State
and Activation Regimes in Europe** 35
  Colin LINDSAY

**Activation in the Netherlands:
The Gradual Introduction of a Paradigm Shift** 71
  Rik VAN BERKEL

**Danish Activation Policy: The Role of the Normative Foundation,
the Institutional Set-up and Other Drivers** 99
  Flemming LARSEN and Mikkel MAILAND

Activation Policy in Sweden 127
  Eskil WADENSJÖ

**The French Activation Strategy
in a Comparative Perspective** 145
  Jean-Claude BARBIER

**The Commitment to Be Actively Available
for Work and Employment Policy in Spain** 173
  Jorge ARAGÓN, Fernando ROCHA, Ana SANTANA
  and Jorge TORRENTS

**The Activation Trend in Portuguese Social Policy.
An Open Process?** 207
  Pedro HESPANHA

**Activation Policies and Shaping Factors
in the Czech Republic** 241
  Tomáš SIROVÁTKA

Activation Regimes in Europe: A Clustering Exercise 275
  Amparo SERRANO PASCUAL

Notes on Contributors 317

Acknowledgments

This book has been prepared as a result of interdisciplinary research supported by the Swedish Saltsa research programme and the Research Department of the European Trade Union Institution for Research, Health and Safety (ETUI-REHS). As a follow-up to previous study on the implementation of the activation concept in a number of European countries, the Swedish Saltsa programme, together with the ETUI-REHS, organised a collective research project in order to identify different activation regimes within the EU. We have invited groups of National experts to identify the main items characterising the way activation has been implemented at a national level. We met twice in Brussels to discuss the framework for the research project, as well as national reports.

First of all, we would like to thank the Saltsa programme and ETUI-REHS, whose financial and intellectual support have made this research project possible. We are also very grateful to the contributors to this volume for the quality of their contributions and their commitment to the research work.

The ETUI-REHS is financially supported by the European Commission.

Reshaping Welfare States: Activation Regimes in Europe

Amparo SERRANO PASCUAL

Introduction

Welfare models shape the 'social question' at a symbolic level in any community and affect the way in which social responsibility for tackling social exclusion is shared among the various core institutions in society (the Welfare State, the family, the individual and the market). They also bring communities together, giving them a sense of cultural identity and providing their representatives with political legitimation. All these models form the essence of the hegemonic interpretations made to determine the most pressing social problems (i.e. the ones considered 'unfair' and therefore labelled 'problematic', a *social problem*), as well as who is responsible for solving them (the individual, the Welfare State, the market or the family, etc.). Welfare policies aimed at tackling issues such as unemployment, social exclusion and poverty are a good example of this situation.

Government intervention in the political regulation of markets is currently being affected by different trends, such as the onward march of European economic integration and globalisation, demographic changes and ideological regulation promoted by supranational institutions. A state's ability to invest in welfare measures is being curbed by the requirements of the Economic and Monetary Union EMU) process, where budgetary austerity is often the leading principle. Consequently, we are faced with new conditions and a new set of rules that are placing significant limits on the implementation of Keynesian-oriented policies.

At the same time, the demands placed on the Welfare State are being transformed as a result of the changing qualifications and skills required by the production system, the ageing population and companies' 'vocal' demands for changes to be made to social regulation standards (flexibility). These demographic phenomena and changes in the structure of industry are resulting in a transformation of welfare models at both an ideological and institutional level. On the one hand, there have been changes in regulatory benchmarks and in the hegemonic understanding of the nature of the problem and who is responsible for dealing with it. On the other, there is a shift in the precarious (im) balance of power among social actors, putting workers/citizens in a more vulnerable position *vis-à-vis* industry's new demands. In this context, we are witnessing an exhaustive regulatory reassessment of welfare models, resulting in what could be described as a new activation paradigm. This paradigm goes beyond mere intervention in the labour market in order to help unemployed people into work. It involves a policy of producing individuals and identities that conform more readily to industry's new rules and as such it also involves a new understanding of citizenship.

This activation paradigm redefines 'what is normal at work'. It also redefines the representation of citizenship and our understanding of what is fair and justifiable or unfair and unjustifiable, as well as what rights people should be entitled to and the extent to which State intervention should be possible.

This book analyses the extent of these changes from a cross-cultural perspective. Researchers from eight EU member states have studied the complex nature of these regulatory changes and the extent to which they have been influenced by supranational actors, such as the European institutions. A previous study (Serrano Pascual (ed.) 2004) showed that there has been a process of convergence towards a common regulatory paradigm, but that this has nevertheless resulted in very different policies, depending on the role played by various institutional and ideological factors.

This conclusion led to a desire to identify possible activation regimes within the European Union that might explain these diverse responses. These activation regimes represent the social, regulatory and institutional frameworks a given community relies on to tackle problems construed as being social. Identifying activation regimes will enable us to resolve the contradiction characterising the debate on the direction of current changes. On the one hand, there is an analytical perspective focused on convergence processes arising mainly from the role of supranational institutions, other hegemonic discourses and the spread of certain ideologies. On the other, there is a perspective based on the role of historical and institutional contexts in interpreting the process, focusing on the diverse nature of these changes due to their specific historical development (path dependency).

Section 1 of this introductory chapter will begin by describing the nature and principles of this new activation paradigm. Section 2 will look at the issue of supranational regulation by EU institutions, one of the factors that have influenced the trend towards the adoption of the activation paradigm, at least in certain EU member states.

Following on from the introduction, chapters 2 to 9 will examine the key activation approaches and policies in various European countries, as well as look at the role played by institutional, sociological and economic factors in the development of each country's specific activation measures. Eight countries participated in this study: the United Kingdom (Lindsay, Chapter 3), the Netherlands (van Berkel, Chapter 4), Denmark (Larsen and Mailand, Chapter 5), Sweden (Wadensjö, Chapter 6), France (Barbier, Chapter 7), Spain (Aragón, Rocha and Torrens, Chapter 8), Portugal (Hespanha, Chapter 9) and the Czech Republic (Sirovátka, Chapter 10). These countries have different welfare regimes, as defined by Esping Andersen (1996) and Ferrera (1996), and are intended to be representative of the huge diversity of regimes found in the European Union. At the same time, however, in the interests of identifying intra-cluster differences, some countries which have the same regime were also selected (France and the Netherlands from the continental regime; Sweden and Denmark from the Scandinavian regime; Portugal and Spain from the Mediterranean regime). The remaining two countries are the UK, which represents the liberal regime, and the Czech Republic which represents the new EU member states.

The concluding chapter, chapter 10, will outline a typology of activation regimes based on the information presented in the country chapters in this book. To this end, this chapter explores what is meant by a 'regime', and the characteristics of what we have chosen to call 'activation regimes'. These characteristics can be divided into two main groups. Firstly, what could broadly be described as institutional and political factors: modes of institutional governance (i.e. the role of the various institutions and the balance of power between them), as well as the various historical agreements between the social actors. Secondly, sociological factors: the prevailing ideological and cultural traditions in a given country. These play an important role in how the problem is defined and who is seen as being responsible for tackling it. By considering these two groups of factors, we are adopting a multidisciplinary approach that will allow us to present a pluralistic analysis of the transformation process. Chapter 2 will conclude by proposing an activation regime typology based on the three groups.

Using the *activation regimes* approach as the basis for analysing changes in the intervention models will enable us to offer an explanation for certain trends within the EU that all converge on the adoption of the activation paradigm (e.g. the increase in availability assessments, shortening of benefit periods, increasing use of sanctions, wider redefinition of suitable jobs, expansion of the group of activation policies), while at the same time also stressing the significant national differences in the content of these activation programmes.

Activation Policies: A New Intervention Paradigm?

The intervention paradigm based on the concept of activation[1] is characterised by three fundamental features:

- an *individualised approach*: rather than creating appropriate political conditions for the fair redistribution of wealth, the aim is to change individual behaviour, motivation and attitudes. These policies favour increased individualisation of interventions (tailored, client-centred services) and greater involvement of the beneficiary. The regulatory and legitimating benchmark for these policies is the individual.

- an emphasis on *employment*: the goal of these policies is employment (work focus) and autonomy. The policies are targeted at influencing individual behaviour in the labour market (providing incentives, persuading and motivating individuals). The focus is on the economic aspects of citizenship rather than on political or social ones.

- *contractualisation as a core principle*, in two respects: firstly, the contract has become the fundamental metaphor as far as guiding and legitimating these policies is concerned, and secondly, it involves a change in the terms of the social contract that has traditionally been used to define the concept of citizenship. It has become more of a moral contract than a social or political one. Citizens' access to their rights is now conditional on their attitude and behaviour with regard to their employment. In addition to the contract as a key social regulation mechanism, the 'reciprocity norm' is reaffirmed, and 'deservingness' becomes one of the key principles underpinning the legitimacy of citizenship itself. This explains why social partners' political campaigns for legitimate welfare intervention are focusing on the concept of 'suitable jobs'.

The following table attempts to summarise this paradigm shift[2] in the intervention model:

---

[1] We are using the concept of 'activation' in a different sense to related concepts such as 'active policies' (which covers almost all labour market policies) or 'workfare policies' (which has an excessive focus on the punitive aspects of some activation policies). Our definition of the term is a general and comprehensive, designed to allow us to identify the changes in the principles according to which Welfare States are run with a view to drawing up a classification of activation regimes. A disciplinary or emancipatory aim-based definition, for example, or definitions based on the intervention method (punishment, obligation) could be problematic, since other studies (see, for example, Serrano Pascual 2004) have shown that aims and methods vary from one country to another. In the context of this analysis, activation policies may be understood as a *new intervention paradigm*

[2] Hall (1993) argues that in order to be able to talk of a *paradigm shift*, the changes need to go beyond simply modifying existing instruments or political strategies; a

Table 1. Changes in Intervention Paradigms

	Intervention paradigm based on the provision of welfare	Intervention paradigm based on the provision of activation
Location of the problem	Political economy. Wrong functioning of the market	Personal behaviour Individual attitudes
Meaning of social integration	Political, social and economic integration	Economic integration
Concept of citizenship	Condition which entitles citizens to rights	Status to be deserved. Rights are conditional on responsible behaviour

Individualisation of Interventions Targeted at Managing Behaviour

The activation-based intervention model is leading to an increasingly individualised approach to tackling the problem of labour market exclusion. Individualisation can be understood in two ways. On the one hand, the individual is the primary focus of interventions (and is consequently also viewed as part of the problem) (supply side policy) and, on the other, there is a growing tendency to promote the individual's involvement in his own integration. What both of these aspects share is a growing emphasis on requiring 'clients' (i.e. benefit recipients) to behave like responsible citizens. The result is a shift in the nature of the problem being tackled: rather than being a fight against poverty, it is now, above all, a fight against (welfare) dependency.

This emphasis on the individual as the primary focus of interventions is related to a change in prevailing ontological assumptions and the resulting transformation in the social representation of citizenship and agency. Dean (Dean 2003) distinguishes between two hegemonic concepts of what constitutes an individual. The first is the liberal/contractual standing of the human condition that stresses the importance of individual responsibility. Social order among autonomous individuals can only be maintained if dependency is combated and prevented. This Hobbe-

---

paradigm shift involves redefining policy goals and the institutional setting. Table 1 presents the arguments that we feel indicate the existence of a paradigm shift: there has been a fundamental change in the basic concepts underpinning intervention models, for example the way in which the problem is explained and justified, the concept of citizenship, and the very meaning and goals of intervention itself. As demonstrated by the country chapters in this study (see in particular the chapter on the Netherlands by van Berkel), this intervention paradigm has repercussions not only for the goals of welfare intervention, but also for the institutional framework of the Welfare State.

sian approach is likely to favour policies geared towards labour market attachment. In contrast, the second type of policy favours a concept of solidarity in recognition of the fact that human beings are interdependent. In this case, individuals are perceived as vulnerable to exploitation. While the first notion is typical of activation policies, the second ontological assumption can be said to characterise social welfare policies.

These different understandings of human nature influence the terms defining the prevailing representation of social inequality. While industrialised societies have traditionally regarded inequality as a social problem, the new social paradigm attributes social inequality to individual shortcomings (in terms of motivation, ethical will, training and personality) and this in turn contributes to the legitimation of certain types of intervention. Consequently, these practices are noted for transforming the approach to intervention and how the problem is viewed. Instead of interventions tackling the factors that affect the demand for labour through Keynesian macroeconomic policies, the focus of intervention has shifted to the supply side, i.e. interventions concerning individuals' motivation and desire to work. In other words, the tendency is for there to be a greater and more explicit emphasis on individual responsibilities.

The spread of this activation model has led to a regulatory reassessment of the principles underpinning previous intervention models, principles based on the hegemonic representations of unemployment. 'Un-employment', or the lack of employability ('un-employability') is now represented as an individual problem. Unlike the old paradigm, this new representation of unemployment does not appeal to society's moral and political awareness, since it is regarded as the worker's individual responsibility. Instead of promoting moral awareness, it generates interventions with a significant punitive content. Individual willingness and responsibility are fundamental principles of this model, making it appear only fair that individuals fulfil their duty to tackle their problems themselves. The individual is considered to be mainly responsible for managing risk (of losing his job, for example) and this risk is viewed as something that is inevitable. This approach to understanding the social question results in citizenship being regarded not as an inalienable right but rather as a status[3] that individuals have to earn for themselves. It sees citizenship mainly in individual rather than social terms, i.e. as something that is determined by individual behaviour (individual choices and attitudes), with the focus more on individual responsibilities

---

[3] This concept opposes the notion of citizenship in industrialised societies, where, according to Marshall's definition (1950), it is the status conferred upon those who are members of a community (Handler 2006).

than on those of society as a whole. At the same time, it considers that the role of the Welfare State is to combat 'dependency'. The core of the social question is no longer the relationship of dependency between workers and the market. Rather, the issue is increasingly the problem of dependency on the Welfare State.

Consequently, we are witnessing a transformation of the concept of social citizenship and its relationship with the Welfare State. The State as the guarantor of social rights (the 'entitlement State') is being replaced by the State as the regulator of individuals' behaviour (the 'enabling State'), i.e. a State whose main role is to ensure responsibilities, values and opportunities. The socialisation of responsibility is being replaced by the concept of 'individual responsibility', where the individual becomes the focus of the debate and of the interventions aimed at tackling the problem.

Thus, the spread of this intervention paradigm is not only leading to new intervention instruments (introduction of punitive measures, tightening of the rules governing access to social welfare), but also to new arguments for justifying and legitimating these instruments, and indeed to a new understanding of social rights. In other words, we are seeing a major shift in the distribution of social responsibilities between the individual and the Welfare State.

Solidarity (or collective responsibility) is being replaced as the principle underpinning State action by a growing emphasis on individual responsibility, a trend that is legitimating the coercive nature of the majority of activation programmes. Their justification rests on the moral (and therefore universal) principle derived from the duties contained in each individual's (citizen's) contract with the State.

This approach is based on a psychologistic concept of social relationships, according to which activation would comprise a process of individualisation aimed at increasing the individual's autonomy (Franssen 2003). In this discourse on dependency and responsibility, the language of 'rights', based on the view that the provision of social security is a collective responsibility, is gradually being replaced with a discourse that stresses the morality of responsibility (Dean 2003).

It would seem, therefore, that although the State is required to intervene, the nature of the intervention changes. Rather than consolidating the political and institutional conditions for the redistribution of wealth, it is designed to emphasise personal responsibilities, exert influence through incentives, and coerce people's will. As a result, political problems are turned into a matter of personal motivation and will (Crespo Suárez and Serrano Pascual 2004 and forthcoming), thereby promoting a *depoliticisation* of the management of social conflict. This approach prevents social exclusion from emerging as a socio-political issue by eliminating any suggestion of a causal link between it and relationships based on power and oppression.[4]

In this context, active involvement will not necessarily lead to social emancipation, since activation policies contain a dual element of complementary exogenous and endogenous pressures.[5] On the one hand, they use punitive measures in order to influence the behaviour of individuals, while on the other hand they are designed to create standardised individuals. Three practices are employed to produce individuals in this way: punishment, standardisation and supervision.

Welfare recipients are considered to be likely to have a range of shortcomings, in their training in some case, and in their willingness to participate or their personality, in others. Consequently, in many countries, a paternalistic intervention model is gaining currency, the key feature of which is *therapeutic medicalisation* (Schram 2000). Schram suggests that this medicalisation goes beyond individualisation, since it consists in

> the tendency to construct welfare dependency as an illness. [...] It legitimates new forms of power, procedures and processes in the administration of welfare that deemphasise the allocation of income and emphasise the treatment of poverty in terms of correcting personal problems and monitoring behaviour. To medicalise welfare dependency is to create the conditions for moving welfare from an income redistribution scheme to a behaviour modification regime (Schram: 82).

The influence that this activation paradigm is having on people's analysis and understanding of the problem helps to explain the fact that individualised punitive models based on activation are even spreading into geographical areas suffering from high levels of job insecurity and unemployment, where one would think that the important social aspects of the problem would be particularly apparent. Lindsay's contribution to this book shows that even when activation measures are implemented in parts of Britain with high levels of poverty and unemployment, the focus of the intervention and the way in which the problem is diagnosed still favour supply-side policies and a greater emphasis on compulsory elements. Indeed, in some countries the debate is starting to focus on questions linked to the 'culture of worklessness' and 'poverty of aspira-

---

[4] For an interesting analysis of the emergence of social categories that have polarised the debate concerning "involuntary" exclusion from work, as well as the social and political nature of the problem, see Salais *et al.* (1986) and Topalov (1994).

[5] For more on the difference between exogenous and endogenous pressures, see Foucault (1975).

tions', strengthening still further the moralistic dimension in dissecting the problem.

Rather than promoting citizenship, this tendency to control the behaviour of unemployed people systematically as part of the assistance offered to help them find work and gain economic independence may in fact impede it, since it causes individuals to feel that they are being controlled, thereby reducing their ability to act independently (Goul Andersen 2001).

The Economic Interpretation of Social Exclusion: Work as a Civil Duty

The standard solution proposed for the majority of both individual and social problems (social exclusion, lack of equal opportunities, lack of competitiveness, psychosocial problems, etc.) is for people to find work.[6] The creation of this work myth explains why most strategies for combating social exclusion focus on providing incentives for people to enter the workforce. As such, work is presented as a remedy that will solve everything. The cases of the Netherlands and France show that there has been a gradual decline in forms of intervention such as voluntary work or supported employment, which were conceived both as stepping stones to employment and also as a means of promoting social and political participation. Instead, the current trend is to favour measures exclusively geared towards finding regular work in the labour market. Despite the questionable nature of the argument that employment is the only path to citizenship,[7] this type of activation policy presents it as an indisputable fact. Nevertheless, policies that are branded with the misnomer of 'passive' can also be (and indeed have been) understood as a means of promoting the participation of unemployed people in society (Serrano Pascual 2003).

Under this paradigm, the social citizenship that allowed individuals to be protected in the face of the unequal balance of power in the market is transformed into an economic citizenship that is based on participa-

---

[6] Goul Andersen questions this underlying premise of activation policies. In an empirical study of unemployed Danish people in the 1990s, he shows that many of the negative psychosocial effects observed in studies of unemployed people are not so much due to the fact that they are out of work as to the fact that they do not have enough money. Activation policies nevertheless take the exact opposite approach, by assuming that personal wellbeing can only be achieved through work, while financial security offers nothing more than passive support (Goul Andersen 2001).

[7] For a well-reasoned discussion of the questionable correlation between employment and personal wellbeing and of whether or not passive policies act as a disincentive to labour integration, see Goul Andersen (2001) and van Berkel and Moller (2002).

tion in the market (Saint Martín 2001). This economic citizenship not only requires workers to be more or less (un)conditionally available to meet the demands of the market, it also expects them to show that they are available (i.e. to show willing). As such, this intervention paradigm is based on a moral understanding of work as a *civil duty*. Work is therefore seen as a prerequisite for citizenship, a fact that constitutes a paradigm shift away from previous ideas about exclusion and access to citizenship. At the same time, the meaning of the social question is also changing. The emphasis is no longer so much on guaranteeing people the provision of financial support and security throughout their lives but rather on guaranteeing them the chance to work. As for the Welfare State, its role is now to socialise individuals to be workers rather than to be individuals (Holden 2003).

As a result, the policies based on this new way of perceiving social problems are geared towards increasing the economic activity rate and not just the employment rate (by discouraging people from taking early retirement, promoting work-life balance in order to encourage more women into employment, introducing tax and social security reforms, tightening access to unemployment benefit or incapacity benefit, etc.). In addition to encouraging unemployed people to find work, these policies are also increasingly questioning the legitimacy of economic inactivity (on the grounds of sickness, childcare, old age, training, etc.) (Bonvin 2004). This process is having major repercussions in terms of the role that work is acquiring in our societies as something that legitimates and gives meaning to our existence. The trend is for employment to be seen more as a civil duty than as a right, while rights and responsibilities are viewed as part of a reciprocal exchange whereby social rights can be reduced to nothing more than having the opportunity to work. According to Dean (2003), this view is based on viewing the individual as an independent, competitive being rather than as a social being subject to interdependent relationships and consequently also vulnerable to exploitation. Consequently, economic and market operation problems become individual, moral and psychological concerns (Crespo Suárez and Serrano Pascual, forthcoming).

The term 'security' (protection against risk), which was the basis of the structure of the protective Welfare State, is now changing its meaning to 'the ability to adapt to change'. The Welfare State's purpose is, therefore, no longer to protect against the risks inherent in a market economy, but rather to create the right conditions and attitudes for people to adapt to the requirements of an ever-changing economy. In other words, its role is to motivate the workforce and teach people how to sell and market themselves, how to 'turn themselves into entrepreneurs'. Paradoxically, this approach appeals to a semantic register based on individual freedom, personal choice, self-fulfilment and initiative. The idea is to tap into individuals' potential and ability to act in order to increase their autonomy, in other words to produce individuals who are capable of independently managing their own integration and participation in society (Franssen 2003), in other words, individuals capable of taking control of their own lives.

What we are witnessing here is the Welfare State turning into a modern project, into a 'tutor' State that implements supply-side interventions. It reinforces human capital and fosters 'individual agency': providing people with ethical skills (self-management, self-help and self-reliance) so that a new kind of worker can be created, who is more flexible, active, employable, etc. As a result, the Welfare State's main purpose is to regulate behaviour, basing its intervention on the principle of welfare as a moral issue (Serrano Pascual 2003).

Consequently, the State's role is not to offer protection against market forces but rather to encourage a more dynamic market. As such, this discourse is proposing a redistribution of responsibilities between the individual and the Welfare State, while at the same time conspicuously failing to make any mention of the role of businesses in the fight against social exclusion. While this regulatory reassessment redefines the position of individual citizens and the Welfare State, however, it not only fails to question the laws of the market but actually contributes to consolidating them and establishing them as something that is to be taken for granted (Alonso 1999).

A Moral Contract with the Community: Creating a New Kind of Worker

In order to understand the nature of the changes arising from this concept, it is important to begin with a brief outline of the principles on which social welfare in industrialised societies was founded. One of the authors who has most successfully analysed the link between social welfare and the Welfare State is Esping Andersen (1996). According to this author, the main goal of the Welfare State has traditionally been to afford protection against market forces, meaning that social service provision was therefore an inalienable right. Consequently, social citizenship was a status enjoyed by everyone (Marshall 1950). The fact that it was a social right meant that individuals could make their own choices free from the constraints of market forces. Social rights varied from one country to another, depending on the extent to which they enabled individuals to maintain a certain standard of living independently of market forces. This protection of workers against market forces was intended to act as a safety net to prevent them from being exploited in the market, in view of the unequal balance of power that characterises the commercial relationship between employers and employees. As such, it strengthened the position of the worker and curbed the authority of employers (Esping Andersen 1996). Recognition of the imbalance in the contractual relationship between employer and employee led to the socialisation of risk, with risk being defined as a social (mutualisation of risk) rather than an individual matter. The Welfare State's main role has, therefore, been to guarantee individual autonomy with respect to the market.

This is the background to understanding the change in the meaning of social welfare that is brought about by the activation paradigm. Rather than providing protection against market forces, social welfare's main goal under the new paradigm is to help workers adapt to market requirements. The activation paradigm therefore involves a transformation of the principles solidarity is based on. It ignores the social causes of poverty and alters the fundamental approach to the issue, moving from a political analysis to a more individual or moral interpretation (every individual's moral duty to take responsibility for himself).

The result is a change in the construction of the problem. Rather than focusing on 'un-employment', which could lead to a social analysis of the social and structural causes of job shortage, the problem is instead being defined in terms of lower economic activity rates. Welfare policies based on a social concept of risk (unemployment benefit, sick pay, early retirement, sabbaticals, etc.) are described as (or perhaps it would be more appropriate to say *branded*) 'passive'. Attempts to provide ideological justification for this approach go beyond purely financial arguments of the ilk that the Welfare State is in the throes of a financial crisis, since passive measures account for only a small percentage of total national welfare spending.[8] Neither are social reasons the main justification put forward, given the fact that various evaluation studies[9] have shown this type of measure to have limited effectiveness in combating unemployment and social exclusion. Rather, the focus is on the moral side of the question, whereby passivity is understood to generate dependency and an abdication of social responsibility. These moral aspects form part of a broader social demand: the moral obligation for people to be *self-governed individuals* (Bauman 1998). The following table offers a summary of the various concepts underpinning the new social contract with the community:

---

[8] See Barbier and Theret (2004) for details of the French situation.
[9] Barbier (2006); De la Porte and Pochet (2003a); Serrano Pascual (2004).

Table 2. Social Contract

	Welfare State	Enabling State
Main principle underlying the institutionalisation of solidarity: theoretical approach to agency and dependency	Asymmetrical relationship between citizen/market: need for protection against market forces Dependency on the market: risk of exploitation	Ensuring individual agency (economic independence) Dependency on the State, passivity promoted by previous ways of dealing with risk
Main concept of risk	Social risk: individual is not responsible for risk Socialisation of risk	Individual risk: moral principles – understanding of work – and the individual's behaviour regarding his own transition into the labour market
Role of the State	Decommodification	Enhance individual responsibility

Consequently, this type of intervention can be geared towards both developing human capital and increasing the reserve workforce, as well as towards providing people with moral skills, such as self-management, self-help and self-reliance, in order to create a new kind of worker who is more flexible, responsible and active.

Factors Explaining the EU Convergence towards the Activation Paradigm: The Role of the European Employment Strategy

Most European countries are undergoing a review of the rules governing incentives to work and the limits on unemployment insurance (level and duration of unemployment benefit, terms of access, etc.), changes in eligibility criteria (limitation of entitlement to unemployment benefits, tightening of entitlement conditions) and in benefit rates and duration. Some elements of convergence may also be identified in the type of approach (client-centred approach: services tailored to fit the individual's needs). In many countries a process of 'standardisation' of non-standard conditions can be observed, which has gone hand in hand with the spread of these activation measures, thereby contributing in some countries to labour deregulation. But in all cases, there seems to be a close interrelation between the regulatory tools used and the quality of jobs offered to unemployed people (Serrano Pascual 2004). Consequently, despite the fact that the paradigm is implemented in very different ways depending on which activation regime is in force, a common trend can nevertheless be identified towards individualisation of interventions, greater emphasis on the economic aspects of citizenship and the contractualisation of social welfare, all of which are features of the activation paradigm. How can we explain the fact that countries with such different social traditions and divergent political philosophies have all adopted this paradigm?

There is currently an interesting ongoing debate on the possible convergence of social responses to economic changes. Together with the role played by demographic factors (such as population ageing) and economic factors (changes in industry, economic crisis), it also focuses on the influence of the supranational level of government. There are four main camps in this debate. Some authors (Finn 1999; Jessop 2002; Handler 2006; Palier 2001) claim that we are seeing the emergence of similar arrangements as well as a process of convergence towards a paternalistic and 'workfarist' approach similar to that in the USA (neoliberal globalisation). Others (Barbier 2002; Castells 1996; Esping Andersen 1996; Pierson 2001) stress the diversity of responses that are emerging depending on a country's institutions, macroeconomic policies, etc. (institutionally path- and past-dependent responses). Another group (Hall 1993; Hemerijk *et al.* 1999; etc.) argues that convergence is dependent on levels and dimensions (overarching goals, policy instruments, the setting of these instruments, institutions). Finally, the last group (including authors such as van Berkel (2005) for the Dutch case, Barbier *et al* (2006) for France and Natali (2004) on the subject of pensions) stresses the hybridisation of national trends and approaches that typifies these recent developments.

This study could be placed somewhere between the third and fourth groups. On the one hand, *convergence* processes can be identified when the regulatory activation paradigm is adopted. However, these processes *differ* greatly when citizens are placed in a vulnerable position or offered support. On the other, we are also witnessing a growing trend towards *hybridisation* of activation approaches, to such an extent that there is a gradual diverse mix of elements from very different cultural backgrounds and social models. This could be leading us towards a reassessment of Esping Andersen's classic typology. In some cases, the EU institutions have had an important role to play in this process.

This section is going to focus on the role of the EU institutions in this convergence process of interventions towards the same activation paradigm. It is not our intention to suggest that the supranational level of the European institutions is the only or indeed the most important in terms of influencing convergence. However, we do believe that EU institutions are playing an important role in some countries in disseminating some of the key concepts in the political debate on social exclusion and that it is, therefore, important to analyse this role.

The regulation put in place by EU institutions is an approach which, rather than seeking to homogenise specific policy measures designed to tackle labour market problems, is based on *persuasion* (in an effort to build up 'epistemic communities' Pochet and Natali 2005). The main regulatory tool is based on the provision of a common discourse and analytical framework to frame the debate on labour market crises and guide diagnosis of the problems, legitimating principles and intervention goals, as well as defining the role of the Welfare State/individuals – albeit not of firms.

There have been a number of reviews of the employment guidelines since their launch following the Luxembourg Summit in 1997. If we trace the development of their content, we can see a gradual trend towards emphasising the activation element. The new guidelines approved in July 2005 contain various statements promoting the three issues that we have identified as being typical of the activation content: individualisation (the idea that unemployment and exclusion problems can be solved by modifying people's motivation and personal attitudes) based on labour integration (where issues related to the protection of workers, the distribution of financial resources, fair pay, etc., are subordinate to the goal of increasing the employment rate) and contractualisation (recognising both parties' responsibility in the integration project). The greater emphasis on activation is especially noticeable in the most recent guidelines, where we can find expressions such as: 'achieving full employment', 'attract and retain more people in employment', 'increase labour supply and modernise social protection systems', 'improve adaptability of workers and enterprises', 'increase investment in human capital through better education and skills' (guideline No. 17), 'increase female participation', 'better reconciliation of work and private life', 'support for active ageing', 'modern social protection systems [...] to support participation and better retention to employment' (guideline No. 18), 'to safeguard economic and fiscal sustainability as a basis for increased employment' (integrated guideline No. 2), 'enhance work attractiveness', 'make work pay', 'guidance and training as part of personalised action plans', 'review of the incentives and disincentives resulting from the tax and benefit systems, including the management and conditionality of benefits' (guideline No. 19), 'modernisation of labour market institutions', 'remove obstacles to mobility for workers' (guideline No. 20), 'reduced non wage labour costs', 'review the tax wedge' (guideline No. 21), 'ensure employment friendly labour cost development and wage setting mechanism' (guideline No. 22), 'increase and investment in human capital' (guidelines No. 23 and 24).

The use of this approach reveals that three main tools are employed in relation to activation policies in the framework of the European Employment Strategy (EES)

a) Ideological persuasion;
b) The provision of political resources;
c) Reflexive deliberation and promotion of policy learning.

Concerning the first aspect, *ideological persuasion*, the adoption of the discourse of EU institutions has had an important impact in Portugal and Spain, and to some extent also France, the Czech Republic and the UK, on the construction of the terms of unemployment and poverty issues, influencing the main lines along which the debate has been conducted and the way in which the problems are described. In some countries, such as Spain, the concepts contained in the EES have even entered the public debate and have been taken up by the mass media (Mailand 2005). As a result, we could say that EU institutions are affecting the direction taken by the debate, influencing the selection of the terminological constructions employed to refer to and reflect upon the problem of labour market exclusion and proposing common frames of reference. The main conclusions of the chapters in this book on the role played by EU institutions in this respect are:

- It can promote important changes in member states' policy thinking, establishing forms of linear causality between aspects such as employment and taxation, activity and economic growth, or unemployment benefit and activity rate. In some countries, such as Spain and Portugal, it has influenced the decision to merge the Ministry of Labour and Employment with the Ministry of Social Affairs, thereby reinforcing the view of social exclusion that focuses on economic and employment factors, which is so characteristic of the activation paradigm.

- It can help to ensure that certain items are placed on the agenda: the activity rate replaces the unemployment rate as the key reference point and lifelong learning becomes a central topic. In the United Kingdom, Denmark and Portugal, EU institutions have contributed to a greater emphasis on preventive measures.

- It can lend additional force to certain policy decisions, for example the need to have tighter rules for unemployment benefit entitlement or, more indirectly, the need to cut spending in order to meet the demands of the Economic and Monetary Union. EU institutions are playing an important role in the legitimation of major changes to the Welfare State and in the legitimation of the reform agenda in countries such as

Portugal, Spain, the United Kingdom and the Netherlands. Indeed, some governments cite the supranational level in their rhetoric in order to divert blame from themselves (Pierson 2001). By claiming that the issues are supranational, they can assert that welfare reform is inevitable and present the national government as a victim of these 'necessary' changes (such as cuts in welfare spending, postponing the retirement age and promoting the participation of 'dependent' members of society).

As far as the second point is concerned, it is important to note that the concepts promoted by the EES can serve as *political resources* in the hands of civil society, enabling asymmetrical power relationships to be challenged. Ensuring the political mobilisation of different social groups is a precondition for successful intervention.

The conclusions of the national cases in this book show that:

• The EES may well assist in *awareness-raising* regarding the situation of specific groups in the labour market, causing certain types of issues and situations to be regarded as problematic rather than taken for granted. The EES may act as a catalyst in some areas and push certain Welfare State issues and reforms higher up the political agenda. This has proven to be particularly true for the integration of women into the labour market in the Netherlands, Spain and Portugal, where the guidelines have led to equal opportunities and work-life balance becoming political priorities. The influence of Europe is especially significant in Portugal, in particular in areas such as active measures or programmes to combat poverty (Guillén *et al.* 2002).

• For some civil society groups, the EES may provide *political tools and strategic resources*. Trade unions and women's movements, etc., are able to use the EES to promote certain items on their agendas. Guidelines on gender mainstreaming, for instance, have been useful in promoting calls for government action in this area.

• In relation to the *setting up of institutions and institutional innovation*, the EES may actually facilitate the establishment of new institutions, for example the inter-ministerial commission for drafting the National Action Plans (NAPs) in the Czech Republic, which will enable a more co-ordinated and comprehensive approach to developing employment policy. A similar effect has sometimes occurred with the implementation of gender mainstreaming, while in other cases the EES may replace previous institutions (Behning and Serrano Pascual 2001).

• The EES may assist the *empowerment* of certain social groups. In some cases it has facilitated the participation of specific civil society groups (cf. the emphasis on partnership). In Spain and Portugal, the EES has contributed to the establishment of some measure of partnership culture. However, one of the main weaknesses of the EES has been the limited extent to which a wide range of actors has been genuinely involved and, therefore, the limited scope for learning from each other. Local and regional actors have not been adequately integrated into the process (de la Porte and Pochet 2003b). The top-down approach to the drafting of the NAPs represents an obstacle to local actors' greater involvement in the EES, while the space for social partner participation is also rather limited. The latter has improved in comparison with the first few years when EU guidelines were implemented, but it varies considerably from country to country, depending on the participative and social dialogue culture and traditions existing at national level. While the social partners may be invited to respond to the proposed content, they have little opportunity to take part in establishing the terms of the debate. In fact, the EU has promoted the involvement of social partners in a deliberate effort to internalise the terms of the debate. The participation of other civil society groups is rather limited and selective (with the possible exception of some influential lobbies).

As regards the third point, i.e. *reflexive deliberation*, the EES may enhance policy learning by means of policy transfer/exchange between member states and by providing the methodological prerequisites for a reflexive stage. The main tools for achieving this stage have been, firstly, the opportunity to call on experts and stakeholders (expertocracy); secondly, the use of benchmarking; and, thirdly, the spread of calls for an evaluation culture. In the Czech Republic, Portugal and Spain, this appears to have led to a more co-ordinated approach and more successful identification and framing of labour market problems, contributing to a process of institutional learning. Nevertheless, some of the procedures promoted by EU institutions (for example personalised interventions) have not been implemented very effectively in these countries owing to the fact that they have not been accompanied by the necessary funding and resources.

In certain countries at least, it would appear that EU institutions have contributed to the spread of the activation paradigm (through an increased emphasis on the individualisation of interventions, the condemnation of passive measures, the growing tendency to insist on participation in the labour market as a cure-all, the dissemination of the 'activation' concept and ideology, the increasingly personalised nature of intervention types, etc.). Nevertheless, the extent and nature of their influence varies from country to country. In Spain and Portugal, Europe has been synonymous with modernisation and the consolidation of democracy (Crespo Suárez *et al.* 1998). Furthermore, both Spain and Portugal have been net beneficiaries of the EU Structural and Cohesion Funds, which have provided them with the funding needed to implement a range of active policies, as well as with additional pressures

(Mailand 2005). There are indeed two sides to the influence of EU institutions in these countries. On the one hand, it has fostered the development of the Welfare State by encouraging greater investment in employment measures and the development of the corresponding institutions. Furthermore, EU membership has constituted an important source of legitimation for new democratic regimes. On the other, however, the austerity measures imposed by EU institutions have resulted in cuts in government welfare spending.

Compared to Spain and Portugal, countries such as Denmark and the Netherlands have a much more Eurosceptic attitude, and this to some extent explains the limited influence of EU institutions in these countries. It appears that EU institutions have been more influential in countries like Spain and Portugal, where government welfare spending was traditionally lower, whereas it is much harder to trace their influence in countries such as Denmark, Sweden or the Netherlands. The varying degrees of influence of the EES may also partly be due to differences in countries' collective identities and in the amount of confidence that different countries have in the effectiveness of their welfare intervention models. Consequently, while countries like Denmark, Sweden, the Netherlands and the United Kingdom would argue that in fact it is they who have done the influencing, in other words that the EU's priorities have in many cases been influenced by these countries, the reverse is true in the Mediterranean countries and the new EU member states.

In addition, the fact that certain countries have come to be regarded as 'best-practice models' means that they are to some extent under pressure to maintain their status, making them more likely to ignore any criticisms or recommendations made by European institutions. In countries such as Denmark and the Netherlands, which are treated as 'models' by various institutions such as the OECD, there can be considerable pressure to maintain their status as it is often as a source of political legitimation for the current government. Larsen and Mailand's contribution in this book draws attention to this apparent contradiction between the lack of supranational influence on domestic policy on the one hand, and the significant efforts made by the Danish government to modify or ignore any recommendations received, on the other.[10] We could therefore state that in Denmark's case, EU institutions only have an indirect legitimising influence, with pros (endorsement of a model based on high welfare expenditure) and contras (for example, diminishing the importance of issues such as gender inequality by considering that, based on

---

[10] Larsen and Mailand highlight the fact that there have been a lot of informal negotiations with EU institutions geared towards ensuring that the Community 'evaluation' procedures (recommendations, joint reports) perpetuate this model.

EU indicators, these problems have already been solved in countries like Denmark; Mósesdóttir and Erlingsdóttir 2006).

Consequently, the main, albeit weak and indirect, source of influence in countries such as the UK, France, Denmark, the Netherlands and Sweden could be due to the fact that EU institutions' adoption of many of these countries' regulatory premises may increase their symbolic importance, thus confirming and legitimating the direction taken by their welfare models. As far as the other countries are concerned, it appears that European institutions have played a significant standardising role by acting as a benchmark for employment policy (disseminating concepts, priorities and procedures).

Notwithstanding the above, another possible source of supranational influence that could explain this convergence with regard to the adoption of the activation principle in several different European countries is the role of transfers between countries. Exchanges have been observed between Denmark and the Netherlands (cf. Larsen and Mailand in this book), France and Spain (cf. Aragón *et al.* in this book), and Denmark and France (Barbier *et al* 2006).

The following list summarises the different strands that explain this convergence trend in the activation paradigm and the role played by EU institutions:

1. persuasion role of EU institutions,

2. national governments' (and other social groups of the civil society) strategic use of concepts, arguments and recommendations proposed by EU institutions in the interests of blame avoidance; the role of supranational regulation as a legitimator of social changes that would otherwise have met with major opposition from society,

3. consolidation of traditions and ways of implementing policies: EU guidelines are an amalgam of different welfare measures and, therefore, they largely reinforce existing trends,

4. dissemination of experiences across different member states,

5. pressure to maintain status as a 'country model' for the EES in order to further consolidate this model.

Conclusion

As stated above, the spread of the activation principle has resulted in a new concept of individual citizenship gaining currency. Its core principles are individualisation (an emphasis on greater self-reliance), contractualisation (more emphasis on the principle of reciprocity, i.e. the requirement for individuals to show willingness when it comes to finding work), and the predominance of economic factors (with greater emphasis being placed on the economic aspects of citizenship rather than on socio-political ones). This in turn has led to a new social contract between the State and its citizens, prompting a change in the way that social responsibilities are structured and shared among the individual, the family, the Welfare State and the market or industry. In other words, it involves not just a new understanding of rights and duties, but also a new balance between them.

The decision by countries to adopt the activation paradigm for their welfare response to tackling problems such as unemployment, economic inactivity, etc., has led them to experience a number of common trends. Firstly, there is a growing trend for intervention mechanisms to become individualised. As a result of this process, the targets of interventions are increasingly individuals with their own personal backgrounds rather than social groups, leading to adopt a more personalised approach, that is, at least at rhetorical level, better tailored to individual circumstances. Secondly, and to some extent as a result of the above, there is a trend to enlarge the instruments employed for these purposes (guidance, mediation, work experience, job subsidies, wage subsidies, etc.) as incentives to encourage labour integration. Thirdly, greater use is being made of punitive measures, while the fourth trend is the spread of the principle of contractualisation as the basis for structuring and legitimating interventions and the term 'suitable job' is being given a broader definition. Consequently, we are faced with two apparently contradictory trends: on the one hand, the promotion of flexible solutions tailored to the individual's specific circumstances and, on the other, the greater role played by coercion in the incentives offered to jobseekers.

Although several factors can explain the spread of the activation paradigm, one of the most important, at least in some countries, is the influence of the persuasion-based regulations promoted by EU institutions. However, the nature of this influence can be very varied and rather than the EU simply influencing member states directly, the issue is in fact far more complicated. Four kinds of influence have been identified: persuasive (i.e. the adoption of the 'language' used by the EU institutions), political (the reinforcement of certain political decisions and collective actors), intercultural (the dissemination of experiences among different countries) and finally symbolic/cultural (reinforcing the legitimation of a given social model).

The fact that several countries have adopted this activation model does not mean that it has resulted in similar policies. Only a brief look at government commitments to and investment in social welfare and the rights provided by labour market regulation policies in different countries is enough to realise that there are major disparities across Europe. This means that we can only talk of regulation in a context of diversity. As we shall see in the country cases and the concluding chapter, very diverse activation regimes can be identified, based mainly on institutional agreements and modes of governance structuring the balance of power between the different actors and regulatory and cultural assumptions regarding work, unemployment and citizenship.

References

Alonso, L.E. (1999), *Trabajo y ciudadanía*, Madrid, Editorial Trotta.

Barbier, J.C. (2002), "Europe sociale : l'emploi d'abord", *Centre d'Études de l'Emploi*, No. 44.

Barbier, J.C. (2004), "Activation policies: a comparative perspective», in A. Serrano Pascual (ed.), *Activation Polities for Young People in International Perspective*, Brussels, ETUI, pp. 47-83.

Barbier, J.C., N. Samba Sylla and A. Eydoux (2006), *Analyse comparative de l'activation de la protection sociale en France, Grande Bretagne, Allemagne et Danemark, dans le cadre des lignes directrices de la stratégie européenne pour l'emploi*, Research report to the DARES.

Barbier J.C. and B. Théret (2004), "Le nouveau système de protection sociale", *La lettre de la Régulation*, No. 49, July, pp. 1-5.

Bauman, Z. (1998), "Europe of stranger", *Working Paper Series. Transnational Communities Programme*, WPTC-98-04.

Behning, U. and A. Serrano Pascual (2001) (ed.), *Gender Mainstreaming in the European Employment Strategy*, Brussels, ETUI.

Berkel, van R. (2000), "Activering in Nederland. De toenemende hybridisering van het beleid", *Tijdschrift voor Arbeid en Participatie*, Vol. 21, No. 2/3, pp. 95-107.

Berkel, van R. and I.H. Moller (2002), *Inclusion through Participation*, Bristol, The Policy Press.

Bonvin, J.M. (2004), "The rhetoric of activation and its effects on the definition of the target groups of social integration policies", in A. Serrano Pascual (ed.), *Activation Polities for Young People in International Perspective*, Brussels, ETUI, pp. 101-126.

Castells, M. (1996), *La era de la información*, Madrid, Alianza Editorial.

Crespo Suárez, E., F. Moreno and A. Serrano Pascual (1998), "From the logic of permanence to the logic of fragmentation: Socio-productive conditions and rearticulation of the middle-class", in B. Steijn, J. Berting and M. de Jong (eds.), *Economic Restructuring and the Growing Uncertainty of the Middle Classes*, Dordrecht, Kluwer Academic Publisher, pp. 93-115.

Crespo Suárez. E. and A. Serrano Pascual (2004), "The EU's concept of activation for young people: toward a new social contract?", in A. Serrano Pascual (ed.), *Activation Policies for Young People in International Perspective*, Brussels, ETUI, pp. 13-47.

Crespo Suárez, E. and A. Serrano Pascual (forthcoming), "Political production of individualised subjects in the paradoxical discourse of the EU institutions" in R. van Berkel and B. Valkenburg (eds.), *Making It Personal. Individualising Activation Services in the EU*, Bristol, Policy Press.

De la Porte, C. and Ph. Pochet (2003a), "A twofold assessment of employment policy coordination in light of economic policy coordination", in D. Foden and L. Magnusson (eds.), *Five Years' Experience of the Luxembourg Employment Strategy*, Brussels, ETUI, pp. 13-69.

De la Porte, C. and Ph. Pochet (2003b), "The participative dimension of the OMC", Paper prepared for the conference *Opening the Open Method of Coordination*, 4-5 July, 2003.

Dean, H. (2003), "Human rights and welfare rights. Re-conceptualising dependency and responsibility", Paper prepared at the First Conference of the European Social Policy Research Network, Social Values, Social Policies, Tilburg, 29-31 August 2003.

Esping Andersen, G. (1996) (ed.), *Welfare States in Transitions*, London, Sage.

Ferrera, M. (1996), "The 'Southern Model' of Welfare in Social Europe", in *Journal of European Social Policy* 6(1), pp. 17-37.

Finn, D. (1999), "Welfare to work: the local dimension", *Journal of European Social Policy*, Vol. 10, No. 1, pp. 43-57.

Foucault, M. (1975), *Surveiller et punir*, Paris, Éditions Gallimard.

Franssen, A. (2003), "Le sujet au coeur de la nouvelle question sociale", *La revue nouvelle*, December, No. 12, Vol. 17, pp. 10-50.

Goul Andersen, J. (2001), "Coping with long-term unemployment: Economic security, labour market integration and well-being". Results from a Danish panel survey, 1994-1999. Paper prepared for the ESF/EURESCU conference. Labour market change, unemployment and citizenship in Europe. Helsinki, 20-25 April 2001.

Guillén, A., S. Álvarez and P. Adão e Silva (2002), "European Union membership and social policy. The Spanish and Portuguese experiences", *Center for European Studies Working Papers*, Harvard University, No. 85.

Handler, J. (2006), "Activation policies and the European social model", in M. Jepsen and A. Serrano Pascual (eds.), *The European Social Model*, Bristol, Policy Press.

Hall, P.A. (1993), "Policy paradigms, social learning and the State: The case of economic policy-making in Britain", *Comparative Politics*, Vol. 25. No. 3, pp. 275-296.

Hemerijck, A. and K. van Kersbergen (1999), "Negotiated policy change: towards a theory of institutional learning in tightly coupled welfare states" in D. Braun, and A. Busch (ed.), *Public Policy and Political Ideas*, Cheltenham, Edward Ekgar Publishing, pp. 166-185.

Holden, C. (2003), "Decommodification and the Workfare State", *Political Studies Review*, Vol. 1, pp. 303-316.

Jessop, B. (2002), *The Future of the Capitalist State*, Cambridge, Polity Press.

Mailand, M. (2005), *Implementing the Revised European Employment Strategy – North, South, East and West*, First working paper of the research project:

Danish employment policy in a European perspective. Available at http://www.sociology.ku.dk/faos/fnotat58.doc.

Marshall, T.H. (1950), *Citizenship and Social Class and Other Essays*, Cambridge, Cambridge University Press.

Mósesdóttir, L. and Erlingsdóttir, R. (2006), "Gender mainstreaming the transition to the knowledge-based society", in L. Mósesdóttir, A. Serrano Pascual and C. Remery (eds.), *Moving Europe towards the Knowledge-based Society and Gender Equality*, Brussels, ETUI-REHS.

Natali, D. (2004), "The hybridation of pension systems within the EU enlarged. Recent reforms in old and new members", *Belgian Review of Social Security*, No. 2/04.

Palier, B. (2001), "Europeanising Welfare States: From the failure of legislative and institutional harmonisation of the systems to the cognitive and normative harmonisation of the reforms", Paper presented at the conference Ideas, Discourse and European Integration, Center for European Studies, Harvard University, May, 11-12 2001.

Pierson, P. (2001) (ed.), *The New Politics of the Welfare State*, Oxford, Oxford University Press.

Pochet, Ph. and D. Natali (2005), "Hard and soft modes of governance: The participation of organised interest to the European network on pensions", Third contribution to the research project *The Open Method of Coordination in the Field of Pensions and European Integration*, carried out by the Observatoire Social Européen and financed by the Belgian Federal Public Service Social Security.

Salais, R., N. Baverez and B. Reynaud (1986), *L'invention du chômage. Histoire et transformation d'une catégorie en France des années 1890 aux années 1980*, Paris, Presses universitaires de France.

Saint Martin, D. (2001), "De l'État-providence à l'État d'investissement social: Un nouveau paradigme pour *enfanter* l'économie du savoir?", L. Pal (ed.), *How Ottawa Spends, 2000-2001*, Ottawa, Carletton University Press, pp. 33-57.

Schram, S. (2000), "The medicalisation of welfare", *Social Text*, 62, Vol. 18, No. 1, pp. 81-107.

Serrano Pascual, A. (2003), "The European strategy for youth employment: a discursive analysis", in A. López Blasco, W. McNeish and A. Walther (eds.), *Young People and Contradictions of Inclusion: Toward Integrated Transition Policies in Europe*, University of Bristol, Policy Press, pp. 85-105.

Serrano Pascual, A. (2004) (ed.), *Are Activation Policies Converging in Europe? The EES for Young People*, Brussels, ETUI.

Topalov, C. (1994), *La naissance du chômeur 1880-1910*, Paris, Albin Michel.

The United Kingdom's 'Work First' Welfare State and Activation Regimes in Europe

Colin LINDSAY

Introduction

The United Kingdom sees itself as a 'world leader' in the development and delivery of active labour market policies (DWP 2004a). The UK National Action Plan for Employment (DWP 2004b) and recent policy documents outlining the 'next steps' in the current government's employment policy agenda (DWP 2004a; 2005) confirm the UK's position as a leading European state in the development of innovative, aggressively supply-side labour market strategies, a position that reflects the priorities of the European Employment Strategy (EES) in promoting employability through the activation of excluded groups (European Commission 2004).

Early concerns that the current government's 'welfare to work' agenda – with the New Deal activation policies at its centre – marked merely a 'newness of rhetoric' (Foden 2000) appear to have underestimated the commitment of the Labour government to fundamental reform of the unemployment policy around the concept of 'Work First'. Some labour market analysts have been willing to concede that the New Deal's emphasis on personalised, tailored services and the offer of a choice of training options, combined with policies to *'make work pay'* that have had a significant impact on in-work poverty, form the basis of a new type of 'ethical employment policy' (White 2000) informed by a 'client-centred approach' (Lindsay 2001). It has also been suggested that labour market strategies such as the New Deal, which combine holistic, client-centred services alongside strong compulsion, reflect the 'progressive re-engineering' of workfare by centre-left policy makers. That is, social democratic governments such as that elected in the UK in 1997 have sought to retain the principle of compulsory activities established by previous centre-right governments, while investing in the development of high quality, holistic services for the unemployed job seekers who are required to undertake these activities (Lindsay and Mailand 2004).

However, even among those who acknowledge some progress from what Gray (1998) has termed the 'maximum deterrence, least cost' approach taken by the previous UK government in the 1980s and early 1990s, there remain considerable concerns regarding the activation policy agenda as currently formulated in the UK. Support for such compulsory activation policies – on the grounds of their social value or effectiveness in promoting labour market inclusion – must therefore be grounded on the concept of *quality*, that is, the quality of labour market and training interventions, and the quality of the outcomes achieved for both individual job seekers and the wider economy. If the quality of services, range of support and choice of options promised to unemployed job seekers is not fully realised, or the results achieved are undermined by a lack of accessible or sustainable job opportunities, then activation policies offer little more than a workfarist drive to force the unemployed into any available work. The need to provide better quality interventions, outcomes and jobs has emerged as an important theme of the European Employment Strategy (EES) as revised in 2003 (European Commission 2003).

This chapter focuses on recent progress in UK activation policy, the ideological and institutional factors influencing these policy developments, and the extent to which the UK's 'activation regime' has delivered high quality services and outcomes. Following this introduction the chapter is structured as follows. Section 2 describes the evolution of activation in the UK in the period immediately before, and since, the development of large-scale active labour market policies (under the 'New Deal' banner) by the current government. Section 3 evaluates the extent to which the UK approach has delivered quality in terms of the content of programmes and the outcomes experienced by participants. Section 4 discusses the ideological and institutional context of the UK's approach to activation, and changes in labour market policy institutions and the roles of different actors (including the social partners). Finally, section 5 draws conclusions and seeks to place UK activation in a European context.

Activation Policies in the UK: The 'State of the Art'?

The Evolution of Activation Policies in the UK

'Activation' has tended to be viewed as an 'umbrella concept', comprising a multitude of schemes and policy approaches (Abrahamson 1999). Accordingly, as activation policies have grown in number and importance across the EU, policy analysts have sought more clearly to define and classify the range of active measures applied by governments seeking to address long-term unemployment (Lødemel and Trickey 2000). In particular, efforts have been made to distinguish between universalistic active labour market policies, in the tradition of the so-called 'Swedish Model' (Fraser 1999), and targeted workfare initiatives such as those pioneered in the United States in the 1980s and 1990s (Peck 1998). It has been suggested that, in general terms, whereas 'active labour market policies' apply a mix of positive and negative sanctions, idealised 'workfare' has a greater emphasis on negative sanctions (Hvinden 1999). Lødemel and Trickey (2000) seek to differentiate workfare from active labour market policies in three further ways: workfare is compulsory; it is primarily about work rather than training; and it is tied to the lowest tier of public income maintenance.[1] Accordingly, arriving at a consistent definition of activation is central to any attempt to establish an 'activation regime' model. This chapter will adopt a broad working definition of activation, here defined as any policy seeking to integrate unemployed people into the labour market, particularly by requiring some form of compulsory job search, training or work-based activity (Lindsay and Mailand 2004).

The evolution of activation policies in the UK has been discussed in great detail elsewhere (Peck 1999, 2001; Trickey and Walker 2000; Lindsay 2001, 2002; Annesley 2003; Finn 2003; Daguerre 2004). To some extent, the origins of the UK's aggressively supply-side activation policies can be traced to the Conservative government's response to the country's unemployment crisis of the 1980s. Throughout the early 1980s, the Conservative government established a range of new training programmes targeted at young people and the long-term unemployed. Yet, prior to 1986, the *stricter regulation* of unemployment benefit claimants was not seen as a particularly important element in labour market policy (Lindsay and Mailand 2004). Indeed, between 1982 and 1986 unemployed people were not even required to attend public employment service (PES) job centre offices to 'sign on' as actively seeking work. Given the long-standing practice of requiring just such an act on the part of job seekers (practically and symbolically underlining the conditionality that, arguably, has consistently characterised the UK's approach to unemployment protection) this relaxation was significant (King 1995). From the perspective of the current UK government, the result was a system that failed to engage with job seekers – a system that

---

[1] Lødemel and Dahl (2000) have added that workfare is more often part of local social services than the remit of labour market authorities.

was 'essentially passive, with no responsibilities to counterbalance the rights of benefit receipt' (Wells 2001, 8).

However, as unemployment declined in the late 1980s and the influence of the 'underclass' debate spread amongst policy-makers, the Conservative government turned to more punitive and restrictive measures. The objective was simple: to activate the long-term unemployed by making life on benefit as unattractive as possible, thus encouraging job seekers to take the most direct route possible into work. A number of changes to the regulation of benefits after 1986 imposed a far stronger degree of compulsion on the behaviour of *all* job seekers, and particularly young people and the long-term unemployed. The so-called 'stricter benefit regime' that emerged over the next decade rendered participation in a range of activities compulsory in all but name (Deacon 2000).

These reforms culminated in the introduction of the Jobseeker's Allowance (JSA) in 1996 as the main benefit for unemployed people. The JSA reform dramatically increased the proportion of social assistance claimants within the unemployed client group by reducing the period of entitlement to contributions-based benefit from twelve to six months. Perhaps more importantly, the JSA resulted in the strengthening and legal codification of many of the restrictive measures applied to job seekers during the preceding years. Where once job seekers worked with PES advisers to develop voluntary 'Back to Work' action plans, claimants were now required to sign a legally binding 'Jobseeker's Agreement' detailing a range of (often extensive) activities to be carried out in order to retain benefit entitlement, and to demonstrate that they were 'actively seeking work'. The 1995 Jobseeker's Act, which established the legal framework for the reform, allowed for compulsory 'directions' (orders to undertake job search or other activities) to be issued by PES advisers and made benefit receipt conditional on the job seeker complying with such instructions, in line with a legally binding 'Jobseeker's Agreement'.

The JSA reform made unemployment benefits less generous and more onerous to claim, especially for those with health problems or caring responsibilities, who were not permitted any relaxation in compulsory job search activities. 'The policy did not encourage work, as was intended, but effectively pushed lone or single mothers and the long-term sick and disabled away from the labour market and increased their reliance on social assistance' (Evans 2001, 261). At the same time, there was a substantial increase in the take-up of sickness-related benefits, as older, mainly manual workers made redundant through processes of industrial restructuring sought to avoid the low levels of benefit and greater compulsion associated with unemployment benefits (Beatty *et al.* 2000; Beatty and Fothergill 2004). The last decade of the Conservative government also saw a significant withdrawal of support from the work-based training policies that had been promoted during the early to mid-1980s (Lindsay 2001). Those programmes that were still provided increasingly focused on job search and motivation, and were therefore considerably less expensive to operate than work-based training schemes (Jones 1997).

The election of a new Labour government in May 1997 marked a significant change in the direction of British activation policies. A substantial investment in 'New Deal' active labour market policies, the amalgamation of social security and public employment service (PES) facilities into a single 'work-focused' benefits and job placement agency, and the introduction of tax/benefit reforms designed to 'make work pay' have radically transformed the employment policy landscape in the UK. It is to the detail of this current policy agenda that we now turn.

Recent Trends in Activation

The UK approach to promoting welfare to work has, since 1997, relied upon a combination of three key elements (DWP 2003a, 2004b): the enforcement of job seeking requirements under the main benefit for unemployed people, the Jobseekers' Allowance (JSA), as part of a 'stricter benefits regime' (Blackmore 2001); a range of activation policies following under the 'New Deal' banner (Hasluck 2001); and a series of tax/benefit measures designed to 'make work pay' (Blundell 2001). Table 1 provides a brief, and by no means definitive, summary of key reforms since 1997.

Table 1. Activation in the UK since 1997: Key Measures

1997	New Deal for Lone Parents (voluntary)
1998	New Deal for Young People (compulsory)
	New Deal for Long-term Unemployed, aged over 25 (compulsory)
	New Deal for Disabled People (voluntary)
	Prototype Employment Zones
1999	National Minimum Wage
	Working Families Tax Credit (WFTC)
	Disabled Person's Tax Credit (DPTC)
	New Deal for Partners of Unemployed (voluntary)
	New Deal for those aged over 50 (voluntary)
2000	Welfare Reform and Pensions Act: requires attendance at compulsory work-focused interviews
	ONE pilots: single work-focused gateway and interviews for all new benefit claimants of working age

2001	Reform of JSA for partners without children: both partners required to demonstrate that they are actively seeking work
	Learning and Skills Councils replace TECs in England and Wales
2002	Jobcentre Plus established
	Step Up pilots
	Reform of New Deal 25+
	Compulsory work-focused interviews for new Income Support clients
2003	Working Tax Credit/Child Tax Credit (replacing WFTC/DPTC)
	Pathways to Work, first wave pilots
2004	Reform of New Deal for Young People
	Pathways to Work, second wave pilots
	Working Neighbourhoods pilots
2005	'Building on New Deal' prototype areas
	Pathways to Work roll out/expansion

There has been little in the way of change in the manner in which the *JSA regime* established by the Conservative government in 1996 operates. Unemployed job seekers are required to attend PES Jobcentre offices every two weeks to demonstrate that they have been actively seeking work, and to follow any 'Jobseeker's Direction'. Failure to comply continues to result in benefit sanctions. The current government has therefore openly supported the pre-existing 'stricter benefits regime' as an appropriate starting point for its own labour market policy reforms. The logic of the JSA regime has been entirely accepted – the only criticism is that the JSA regulations were not 'sufficient' to ensure a successful transition to work for the long-term unemployed (DWP 2004a).

The *New Deal* programmes provide the main focus for activation policies in the UK. The New Deal for Young People was the first and best-funded of the UK's welfare to work programmes, compulsory for those aged 18-24 and unemployed for more than six months. Of the £5.2 billion (then approximately €7.4 billion) initially allocated to the New Deals in 1998, 70% was targeted at the programme for young people, 15% at the 'long-term unemployed 25+' programme (see below), and 15% at other New Deal initiatives (for disabled people, partners of the unemployed and lone parents). The flagship programme for young people offers an intensive 'Gateway' period of counselling and job search help for up to 13 weeks. This was initially followed by a choice of training across 'four options', ranging from year-long education courses or subsidised work placements to shorter training on voluntary sector or environmental projects (with a minimum of one day per week allocated to the delivery of accredited training). When the programme was introduced in 1998, these options lasted a minimum of approximately six months (26 weeks). A reform in April 2004 saw the minimum option period reduced to 13 weeks in an attempt to improve the flexibility of the programme and allow participants to experience a range of different training options. Sanctions – in the form of recurring temporary benefit suspensions – are applied to those refusing to participate. As noted below, the 'employment option' or subsidised work placement option – initially a prominent design feature of the programme – has become far less central to the New Deal's implementation. Employers continue to be paid a weekly training subsidy of £60 (approximately €88 at the time of writing) for placing New Deal 18-24 participants and £75 (approximately €111 at the time of writing) for New Deal 25+ trainees (based on the idea that young people are generally paid less).

The New Deal for Long-term Unemployed People aged over 25 (or 'New Deal 25+') was introduced in June 1998. Initially targeting those unemployed for two years or more, since 2001 the programme has been compulsory for those receiving JSA for 18 months or more. This reform clearly reflected the call for a 'fresh start for long-term unemployed people' within the European Employment Strategy guidelines, but was also influenced by evaluation evidence that showed that the New Deal 25+ was not working effectively (Lindsay 2002). Accordingly, the provision offered through New Deal 25+ has been substantially redesigned. Previously denied the intensive support of a 'Gateway' period (which, with its focus on building a personal relationship between Adviser and unemployed clients, has proved popular with job seekers), New Deal 25+ clients now receive these services. Since April 2001 this has been followed by an 'Intensive Activity Period' (at first mainly focusing on intensive job search activity, confidence-building, counselling and advice, but then offering training options similar to those available to young people). This Intensive Activity Period lasts a minimum of 13 weeks and can last up to 26 weeks. In *exceptional* cases, trainees can be sent on a further or higher education course for up to one year.

There are also New Deal programmes for those aged over 50, lone parents, the partners of the unemployed (who, if they do not have children, are subject to similar job seeking regulations) and disabled people, with the latter programme set to rapidly expand as the government refocuses its welfare to work strategy on those claiming sickness-related benefits. In most cases these programmes have been limited in scope and scale, and have largely not involved compulsory participation, although increasing compulsion appears to be a feature of recently proposed reforms (DWP 2004a; DWP 2005).

Reforms to the tax/benefit system designed to *make work pay* form the third main element of the UK approach to activation. The Working Tax Credit (WTC) is a system of in-work support designed to tackle poor work incentives and persistent poverty among working people. It came into effect in April 2003 and extended existing support available under the Working Families Tax Credit and Disabled Persons Tax Credit (both established in 1999) to childless and non-disabled workers aged 25 and working 30 hours per week or more. The WTC also provides help with childcare, covering up to 70% of childcare costs up to a maximum cost of £200 per week (or £135 per week for one child). The Tax Credit system introduced since 1998 replaced a range of means-tested 'top-up' benefits, and has been credited with making in-work financial support more accessible and less stigmatised.

The introduction of Tax Credits has encountered some problems, and administrative delays (due to inadequate IT systems) and errors in payments to claimants have undermined the credibility of the policy. Nevertheless, combined with the establishment of a National Minimum Wage, the system of Tax Credit reforms has formed the basis of a national strategy to *make work pay*.[2] The government maintains that, despite the problems, these reforms have effectively begun to address in-work poverty: it has been suggested that single working people earning the National Minimum Wage have seen an 18% increase in their income since the WTC reform (DWP 2003b). There is little doubt that the Tax Credit reforms do represent an acknowledgement by government of the need for additional financial support for those making the transition from welfare to work (Bryson 2003).

The extensive programme of reform introduced since 1997 marks a break with standard labour market policy interventions in the UK. There has undoubtedly been an attempt to place further obligations on unemployed people, and the New Deal clearly represents the first major compulsory work-focused activation programme for unemployed 'adults' in the UK (Lindsay 2001). However, the stronger conditionality and compulsion associated with the New Deal reforms has been balanced by attempts to provide incentives to make work pay that arguably amount to the most redistributive economic policy measure introduced by the current government (McLaughlin *et al.* 2001). Furthermore, the content of the New Deal, and in particular the tailored services provided by personal advisers, appear to represent a shift towards a more client-centred, 'needs oriented' approach (Hasluck 2001; see also below). This

---

[2] The National Minimum Wage (not recommended by the EES until 2003, but introduced in the UK in 1998) is currently £4.85 per hour for those aged 22 and over, and £4.10 per hour for young workers.

(arguably contradictory) combination of strong compulsion and holistic, client-centred services at the heart of the UK's approach to activation continues to inform recent policy developments.

The Emerging Policy Agenda

It has been suggested that recent developments in UK labour market policy can be seen as amounting to a state of 'permanent revolution' (Bryson 2003). The activation policy agenda in particular continues to change and adapt to new political and economic priorities. As general registered unemployment has declined, the government has been increasingly concerned with dealing with concentrations of 'worklessness' in small geographical areas, or among members of particularly disadvantaged client groups (Ritchie *et al.* 2005). In particular, the concentration of economic inactivity (often mainly due to high rates of claiming sickness-related benefits) in certain regions and localities has emerged as a key issue. The greater propensity in the UK for unemployment to be concentrated within households in which none of the adult residents work (Gregg and Machin 2003) has also led policy-makers to seek to intensify the focus of locally targeted employability polices. It should be noted that the policy response has retained an almost completely supply-side focus, reflecting analyses that continue to diagnose the problem of worklessness in terms of the skills gaps of former manual workers (Nickell 2004).

Nevertheless, the government's most recent reforms suggest that there has been an acceptance among policy-makers that the 'standard' New Deal activation model may have reached its 'logical conclusion'. There are active efforts to refocus welfare to work to target local areas in greatest need, make major programmes and funding streams more flexible and accessible, and reform the content of provision to address the needs of the most vulnerable. Perhaps predictably, this agenda has thrown up a number of policy programmes which are again defined by an arguably contradictory combination of client-centred individual support and strong compulsion.

Working Neighbourhoods

'Working Neighbourhoods' is a two-year pilot programme which started in April 2004. Twelve local authority neighbourhoods are being targeted (mostly in inner cities, with each neighbourhood reporting around 2,000 people of working age receiving benefits). The programme recognises that the performance of the New Deal has varied at the local level, and purports to link the regeneration and employability policy agendas. However, the solution remains firmly on the supply side, based on a more intensive targeting of the New Deal on high-unemployment postcode areas. Innovative features include the use of peripatetic personal advisers visiting clients in their own neighbourhood and the establishment of area-based service centres. Help is provided in the form of standard New Deal counselling, training, job search and advice services, but personal advisers also have discretion to provide assistance with childcare, transport and other financial barriers. Each neighbourhood has a flexible discretionary fund of £1 million per year.

While Working Neighbourhoods represents a welcome acknowledgment that some local areas require greater assistance than others, it has also seen an increase in compulsion – all JSA claimants are required to participate in New Deal or Employment Zone options after three months, and most economically inactive people of working age claiming benefits are required to attend quarterly work-focused interviews and to complete an Action Plan focusing on steps to a return to work (DWP 2003a). The introduction of the programme also saw an unusual hardening of rhetoric, as ministers spoke of the need to address the 'culture of worklessness' and the 'poverty of aspirations' in some areas, promising to tackle 'the worst concentrations of unemployment, street by street, estate by estate' (Brown 2002). The Trades Union Congress apparently does not see Working Neighbourhoods as a 'blame the victim' approach, and has supported the government's argument that 'the problem lies at the level of the (local) community' (TUC 2004).

StepUp

'StepUp' has been operating since April 2002 in 20 pilot areas characterised by higher than average rates of long-term unemployment. Like Working Neighbourhoods, the programme has seen progressive ideas (in this case built around supported/subsidised employment within 'intermediate labour markets') mixed with high levels of compulsion. Those who have not found work during or within six months of completing New Deal training are required to participate in StepUp, which offers intensive support through a personal adviser and an in-work support worker, and a paid work placement within an intermediate labour market setting for up to 50 weeks. While the 'real work' focus of the programme has been welcomed, the compulsion to undertake workplace-based activities (without the option of other training routes) is perhaps the nearest the UK has come to a fully functioning workfare programme. The results have been modest, with job entry rates standing at around 26% (CESI 2004).

Pathways to Work

'Pathways to Work' is a pilot programme that has been tested in seven 'New Deal delivery areas' in the UK since 2003. Target areas were selected on the basis of their relatively high levels of claimants on sickness-related benefits (Incapacity Benefit and its means-tested social assistance equivalent, Income Support). The government has described Pathways to Work as offering 'a new intervention regime to activate peoples' aspirations to return to work' (DWP 2004a, 16) – the first step in a process of activating the sickness and disability benefits regime in the UK in order to 'focus on what people are capable of doing'. Participants in pilot areas are required to attend a 'work-focused interview' and can gain access (on a voluntary basis) to New Deal training and support services. Early evaluation evidence suggests that the pilots have been modestly successful in encouraging greater participation in the New Deal for Disabled People, and have produced an increase in exits from Incapacity Benefit of around 8-10% (NCSR 2004). The programme will be rolled out in a further 15 areas characterised by high levels of economic inactivity in 2005 and 2006.

Building on New Deal

The emphasis of the government's recent policy document on the future of the New Deal 'Building on New Deal – local solutions meeting individual needs' is an increasing focus on sustainable, high quality outcomes: 'helping people not only to re-enter employment, but to acquire the skills they need to secure long-term, sustainable and rewarding employment' (DWP 2004a, 1). Of course, the heavily supply-side emphasis remains – long-term, sustainable and rewarding employment is seen as following from the efforts of individuals to acquire skills rather than the product of a labour market where such opportunities are consistently available. The policy document describes a proposed move towards a more flexible, localised delivery model for the New Deal, reflecting an acceptance among policy-makers that: (a) the benefits of New Deal have not been felt across all areas; and (b) the client group now being targeted by New Deal are increasingly likely to have multiple or severe barriers to work (DWP 2004a).

'Building on New Deal' (BoND) prototype areas were launched in October 2005. The government has suggested that this major reform of welfare to work is to be informed by three 'core principles' (DWP 2005):

1. A national framework for rights and responsibilities, through:

• the continuing implementation of a nationally consistent JSA regime;

• a more accessible New Deal (still with mandatory participation for 18-24 year olds unemployed for 6 months and the 25-49 age group at 18 months, but also offering services on a voluntary basis to those aged 25 and over at 6 months, and to particularly vulnerable groups at any time during their unemployment);

• the increasing use of mandatory 'work-focused interviews' for lone parents (upon claiming, after 6 and 12 months, and then annually for those with children under 14; and every 3 months for those with children over 14);

• the increased use of 'work-focused interviews' for claimants of sickness-related benefits (upon claiming, and then at a series of 'trigger points');

• and the more extensive piloting of 'Pathways to Work', which (in target areas) will provide mandatory monthly work-focused interviews, specialist provision from the New Deal suite of services (such as supported employment services), and newly-developed work-focused rehabilitative health services.

2. Greater local flexibility, devolution and discretion, through:

• the use of Discretionary Funds that Jobcentre Plus Personal Advisers will have budgetary control over, and which can be used to provide 'early help' to any job seeker judged to be in need of additional assistance, irrespective of benefit status or duration of unemployment;

• a more flexible New Deal, with the rigid 'training options' system replaced with a 'mix and match' menu of provision (see Box 1) with more accessible specialist services for disadvantaged groups.

3. Accountability, targets and contestability, through:

• the use of Discretionary Funds that Jobcentre Plus Personal Advisers will have budgetary control over, and which can be used to provide 'early help' to any job seeker judged to be in need of additional assistance, irrespective of benefit status or duration of unemployment;

• increasing 'contestability' at the local and regional level, so that local District Managers can choose to outsource service provision traditionally delivered by Jobcentre Plus, so that in some areas Jobcentre Plus services themselves may be 'opened up' to competition from voluntary or private sector providers.

Interestingly, as Watt (2004) notes, the weakening of the EES's emphasis on 'meeting individual needs' has been identified as an important 'qualitative' difference emerging from the 2003 review process. The UK approach appears to be moving towards an increasing focus on the individual, facilitated by a devolution of responsibilities and budgets. There are sound reasons for the reforms suggested by the government – the level of incapacity benefit claims in depressed urban labour markets suggest that high levels of sickness mask a problem of hidden unemployment (Beatty *et al.* 2002), while the need for a more flexible approach to dealing with the problems of job seekers *before* they become long-term unemployed has long been acknowledged by both service providers and unemployed people alike.

The more flexible approach to delivering New Deal that has been developed to address these concerns implies that the 'training options' approach that defined the programme's previous incarnations is to be dropped. There is much to be commended in the government's commitment that it does not wish to see job seekers 'slotted into existing [...] standard provision if this is not appropriate' (DWP 2004a, 20). For the government: 'The essence of the flexible menu approach is that people should be treated as individuals and that they should receive the customised support they need' (DWP 2004a, 21). In place of the standard training options, both New Deal for Young People and '25+' clients will, working with personal advisers, select from a broader range of generally shorter training and development services (see Box 1).

Box 1. New Deal Menu of Help

Jobsearch assistance/support – Individually tailored help focusing on job search resources, including help with compiling CVs or letter writing.
Motivational assistance – Helping to address individual motivational barriers to finding work, including better-off-in-work calculations.
Employability skills – Addressing generic skills gaps such as self-presentation, team work, or understanding customer service.
Skills training for local labour markets – Work-focused training linked to current and anticipated local labour market demand.
Wage subsidies – Financial incentives to encourage employers to offer work to clients that they may not otherwise consider.
Work trials – Providing an opportunity for clients to engage in employment without fear of losing their benefits, providing valuable work experience and allowing employers to view potential candidates to fill their vacancies.
Adviser Discretion Fund – A flexible fund allowing Personal Advisers to assist clients in overcoming minor financial barriers to work.
Work experience – Placements providing an opportunity for individuals to gain valuable work experience and relevant job skills.
Self-employment – A range of support and advice to enable people to set up their own businesses, including test-trading while still in receipt of benefits.

> *Career direction* – Advice and guidance about types of work available locally.
> *In-work support* – Advisory support where judged by Personal Advisers as appropriate for individual clients.
> *Specialist support for those with health conditions and disabled people* – Assistance for those who require more intensive help, for example through 'Access to Work' (a subsidy programme assisting employers with the costs of employing disabled workers), residential training, and supported employment opportunities.
> *Specialist support for the most disadvantaged people* – Services such as 'progress2work' – an initiative to help people recovering from illegal drug misuse into work providing support, counselling and specialist training.

However, for those who supported the New Deal because of its supposed 'real work' focus (that is, that it provided work opportunities paid at the 'rate for the job', rather than low quality training courses) there remain concerns that more flexibility and discretion will undermine the quality of the training experience for many participants. The employment subsidy option (already of marginal importance within the overall programme) may become increasingly irrelevant as advisers direct clients towards a wider range of less intensive services. The government has also acknowledged the danger that a more flexible approach to delivering services could produce arbitrary allocation of resources and increasing deadweight effects (DWP 2004a, 2005). There is an acceptance that both Managers at district level and Personal Advisers at local level will require substantial additional training if such an approach is to be workable. The government has indicated that there will be tight controls on the proportion of flexible funding available.

The UK approach to activation continues to be characterised by a combination of strong compulsion and conditionality, but also the expansion of holistic, client-centred services for unemployed job seekers. While the compulsory work-focused activity imposed by the current Labour government represents a strengthening and extension of the conditionality introduced into the UK's system of social protection by the preceding Conservative administration, the substantial investment in training under the New Deal – in itself the result of a highly redistributive policy – and the shift towards a more client-centred approach (characterised by a wider range of tailored training options and one-to-one counselling provided by 'Personal Advisers') cannot be ignored. These trends have continued to dominate UK activation as the focus for welfare to work has shifted from the young and long-term unemployed to 'harder to reach' workless groups and communities.

Is it Working? Outputs and Impacts of Activation in the UK

A Record of Success?

The UK approach to promoting employability through activation has been viewed as a success story within the EU context (Nickell and van Ours 2000). The UK currently has approximately 28 million people in employment, an increase of over 1.9 million since 1997, while both ILO and claimant unemployment have fallen by over 600,000 during the same period (DWP 2004b). The UK's registered unemployment was the lowest of the G8 countries in 2003 (standing at 5%, compared to an EU average of 8%), while the employment rate (then 72%, now 75%) exceeds the EU average (around 63% in 2003). The UK exceeds all the Lisbon employment rate targets, including those for women and older workers. Area-based differences are problematic (see below), but all local authority areas are within 10% of the UK average in terms of economic activity rates. All but 14 local authority areas have employment rates above the EU average (DWP 2003b).

The European Commission (2004) has noted the need for further action in the UK in 'attracting more people to the labour market and making work a real option for all', and specifically in policies to:

• ensure that active labour market policies and benefit systems prevent de-skilling and promote quality in work, by improving incentives to work and supporting the sustainable integration and progress in the labour market of inactive and unemployed people;

• address the rising number of people claiming sickness or disability benefits, and give particular attention to lone parents and people living in deprived areas;

• improve access to and affordability of childcare and care for other dependants, increase access to training for low paid women in part-time work, and take urgent action to tackle the causes of the gender pay gap.

However, advocates of the aggressively supply side-oriented labour market policy approaches adopted in the UK (and other leading 'active' states such as Denmark and the Netherlands) have compared their own countries' performance with that of other EU nations such as France, Germany, Italy and Spain, concluding that the 'European unemployment problem' is in fact the problem of these insufficiently 'active' welfare systems (Koning *et al.* 2004). Similarly, the UK government's submission on the future of the Lisbon Process calls for a 'sharpening of the agenda', pointing to the combination of labour market deregulation and aggressive activation at the centre of the UK approach: 'This means ensuring that the labour force is equipped with transferable skills, that tax and benefit systems provide incentives for people to enter and remain in work, that firms have the capacity to create and vary employment, and that the institutional environment encourages labour market participation' (HM Treasury 2004, 7).

UK spending on activation remains below the EU average (see below), but the New Deal has seen a substantial expansion in welfare to work provision, and the extension of support (which can be taken up on a voluntary basis) to client groups previously excluded from training. Many of those reviewing the evaluation evidence have concluded that the New Deal has fostered social inclusion, expanded activation, and (at the very least) widened the reach of employability programmes to take in previously excluded groups, such as lone parents (Millar 2000; Evans 2001). Early evaluations suggested that the New Deal's performance in terms of achieving job entry for participants, especially young people, has been impressive (Riley and Young 2001), and that the number of young long-term unemployed people would have been double without the impact of the New Deal (NIESR 2000). There is little doubt that since the introduction of activation policies registered youth and long-term unemployment have declined substantially (NAO 2002). One evaluation even suggested that the New Deal for Young People alone had the potential to benefit the economy by £500 million (then approximately €790 million) per year (NIESR 2000). The success of the New Deal for Young People in particular has led the government to claim that 'youth long-term claimant unemployment has been virtually eradicated' (DWP 2003a, 11).

A summary of the destinations of those leaving the main New Deal programmes (for young people and the long-term unemployed) as at September 2004 is provided in Table 2. The results demonstrate that the New Deal has had a significant impact, but that its success has been limited. The New Deal's performance has been affected by economic downturn and the growth of the 'hardest to help' as a proportion of the general unemployed client group. As a result, job entry rates have been declining. In 1998, 47% of young New Deal leavers moved into unsubsidised work, compared to 38% in 2004. It should, however, be noted that follow-up surveys of 'leavers to unknown destinations' suggest that just over half of these clients enter work (O'Donnell 2001).

Table 2. Destinations of People Leaving Main New Deal Programmes, to September 2004

Leaving New Deal for Young People		Leaving New Deal 25+	
Destination	%	Destination	%
Employment	38	Employment	26
Return to JSA	–	Return to JSA	28
Other benefits	11	Other benefits	16
Other known destination	20	Other known destination	8
Unknown destination	30	Unknown destination	22
Total (rounded)	100	Total (rounded)	100
n = 1,147,590		n = 334,540	

In terms of the *quality* of services delivered to unemployed job seekers, the evidence is to some extent clearer. From the programme's outset, supporters of the New Deal and related policies pointed to elements of the new government's welfare to work strategy that marked it out from its predecessors, namely its combination of activation with tax/benefit reforms, and its 'client-centred' approach to dealing with individuals (Oppenheim 1997). Qualitative evaluation evidence has confirmed that the emphasis within New Deal on building relationships between clients and Personal Advisers has been welcomed by both groups (Hasluck 2000; Millar 2000). The Personal Adviser role has emerged as the 'linchpin of success' within the New Deal (Walker and Wiseman 2003). While individual clients' experiences have been diverse, the majority appear to have noted a genuine shift in the way that PES officials deliver job search services, with provision under the New Deal for Young People apparently of a particularly high standard – 'the client-centred experience of the New Deal for Young People seems to be far more positive than the monolithic instrument of social control suggested by some critics' (Finn 2003, 721).

Similarly, whatever the problems around the implementation of certain elements of training provision (see below for a discussion of problems affecting the 'employment subsidy' option of the New Deal), the introduction of greater choice and a broader range of support services for the unemployed has reaped positive results (Hasluck 2001). There is also a consensus that the 'opening up' of employment services to include the voluntary and private sectors (delivered by the first wave of New Deal reforms) has generally had a positive impact on the quality of services (Hoogevelt and France 2000). The New Deal partnerships which coordinate and implement services across 144 'delivery areas' across the UK provide an extensive delivery role for local government, voluntary organisations and private training providers (with the latter leading the delivery of provision in a small number of areas).

Nevertheless, there remain considerable concerns about the extent of private sector penetration in activation and training provision. The replacement of private sector-dominated 'Training and Enterprise Councils' (which the preceding Conservative administration charged with planning local training provision) with Learning and Skills Councils (which include representation from employers, trade unions and the education sector) has been welcomed. However, the relatively low cost-per-client of most New Deal training options, and the continuing focus on 'soft' skills and early job entry, suggest that the long-term impact of the training provided by many private contractors may be limited. This is particularly the case for long-term unemployed people participating in the 'New Deal 25+', which has always emphasised shorter training interventions and a faster transition to work: 'For the older unemployed [...] the emphasis has not been on improving human capital' (Evans 2001, 265).

Furthermore, while the devolution of decision-making and budgetary control implied by 'Building on New Deal' marks a step change towards a more localised, but also potentially more professionalised, approach to dealing with the unemployed, the government's call for increased 'contestability' in the delivery of services has raised concerns (DWP 2004a). The reform of the New Deal which commenced in late 2005 may eventually lead to key services, including the Personal Adviser function performed in most areas by the PES, being outsourced to private or third sector providers. Given the apparent value of these services, there is clearly a need for caution. Evidence from the evaluation of 'single work-focused gateway' services for lone parents has already suggested that the quality of service provision is more likely to be maintained where Jobcentre Plus (PES) staff lead delivery, rather than where private sector agencies are heavily involved (Kirby and Riley 2001).

Challenges for UK Activation

Despite the apparent success of UK activation policies, there remain serious challenges to the sustainability of the current approach. Policy-makers have sought to address some of the weaknesses of the standard New Deal model through continuing reforms (some of which are discussed above). However, the severity of the barriers to work faced by some clients, the lack of decent quality job opportunities in some areas, and a labour market that for some offers work without the chance to escape from poverty, have combined to limit the overall impact of activation policies such as the New Deal, and raise new questions about the future direction of welfare to work in the UK.

While initial job entry figures were encouraging, it is clear that the New Deals, and some other employability programmes provided by the PES, Jobcentre Plus, face an increasing problem of 'revolving door' participation, where clients move from training programmes into short-term employment, and then back into unemployment, eventually repeating their participation in training programmes. Approximately 20% of those currently participating in the flagship New Deal for Young People are attending the programme for at least the second time. In more general terms, two-fifths of those claiming Jobseeker's Allowance are experiencing their second spell of unemployment in a six-month period (ONS 2004).

In broader terms, the role of activation policies in producing positive labour market outcomes in the UK remains subject to debate. For example, an independent study in 2001 found that unemployed young people were 20% more likely to enter work as a result of the New Deal, but also pointed out that the vast majority of participants were likely to have found work without the programme (Institute for Fiscal Studies 2001). The employment-creation impact of the New Deal for Young People has been estimated as approximately 17,000 jobs per year during its first four years of operation, rather more modest than the government's claim that the programme had placed 250,000 people in work (Blundell *et al.* 2003). The main impact of the New Deal for Young People has been on reducing long-term unemployment, rather than increasing participation rates among the young – between 1993 and 2001 the employment to population ratio for 18-24 year old men remained virtually unchanged at around 61% (Blundell *et al.* 2003). A National Audit Office (NAO) report in 2002 similarly estimated a substantial 'deadweight' effect – at a time when government sources were noting that the New Deal for Young People had moved 340,000 people into work, the NAO suggested that the programme had resulted in an increase in employment of no more than between 8,000 and 20,000 (NAO 2002).

Furthermore, Martin *et al.* (2003) have shown that the impact of policies such as the New Deal (in all its forms) has varied dramatically across regions of the UK – predictably, in areas which have experienced the massive job losses associated with de-industrialisation, the New Deal's performance has been least effective. This research suggests that the New Deals have underperformed in many inner urban and depressed industrial labour markets. 'In such areas the "recycling and churning" of participants through the programme are more significant, and suggest that local labour market structures play a significant role in shaping policy outcomes' (Sunley *et al.* 2001, 484). There is little evidence that recent additions to the New Deal to improve job search and matching will address these local variations. It remains clear that local demand continues to impact significantly on the outputs of centralised national welfare to work programmes (Martin *et al.* 2003; Fletcher 2004). Research carried out for the Department for Work and Pensions (DWP) has similarly confirmed that variations in the performance of all Jobcentre Plus services can largely be traced to the impact of local labour market demand (measured as notified vacancies) and levels of socio-economic deprivation within local communities (GHK 2004).

There remain pockets of high unemployment where low claimant unemployment masks a problem of many older workers claiming non-work related sickness and disability benefits (Beatty *et al.* 2002). As noted above, in areas where 'official' unemployment has fallen while job creation remains stagnant, the explanation appears to lie in the transfer of many (particularly older male) job seekers to sickness-related benefits. More than 2.5 million non-employed adults of working age in Britain (excluding Northern Ireland) currently claim sickness-related benefits, and the numbers have risen steeply since processes of industrial restructuring resulted in major job losses during the 1980s (Beatty and Fothergill 2004). The diversion of older, male job seekers from unemployment to sickness benefits has been identified as substantially reducing 'official' unemployment in declining former mining areas, major cities (Turok and Edge 1999), isolated rural areas (Beatty and Fothergill 1997) and seaside towns (Beatty and Fothergill 2003). Even the most ardent believers in the UK's 'unemployment miracle' have acknowledged the 'debacle' represented by the continuing expansion in the numbers claiming Incapacity Benefit (Nickell and van Ours 2000).

These results again highlight a fundamental problem with the UK approach to activation – that welfare to work initiatives which focus solely on improving the individual aspects of employability fail to acknowledge the strong link between weak labour demand and high 'welfare usage' in disadvantaged communities (Peck 2001). It might be argued that these problems are common to all supply-side labour market policies. Activation policies essentially seek to 'individualise a collective problem' (Foden and Magnusson 2003), and thus fail to adequately acknowledge the importance of the geography of labour markets, employer attitudes and behaviour, demand within local economies, and other 'context' factors impacting on the experiences of job seekers. Recent reforms appear to point towards a growing understanding of the need for targeted, area-based solutions. Plans outlined in 'Building on the New Deal' accept that 'the benefits of recent labour market improvements have not been felt ... across all geographical areas', and suggest that the solution may lie in the targeted expansion of New Deal services and the increasing devolution of policy and decision-making on local interventions to the community level (DWP 2004a). However, the link between activation and policies to regenerate disadvantaged communities and develop local economies remains weak.

There are also issues around the quality of provision offered through the New Deal model. The lack of investment in training provision, by government and employers, has long acted as a barrier to achieving sustainable job outcomes and labour market progression for vulnerable groups in the UK (King and Wickham-Jones 1998). Using the broadest measure, activation spending remains well below the EU average (0.2% GDP by % unemployed) in the UK (0.1%) and considerably below that of leading 'active' welfare states such as Denmark (0.3%) and Netherlands (0.7%). The government regularly highlights these figures as evidence of the cost-effectiveness of programmes such as New Deal (DWP 2003b), but it is clear that the New Deal has done little to challenge the 'least cost' culture within UK training policy.

In terms of quality of content, the assumptions surrounding the distinctiveness of the New Deal's commitment to 'real work' experience have come under pressure as the programme has developed. The employment subsidy option of the New Deal was seen, depending on authors' perspectives, as an innovative attempt to deliver training of value and dignity at work (Lindsay 2001), or a dangerous subsidisation of low-paid work with implications for job substitution (Holden 1999). But in reality the 'real work' employment subsidy option has operated on the margins of the New Deal, with a small minority of participants entering this (supposedly crucial) training option throughout the life of the programme (Hasluck 2001). Latest figures show that only 3% of New Deal for Young People participants in total and 9% of those undertaking a training option are currently engaged in an employment subsidy placement. Although this is partly due to the success of the New Deal's 'Gateway' job search service in placing clients in unsubsidised work, there is also evidence that some (particularly larger) employers remained sceptical about the value of the programme, so that opportunities within the employment option have been limited in many areas (Elam and Snape 2000).

There is some evidence that current supply-side initiatives have not been as effective in addressing the needs of people with multiple or severe disadvantages (Millar 2000). While policies such as the New Deal have seen a general improvement in the personal adviser services available to clients, the most disadvantaged are likely to require longer term, more intensive support of a type that, even with the increasing flexibility introduced by successive reforms, the New Deal is unable to provide. Relatively short-term employability programmes that emphasise a work-first approach cannot be expected to assist people facing severe health, personal or social problems requiring interventions that are personalised, intensive, flexible and (if necessary) long-term (Lakey et al. 2001; Dean 2003). Research with drug users (another target group for the New Deal and local employability policies) confirms that welfare to work strategies struggle to address the complex combination of barriers to work faced by such individuals. Nor is the situation of the most vulnerable assisted by 'the corrosive effects of an ideological ethos that encourages people with multiple needs and problems to blame themselves for their failure in the labour market' (Dean et al. 2003, 24).

Finally, for those entering low-paid work through activation programmes, there is evidence that work does not necessarily provide a route out of poverty (Millar and Gardiner 2004). Finn (2003), reviewing evaluation evidence on the New Deal, notes that there is little evidence that clients have been 'forced' to take low paid jobs during the Gateway phase of the programme. However, the combination of insecurity, low pay and lack of opportunities for progression that characterise vacancies in some areas of the UK labour market – and particularly in certain sectors of the service economy – present many job seekers with an unpalatable choice between low quality work and continued unemployment. These factors affect the opportunities open to job seekers, and there is substantial evidence that unemployed people are resistant to the idea of pursuing entry-level, low paying work in expanding service-oriented sectors (Lindsay and McQuaid 2004).

Cook et al. (2001) conclude that the preponderance of low-paid, casualised work within the UK economy means that work-first approaches have the potential to accentuate rather than mitigate social exclusion. The establishment of a minimum wage and tax credit systems is the most obvious policy response to these issues, although the level at which the National Minimum Wage has been set in the UK has had only a minimal effect on income differences (Goos and Manning 2003). Two-fifths of the UK's low-income households (defined as below 60% of median income) have some or all of their adult members working. Approximately 25% of working households are also low-income households (Palmer et al. 2003). These problems have tended to be exacerbated by 'gaps' in the UK strategy on 'making work pay'. The benefits of government policies to make work pay have been denied to many young people – those aged under 25 are not entitled to the Working Tax Credit; and those aged under 22 are eligible only for a lower rate of National Minimum Wage protection. Employers have taken advantage of these systemic weaknesses – it has been estimated that 250,000 young people earn less than the 'adult' minimum wage (Palmer et al. 2003). As noted above, low pay therefore continues to present a major problem for young people and working families alike.

Understanding the UK's 'Work First' Welfare State

The UK Approach to Activation: 'Work First'?

Rhodes (2000, 180) has suggested that the New Deal follows and replicates 'the logic and method of Conservative employment and benefits policy'. The logic is indeed at least similar, but the method is arguably distinct. The current government in the UK has extended and broadened the policies of its predecessor in making compulsory work-oriented activity (whether active job seeking or basic skills training) a condition of financial support for many unemployed people. Indeed, with the introduction of large-scale active labour market policies such as the New Deal, the UK has arguably seen a definitive shift towards 'a work focused approach' to social protection (Evans 2001) within an 'employment-first welfare state' (Finn 2003), where labour market participation is arguably viewed as the ultimate solution to social and economic exclusion. From the government's perspective 'work is the best form of welfare' (DfEE 2001), 'the best defence against social exclusion' (Hewitt 2005), 'the best route out of poverty' (DWP 2005) and 'the best [...] anti-crime and pro-family policy yet invented' (Labour Party 2001). The objective of the government is to provide 'work for those who can and security for those who cannot', by 'rebuilding the welfare state around work' (DSS 1998). The apparent (if limited) success of the New Deal programmes has reinforced policy-makers' commitment to these values – recent NAPs have used the terminology of 'Work First' to describe the government's overall approach to labour market policy (DWP 2003a, 2004b).

The measures discussed above clearly represent a challenge to existing policy structures, and arguably mark a paradigmatic shift in the manner in which UK policy-makers address the problem of unemployment. Those who are convinced that the emergence of a new 'activation regime' in the UK does mark a break with previous approaches to unemployment policy have identified three broadly distinctive themes:

1. new policies seek to alter the balance of rights and responsibilities between the individual and the state;

2. welfare rights have increasingly become subject to conditionality as a result;

3. and the institutions of the welfare state have been refocused on supporting economic autonomy and labour market participation, giving rise to a fundamental transformation in forms of governance.

That the UK approach to activation has seen a rebalancing of rights and responsibilities – typified in the compulsory activation of those registered as unemployed and work-focused interviews for other inactive people of working age – is clear. The current welfare to work agenda fits in with a long-standing tradition of conditionality within the UK benefits system. Yet there is now a stronger consensus that responses to unemployment must focus on the attributes and responsibilities of the individual (Peck 1998). The 'notion of causation [has] moved from the structural to focus on individual character as shaped by personal circumstance', with the result that receivers of welfare are now required to enter into a 'contract' that provides assistance only if 'character' is also enhanced (Lund 1999, 458).

The UK's 'Work First' approach is also perhaps the most distinctive within the EU context in its relative independence of the values of the tax/benefit system (and benefits arrangements in particular). The European Commission (2004) has noted that many member states' activation policies serve mainly to requalify participants for unemployment insurance benefits rather than to assist them into work. The extensive use of social assistance benefits, and the restrictive nature of unemployment insurance within the UK system, has ensured that the primary objective of 'Work First' policies is exactly that – to insert participants in work.

The rebalancing of rights and responsibilities in itself implies that welfare rights are increasingly defined by conditionality. It is clear that the refocusing of unemployment policy (and even non-work-related benefits arrangements) on activity to promote employability represents a central element in the introduction of conditionality of social protection in welfare states across the EU – part of a paradigmatic change from addressing poverty as a problem in its own right to viewing labour market inclusion as key to social inclusion (Serrano Pascual 2003). Within the UK, access to social protection is more than ever before conditional on the individual agreeing to a range of activities to enhance their employability. Non-compliance results in benefit sanctions. The New Deal initially operated within the existing sanctions regime of the JSA. After an intensification of the sanctions regime in 2000, participants can now see their benefits completely withdrawn for six months following a 'third offence' (that is, following a third refusal to follow a 'Jobseeker's Direction' or participate in some form of work-focused activity). It has been estimated that around 10% of New Deal participants were sanctioned during the programmes' first two years. However, third offence withdrawals of all benefits are more rare.

Institutional change has also been a feature of the shift towards activation in the UK. The amalgamation of Benefits Agency and Employment Service within a single 'working age agency', Jobcentre Plus, is significant. Jobcentre Plus was established in October 2001, building on a series of pilot initiatives providing a 'single, work-focused gateway' for all new benefit claimants. The amalgamation process will conclude in 2006. The amalgamated single agency will deal with the benefits of up to 6 million people through an extensive network of 1,000 local and regional offices. The tensions involved in a single agency adopting the dual role of delivering counselling and job-matching services, while also 'policing' and regulating the benefits system, are well known (King and Wickham Jones 1998). Critics of the amalgamation of job matching and welfare benefits services point to the refocusing of social policy interventions on enhancing employability, and suggest that this new working age agency reflects an analysis that assumes that paid work is essential to social participation and the solution to social exclusion (Lister 2001; Finn 2003). It remains to be seen how new initiatives extending the local focus of welfare to work and targeting those claiming non-work-related benefits feed into the process of organisational change.

Explaining the UK Approach to Activation

The *ideological* bases for the UK approach to activation have been popularly cited as, among other things: the 'underclass' thesis popularised by right-of-centre social theorists during the 1980s and 1990s (see, for example, Murray 1990); and the arguments surrounding the balancing of social good and individual rights at the heart of social communitarianism (see, for example, Etzioni 1993). For critics of the current UK government's welfare to work agenda, policies such as the New Deal combine these diverse intellectual traditions in an 'unpleasant cocktail' – 'Murray's character assassination of the poor', mixed with communitarian rhetoric (Prideaux 2001, 97).

However, a review of activation in the UK suggests that, in terms of any direct impact on policy, the 'classic' formulation of the underclass thesis has had limited influence: Murray's (1990, 71) call to 'reintroduce the notion of blame' was never followed through in terms of fully functioning workfare policies or US-style welfare retrenchment. Indeed, as Lindsay and Mailand (2004, 202) note: 'Murray's vision of an underclass choosing to avoid work because of the overgenerous nature of welfare benefits had limited direct impact in most European countries (where the author's obsessions with race and "illegitimacy" were shared by few moderate policy makers)'. Furthermore, perhaps predictably, the currency of the underclass thesis suffered a severe blow with the economic recovery of the early 2000s, as many supposedly unemployable members of the underclass made their way back into work, having been given the opportunity to do so by expanding labour demand (Freeman 2000). Mead's (1986) arguments about the 'culture of poverty', and the defeatism and passivity of the long-term unemployed may have been more influential – indeed, the logical conclusion of Mead's thesis is that a re-balancing of social rights and obligations is required, and that compulsory activation should be used to re-integrate and motivate the unemployed poor (Lindsay and Mailand 2004).

The idea that long-term unemployment in itself inevitably results in personal decline and de-motivation is one that has been adopted (albeit in different forms) by a number of leading economic theorists in the UK. Indeed, a more likely intellectual foundation for the UK's activation agenda is the influence of supply-side economists (see, for example, Layard 1997, 2000; Nickell and van Ours 2000), who have successfully argued that duration of dependency – the increased likelihood of continued unemployment amongst the long-term jobless due to the deterioration of skills, work habits and commitment over time – has a major role to play in explaining high levels of structural unemployment. Once accepted, this 'withering flowers' argument leads to the logical conclusion that effective active labour market programmes, aimed at activating and improving the skills of the long-term unemployed, have the potential both to positively impact on the employability of individual clients, and permanently ratchet down the rate of unemployment in the wider economy. The UK government has explicitly identified concerns over structural joblessness and the impact of poor basic skills attainment on national productivity as informing its approach to promoting employability policy agenda, and the activation strategies deployed as a central element of that agenda (DWP, 2002, 2003, 2004). This fundamentally supply-side argument has continued to inform UK policy, while regional variations in unemployment tend to be explained with reference to insufficient wage discipline and local disparities in the treatment of the unemployed (Koning *et al.*, 2004).

In terms of the *institutional* foundations of UK activation, the New Deal's introduction in 1998 reflected the EES's emphasis on providing a 'fresh start' for young people before six months of unemployment, and older unemployed people before twelve months of unemployment. Measures to make work pay and widen the scope of welfare to work to address different client groups have also reflected EES priorities. However, in reality, the foundations of the UK approach had been laid well before the Luxembourg Jobs Summit of November 1997, as the Labour Government elected the preceding May prepared to build on the existing 'stricter benefits regime' and apply lessons learned from other 'active' welfare states, such as Sweden, Denmark, the United States and Australia (Lindsay and Mailand 2004).

The EES can therefore be seen as reinforcing and supporting, rather than directly inspiring, the UK government's expansion of active employability policies. Furthermore, while there is some evidence of experience from Nordic welfare states informing the early development of the New Deal (Giddens 1998), the link is less clear between formal policy learning through the EES's peer review systems and the emergence of new activation strategies. Research analysing the peer review activities undertaken under the EES has identified limited direct policy transfer, with most EU states 'relying on home-grown means' (in terms of administrative and institutional frameworks) to meet national and EES labour market policy goals. For Casey and Gold (2005, 36) the peer review process 'might have produced a degree of "tweaking" of existing policies, but it hardly acted as a catalyst for policy transfer'. Nevertheless, the analysis of Europe's unemployment problem implicit in the EES has long held that activation measures are the key to reducing the numbers who are out of work. It is an analysis that has been welcomed and replicated within UK policies to promote employability and labour market inclusion. This process of mutual reinforcement and legitimisation has continued as both the EES and UK strategies have been reconfigured to take account of falling unemployment and rising concerns over retention and work conditions.

In terms of cross-national policy transfer, the US is most often seen as inspiring the UK's approach to activation. There is some evidence of successive Conservative governments (1979-1997) apparently 'learning from America' in targeting a perceived culture of welfare dependency and piloting specific initiatives such as the short-lived Employment Training scheme and Training and Enterprise Councils (Peck and Jones 1995). Critics have argued that the current Labour government's welfare to work programme reflects a continuing fascination with American style workfare (Peck and Theodore 2001; Annesley 2003). In particular, the close relationships established between the UK Labour and US Democrat administrations in the mid 1990s has led some to speculate that the Clinton presidency's extension of workfare inspired UK activation (Dolowitz *et al.* 1999). However, although UK ministers have used similar rhetoric – for example, the welfare system should offer 'a hand up not a hand out' (Harman 1997) – evidence of specific elements of policy transfer is less obvious.

The reality is one of substantial differences between US workfare and the application of activation in European states, including the UK (Lødemel and Trickey 2000). Accordingly, we might conclude that whilst the recent debate on labour market policy has – to an extent – been framed by the rhetoric of American workfarism, other political ideas have also impacted on the policy arena. More importantly, as Lødemel (2000, 307) suggests: 'cross-Atlantic diffusion has been a proliferation of *ideas* about the need to re-balance rights and obligations, more than the application of *lessons learnt* from US programmes'.

The reasons for the UK's divergence from the US workfare model clearly include the breadth of the UK welfare to work client group, compared with the targeting of marginalised groups such as lone parents in the US (Lødemel 2004). Indeed, Lødemel (2000, 2004) makes a convincing case that 'policy inheritance matters' when considering the institutional foundations of activation policies. However, Lødemel seeks to move beyond the generalisations of regime theories that have lumped the UK together with the US and other Anglo-Saxon nations under an ideal-typical 'liberal' world of welfare (Esping-Andersen 1990), or similar policy regimes in relation to unemployment protection (Gallie and Paugam 2000), social assistance (Gough 2001) or youth transition policies (McNeish and Loncle 2003).

Rather than straining to maintain the divisions that form the orthodoxy of welfare regime theory, Lødemel is interested in explaining the convergence of *diverse* welfare states around activation, and the reasons why some states – including the UK – have combined strong compulsion with measures that seek to genuinely improve individuals' employability or promote 'human resource development' (HRD) rather than simply force them to return to work by the quickest route (a 'labour market attachment' approach). For Lødemel (2000) the 'centralised programmes' found in Denmark, the UK and the Netherlands represent a clear case of convergence in active labour market policies: a 'shared HRD approach' has emerged from quite different unemployment and social assistance schemes, and indeed regimes.

Lødemel argues that the integration of social assistance with insurance-based provision for the unemployed is a potentially important determinant of progressive, HRD-oriented activation. As noted above, in a linked argument, it is suggested that 'target group matters' – that countries with large client groups subject to compulsory activation are likely to have more progressive and less stigmatising activation policies. This theory may help to explain the UK's convergence with other countries with 'centralised programmes' to activate social assistance claimants, such as Denmark and the Netherlands (see also Trickey 2000). Denmark, for example, had an existing active labour market policy structure in place when activation was expanded in the mid 1990s to engage a larger proportion of social assistance claimants, leading Lødemel to speculate that the Danish system's overall HRD-oriented focus may result from the 'trickle down' of progressive approaches to activation from labour market policy directed towards those claiming insurance-based unemployment benefits. While the UK prior to 1997 pursued a more 'labour market attachment'-focused approach to activation, increasing compulsion was at least applied to all job seekers, after the regime governing social assistance and contributory unemployment benefits was integrated under the JSA reform.

Finally, however, it is important to remember that 'politics matters' when tracing the development of activation in the UK. Lindsay and Mailand (2004) suggest that the mix of strict compulsion and client-centred services in the UK can be partially explained by the strong centre-left Labour government's 'progressive re-engineering' of activation after a strong centre-right government had established the case for increasing compulsion. Indeed, it has been argued that such centre-left governments are in a stronger position to introduce active labour market policy reforms because they are less open to charges of welfare retrenchment that might be levelled at the political right (Ross 2000). Others see the expansion of activation in the UK as a signal of the Labour Party's shift to the political right (Lund 1999). But it is as plausible to suggest that policies promoting work as both a right and a duty tie in with traditional values of the British Labour movement. As a 'Labour' party (emerging from the trade union movement) rather than a 'social democratic' party, there is much continuity between the current governing party's valuing of paid work and the traditions of Labour thinking in the UK, based on an enduring belief that employment is the best way of securing economic and social well-being. It is a tradition that has long recognised 'the importance of work incentives, the obligations of the workless and the need for proactive government measures to improve employability' (Page 2003, 9).

Conclusion

The UK has recently seen a strengthening and expansion of compulsory activation. This amounts to a crucial shift in the way that unemployment is understood and addressed: new policies have altered the balance of rights and responsibilities between the individual and the state; welfare rights have become subject to increasing conditionality as a result; and the institutions of the welfare state have been refocused on supporting labour market participation.

The UK has faced similar labour market problems to its European neighbours in recent years. During the 1980s and 1990s recurring high youth and long-term unemployment were key problems. More recently, as participation rates have gradually risen, concerns over retention and in-work poverty have come to the fore. It is hardly surprising that the UK, having reflected – and helped to legitimate – the EES's focus on active measures to promote employability in the 1990s, should now share the reconfigured Strategy's emphasis on improving the quality of outcomes for those successfully making the transition to work. Policies introduced since 1997 have retained and built upon the stricter benefit regime established in the 1980s, but have also produced more client-centred or HRD-focused services for job seekers.

The combination of these active policies to promote employability and a range of recent initiatives to make work pay (including the National Minimum Wage) appear to have enjoyed some, albeit limited, success in the UK. But problems remain: too many working families and young people continue to have to cope with very low incomes, combined with insecurity at work and few opportunities for progression. Furthermore, success rates for key activation schemes have been declining as standardised, short-term training interventions have struggled to address the problems of more disadvantaged individuals. New interventions 'building on the New Deal' promise to offer more flexible and intensive services, but also increased compulsion targeted at specific workless groups and communities. Meanwhile, it remains unclear as to whether the increasing 'contestability' promised in public employment services will herald the privatisation of PES provision, and whether the marketisation of these interventions is compatible with the need to address the problems of more vulnerable job seekers.

Finally, and crucially, there remains a reluctance within government to accept that the employability of individuals is a function of both supply and demand: the unemployment problem in many urban areas reflects a problem of weak local labour demand that cannot be addressed through supply-side policies alone. Effective labour market policies must address the full range of issues affecting the employability of unemployed people. Activation policies clearly have a role to play, but only as part of a package of measures that also address economic hardship and social exclusion amongst the unemployed and demand deficiency in depressed labour markets (Lindsay and Mailand 2004). If the UK is to deliver on its promise of high quality services and outcomes for job seekers, policy-makers must re-state the importance of interventions that are client-centred, offering a choice of provisions tailored to the needs of individuals, and which form part of a coherent strategy to promote sustainable employment in all regions.

References

Abrahamson, P. (1999), "Activation and social policies: comparing France and Scandinavia", in D. Bouget and B. Palier (eds.), *Comparing Social Welfare Systems in Nordic Europe and France*, Paris, MIRE, pp. 403-417.

Annesley, C. (2003), "Americanised and Europeanised: UK social policy since 1997", *British Journal of Politics and International Relations* 5 (2), pp. 143-165.

Beatty, C. and S. Fothergill (1997), *Unemployment and the Labour Market in RDAs, Rural Research Report 30*, Salisbury, Rural Development Commission.

Beatty, C. and S. Fothergill (2003), *The Seaside Economy*, Sheffield, Sheffield Hallam University.

Beatty, C. and S. Fothergill (2004), *The Diversion from 'Unemployment' to 'Sickness' across British Regions and Districts*, Sheffield, Sheffield Hallam University.

Beatty, C., S. Fothergill and R. MacMillan (2000), "A theory of employment, unemployment and sickness", *Regional Studies* 34 (7), pp. 617-630.

Beatty, C., S. Fothergill, T. Gore and A. Green (2002), *The Real Level of Unemployment*, Sheffield: Sheffield Hallam University.

Blackmore, M. (2001), "Mind the gap: exploring the implementation deficit in the administration of the stricter benefits regime", *Social Policy and Administration* 35 (2), pp. 145-162.

Blundell, R. (2001), "Work incentives and in-work benefit reforms: a review", *Oxford Review of Economic Policy* 16 (1), pp. 27-44.

Blundell, R., H. Reed, J. Van Reenan and A. Shephard (2003), "The impact of the New Deal for Young People on the labour market: a four year assessment", in R. Dickens, P. Gregg and J. Wadsworth (eds.), *The Labour Market under New Labour: The State of Working Britain*, Basingstoke, Palgrave, pp. 17-31.

Brown, G. (2002), *Speech by the Chancellor at the Urban Summit*, Birmingham (1 November), at: http://www.hm-treasury.gov.uk/newsroom_and_speeches/

Bryson, A. (2003), "Permanent revolution: the case of Britain's welfare to work regime", *Benefits* 11 (1), pp. 11-17.

Casey, B. and M. Gold (2005), "Peer review of labour market programmes in the European Union: what can other countries really learn from each other?", *Journal of European Public Policy* 12 (1), pp. 23-43.

CESI (Centre for Economic and Social Inclusion) (2004), *Evaluation of StepUp: Interim Report*, London: CESI.

Cook, J., M. Roche, C.C. Williams, and J. Windebank (2001), "The evolution of active welfare policies as a solution to social exclusion in Britain", *Journal of European Area Studies* 9 (1), pp. 13-26.

Daguerre, A (2004), "Importing workfare: policy transfer of social and labour market policies from the USA to Britain under New Labour", *Social Policy and Administration* 38 (1), pp. 41-56.

Deacon, A. (2000), "Learning from the US? The influence of American ideas upon 'New Labour' thinking on welfare reform", *Policy and Politics* 28 (1), pp. 5-18.

Dean, H. (2003), "Reconceptualising welfare to work for people with multiple problems and needs", *Journal of Social Policy* 32 (3), pp. 441-459.

Dean, H., V. MacNeill and M. Melrose (2003), "Ready to work? Understanding the experiences of people with multiple problems and needs", *Benefits* 11 (1), pp. 19-25.

Dolowitz, D., S. Greenwold and D. Marsh (1999), "Policy transfer: something old, something new, something borrowed, but why red, white and blue?", *Parliamentary Affairs* 52 (4), pp. 719-730.

DWP (Department of Work and Pensions) (2003a), *The UK Employment Action Plan*, London, DWP.

DWP (2003b), *Full employment in every region*, London, DWP.

DWP (2004a), *Building on New Deal: Local Solutions Meeting Individual Needs*, London, DWP.

DWP (2004b), *The UK Employment Action Plan*, London, DWP.

DWP (2005), *Department of Work and Pensions Five Year Strategy: Opportunity and Security through Life*, London, DWP.

Elam, G. and D. Snape (2000), *New Deal for Young People: Striking a Deal with Employers*, Sheffield, Employment Service.

Esping-Andersen, G. (1990), *The Three Worlds of Welfare Capitalism*, Cambridge, Polity Press.

Etzioni, A. (1993), *The Spirit of Community: The Reinvention of American Society*, New York, Touchstone.

European Commission (2003), *Proposal for a Council Decision on Guidelines for the Employment Policies of Member States*, Brussels, Commission of the European Communities.

European Commission (2004), *Benefit Systems and their Interaction with Active Labour Market Policies*, Brussels, European Commission.

Evans, M.E. (2001), "Britain: moving towards a work and opportunity-focused welfare state", *International Journal of Social Welfare* 10 (4), pp. 260-266.

Finn, D. (2003), "The 'employment first' welfare state: lessons from the New Deal for Young People", *Social Policy and Administration* 37 (7), pp. 709-724.

Fletcher, D.R. (2004), "Demand-led programmes: challenging labour market inequalities or reinforcing them?", *Environment and Planning C: Government and Policy* 22 (1), pp. 115-128.

Foden, D. (2000), "The New Deal for young workers: some reflections", in A. Serrano Pascual (ed.), *Tackling Youth Unemployment in Europe*, Brussels, ETUI, pp. 121-124.

Foden, D. and L. Magnusson (2003), "The European Employment Strategy: five years on", in D. Foden and L. Magnusson (eds.), *Five Years' Experience of the Luxembourg Employment Strategy*, Brussels, ETUI.

Freeman, R. (2000), "The US underclass in a booming economy", *World Economics* 1 (2), pp. 89-100.

Gallie, D. and S. Paugam (2000), "The experience of unemployment in Europe: the debate", in D. Gallie and S. Paugam (eds.), *Welfare Regimes and the Experience of Unemployment in Europe*, Oxford, Oxford University Press, pp. 1-25.

GHK et al. (2004), *Understanding Performance Variations: Synthesis Report for Jobcentre Plus*, Research Report 196, London, DWP.

Giddens, A. (1998), *The Third Way: The Renewal of Social Democracy*, London, Polity.

Goos, M. and A. Manning (2003), "McJobs and MacJobs: the growing polarisation of jobs in the UK", in R. Dickens, P. Gregg and J. Wadsworth (eds.), *The Labour Market under New Labour: The State of Working Britain*, Basingstoke, Palgrave, pp. 70-85.

Gough, I. (2001), "Social assistance regimes: a cluster analysis", *Journal of European Social Policy* 11 (2), pp. 165-170.

Gray, A. (1998), "New Labour, new labour discipline", *Capital and Class* 65, pp. 1-8.

Gregg, P. and S. Machin (2003), "Workless households and the recovery", in R. Dickens, P. Gregg and J. Wadsworth (eds.), *The Labour Market under New Labour: The State of Working Britain*, Basingstoke, Palgrave, pp. 32-39.

Harman, H. (1997), "New Deal for Lone Parents is welfare reform in action", Department of Social Security Press Statement (23 October).

Hasluck, C. (2000), *New Deal for Young People: Two Years on*, Sheffield, Employment Service.

Hasluck, C. (2001), "Lessons from the New Deal", *New Economy* 8 (4), pp. 230-234.

Hewitt, P. (2005), Remarks by Rt. Hon. Patricia Hewitt MP, Secretary of State for Trade and Industry, to New Policy Institute Conference on "More and Better Jobs", London (31 January).

HM Treasury (2004), *Mid-term Review of the Lisbon Strategy: UK Submission to the High-Level Group*, London, HM Stationery Office.

Holden, C. (1999), "Globalisation, social exclusion and New Labour's work ethic", *Critical Social Policy* 19 (4), pp. 529-538.

Hoogvelt, A. and A. France (2000), "New Deal: the experience and views of clients in one Pathfinder city (Sheffield)", *Local Economy* 15 (2), pp. 112-127.

Hvinden, B. (1999), "Activation: a Nordic perspective", in M. Heikkilä (ed.), *Linking welfare and work*, Dublin, European Foundation for the Improvement of Living and Working Conditions, pp. 27-42.

Institute for Fiscal Studies (2001), *No more Skivvy Schemes? Active Labour Market Policies and the British New Deal for Young Unemployed in Context*, London, Institute for Fiscal Studies.

Jones, M. (1997), "The degradation of labour market programmes", *Critical Social Policy* 17 (3), pp. 91-104.

King, D. and M. Wickham-Jones (1998), "Training without the state? New Labour and labour markets", *Policy and Politics* 26 (4), pp. 439-455.

Kirby, S. and R. Riley (2001), *The Employment Effects of ONE: interim Findings from the Full Participation Phase*, London, DWP.

Koning, de, J., R. Layard, S. Nickell and N. Westergaard-Nielsen (2004), *Policies for Full Employment*, London, DWP.

Lakey, J., H. Barnes and J. Parry (2001), *Getting a Chance: Employment Support for Young People with Multiple Disadvantage*, York, Joseph Rowntree Foundation.

Layard, R. (1997), "Preventing long-term unemployment", in J. Phillpott (ed.), *Working for Full Employment*, London, Routledge, pp. 190-203.

Layard, R. (2000), "Welfare to work and the New Deal", *World Economics* 1 (2), pp. 73-87.

Lindsay, C. (2001), "A new deal through partnership, a new approach to employability: the case of the New Deal for Young People in the United Kingdom", in A. Serrano Pascual (ed.), *Enhancing Youth Employability through Social and Civil Partnership*, Brussels, European Trade Union Institute, pp. 173-190.

Lindsay, C. (2002), "Long-term unemployment and the employability gap: priorities for renewing Britain's New Deal", *Journal of European Industrial Training* 26 (9), pp. 411-419.

Lindsay, C. and M. Mailand (2004), "Different routes, common directions? Activation policies for young people in Denmark and the UK", *International Journal of Social Welfare* 13 (3), pp. 195-207.

Lindsay, C. and R.W. McQuaid (2004), "Avoiding the "McJobs": unemployed job seekers and attitudes to service work", *Work, Employment and Society* 18 (2), pp. 297-318.

Lister, R. (2001), "New Labour: a study in ambiguity from a position of ambivalence", *Critical Social Policy* 21 (4), pp. 425-48.

Lødemel, I. (2000), "Discussion: workfare in the welfare state", in I. Lødemel and H. Trickey (eds.), *An Offer You Can't Refuse: Workfare in International Perspective*, Bristol, Policy Press, pp. 294-343.

Lødemel, I. (2004), "The development of workfare within social activation policies", in D. Gallie (ed.), *Resisting Marginalization: Unemployment Experience and Social Policy in the European Union*, Oxford, Oxford University Press, pp. 197-222.

Lødemel, I. and E. Dahl (2000), *Public Works Programs in Korea: A Comparison to ALMP and Workfare in Europe and the United States*, New York, World Bank.

Lødemel, I. and H. Trickey (2000), "A new contract for social assistance", in I. Lødemel and H. Trickey (eds.), *An Offer You Can't Refuse: Workfare in International Perspective*, Bristol, Policy Press, pp. 1-40.

Lund, B. (1999), "'Ask not what your community can do for you': obligations, New Labour and welfare reform", *Critical Social Policy* 19 (4), pp. 447-462.

Martin, R.L., P. Morrison and C. Nativel (2003), "The local impact of the New Deal: does geography matter?", in R.L. Martin and P. Morrison (eds.), *Local Labour Markets: Processes, Problems and Policies*, London, Routledge, pp. 175-207.

McLaughlin E., J. Trewsdale and N. McCay (2001), "The rise and fall of the UK's first tax credit: The Working Families Tax Credit 1998-2000", *Social Policy and Administration* 35 (2), pp. 163-180.

McNeish, W. and P. Loncle (2003), "State policy and youth unemployment in the EU: rights, responsibilities and lifelong learning", in A. Lopez Blasco, W. McNeish and A. Walther (eds.), *Young People and the Contradictions of Inclusion: Towards Integrated Transition Policies in Europe*, Bristol, Policy Press, pp. 105-126.

Mead, L. (1986), *Beyond Entitlement*, New York, Free Press.

Millar, J. (2000), *Keeping Track of Welfare Reform: The New Deal Programmes*, York, Joseph Rowntree Foundation.

Millar, J. and K. Gardiner (2004), *Low Pay, Household Resources and Poverty*, York, Joseph Rowntree Foundation.

Murray, C. (1990), *The Emerging British Underclass*, London, Institute of Economic Affairs.

NAO (National Audit Office) (2002), *New Deal for Young People: Report by the Comptroller and Auditor General*, London, NAO.

NCSR (National Centre for Social Research) (2004), *Incapacity Benefit Reforms: The Personal Adviser Role and Practices*, London, DWP.

Nickell, S. (2004), "Poverty and worklessness in Britain", *The Economic Journal* 114 (494), C1-C25.

Nickell, S. and J. van Ours (2000), "Why has unemployment in the Netherlands and the United Kingdom fallen so much?", *Canadian Public Policy* 26 (Special Supplement), pp. 201-220.

NIESR (National Institute for Economic and Social Research) (2000), *The New Deal for Young People: Implications for Employment and Public Finances*, Sheffield, Employment Service.

O'Donnell, K. (2001), *New Deal Survey of Leavers to Unknown Destinations*, Sheffield, Employment Service.

ONS (Office for National Statistics) (2004), *New Deal for Young People and Long-term Unemployed Aged 25+: Statistics to December 2003*, London, ONS.

Oppenheim, C. (1997), "Welfare and work", *Renewal* 5 (1), pp. 50-62.

Page, R. (2003), "New Labour and paid work: a break with the past?", *Benefits* 11 (1), pp. 5-9.

Palmer, G., J. North, J. Carr and P. Kenway (2003), *Monitoring Poverty and Disadvantage*, York, Joseph Rowntree Foundation.

Peck, J. (1999), "New Labourers? Making a New Deal for the workless class", *Environment and Planning C: Government and Policy* 17 (3), pp. 133-161.

Peck, J. (2001), *Workfare states*, London, Guildford.

Peck, J. and M. Jones (1995), "Training and Enterprise Councils: Schumpeterian workfare state or what?", *Environment and Planning A* 27 (9), pp. 1361-1396.

Peck, J. and N. Theodore (2001), "Exporting workfare/importing welfare to work: exploring the politics of Third Way policy transfer", *Political Geography* 20, pp. 427-460.

Prideaux, S. (2001), "New Labour, old functionalism: the underlying contradictions of welfare reform in the US and the US", *Social Policy and Administration* 35 (1), pp. 85-115.

Rhodes, M. (2000), "Desperately seeking a solution: Social Democracy, Thatcherism and the Third Way", *West European Politics* 23 (2), pp. 161-186.

Riley, R. and G. Young (2001), *Does Welfare to Work Policy Increase Employment? Evidence from the UK New Deal for Young People*, London, NIESR.

Ritchie, H., J. Casebourne and J. Rick (2005), *Understanding Workless People and Communities: A Literature Review*, London, DWP.

Ross, F. (2000), "Framing welfare reform in affluent societies: rendering restructuring more palatable?", *Journal of Public Policy* 20 (2), pp. 169-193.

Serrano Pascual, A. (2003), "The European strategy for youth employment: a discursive analysis", in A. Lopez Blasco, W. McNeish and A. Walther (eds.), *Young People and the Contradictions of Inclusion: Towards Integrated Transition Policies in Europe*, Bristol, Policy Press, pp. 85-103.

Sunley, P., R. Martin and C. Nativel (2001), "Mapping the New Deal: local disparities in the performance of welfare to work", *Transactions of the Institute of British Geographers* 26 (4), pp. 484-512.

Trickey, H. (2000), "Comparing workfare programmes: features and implications", in I. Lødemel and H. Trickey (eds.), *An Offer You Can't Refuse: Workfare in International perspective*, Bristol, Policy Press, pp. 249-293.

Trickey, H. and R. Walker (2000), "Steps to compulsion within British labour market policies", in I. Lødemel and H. Trickey (eds.), *An Offer You Can't Refuse: Workfare in International Perspective*, Bristol, Policy Press, pp. 181-214.

TUC (Trades Union Congress) (2004), *Working Neighbourhoods*, Welfare reform briefing 52, London, TUC.

Turok, I. and N. Edge (1999), *The Jobs Gap in Britain's Cities: Employment Loss and Labour Market Consequences*, Bristol, Policy Press.

Walker, R. and M. Wiseman (2003), "Making welfare work: UK activation policies under New Labour", *International Social Security Review* 56 (1), pp. 3-29.

Watt, A. (2004), "Reform of the European Employment Strategy after five years: a change of course or merely presentation?", *European Journal of Industrial Relations* 10 (2), pp. 117-137.

Wells, B. (2001) *From Restart to New Deal: A Recent History of Labour Market Intervention*, paper presented at the Institute for Labour Research Conference, Leicester (2-4 July).

White, M. (2000), "New Deal for Young People: towards an ethical employment policy?", *Policy Studies* 21 (4), pp. 281-295.

Activation in the Netherlands: The Gradual Introduction of a Paradigm Shift

Rik van Berkel

Introduction

The focus in this chapter will be on the period during which the European Employment Strategy has been in force. However, in terms of describing the history of Dutch activation policies, the launch of the European Employment Strategy in the late 1990s does not signify an important moment in the sense of somehow marking a significant change in the direction or intensity of Dutch activation. As the Dutch evaluation report on the EES's first five years concludes, its impact on Dutch policies has been quite moderate (Zijl *et al.* 2002). In other words, in the historical development of Dutch activation policies, the introduction of the EES constitutes a rather arbitrary moment. Of course, some important reforms have taken place since then, but in general they were not triggered by the EES and its guidelines and recommendations.

This paper will first provide an overview of the origins of Dutch activation policies and some developments in the period preceding the EES. We will then look in more detail at the reforms that have taken place during the EES period. In analysing developments in Dutch activation, we will make a distinction between what has been called 'formal policy' – that is, changes in the nature and content of social policy programmes – on the one hand, and 'operational policy' (that is, changes in the management, administration and organisation of these policies) on the other (Carmel and Papadopoulos 2003). During the last decade or so, the latter type of development in activation and social policy more generally has become increasingly important. Put differently, in the course of its history, activation has become a two-sided process of activating both the unemployed and the institutions involved in the administration and delivery of social security and activation services, as it has become increasingly clear that the latter is a *sine qua non* of the former. After our analysis of developments in activation, we will look at its effects. Specific attention will be paid to the effects of reforms of operational policy, as these have dominated reforms during the last five years, and have managed to attract international attention – some even talk of a 'Dutch model'. Then, drawing upon the Dutch evaluation report on the European Employment Strategy, we will assess the impact of the EES on Dutch activation policies. Finally, we shall present some concluding comments, as well as some tentative remarks on the future of activation in the Netherlands.

The Origins of Activation in the Netherlands: The Pre-EES Period

Debates on the sustainability of the Dutch welfare state date back to the 1970s. Rising unemployment – including long-term unemployment – and, more specifically, the increasing use of disability benefits as a relatively generous exit option for older workers made redundant in times of economic crisis, were sources of concern for successive Dutch cabinets. Initially, this resulted in a period of reform, mainly focusing on welfare state retrenchment, for example by lowering the wage replacement levels of social insurance, reducing entitlement periods, sharpening eligibility criteria, and so on. Increasing the selectivity of Dutch social insurance by making access more difficult and by differentiating entitlements according to individual employment record was an important objective of these reforms (Van Oorschot 1998). Nevertheless, some elements of a more thorough and fundamental modernisation of Dutch social security were already present, although still in embryonic form. On the one hand, some reforms revealed a shift in the objectives of social security from protection and financial compensation towards activation and labour market participation. Examples include an expansion of (re)qualification programmes for the unemployed and an act on promoting the labour market participation of the partially handicapped. Another example is the gradual sharpening of sanctions against people dependent on unemployment benefits. These examples show that Dutch social security was gradually being reformed into a system of incentives and disincentives aimed at influencing the behaviour of the unemployed, especially their motivation to (re-)enter the labour market. On the other hand, a process of activating the social partners was also visible. This took the form of an increasing emphasis on private, supra-statutory social security regulated through collective agreements rather than law (for an analysis of Dutch social security reforms during the 1980s and 1990s see Teulings *et al.* 1997).

These more fundamental elements in the reform of the Dutch welfare state, and specifically the shift from protection to labour market participation as the core objective of welfare state arrangements, came explicitly to the fore in a report by the Netherlands Scientific Council for Government Policy, published in 1990 (WRR 1990). This report had a significant impact on Dutch welfare state and social security reforms during the 1990s, and it is probably no exaggeration to say that it heralded a new era of reform with the explicit aim of transforming the welfare state from 'passive' to 'active'. The central argument of the report – which is still heard today – was that not unemployment but low labour market participation levels are the most significant threat to the sustainability of the Dutch welfare state. From that time onwards, almost every social policy reform has somehow been legitimised by referring to the need to increase labour market participation – and reduce social security dependence – in order to safeguard the sustainability of Dutch social security.

Initially, the reforms focused mainly on formal policy. On the one hand, the reforms of the social security system that started in the 1980s continued. In this process, Dutch disability benefits received most attention, as the number of people dependent on them had increased dramatically, reaching almost one million in the early 1990s. This became notorious internationally as the 'Dutch disease'. On the other hand, a relatively new generation of social policies was introduced: active labour market policies or activation policies. Together with social security reforms, considered part of the transformation process required to make the Dutch welfare state more activating, these were aimed at promoting the labour market participation of those dependent on benefits and social assistance. Besides this 'programmatic' orientation of reforms, however, an 'institutional' approach to the central problem of low labour market participation became increasingly important from 1992 onwards. In other words, after the Scientific Council's report advocating a redefinition of the core problem of the Dutch welfare state from unemployment to low labour market participation, we now saw the emergence of a new approach to identifying the problem's main causes. In order to increase labour market participation, the modernisation not only of formal policy was needed (reforms of social assistance and social insurance, the introduction of activation policies), but also of operational policy, that is, the institutional context of the administration and delivery of social policies. Once again, Dutch disability benefits functioned as a trigger. A parliamentary inquiry into the administration of social security reached the conclusion that the strong involvement of the social partners in the administration of disability benefits played a major role in the dramatic increase in the number of people dependent on disability benefits during the 1990s. The social partners, according to the report in which the results of the parliamentary inquiry were published, had 'misused' and 'abused' disability benefits by opening the gates to social security in order to deal with massive redundancies and dismissals. In those days, disability benefits offered redundant workers relatively generous social protection and so reduced social unrest. This inquiry would become the starting point of a whole range of institutional reforms which we shall discuss in more detail below. Here it should be noted that although the inquiry blamed the social partners for the 'Dutch disease', reduction of the labour supply – for example, by offering older workers relatively generous labour market exit options to 'make room' for young job seekers – was a nationally endorsed strategy for dealing with unemployment until the late 1980s. In terms of welfare state regimes and the classification of the Netherlands as a 'hybrid' model (Esping-Andersen 1999), Dutch labour market policy had clear conservative characteristics until the late 1980s.

We will now look in more detail at these reforms of formal and operational policy.

Formal Policy: Social Security Reforms

In their analysis of social security reforms in the period 1987-1997, Teulings *et al.* (1997) distinguish three types of reform:

1. Reforms affecting access to the social security system. In this context, three examples can be mentioned. First, the accessibility of social assistance to young unemployed school leavers has been reduced. For them, the right to social assistance has been replaced by a right to activation (see below), which implies that they will only receive an income when they accept a work experience placement. Secondly, later in the 1990s Dutch sickness benefits (the gateway to Dutch disability benefits) were privatised for most workers. This meant that during the first year of sickness, employers were obliged to pay their sick employees at least 70% of their wage.[1] This reform is supposed to have an activating effect as well: it is supposed to stimulate employers to invest in the rapid return of sick workers to work, so preventing disability benefit dependency. A final example concerns reform of the Disability Act. On the one hand, the criteria used in determining whether someone is disabled have been sharpened in order to reduce the inflow into disability benefits. On the other hand, the concept of 'suitable job' has

---

[1] In collective agreements between unions and employers' organisations, suprastatutory arrangements have been created so that most employees will receive their full wage for a maximum period of 1 year of sickness.

been broadened. This means that in determining the remaining earning capacity of a disability benefit claimant (which affects the amount of money they are entitled to), a broader range of jobs will be taken into account than those matching their qualifications and work experience.

2. A second group of reforms concerns the period of benefit dependency for those eligible for benefits. On the one hand, these reforms are intended to make a period of benefit dependency less attractive, which is seen as an incentive to find a job and become financially independent from social security. Thus, the periods during which people are entitled to social insurance and to the wage-related component of social insurance benefits have been curtailed.[2] On the other hand, tests during periods of benefit dependency to determine whether people still meet the eligibility requirements have been intensified. Thus, disability benefit claimants are tested more frequently to see if their earnings capacity has increased. And unemployed people on unemployment benefits or social assistance are supervised more vigorously as far as their efforts to increase their employability and to apply for jobs and their willingness to accept job offers are concerned.

3. A final group of reforms is aimed at promoting exit from benefits or social assistance. The expansion of activation programmes and of their target groups (see below) is one measure taken in this context. Another is broadening the concept of a 'suitable job', which has been introduced not only in relation to disability benefits but also, for example, social assistance. A new Social Assistance Act introduced in 1996 implemented a system in which the unemployed had to accept a broader range of jobs the longer their unemployment went on.

Partly, these reforms are a continuation of the type of reforms introduced during the 1980s. However, as Teulings *et al.* argue, they also differ from prior reforms in that they are more explicitly aimed at promoting labour market participation and independence of the welfare state, and focus much more strongly on the individual responsibility of benefit claimants to increase their employability and promote benefit exit. In Dutch policy rhetoric, the paradigm shift towards a more activating welfare state consists of a mixture of sticks and carrots: that is, a blend of measures aimed at strengthening the obligations of social security claimants and making social security dependence less attractive

---

[2] In the context of the Dutch social security system this means that people will end up in the income safety net of the Dutch social security system – social assistance: a flat-rate rather than wage-related benefit linked to statutory minimum income – sooner than formerly. In addition, as social assistance entitlements are not individualised, they may run out of public income transfer entitlements if they have a working spouse, for example.

on the one hand, and supportive measures in the form of activation programmes on the other.

Formal Policy: Introduction and Expansion of Activation Policies

The introduction of activation and reintegration programmes is the second type of formal policy reform accompanying the Dutch paradigm shift in social policies. Earlier in this paper we characterised these programmes as relatively new: in contrast to the Scandinavian countries, the Netherlands has no rich history of (supply-oriented) active labour market policies. The first experimental activation programmes started in the late 1980s, although there were predecessors, which makes identifying an exact starting point a bit arbitrary. It would be impossible to give a full overview of the numerous changes *of* programmes and *in* programmes that have taken place during the last 15 years. Instead, we will focus on some of the main developments.

The first development has been the gradual enlargement of the target groups of activation programmes. Initially, the programmes focused on the young unemployed, specifically young people receiving social assistance. This seems to be quite common in Europe: partly because – at least in some countries – young people are hit particularly hard in periods of rising unemployment; partly because the social and individual consequences of youth unemployment are considered to be more serious than those of adult unemployment; and partly because the adoption of a stricter approach to social security recipients meets less resistance when focused on the young unemployed (see, among others, Kieselbach 2002; López Blasco *et al.* 2003; Serrano Pascual 2004). Also comparable to the situation in other countries (for example, the British New Deal – Stafford and Kellard 2004), the programmes for the young unemployed received most attention and most funds. They were turned into full-coverage programmes in the early 1990s, which was not the case for the programmes aimed at the long-term unemployed also being developed in the early 1990s. During the 1990s, more and more target groups – apart from the young and long-term unemployed – were subjected to activation programmes. In the period under consideration here (up to 1998), this particularly affected the position of (partly) disabled people and single parents dependent on social assistance. As far as the latter group is concerned, the new Social Assistance Act of 1996 is important. Before 1996, single parents dependent on social assistance (95% of whom are women) were categorically relieved of the work obligation until their youngest child reached the age of 12. The 1996 Act lowered the age threshold to 5 (Knijn and Van Wel 2001). Thus, as soon as their youngest child turned 5, single parents on social assistance were treated as 'normal' unemployed. This reflects a more general trend taking place in the context of 'activating' the Dutch welfare state: a redefinition of the status of various categories of social security claimants. Groups of people who used to be considered as legitimately drawing benefits or social assistance because they were single parents, widows or partly disabled were redefined as 'regular' unemployed.

The second development concerns the instruments available for activation programmes. On the one hand, a differentiation of instruments has been taking place. During the 1990s, the range of instruments available gradually expanded, and came to include job-search guidance, job mediation, work experience placements, temporary and permanent subsidised jobs, wage subsidies to make low-paid jobs more attractive and to promote the labour market participation of the long-term unemployed, supported employment, training courses for professional and soft skills, voluntary work, and so on. On the other hand, a flexibilisation of instruments took place, so that activation agencies had more discretionary power in deciding the content of the activation programme of a particular individual. Even a differentiation of the *objectives* of activation could be observed. Although participation in the regular labour market remained the main objective of activation programmes, it was recognised that for some groups of unemployed, this might be a bridge too far. Therefore, subsidised employment could in certain cases be considered an end station of activation. The 1996 Social Assistance Act went one step further in differentiating the objectives of activation. The Act allowed municipalities to experiment with so-called social activation programmes, which were aimed at the category of unemployed furthest from the labour market. These social activation programmes were aimed at promoting the participation of this category of unemployed in unpaid activities, for example, voluntary or community work. These activities could be considered a stepping stone towards labour market participation, but they could also be aimed at promoting social participation and preventing or combating social exclusion and social isolation. In the latter case, labour market participation was not an explicit objective. Participation in the latter type of social activation programmes was voluntary (cf. van Berkel and Hornemann Møller 2002).

The third development is a clear shift in activation from target groups towards more individualised or personalised approaches. The first activation programmes were aimed at target groups that were defined in a traditional way, such as the young unemployed and the long-term unemployed. Over the years, it became clear that this way of defining target groups was of limited use in activation programmes. The heterogeneity within these target groups was considerable and uniform social intervention instruments were not very successful in dealing with highly differentiated ones. The abovementioned flexibilisation of activation instruments was one policy response to this situation. The development of a new, more refined system of defining target groups, introduced nationally, was another. This system assigned each individual unemployed person to a group at a 'similar distance' from the labour market. On the basis of information gathered during intake interviews with the help of a so-called labour market measuring rod, each activated individual would be assigned to one of four groups, each of which represented a different labour market 'distance'. In this way, decisions regarding the nature of activation interventions could – at least theoretically – be based on a broader insight into the situation and the characteristics of the individual unemployed person than was possible under a traditional target group approach. The activation programmes and instruments available for an individual were dependent on the group to which they were assigned. Thus, people assigned to category 1, the group closest to the labour market, were considered able to find a job on their own and did not receive any support. For the unemployed in category 2, a short period of activation was considered to be sufficient. Unemployed persons in category 3 were confronted with multiple problems and barriers to labour market participation. Temporary or permanent subsidised jobs were considered adequate activation instruments for this group. Category 4, finally, were considered as at such a distance from the labour market that they could only return to it with help. The abovementioned social activation programmes were mainly aimed at this group.

The fourth development concerns the obligations of persons dependent on benefits and social assistance. As already mentioned, an increasing proportion of social security claimants were redefined as 'normally' unemployed. This implied that they were subject to the work and activation obligations. In addition, the obligations of the unemployed were sharpened and sanctions for non-compliance were laid down. In most cases, sanctioning would involve a temporary reduction or withdrawal of benefits or social assistance. However, a formal system of sanctions is of little use if administrative agencies – for whatever reason – do not supervise the behaviour of the unemployed. Therefore, national government not only aimed at sharpening the obligations of the unemployed, but also at strengthening their enforcement by administrative agencies, for example, by demanding more frequent interactions between the agencies and the unemployed. This brings us to the next type of social policy reform: reform of the institutional arena.

Operational Policy: Reform of the Institutional Arena

During the 1990s, awareness increased concerning the crucial role of administrative agencies in realising national social policy objectives and enforcing regulations. It became increasingly clear that the central objectives of increasing labour market participation and reducing social security dependency required not only programmatic changes, but also an institutional arena committed to acting in accordance with national government's aims. This awareness instigated a new wave of reforms – stimulated by New Public Management and New Governance ideas – that would lead to a thorough restructuring of the administrative arena, and to the introduction of new forms of steering by national government. In the period under consideration here – before the introduction of the European Employment Strategy – two reform processes should be mentioned. The first concerns reform of the administrative structure of social insurance, that is, unemployment benefits and disability benefits. Until the 1990s, the administrative structure of social insurance had strong corporatist characteristics. Trade unions and employers were in charge of its administration through so-called industrial insurance boards which were organised on a branch basis. They were also strongly represented in the tripartite supervisory body. When successive Dutch governments failed to reduce the number of recipients of disability benefits, this corporatist administrative and supervisory structure came under pressure: the 'Dutch disease' increasingly came to be seen as an *institutional* problem (Van der Veen 2002). The involvement of the social partners in the administration of social insurance was seen as a major barrier to realising the government's social security reform objectives because it allowed the social partners to pursue their own policy priorities. These did not necessarily correspond with – and sometimes even contradicted – national government objectives. Thus, a process of 'disentanglement' was started: 'The various interest groups, particularly the social partners, that are involved in social security administration are kept at a distance from actual case administration, and the process of intertwining the responsibilities of the various parties involved is being reversed' (Van der Veen 2002, 198). The industrial insurance boards were abolished, and the administration of social security was left to independent administrative agencies (five so-called 'uvi's'). In other words, the involvement of the social partners was marginalised.

Interestingly, the second institutional reform – the reform of the public employment services (PES) that started in the 1990s – shows an opposite development, at least temporarily (the reform process is analysed in more detail in Sol 2003). Originally, PES was a public sector organisation functioning independently of the social security administration and governed directly by the Ministry of Social Affairs and Employment. Growing criticism of and dissatisfaction with PES services led to a decision by national government to end direct government control. Instead, a tripartite management structure was established which involved the social partners directly in the management of the PES agencies. However, an evaluation report published in 1995 was very critical of the effects of the reform in terms of effectiveness and efficiency: although the results of activation programmes improved, costs had increased significantly and little attention was paid to the group of unemployed at the greatest distance from the labour market. A new round of reforms followed, which from a present-day perspective can be seen as the first steps towards the introduction of market mechanisms and a purchaser/provider split in employment services. Part of the PES budget was made performance-related; the administrative agencies of social insurance (the 'uvi's') and social assistance (the municipalities) acted as purchasers of employment services. As the purchasers were obliged to purchase 80% of their reintegration services from PES, competition remained limited.

Activation Reforms in the Netherlands since the Introduction of the EES

The conclusions of the European Council summit in 2000 in Lisbon explicitly referred to the development of 'active welfare states' in the EU: 'Investing in people and developing an active and dynamic welfare state will be crucial both to Europe's place in the knowledge economy and for ensuring that the emergence of this new economy does not compound the existing social problems of unemployment, social exclusion and poverty' (quoted in Esping-Andersen 2002, viii). The active welfare state concept was introduced into the EU debate during the Belgian presidency in 1999, and was described by the then Belgian Minister for Social Affairs and Pensions as follows:

> First, it refers to a goal, namely a state of *active* people. We want to enable all citizens to participate in the mainstream of social and economic life. Second, it is no coincidence that our objective is called a *welfare* state: the traditional ambition of providing adequate social protection for those who cannot participate actively, or who have reached the age of retirement, is entirely preserved. Third, the notion suggests that we need an '*intelligently active* state', i.e. it refers to the way in which government should conduct and manage its social policy. (Esping-Andersen 2002, ix; italics in original)

Before the concept of active welfare state was introduced and became a buzzword in European policy debate, the European Employment Strategy was clearly intended to make EU welfare states more activating and thus to promote an EU-wide shift in the core objectives of social policy from protection to participation. Of course, this did not come out of the blue: several national governments were already advocating or actually implementing social policy reforms in the spirit of this paradigm shift in their national welfare states. In the previous section, we tried to show that the Netherlands was one of these countries, and that the shift towards an active welfare state was well under way by the time the EES was introduced. Because of this, we believe that the Netherlands is a trend setter rather than a trend follower as regards the transformation of European welfare states. This conclusion was also reached in the Dutch evaluation report on the European Employment Strategy (Zijl *et al.* 2002). Against the background of the central role of policy learning in the Open Method of Coordination underlying the EES, the authors of the Dutch evaluation report distinguish three 'levels' of policy learning:

> First-order changes are no more than minor adjustments in the policy instruments. [...] Second-order changes involve a form of retooling and the introduction of new policy techniques. [...] Third-order changes concern a shift in 'the hierarchy of goals and instruments employed to guide policy' [*author's note*: reference omitted]. In agreement with Kuhn's paradigm of 'normal science' and paradigm shifts, Hall conjectures that a third-order change comes close to a paradigm shift. (Zijl *et al.* 2002, 20-21)

They conclude that no third-order changes have taken place in Dutch social policies as a consequence of the EES. This statement can be substantiated by looking at the policy reforms that have been taking place since 1998 which, as we will try to show, reveal an intensification and continuation of the line of reforms started in the late 1980s rather than a fundamental shift. In addition, an important part of the reforms in the period since 1998 has focused on institutional reforms, whereas the EES guidelines mainly focus on programmatic issues. Only since the guidelines of 2003 has the EES paid specific attention to issues of governance. However, the EES governance guidelines strongly focus on partnerships, which are not the central element of the Dutch institutional reforms.

Formal Policy: Social Security Reforms

Since 1998, several new reforms have been introduced in the Dutch social security system. As in the pre-1998 period, these reforms aim at making social security less attractive and at promoting the labour market entry of people dependent on social security – in short, they aim to make social security more activating. Reforms of the unemployment benefit system, for example, make certain groups of unemployed dependent on social assistance sooner than before. In the coming years, drastic changes in disability benefits will be introduced – the marginalisation of the social partners in the administration of social insurance has not had the curative effect on disability benefit dependency that was expected – which will make these benefits accessible only to permanently and fully disabled people. Furthermore, 2004 saw the introduction of yet another new Social Assistance Act, the Act on Work and Assistance. Apart from the institutional reforms this act introduced (see below), two new elements should be mentioned here. First, it put an end to categorical exemptions from the work obligation. This implies that single parents with young children (irrespective of their age) and unemployed persons of 57.5 years or older (formerly exempt from the work obligation) are now obliged to seek work and accept job and activation offers. Secondly, the new act replaced the concept of 'suitable' job with that of 'generally acceptable' job. This means that unemployed social assistance recipients have to accept any job offer that is made to them, irrespective of their qualifications or prior work experience. In the area of the privatisation of social security, employers are now obliged to continue paying sick employees 70% of their wages for a maximum period of 2 years. This is supposed to act as an incentive for employers to increase their efforts to reintegrate sick employees. Finally, national government will abolish the subsidisation of early retirement schemes. That way, it intends to promote the labour market participation of older workers and to discourage early labour market exit.

Formal Policy: Activation Programmes

Although the period since 1998 has not seen the introduction of (major) new activation programmes, reforms have been taking place that aim at intensifying the activation efforts of Dutch social policies. Let us look at some examples. Comprehensive approaches have been introduced for unemployed persons aged 24 or above, not only newly unemployed individuals, but also those already dependent on social assistance or benefits. In addition, changes in the status of people dependent on social security have also continued: as already mentioned, the obligation to look for a job and accept job offers has been extended to groups of people formerly exempt from the work obligation. Older unemployed people were a 'new' category affected by this strategy, and this reflects the concerns about an ageing society that are at the top of the social policy agenda of many European countries. Activation has also become more focused on regular labour market participation. For example, the obligatory nature of the social activation programmes mentioned above has been strengthened for people with work obligations, and these programmes are increasingly seen as stepping stones towards paid labour. Furthermore, the present government has decided to reduce the number of subsidised jobs considerably, as these were considered to be 'participation traps': the number of people exiting subsidised jobs and finding a regular job was seen as too low. Whether subsidised jobs might be the best available participation form for certain groups of unemployed people was not considered during the preparation of this government decision. A final development that should be mentioned is that national government has been reducing the budget available for activation in recent years. In the context of increasing unemployment, the reduction of activation budgets has inevitable consequences for the implementation of activation programmes. We will return to this later.

Operational Policy: Institutional Reforms

In the previous section we saw how the structure and management of the institutional arena of the administration and delivery of social security and employment and activation services was increasingly identified as a major barrier to transforming the Dutch welfare state. In the period 1998-2004, the institutional reforms that started in the early 1990s were significantly intensified, leading to an overhaul of the institutional structure, leaving no part of the administration of social insurance, social assistance and employment and activation services untouched.

After having marginalised the role of the social partners in the administration of social insurance, the Dutch government intended to privatise the administrative structure. The five 'uvis' were to be sold to commercial providers, and newcomers would be allowed to enter the administration market as well. However, this proposal was rejected by the Dutch parliament which was particularly anxious about the way the commercial providers would use data on beneficiaries (cf. Gilbert 2002). The Dutch government therefore decided to establish an institution for the administration of social insurance – the Administrative Agency for Employees' Insurance (UWV) – functioning under the direct responsibility of the Ministry of Social Affairs and Employment, and involving a merger of the five 'uvis'. This development towards centralisation and an expansion of national government control differs from developments in the areas of social assistance and activation services, and seems to contradict principles of New Government and New Public Management which advocate decentralisation rather than centralisation, and a reduction rather than expansion of the role of the central state in administration and service delivery (Osborne and Gaebler 1993; Newman 2001). However, in the area of social security administration, centralisation and strengthening central state control were seen as the only feasible road towards the creation of an institutional administrative arena that would comply with national government's policy objective of making Dutch social security more activating.

A second wave of institutional reforms took place in the area of social assistance. Once again, the government's main concern was to provide incentives to the municipalities responsible for administering social assistance to cooperate in realising a more activating social security system. This required central steering mechanisms, in a context in which it was recognised that decentralisation and local discretion were necessary to adjust general policy programmes to local and individual circumstances. Reforms aimed at balancing centralisation and decentralisation have characterised the reform of Dutch social assistance for a long time (see, for example, van Berkel and Van der Aa 2004). In the first few years of the millennium, a performance-based funding system for the activation of social assistance recipients was introduced. In the so-called Agenda for the Future agreements the government agreed with the municipalities that they would receive extra funds for activation if they achieved a specified number of activation trajectories, of which a certain proportion should result in labour market entry.

However, even before the first results of this performance-based funding system were known, a new system was being prepared. This was introduced with the implementation of a new Social Assistance Act in 2004, the second in a decade. Since the introduction of social assistance in the Netherlands in the 1960s, the Dutch municipalities have been responsible for its administration. However, they were never fully financially responsible. National government refunded most municipal expenses in the context of social assistance: 90% until the introduction of the new Social Assistance Act of 1996. The 1996 Act reduced this proportion to 75%, but this was still considered insufficient to provide financial incentives for municipalities to strengthen their activation efforts aimed at social assistance recipients. Thus, the most recent social assistance reform proceeded with the strategy of increasing the financial responsibility of the municipalities, and made them fully financially responsible for social assistance. Each year, municipalities receive a fixed budget for social assistance from national government, which is calculated on the basis of historical data and economic indicators. When municipalities exceed the budget for social assistance payments, they have to draw on their own resources. If they spend less, they are free to spend the rest of the budget as they like. This system is expected to encourage local authorities to activate social assistance recipients and to reduce spending on social assistance payments. Anticipating the positive results of these reforms – in terms of a reduction of social assistance dependency – the government has reduced the overall budget for social assistance expenditure. This may turn out to be premature, not only because the unemployment situation has deteriorated in recent years, but also because it will take some time for the reforms to take effect.

The third institutional reform concerns the provision of activation services. Until the late 1990s, the public employment services were the main providers of activation services, both for the insured and for social assistance recipients. As mentioned in the previous section, several reforms of PES management took place in the 1990s to improve its role in activating the unemployed. However, these reforms were considered unsuccessful. Therefore, the government decided to radicalise the introduction of market mechanisms and the purchaser/provider split which had already guided the latest reforms in the pre-1998 period by fully liberalising the provision of activation services. Nowadays, activation services are provided mainly by private, for-profit companies. The PES departments providing activation services have been privatised, and what is left is a slimmed down PES that is responsible for some basic services, such as registration of the unemployed, registration of job vacancies and the activation of newly registered unemployed.

In the new institutional arena, a split between purchasers and providers of activation services has been implemented. The main public purchasers are the agencies administering benefits and social assistance. Municipalities have to buy activation services for social assistance recipients, and the new public agency for the administration of employees' insurance has to buy activation services for recipients of unemployment and disability benefits. To promote competition, and to avoid preferred supplier processes, public purchasers are obliged to spend 70% of their activation budgets on the open market, and have to use open tendering procedures in the purchasing process. Apart from these public purchasers of activation services, a group of private purchasers is becoming increasingly important, namely the employers. The privatisation of sickness benefits has increased the responsibilities of employers in the reintegration of sick employees, for which purpose employers can buy the services of reintegration companies. So far, approximately 700 companies have registered as reintegration companies, two thirds of which are smaller companies (employing fewer than ten employees).

What is left of PES has been reorganised into a nationwide network of so-called Centres for Work and Income. These CWIs are the gatekeepers of the Dutch social security system. New social security claimants will enter the system through the CWI, which registers the claimants and determines their labour market 'distance'. The group of unemployed closest to the labour market are serviced by CWI, which offers them information on vacancies, support in making job applications, and so on. CWI provides these services itself; it does not act as a buyer on the activation market. Other unemployed persons – and the unemployed closest to the labour market who have not found a job after six months of unemployment – are referred to the benefit agencies responsible for these groups of 'harder to employ' unemployed. In other words, CWI plays no role in the activation of people who have been unemployed for a period longer than six months.

Some Effects and Implications of the Reforms

During the 1990s, activation efforts increased significantly. This also becomes clear when we look at expenditure on activation policies (Table 1).

Table 1. Expenditure on Activation Policies in the Netherlands and the EU, 1986-1999

	1986-1990	1991-1995	1996-1999
% of GDP			
Netherlands	0.56	0.85	1.07
EU	0.62	0.79	0.78
% of total unemployment expenditure			
Netherlands	16	22	25
EU	28	28	29

Source: Calmfors *et al.* (2001), quoted in Zijl *et al.* (2002, p. 36).

One of the first things Dutch policy-makers will point to when asked about the effects of the reforms are some general data on the labour market participation of the Dutch population. And indeed, as the following tables show, labour market participation in the Netherlands increased significantly during the 1990s. First, unemployment fell to 2.5% in 2001 (see Table 2). Recently, however, it has increased again, and is now around 6%.

Table 2. Unemployment in the Netherlands and the EU, 1993-2003

	1993	1995	1997	1999	2001	2003
NL	6.2	6.6	4.9	3.2	2.5	3.8
EU-15	10.1	10.1	10.0	8.6	7.4	8.0

Source: Eurostat

Secondly, the employment rate of the Dutch population has increased significantly. In the course of 10 years, the overall employment rate increased by 10 percentage points, compared with 4 percentage points in the EU during the same period. There has been a considerable improvement in the employment rates of women and older workers.

Women's employment rate increased 13 percentage points, and the employment rates of older workers by an impressive 16 percentage points. In both respects, the Netherlands performed significantly better than the EU as a whole (see Table 3).

Table 3. Employment Rates in the Netherlands and the EU, 1993-2003

	1993	1995	1997	1999	2001	2003
NL total	63.6	64.7	68.5	71.7	74.1	73.5
EU-15	60.1	60.1	60.7	62.5	64.1	64.4
NL men	74.6	75.3	78.8	80.9	82.8	80.9
EU-15	71.0	70.5	70.7	72.0	73.1	72.6
NL women	52.2	53.8	58.0	62.3	65.2	65.8
EU 15	49.2	49.7	50.8	52.9	55.0	56.0
NL older*	28.8	28.9	32.0	36.4	39.6	44.8
EU-15	35.7	36.0	36.4	37.1	38.8	41.7

Note: * 55-64 years of age. *Source*: Eurostat.

Of course, it is a well-known characteristic of the Dutch labour market that the increasing participation of women is mainly taking the form of part-time work. This is illustrated by Table 4, which shows the large number of part-time jobs and the significant increase in the relative importance of part-time work during the 1990s.

Table 4. Part-Time Work in the Netherlands and the EU, 1993-2003

	1993	1995	1997	1999	2001	2003
NL	35.0	37.3	38.0	39.4	42.2	45.0
EU-15	–	16.0	16.9	17.7	18.0	18.6

Source: Eurostat.

Finally, long-term unemployment has also decreased significantly, from around 50% in the early 1990s to around one third in 2000 (see Table 5).

Table 5. Long-Term Unemployment in the Netherlands and the EU, Men and Women, 1990-2000

	1990	1995	2000
NL men	55	52	32
EU men	47	49	45
NL women	45	42	33
EU women	50	51	48

Source: OECD, quoted in Zijl et al. (2002), p. 10.

However, it is impossible to establish the degree to which activation policies have contributed to these results which, from the point of view of promoting labour market participation, are quite positive. As the Dutch EES evaluation report states, measuring the effectiveness of policies is a 'weak spot' in the Netherlands (which is putting it mildly), and this becomes an even bigger problem in respect of comparative research into the impact of reforms. Of course, it is likely that activation policies have had some effect. For example, the introduction of tens of thousands of subsidised jobs will have contributed to a reduction in long-term unemployment, as these jobs were mainly targeted at this group. However, this does not alter the fact that we cannot make a reliable assessment of the relative impact of activation on labour market participation figures compared to, for example, the impact of economic growth during the second half of the 1990s.

Apart from their direct effectiveness, the Dutch EES evaluation report points out that the reforms may also have had an indirect impact, for example, on the actions and attitudes of relevant actors, such as administrative agencies, employers and the unemployed.

As already mentioned, since 1998 institutional reforms have intensified (see van Berkel and Van der Aa 2005).

One of the main reform objectives was to increase the number of unemployed people involved in activation programmes and to improve their effectiveness. As far as the activation of social insurance recipients is concerned, recent research reveals that the administrative agency for social insurance has not managed to achieve a comprehensive approach to activation (Kok et al. 2004). As regards the activation of social assistance recipients, preliminary evaluation of the contractual agreements between the municipalities and national government shows a similar picture, namely that objectives have not been realised. At the same time, differences between the municipalities are significant (Table 6).

Table 6. Progress in Respect of 'Agenda for the Future' Agreements in the 30 Largest Municipalities, Netherlands, 2002

	Proportion of agreed number of trajectories realised (%)	Proportion of agreed number of job entries realised (%)
Amsterdam	76	104
The Hague	86	194
Rotterdam	72	96
Utrecht	67	68
Alkmaar	36	32
Almelo	93	27
Amersfoort	92	101
Arnhem	61	79
Breda	89	175
Deventer	71	65
Dordrecht	67	99
Eindhoven	90	86
Emmen	86	40
Enschede	101	136
Groningen	98	241
Heerlen	84	102
Helmond	50	69
Hengelo	23	69
Leeuwarden	97	64
Leyden	22	45
Lelystad	43	21
Maastricht	95	100
Nymegen	68	91
's-Hertogenbosch	34	27
Schiedam	60	55
Tilburg	90	166
Venlo	106	225
Zaanstad	89	113
Zwolle	90	45

Source: Ministry of Social Affairs and Employment, *Tweede Voortgangsrapportage Agenda voor de Toekomst* (http://docs.szw.nl/pdf/35/2004/35_2004_3_4921.pdf). One of the municipalities is missing in the tables presented in this report.

As Table 6 shows, the degree to which the municipalities succeeded in realising the number of activation trajectories agreed for 2002 ranges from 22% for the worst performer to 106% for the best performer. There is even greater variation in respect of the agreed number of labour market entries: while the worst performer realised a paltry 21% of the agreed number of entries, the best performer realised 241%. Interestingly, in explaining the disappointing placement results the progress report mentions only implementation and institutional issues, with no reference to growing unemployment. Despite the fact that these results lag behind government targets, the overall impression is that the institutional reforms have substantially increased the number of activated social security and social assistance recipients.

As far as activation outcomes are concerned, the picture is less clear. In the Dutch context, activation is considered successful when it results in a sustainable job placement, which is defined as a job contract for a period of at least six months. It is well known that the majority of activation trajectories are not successful in this sense, at least in the Dutch context. To illustrate this, the Dutch newspaper *NRC Handelsblad* published the following activation results for the first six months of 2004 (*NRC Handelsblad*, 22 January 2005). Of all the recipients of unemployment benefits or disability benefits referred to reintegration companies by the UWV, 28% found a job for a period of at least six months and 45% were referred back to the UWV without success. Of the unemployed social assistance recipients referred to the reintegration companies by the municipalities, 20% managed to find a job for a period of at least six months. One third were referred back to the municipalities without success.

In addition, no data are available about what happens to successfully activated people after six months. That is, we do not know whether activated people manage to keep their jobs or become unemployed again. This issue is becoming increasingly important as there is a clear tendency in Dutch activation to focus on short-term job placements rather than on investing in the qualifications, skills and capacities of the unemployed, that is, their long-term employability. As we will see, this tendency can also be considered a consequence of the institutional reforms. Secondly, activation is increasingly focusing on participation in the regular labour market. Nevertheless, a considerable proportion of the labour market entries of activated social assistance recipients involve subsidised jobs, the volume of which is, as already mentioned, now being reduced. Thus, the reduced availability of subsidised jobs will most likely lower the success rate of activation trajectories. Finally, it is questionable whether finding a job after activation should always be interpreted as a *result* of activation. Reintegration companies are inclined to do so, as they are paid only for successful activation trajectories. However, from the point of view of the unemployed, attributing labour market entry to activation is often doubtful.

Another objective of the institutional reforms was to increase the efficiency of activation, that is, the degree to which activation offers meet the needs of the unemployed. Nowadays, it is hard to find a policy document on activation that does not somehow underline the positive impact of tailor-made, individualised or personalised services on the success of activation. Introducing market mechanisms and competition into the provision of activation services was expected to promote this, but it has not yet happened. The activation services provided by the private reintegration companies continue to be highly standardised (lack of 'allocative efficiency'), and research has pointed out that the companies are reluctant to innovate (lack of 'dynamic efficiency' – Struyven *et al.* 2002; Algemene Rekenkamer 2004). In addition, according to public purchasers there is little differentiation in the services provided by the reintegration companies. This situation can be explained in a number of ways. First, the reintegration companies characterise the market as a 'prize fighter market' (Arents *et al.* 2004). The large number of companies operating on the market and the relatively short period for which contracts are usually concluded (on average, 1-1.5 years) make competition strong. Secondly, most contracts mention success rates of 40% to 50%. This means that the reintegration companies can be unsuccessful in about half of the trajectories that they provide without violating contractual agreements. Thirdly, public purchasers often leave the decisions about the content of activation trajectories to the reintegration companies. The consequence of this is that the public purchasers do not monitor whether individual activation trajectories do indeed meet the needs of the unemployed.

Increasing the quality of activation services has been mentioned as another objective of the institutional reforms in general and of the liberalisation of activation services specifically. The Dutch government does not interfere in this respect, as it relies on the self-regulating power of the market. The branch organisation of reintegration companies has developed a quality mark, but the criteria included in it tell us little about what actually happens in the activation process: for example, how the companies try to design tailor-made and individualised activation interventions, how clients are treated during activation, and so on. Research into the implementation of the institutional reforms has concluded that there is no evidence that liberalisation has indeed improved the quality of activation services (see, for example, Horssen *et al.* 2004; Arents *et al.* 2004). Standardised activation offers predominate and the lack of innovation and differentiation is not encouraging. In addition, the emphasis in the contractual agreements concluded between government and municipalities is on quantitative rather than qualitative targets. This also applies to the aim of taking a comprehensive approach in the activation of both social insurance and social assistance recipients.

A final issue that should be mentioned in this context is choice. It is evident that the liberalisation process has increased choice for the purchasers of activation services. For the clients or users of activation, however, the story is completely different. Despite the policy rhetoric about the importance of clients' choice and how this may improve the functioning of the market, the strong emphasis in the Dutch activation debate on the obligations and responsibilities of activation target groups has contributed to a situation in which policy-makers are not eager to empower clients. It therefore came as no surprise when a National Audit Office study among recipients of unemployment benefit reached the conclusion that clients had virtually no choice (Algemene Rekenkamer 2004). Nevertheless, a number of developments are worth mentioning in this context. For several years now, some regions have been experimenting with a so-called personal reintegration budget for disabled people. Participants in this experiment can design their own reintegration plan and choose their own reintegration company, although the agency administering their benefits has to approve of the plan. Several hundred people have participated. As a follow-up, a new instrument, the so-called Individual Reintegration Agreement (IRO), was introduced in summer 2004. This instrument is aimed at recipients of disability benefits and unemployment benefits (not yet at social assistance recipients). This instrument is another initiative aimed at increasing the choice of activation clients. Research has shown that in the first 6 months of its existence, over 2,000 IRO applications were made and that the IRO users appreciate the possibility of choice (Aarts *et al.* 2004).

Another issue that should be discussed in relation to the introduction of market mechanisms in the provision of activation services concerns 'creaming' (serving those clients who can most quickly and easily be brought to the payment points) and 'parking' (leaving behind clients thought likely to need more services to reach outcomes, and sacrificing later outcome payments). In the literature on the introduction of market mechanisms in the provision of publicly financed social services, creaming and parking are often mentioned as potential risks. Although no studies exist in the Netherlands that specifically address these issues, there are indications that creaming does not take place frequently. Given that the agencies responsible for the administration of social assistance and social insurance have to realise large numbers of activation trajectories, they have to refer as many clients as possible to the reintegration companies. Furthermore, the reintegration companies themselves would stimulate the administrative agencies to ensure sufficient referrals in order to be able to realise the contractually agreed quantitative targets. These processes reduced creaming processes at the administrative agencies. In addition, creaming at the market entrance of reintegration companies was limited as well, as the companies were allowed to refuse clients referred to them only in exceptional cases (for example, if clients behaved aggressively). At the same time, parking does take place. That is, some groups of clients in an activation trajectory receive more attention than others. For example, in a local study of the activation of social assistance recipients in the city of Rotterdam, it was found that there was no relation between duration of participation in a trajectory on the one hand, and the number of contacts participants have with their consultants or the number of activation services offered to them on the other. Furthermore, a national study into the development of the reintegration market found that several reintegration companies admit the use of parking strategies (Arents *et al.* 2004).

As far as the decentralisation of social assistance is concerned, we have already seen significant differences in the performance of municipalities in the context of the Agenda of the Future agreements with national government. And although no data exist on whether intermunicipal differences have increased as a consequence of decentralisation, one may expect this to be the case, as it is an explicit intention of decentralisation to give local authorities more autonomy in adapting national regulations to local and individual circumstances. As yet, no research data have been published on the effects of the most recent decentralisation reform, the new Social Assistance Act introduced in 2004. Nevertheless, some tentative comments are possible on the consequences of this reform for local social policies in the area of activation and social assistance. The municipalities' financial responsibility for social assistance expenses will most likely change local policy priorities.

In terms of the activation of social assistance recipients, this may happen in several ways. First, the government has released the municipalities from the obligation of pursuing a comprehensive approach in the activation of social assistance recipients. This is an interesting decision, given the EES guidelines on the comprehensive approach (see below). Apparently, the government expects that financial responsibility for social assistance will provide the municipalities with sufficient incentives to activate as many social assistance recipients as possible. However, it is not at all obvious that this is what the municipalities will do. They might also decide to focus activation on the most employable, hoping that this strategy will reduce the number of social assistance recipients most quickly, and with relatively low investment in activation programmes. It is usually the case that the greater the distance from the labour market, the more expensive the reintegration intervention will be. The current labour market situation could function as an extra argument for municipalities to take this road. Unemployment has doubled in the last couple of years, and this has certainly contributed to the failure of the majority of activation trajectories, that is, without the activated persons being reintegrated in the labour market. This strategy will definitely produce creaming processes – and since the contracts between national government and the municipalities will not be renewed, and the obligation to realise a comprehensive approach has been lifted, there are no national regulations or binding agreements that prevent the municipalities from employing this strategy. Secondly, the new regime may have an impact on the content of activation interventions. Several municipalities are increasingly focusing activation on rapid job placements, rather than on investing in the skills, qualifications and employability of the unemployed. The recent popularity in the Netherlands of Work First strategies is one indication of this. Another is the experiences of reintegration companies that it is becoming increasingly difficult to include education in activation trajectories (Arents *et al.* 2004). The replacement in the new Social Assistance Act of the concept of 'suitable job' by that of 'generally acceptable job' makes it easier for municipalities to pursue this strategy, as it obliges the unemployed to accept practically any job offered to them. Thirdly, a 'tougher' approach in activation might also result in a stricter sanctioning regime. More generally, stricter application of sanctions might be seen as a relatively 'cheap' activation strategy.

Although it is clear that the municipalities are using these strategies, no overall picture is available that could inform us of the extent to which this is the case. Furthermore, it remains to be seen whether the municipalities will pursue this tougher approach to social assistance recipients, or will soften their approach once they have become experienced in dealing with the new institutional framework.

The Impact of the EES

The Dutch EES evaluation report is quite clear in its conclusions regarding the EES's impact on Dutch social policies. It has not stimulated fundamental changes in the Dutch welfare state ('third order' or paradigmatic changes, in the terminology used in the evaluation report), as the transformation process towards a more active welfare state started long before the EES was introduced. Against the background of the policies discussed in this paper, the evaluation report mentions two issues in respect of which the EES has had an impact (Zijl *et al.* 2002). First, the EES has stimulated the development of a comprehensive approach in activation. A comprehensive approach to the young unemployed has existed since the early 1990s, but EU pressure has been helpful in implementing a comprehensive approach to the older unemployed, especially the newly unemployed. Interestingly, however, in the context of the decentralisation of social assistance in 2004, the Dutch government put an end to the obligation of local authorities to utilise a comprehensive approach. So at least in the area of social assistance, the impact of the EES has been short-lived. The second area in which the EES has had an impact on Dutch social policies is the labour market participation of women. The evaluation report concludes that the EES has been helpful in defining a long-term target for female labour market participation: 65% by 2010. These moderate results bring the authors of the Dutch EES evaluation report to the following overall conclusion: 'All in all this leads to the conclusion that the EES was not without merit for policy-making, but neither was it the powerful tool for improving social economic policy in the Netherlands it could have been' (Zijl *et al.* 2002, p. 66).

The weak impact of the EES is also reflected in Dutch public and political debate on social policies, in which it hardly plays a role – for example, in legitimating policy reforms. This does not mean that the EU is absent from the transformation of the Dutch welfare state, but its impact is rather on setting and legitimating the general reform agenda than at the level of specific reforms. For example, meeting the criteria of the Stability Pact is frequently mentioned as an argument for reducing the generosity of the Dutch welfare state. The Dutch Finance Minister is a strong opponent of any relaxation of these criteria. Another example concerns the ageing of the population, which is high on the political agenda in the EU and is used by the current Dutch government time and again to legitimate reforms aimed at increasing labour market participation and reducing social security dependency and generosity.

Conclusions and Future Prospects

As we have seen, the Dutch welfare state has gone through considerable reforms during the last 15-20 years. The process is still continuing. These include not only programmatic reforms, but also – and increasingly – reforms of the institutional arena. For people of working age dependent on social security, these reforms have had significant consequences. An increasing proportion of them are now considered unemployed: the legitimacy of other reasons for dependency (disability, age, child care, widowhood) has been eroded. The quality of benefits, especially for those considered employable, has decreased. Apart from these developments in the quality of social security, which in themselves are supposed to have an activating effect, work obligations – and the surveillance of the compliance of the unemployed with these obligations – have been sharpened, along with the system of sanctions for non-compliance. The intensification of interactions between the unemployed and social workers, job consultants, and so on, implies that the behaviour of the unemployed is being scrutinised to an unprecedented degree.

In addition, the focus of activation on regular labour market participation has been strengthened, pushing alternative forms of participation (subsidised jobs, unpaid work) into an even more marginalised position. All in all, we may conclude that in terms of approaches to activation (cf. van Berkel and Hornemann Møller 2002), the Dutch activation approach has gradually become tougher. Furthermore, we see a development from, in the words of Lødemel and Trickey (2000), a human-resource to a labour-attachment approach in activation. Short-term job placements have gained priority over investing in long-term employability (the latter being in the first instance considered an individual responsibility, not a responsibility of the welfare state or the social security system); temporary jobs of six months are considered 'sustainable' in the context of activation (although this is a relatively long period compared to, for example, the UK); and the unemployed experience increasing difficulties in refusing job offers they consider unattractive, as the concept of 'generally acceptable job' makes the refusal of job offers virtually impossible. Improving the quality of jobs – especially when the definition of this concept involves the matching of job characteristics and the characteristics, needs and wishes of the individual unemployed person – is not an ingredient of the Dutch activation strategy, despite the policy rhetoric that 'motivated clients' and 'activation offers that meet the needs and wishes of clients' contribute to the success of activation interventions.

As far as institutional reforms are concerned, preliminary results are disappointing. Although they have contributed to a significant increase in the number of unemployed people involved in activation programmes, other reform objectives have hardly been realised. Increasing unemployment and the deterioration of the Dutch economy can only partly explain the disappointing results. The inadequacy of some of the institutional reforms also plays a role. The liberalisation of activation services is a clear example. This standard bearer of the 'Dutch model' has not met the expectations that market optimists had of it. This does not mean that the introduction of market mechanisms and liberalisation cannot contribute to making activation more effective and efficient, however, and that it cannot improve quality and choice.

References

Aarts, L., M. van den Hauten and K. Visscher (2004), *Eerste voortgangsrapportage IRO*, The Hague, APE.

Algemene Rekenkamer (2004), *Bemiddeling en reïntegratie van werklozen*, The Hague, Algemene Rekenkamer.

Arents, M., R. Dorenbos, V. Van Loon and J. Van Velden (2004), *Ontwikkelingen op de reïntegratiemarkt. Ervaringen van reïntegratiebedrijven en opdrachtgevers*, The Hague, RWI.

Carmel, E. and T. Papadopoulos (2003), "The new governance of social security in Britain", in J. Millar (ed.), *Understanding Social Security: Issues for Social Policy and Practice*, Bristol, Policy Press, pp. 31-52.

Esping-Andersen, G. (2002), *Why We Need a New Welfare State*, Oxford, Oxford University Press.

Esping-Andersen, G. (1999), *Social Foundations of Post-industrial Economies*, Oxford, Oxford University Press.

Gilbert, N. (2002), *Transformation of the Welfare State. The Silent Surrender of Public Responsibility*, Oxford, Oxford University Press.

Horssen, C. van, L. Mallee and J. Mevissen (2004), *De reïntegratiemarkt langs de meetlat van SUWI. Derde inventarisatie van stand van zaken*, Amsterdam, Regioplan.

Kieselbach, T. (ed.) (2002), *Youth Unemployment and Social Exclusion. A Comparison of Six European Countries*, Opladen, Leske + Budrich.

Knijn, T. and F. van Wel (2001), "Careful or lenient: welfare reform for lone mothers in the Netherlands", *Journal of European Social Policy* 11 (3), pp. 235-253.

Kok, L., J.A. Korteweg and M. van der Meer (2004), *Evaluatie sluitende aanpak 1998-2003*, Amsterdam, SEO.

López Blasco, A., W. McNeish and A. Walther (2003), *Young People and Contradictions of Inclusion. Towards Integrated Transition Policies in Europe*, Bristol, Policy Press.

Newman, J. (2001), *Modernising governance. New Labour, Policy and Society*, London, Sage.

Osborne, D. and T. Gaebler (1993), *Reinventing Government. How the Entrepreneurial Spirit Is Transforming the Public Sector*, London/New York, Penguin.

Serrano Pascual, A. (ed.) (2004), *Are Activation Policies Converging in Europe? The European Employment Strategy for Young People*, Brussels, ETUI.

Sol, E. (2003), "Government governance and beyond. Reconciling flexibility and accountability in labour market policy in the Netherlands", paper presented at the conference 'Decentralisation of employment policies and new forms of governance: tackling the challenge of accountability', Warsaw, 27-28 March 2003.

Stafford, B. and K. Kellard (2004), "Making it personal: the development of active labour-market programmes in the UK', paper presented at the ASPEN seminar 'Individual approaches in activation in the EU", Växjö, Sweden (December).

Struyven, L., G. Steurs, A. Peeters and V. Minne (2002), *Van aanbieden naar aanbesteden. Marktwerking bij arbeidsbemiddeling en reïntegratie in Australië, Nederland, Verenigd Koninkrijk en Zweden*, Leuven/Leusden, Acco.

Teulings, C., R. van der Veen and W. Trommel (1997), *Dilemma's van sociale zekerheid. Een analyse van 10 jaar herziening van het stelsel van sociale zekerheid*, The Hague, VUGA.

van Berkel, R. and I. Hornemann Møller (2002), *Active social policies in the EU. Inclusion through participation?*, Bristol, Policy Press.

van Berkel, R. and P. van der Aa (2004), "From welfare state to welfare city? A Dutch case study", paper presented at the ESPAnet conference, Oxford (September).

van Berkel, R. and P. van der Aa (2005), "The marketisation of activation services: a modern panacea?", *Journal of European Social Policy* 15 (4), pp. 329-343.

Van der Veen, R. (2002), "From mutualities and factory funds to a comprehensive system of social insurance schemes. A sociological perspective on the history of social insurance administration", in J. Berghman, A. Nagelkerke, K. Boos, R. Doeschot and G. Vonk (eds.), *Social Security in Transition*, The Hague, Kluwer Law International.

Van Oorschot, W. (1998), "From solidarity to selectivity: the reconstruction of the Dutch social security system 1980-2000", in E. Brunsdon, H. Dean and R. Woods (eds.), *Social Policy Review 10*, London, Social Policy Association, pp. 183-202.

WRR (1990), *Een werkend perspectief. Arbeidsparticipatie in de jaren '90*, The Hague, SdU.

Zijl, M., M. van der Meer, J. van Seters, J. Visser and H.A. Keuzenkamp (2002), *Dutch Experiences with the European Employment Strategy*, Amsterdam, UvA.

Danish Activation Policy: The Role of the Normative Foundation, the Institutional Set-up and Other Drivers

Flemming LARSEN and Mikkel MAILAND

Introduction

Due to the general interest in understanding the background to the strong performance of the Danish labour market in the 1990s, Danish activation policy has had its share of attention. This activation policy was seen as one explanation of the rapid and inflation-free reduction in unemployment. Just as Denmark managed to balance high levels of flexibility and a high level of social security in the labour market in general, so the country seemed to have established a successful activation policy by balancing compulsion and work-testing (sticks) with human capital development and a client-centred approach (carrots).

But how should this successful Danish activation policy be understood? Can it be understood within the framework of the universalistic Scandinavian welfare state, one of 'the three worlds of welfare capitalism' (Esping-Andersen 1990)? Or does the 'recommodification' associated with activation policy imply such a challenge for the 'decommodification' associated with the Scandinavian version in Esping-Andersen's typology that the whole theory and the typology would have to be abandoned?

Activation researchers seem to have responded differently to this and other challenges to this the most prominent of all regime theories. Some activation researchers with an interest in regimes have continued to relate their studies to the Esping-Andersen typology, while others have applied Bob Jessop's three variations of the 'workfare state' (Jessop 1994; Peck 1996; Torfing 1999), and others again have preferred Gallie and Paugam's 'unemployment policy regimes' (Gallie and Paugam 2000; Madsen 2003).

The aim of this chapter, however, will not be to test whether and how Danish activation policy fits these theories, but to *describe* key policy contents and key institutions to *explain* why and how the activation policy came into existence and developed further, and to *discuss* the extent to which the key features of the policy will be able to resist current attempts to fundamentally change them.

In compliance with the focus of this volume, this chapter will primarily concentrate on two features of Danish activation policy: its *normative foundation and justifications*, including the problems that activation policy is believed to be able to solve; how unemployment is understood; the role of evaluations and moral issues (section 3); and *the institutional set-up*, including the role of the state, PES, local authorities and, not least, labour market parties (section 4). In addition – and also in accordance with the focus of the present anthology – in section 5 we analyse the impact of the *European Employment Strategy* on Danish employment policy. However, a full understanding of Danish activation policy has to include at least a short description of its *contents* (including the types of active measures applied, target groups, links to benefits, and so on), and with that we shall begin.

The Contents of Danish Activation Policy

First, we need to step back to the late 1980s/early 1990s when a marked shift from a predominantly passive (support) policy to a more active policy was being formed. Overall, Danish labour market policy at that time was very passive; through the second half of the 1970s and 1980s, passive expenditure on unemployment support and early retirement made up approximately 75% of total labour market-related government expenditure (out of total consumption equivalent to 5-6% of GNP). In addition, employment and training schemes were designed to allow individuals to stay in the system rather than for active skills enhancement or disciplining. However, new discourses paved the way for a policy shift in the 1990s. The work capacity and work ethic of the unemployed were called into question, and structural unemployment (manpower shortage concurrent with high unemployment) was high on the political agenda by the late 1980s. Political discussions about the structural problems of the labour market became the starting signal for a new policy development.

The structural problems led to the establishment of several commissions, and a good deal of debate about possible ways of changing the financing of the unemployment benefit system (instead of being primarily financed by the state there would be higher contributions from enterprises and employees), and reducing the generous (by international comparison) level of unemployment benefit. However, both turned out to be unfeasible politically (and have remained so, for the insured unemployed at least). However, it was possible to mobilise relatively broad support for a more active policy.

There was thus a fairly broad political consensus that it was not possible to solve the problems of unemployment within the framework of the existing well-established employment schemes and support systems. This kind of state-run strategy is believed to give rise to problems, especially in connection with 'work ethic' and 'labour market readiness': the former for groups who have chosen to use the support system to lead an 'alternative lifestyle' outside the labour market, and the latter in relation to the group of long-term unemployed who, after years of idleness and passive support, have lost the ability to get and hold down a job. One's understanding of the scope and nature of the two problems is a matter of perspective and political conviction. Nevertheless, when it comes to the cure, there is widespread political agreement: an active labour market policy, and thus activation. This means a more active policy spanning the field between *social disciplining*, in the form of workfare-inspired incentives such as activation obligations, tougher availability rules and shorter benefit eligibility periods, and *social integration*, whose main measures are activation in relation to individually tailor-made initiatives and skills upgrading, and closer links with the labour market. Figure 1 illustrates this activation policy mix:[1]

Figure 1. The Active Line – Policy Alternatives and Strategies

	Active line/Activation		Passive line
	Social disciplining	Social integration	Social compensation
Problem	Insufficient economic incentives to seek and take a job	Insufficient competences and qualifications to get a job	Insufficient income support
Instruments	Obligation to work or meet other demands	Needs-oriented (re)qualification	Income compensation
Incentives for behavioural change	Extrinsic motivation (sanctions)	Intrinsic motivation (help for self-help)	None
Orientation of problem solution	Ordinary labour market	Ordinary labour market and social orientation	Social orientation
Welfare state contract	Conditional (work obligation) 'Quid pro quo'	Conditional (employability) 'Quid pro quo'	Unconditional in relation to work obligation and employability 'Quid without quo'

---

[1] Workfare/welfare or work-first/human-capital approaches are other distinctions which attempt to describe these policy understandings and strategies.

| Partial objective | Work first | Improve employability | Improve life quality |
| Final objective | Self-sufficiency | | Social security and equality |

From the start, Danish activation policy has been a mix of both social disciplining and social integration, although the emphasis has shifted over time. Social disciplining has thus been given more prominence, especially from the late 1990s, as we discuss in section 3.

Development of the Contents of Activation Policy

In 1992, when it became clear that cuts in the unemployment benefit level were not politically feasible, a committee set up by the government (*the tripartite Zeuthen committee*) instead proposed making the policy more active by introducing more individual and tailor-made skill-enhancement initiatives and reducing the unemployment benefit period. This needs-oriented activation effort would be realised through radical regionalisation, including strengthened regional corporatist bodies, and the introduction of individual action plans that would specify activation and function as a contract between the labour market system and the unemployed individual. A new type of labour market 'deal' was then made with the Labour market reform act of 1994. From a period characterised by fiscal tightening and politically accepted high rates of unemployment, compensated by far-reaching protection systems (administered by the unions), a giant leap was made to an expansive fiscal policy, genuine and early individual education and training of the unemployed, and new regionalised corporatist steering arrangements. Furthermore, the almost 'sacred' protection systems came under attack, with shorter periods of eligibility for unemployment benefit, tougher availability assessments and compulsory activation. The benefit level remained unchanged, but the right to unemployment benefit can no longer be regained via activation or employment schemes. The maximum period in the unemployment benefit system was set at seven years, with the possibility of an extension of two years' leave.

In combination with the reform, leave schemes to some extent institutionalise the idea of temporarily exiting the labour market on public support. Leave schemes for up to one year for sabbaticals, childcare and training/education on unemployment benefit (only 80% for the sabbatical scheme) were introduced in order to reduce the labour supply. These rights applied to both the employed and the unemployed. The favourable conditions for taking leave were reduced significantly during the 1990s, and sabbatical leave has now been abolished (educational and child-care leave still exist but at a very low level).

This strategy proved very successful: unemployment was halved in five years, without causing any significant bottleneck or inflationary problems. The problems of structural unemployment and the negative consequences of passive employment and support schemes seem to have been solved. This has been described as a 'job miracle'. Despite its success (or, some would argue, because of it) the 1994 reform has been adjusted several times. Each adjustment has been a step towards a more active policy, primarily in terms of enrolling more and more unemployed persons in activation programmes. This was done by progressively tightening the obligation to provide the unemployed with an activation offer from after four years of unemployment in 1995 to after one year from 1999 (six months for the young unemployed). Other effects of the adjustments are restricted access to the unemployment benefit system, a reduction in the total unemployment benefit period from seven to four years, and generally tougher availability assessments. Also, the possibilities and conditions of the various leave schemes have been reduced significantly, in effect all but abolishing the job rotation scheme. The local authority activation scheme was legislatively expanded to include all non-insured social welfare recipients, and an option to reduce cash benefits in cases where job offers or participation in activation offers were rejected.

The local authorities' activation schemes targeting the uninsured unemployed developed partly along similar lines to the activation schemes of the PES. That is, activation applied to nearly all uninsured unemployed, but it also differed in terms of instruments and target groups.

After a new right-wing government came to power in 2001, a new labour market reform took effect in 2003, in which the upgrading of the skills of the unemployed was considerably reduced. More emphasis is now placed on guidance and contact meetings, and subsidised jobs. In a sense this can be seen as a change of course compared to the active labour market policy of the 1990s. However, due to increasing unemployment and major redundancies in the wake of the offshoring of manufacturing jobs to low-wage countries, the government has opened up the way for more training, especially for the unskilled and low-skilled unemployed.

To sum up developments in the contents of Danish labour market policy since the 1994 reform, throughout the period the policy has included complementary elements of social disciplining and social integration. There is no doubt, however, that developments have been shifting from a significant focus on social integration to a much greater emphasis on social disciplining. This marks a discursive breach in substance in which Denmark's unique form of workfare policy (social disciplining), including strong elements of social integration (welfare), has taken a more traditional turn. Consequently, the social disciplining elements are becoming more and more prominent in Danish labour market policy. However, the fact remains that Danish labour market policy aims to take into account both the supply and the demand sides, and to balance potentials in terms of allocation, welfare and development. One goal is definitely to make employees more flexible in relation to the demands of the labour market, but at the same time to give them options and offers that really improve their chances.

Arguments Underlying Danish Activation Policy (Normative Justifications)

Activation therefore became the new consensus concept in Danish politics. The arguments supporting it were multiple, and to some extent contested politically. At least three main justifications – each linked to different social and economic problems – of activation can be identified, along with an implicit contract between state and citizens. These four considerations have been used to validate the policy and can thus be interpreted as the drivers behind it.

First, as already mentioned, there was widespread political focus on *'structural problems' in the labour market* (where the term 'structural' refers to labour shortages in spite of continuous unemployment), usually based on a concern about macroeconomic balance problems. Two main approaches to solving these problems can be identified, supporting the strategies of social disciplining and social integration respectively. First, the neo-classical approach, pointing to increased incentives to find work. The means of achieving this include wider wage differentials (lower introduction pay), lower unemployment benefit, obligatory activation and generally tighter availability rules (Hansen *et al.* 1997). In the labour market policy of the 1990s this way of thinking has clearly left its mark, primarily in the form of increasing incentives for accepting a job. This reasoning is based on the perception of individuals as driven by rational calculations ('rational choice'): by making it more attractive to take a job than not, more rational and market-conformist behaviour is encouraged. This approach supports a social disciplinary line in activation policy. Second, the interventionist approach which aims at the targeted skills upgrading and social integration of the individual. Under this approach, the public authorities are given an important role in securing societal solutions to problems that have individual implications.

The qualifications dimension has thus been at the top of the political agenda since the mid-1980s, although it may now be changing, as the understanding of unemployment and the requisite forms of activation seems to be changing. Hence, the partial and gradual development from a human-capital oriented social inclusion strategy to a work-first oriented social disciplining strategy should, among other things, be seen in light of the emergence of newly dominant ideas about which activation measures work and which do not, which is also related to the forms of evaluation chosen by the ministry and the use of evaluation studies.

During the first few years of the new social democratic government, the Ministry of Labour understood structural unemployment as caused by a *qualifications deficit*. Therefore, providing the unemployed with education and training to improve their qualifications quantitatively or to upgrade them could solve the problem. This was reflected in the fact that during the 1990s education and training was by far the most frequently used activation measure, at least for the insured unemployed.

The belief in a qualifications deficit, and in education and training as 'magic tools', was eroded during the later years of the social democratic government, and this erosion continued after the change of government in 2001. It has gradually been replaced by the idea of a *motivational deficit* to support the partial and gradual shift towards the social disciplining approach, within the framework of which activation measures to a larger extent build on incentives for the unemployed to take up employment. This idea is not new, but more weight has been attached to it in recent years. The cause of the problem is now more that the unemployed '*won't work*', while during the period of widespread belief in the qualifications deficit it was held that the unemployed '*can't work*' (Joergensen and Larsen 2003, 181). Hence, making work pay by increasing the pressure to actively seek work has become the order of the day (for example, by widening the gap between minimum wages and unemployment benefit).

Although it is not possible to spell out the exact causal relationship between the two, the erosion of the qualifications deficit idea took place concurrently with a development in evaluation studies. In the mid-1990s, the effect evaluations of activation policy were mostly positive, despite a number of weak points. Benefits included increased effective supply of labour, increased labour market mobility and – despite lock-in effects – (limited) positive employment effects of both education and subsidised training (see summary by Larsen and Langager 1998). By the end of the decade, however, Ministry of Labour studies and independent research became less positive. By including the negative effect of lower search activity during activation (lock-in effect) and the negative employment effect due to higher taxes (financing the cost of activation policy), the Danish Economic Council found that only job training in the private sector had a positive net employment effect for the insured unemployed (Det Oekonomiske Råd 2002). Not surprisingly, the Ministry of Labour's evaluations were less negative than the Economic Council's, but its evaluations did start to pay increasing attention to the negative effects. One of the Ministry's more recent effect evaluations distinguishes between a positive motivational effect, a positive qualification effect and a negative job search effect. Among other things, this evaluation shows that whereas all activation measures reduce the clients' dependence on transfer payments, job training in the private sector does so the most. Moreover, it is argued that the lock-in effect was greatest for activation of the short-term unemployed, indicating that it is possible to start activation too soon (Arbejdsministeriet 2000). However, most of the studies regrettably tend to measure the effect only one year after the end of activation, which is too short a time in which to measure the total positive employment effect of education and training, as demonstrated in a recent independent study (Henning *et al.* 2005).

Second, the level of public spending in relation to what might be called *the problems of financing the welfare state* came to be a dominant political issue. Continually rising welfare expenditure does not tally with broad political ideas on the potential for increasing tax revenue. Among other implications – for example, modernisation of the public sector – in a labour market policy context it is a question of reducing the costs of passive transfer payments.

Third, there is a strong focus on the *interaction between social problems and labour market attachment*. It is thus increasingly recognised that a lack of labour market attachment causes more than just financial losses for the individual. It will often have far-reaching social consequences. It implies that the inherent exclusion mechanisms and the resulting social problems of unemployment cannot be solved by passive income support or social security systems. Work has become the cure-all for an individual's lack of qualifications and social problems. During the 1990s, this perception became even more widespread as activation policies were widened to include more and more target groups. Nearly all unemployed people, whether suffering from social, mental or physical problems, came to be included in the target groups for activation, and would – according to this perception – at some point be able to obtain employment in one form or another. Social inclusion became virtually synonymous with labour market inclusion. Hence, in Denmark the perception of social exclusion was not so much a dependency on transfer income – as proposed in the dependency culture thesis in its 'classic' American formulation (Lindsay and Mailand 2004) – but a weak or missing attachment to the labour market, together with concern about the 'lost generation' of unemployed young people (Clasen 2000).

Fourth, while structural unemployment, financial pressure on the welfare state and the social consequences of labour market exclusion were thus used as arguments to justify activation policies in Denmark, the construction of – or reference to – a *moral contract* between citizens and society has also played an important role. The importance of the contract is illustrated by the fact that the concept 'right and duty of activation' became a central term in the activation policies of the mid-1990s. The concept refers to a *quid pro quo* deal between the unemployed and the state, whereby the unemployed receive unemployment benefits and assistance to improve their employability in return for making an effort to find employment, so that they can contribute to society. The 'right and duty' concept is very much in line with the communitarian ideology that flourished in the Western world during the 1990s (Carstens 1999).[2] Just how important this moral contract is can be seen from the fact that political and public indignation about well-off students signing up for social security immediately after secondary school, without even making an effort to find a job, was one of the main drivers of the first compulsory activation programme (the Youth Allowance Scheme), introduced for uninsured young unemployed (Torfing 2004, 173).

Like the activation concept itself, the *quid pro quo* concept is very broad and can comprise very diverse forms of mutual exchange between the state and the unemployed. In the Danish case, the concrete starting point of the 1994 reform was a situation in which stricter availability rules and a reduction of the benefit period to 9 years (it had been practically indefinite: eligibility was automatically regained through obligatory public job training and short educational spells) was replaced by a massive (financial) push on individual needs-oriented (re)qualification. This was the price demanded not least by the trade unions for accepting the deal on activation. This starting point for the *quid pro quo* concept (rights and duties) of the activation policy has since changed in the direction of more emphasis on the duties of the unemployed than on

---

[2] While the rights and duties principle in Denmark is deeply rooted in the welfare state and the history of the Social Democratic Party, the communitarian ideology is of American origin, although it has also played a role in Blair's and Schröder's 'Third Way'. It could be seen as a reaction to both neo-liberalism's rejection of the relevance of communities and moral obligations, and the citizens' lack of obligation in traditional social democratic welfare states. The communitarian ideology emphasises the importance of moral obligations, responsibilities and communities (including local ones) and the reciprocity between society and citizens. In the context of social and labour market policies, the communitarian ideology implies that criteria for full citizenship are altered. Full citizenship is only obtained through economic participation – or at least the demonstration of a willingness to make an effort to achieve economic participation.

their right to be provided for by the state. For instance, the benefit period has been shortened further (to 4 years) and the availability assessment tightened, and there has been a change in the content of the activation initiatives towards less needs-oriented requalification.

However, it should be mentioned that the trade unions in particular have fought hard to maintain the state's obligations in this moral contract, in which activation is understood as a 'right' of the individual. In 1998 in bipartite negotiations prior to the so-called third phase of labour market reform, the trade unions accepted further shortening of the maximum benefit period in exchange for, *inter alia*, a specification that after one year (six months for young people) the unemployed should be in activation programmes for at least 75% of the time, and that the unemployed had the right to six weeks' self-chosen training or other educational activities. In this way, the quantity of activation rather than the quality became the fundamental right for the unemployed. However, paradoxically, the extensive activation measures, with their more standardised and short-term labour market-oriented tools, have in practice come to be seen largely as duties and not rights, by both the authorities and the unemployed. In that sense, this agreement could also be seen as making more demands of the unemployed than of the state. The General Workers' Union's opt-out from the agreement further illustrates that from a trade union perspective this was controversial (Mailand and Due 2003; Winter 2003; Christensen *et al.* 2004).

The '*quid pro quo*' and the 'rights and duties' concepts and ideologies are also present in the new right-wing government's activation policy. While replacing several elements and terms of the social democratic government's activation policies, the new government has developed the concept further. This is most evident in a publication containing future policy principles and cases from February 2004 entitled '*Quid pro quo*' (Regeringen 2004). Here, the government refers directly to the concept 'rights and duties' and emphasises that employment policy is an area in which this concept has already been implemented. In line with the performance-related elements in the labour market reform 'More people into employment', the *quid pro quo* concept is 'graduated', so that citizens and public agencies receive financial resources and services from the state, depending on their *performance*. The original communitarian exchange is in this way mixed up with New Public Management approaches, and citizens are increasingly equated with public agencies as entities whose performance can be optimised if given the right economic incentives.

In sum, these four drivers and ways of justifying Danish activation policy – structural unemployment, fiscal crisis of the welfare state, social exclusion and the moral contract – have all been important in developing the content of the policy. More aspects could be added: international organisations and discourses, learning from other countries, unemployment figures and economic globalisation (Joergensen and Larsen 2003; Mailand and Due 2003; Lindsay and Mailand 2004). However, with the exception of the European Employment Strategy (which will be treated in section 5), analysis of these drivers is beyond the scope of this article.

All the same, one additional driver must to be included. Danish activation policy (and its development) is impossible to understand or explain without looking at the specific Danish institutional set-up, which among other things is characterised by the extensive influence of the labour market actors and a strong consensus-creating capacity. It is thus our assertion that there is a connection between institutional set-up and (feasible) policy content. This is the theme of section 4.

The Importance of the Institutional Set-up

As already mentioned, Denmark has also been affected by international discourse trends in the understanding and solution of problems, and this has had an impact on policy. There is no doubt that the emphasis has shifted from social integration to social disciplining. This marks a substantive discursive breach, in which Denmark's unique form of workfare policy – social disciplining with strong elements of social integration (welfare) – has taken a more traditional turn.

However, Danish activation policy is still substantially different from activation policies pursued in most other EU countries, being more ambiguous in its course of development. On the one hand, there has been a strong focus on activating the unemployed by means of stronger motivation (social disciplining). On the other hand, advocates of the social inclusion strategy, who oppose an individualisation of problems and solutions, have pointed out that (lack of) economic incentives is not the only cause of the problems (more sociological analyses have supported this view, for example, Andersen et al. 2003). The traditional universalism of the Scandinavian welfare state must be maintained, but public initiatives must be made more proactive and labour-market directed. At the same time, qualitative methods must be developed to map the individual unemployed person's situation, potential and motivation, and then initiate situationally adapted measures accordingly. The individual action plans introduced in 1994 can be seen as embodying the idea of giving the unemployed a say in their own fate. It has also been a characteristic of Danish measures that this kind of consideration has been particularly strong in the implementation phase (Larsen *et al.* 2001). Some even claim that this tendency to focus on social integration in the implementation phase has made politicians deliberately design the legislation in a more socially disciplining way than originally planned (Larsen and Andersen 2004).

It can thus be established that the different main arguments and considerations are embedded and to some extent also balanced in the Danish policy mix, particularly if the implementation phase is included. This is a particular characteristic of the management of Danish activation policy. But what are the characteristic features of the steering of Danish labour market policy (viewed in a comparative perspective)? What are the guiding principles of the strategies of public intervention (state-driven strategy) on the one hand, and of neo-classically inspired market solutions on the other? And what is the role of the institutional set-up in this context?

Many have categorised Danish labour market policy as an aggressive workfare strategy (Cox 1998, 1999; Torfing 1999, 2000). Notwithstanding a number of workfare-inspired elements, it is doubtful whether the Danish policy really fits into this category, at least in a narrow definition (a requirement to work in return for social benefits). For example, as a result of its long history, the welfare elements of Danish labour market policy are still very comprehensive by international standards. And despite closer links, the benefit system is not connected exclusively to a *quid pro quo* in the form of work requirements. For example, after the political process preceding the 1994 labour market reform the question of reducing financial support did not really arise until autumn 2003. It was not considered politically feasible. Thus when the right-wing government in autumn 2003 suggested reducing the level of unemployment benefit it restricted the move to high-paid workers, with the purpose of making them finance the first part of their unemployment spell themselves. The minority government managed to establish a narrow majority for its proposal, but heavy criticism, for example from employers' organisations and the trade unions, put a lot of pressure on the government. Prime minister Anders Fogh Rasmussen, however, stood his ground and went on TV to declare that reducing the unemployment benefit level was and would remain government policy. This led to a storm of protests from all sides (including some very influential business people). Labour market experts in particular worried about how such an initiative would affect labour market mobility, while employers worried how it would affect bargaining on pay and working conditions in general. The prime minister then went on holiday to Mexico (conveniently), and finance minister Thor Pedersen, on his own initiative (according to himself and the prime minister), withdrew the proposal. This incident illustrates how difficult it is to alter the level of social security payments in Denmark. Even more so, because both employers and trade unions clearly realise the advantages of balancing the need for flexibility against the need for social security. An extra dimension of this case of 'benefit blunder' is that the collective agreements concluded in 2004 contain a clause for renegotiation in case the government changes the rules governing unemployment benefit. This was a strong signal from the two sides of the labour market that political intervention in the level of social security will have consequences.

However, the social partners' successful protection of the unemployment benefit level is not matched by the case of the uninsured unemployed. In recent years there have been at least three initiatives to reduce the level of benefits or tighten the eligibility criteria for part of this group, justified by the government as make-work-pay initiatives. All three initiatives exhibit a previously unseen willingness on the part of the state to experiment with the toughest form of social disciplining, but, importantly, only in relation to certain groups of unemployed.[3]

Despite these recent initiatives, on the whole, typical either/or strategies have been turned into complementary strategies in Danish labour market policy. Danish initiatives from the 1990s consist of equal parts innovation and imitation. Welfare and workfare elements are mixed in a special way, adjusted to Danish service capitalism's structural traits, institutional and organisational traditions and political norms affecting process solutions. The steering side is therefore also a key factor in the history of the policy. The Danish tradition of corporatist arrangements has been strengthened, while competence for designing activation measures has been significantly regionalised. The Danish reform strength-

---

[3] The first was the introduction in 2002 of so-called Starters Assistance ('Starthjælp'), a reduced level of unemployment benefits for immigrants who have been in Denmark for less than 7 of the last 8 years. The second was the 2004 introduction of the Social Assistance Ceiling ('Kontanthjælpsloftet'), a maximum amount of social assistance benefits which uninsured unemployed persons may receive. Virtually no positive employment effects of this scheme have been found (Graversen and Tinggaard 2005). The third initiative is from 2005. It replaces the unemployment benefit of one person in a married couple where both previously received unemployment benefits for the uninsured with so-called 'Partner Assistance' ('Ægtefælle tillæg'), unless both have worked for more than 300 hours during the last two years. The de facto target group is immigrants. The initiative is remarkable in that it redefines the rights and duties principle so that it is no longer enough for the lowest strata of the unemployed to be willing to accept jobs and activation offers, rather they must account for hours of past employment. The main problem with these new initiatives, of course, is that they are likely to become a source of impoverishment rather than of labour market inclusion, particularly if it turns out that the explanation for the lack of labour market participation is not this group's work incentives, but a lack of demand for their qualifications, discrimination or other explanations that transcend the supply side.

ened the role of labour market actors, especially at regional level. Private interests are institutionalised as part of the public authorities.

The Politics of Industrial Relations and Labour Market Policy

In order to understand Danish labour market policy and the relatively consistent balancing of economic and welfare political considerations built into it, it is therefore necessary to understand the politics of industrial relations. As early as 1899 labour market actors entered into an agreement about labour market disputes and how to resolve them, as well as on the position of organisations in the system (the 'September Compromise'), thus establishing centralised negotiations and mechanisms for dispute resolution. This also laid the foundation for the practice of leaving it to the actors themselves to regulate most matters of importance for the labour market. This is why it was not until the 1960s that we see the formulation of a proper labour market policy, giving the public authorities a more active role.

Generally speaking, the parliamentary situation plays a lesser role than might be expected. A change of government has rarely led to substantial reforms of labour market policy, and, in the event of reform, the norm has been broad political compromise. The Danish tradition of minority and frequently changing governments is an important factor in this aspect of the Danish political system. Another is the deeply rooted corporatist structures, dating back more than 100 years. This applies both to policy-making, in respect of which consultation or participation of the labour market parties have been a tradition, and to administration, with tripartite representation in councils, committees and commissions (Larsen 2002). This is clearly reflected in Danish labour market policy. The 'fingerprints' of the labour market actors are highly visible on the policy side: on the one hand, in a moderate – in an international perspective – degree of public intervention, and on the other in a policy characterised by a balancing of economic and welfare considerations (Larsen and Jorgensen 2002). The parties also play an important role in implementation. When the labour market was emerging as an independent policy area in the late 1960s, corporatist structures were established as well. A national corporatist body (the National Labour Market Board, now the Employment Council) was established along with 14 regional corporatist bodies (the Regional Labour Market Boards, now Labour Market Councils). Despite their restricted competences, this created the framework for the collegiate system. These councils have been given varying, but generally increasing competences. It is remarkable that Denmark further empowered corporatist structures by handing over new steering and implementation responsibilities to them in the 1990s.

Regarding the corporatist institutional set-up, there was an early realisation that it would only be possible to implement labour market policy if the state's consensus-building resources were increased. This had to be done by including the labour market actors in policy-making and implementation. This realisation led to the decision-making system described above. In this way the organisations in question could be integrated and help expand the scope of the state's activities. However, there is another dimension to the institutional setting which can be observed in, for example, the implementation processes (Larsen et al. 1996). Historically, once institutions have been established which influence the orientation and the actions of the actors, feedback mechanisms arise which in turn strengthen institutional regulation. A special policy style therefore evolves with organisational participation and a collectivist culture. The institutionalised role of the labour market actors must thus be recognised as an important driving force behind labour market policy. Also in this connection it is very important that labour market actors are also an institutionalised part of similar steering systems related to other aspects of labour market policy, notably occupational health and safety, and vocational and adult education and training.

However, there are limits to the labour market actors' influence on labour market policy. This is true in an historical context, but also in relation to present developments, starting in the late 1990s. For one thing, the consultative role played by the parties in the political system seems to have diminished. For another, certain 'roll back' tendencies can be observed in the late 1990s in relation to the revitalisation of the administrative corporatism launched by the labour market reform of 1994 (Larsen and Stamhus 2000). Furthermore, the local authorities have been given important labour market tasks and in this set-up the labour market organisations have little influence. However, labour market actors are represented in the social coordination committees for an inclusive labour market in the municipalities, although in general these committees have limited competences.

Finally, it is important to mention a number of new labour market-related problems which the tripartite system has so far found it difficult to cope with in traditional terms. Although the Danish labour market policy of the 1990s can be described as successful in terms of solving structural problems and combating unemployment in general, it is a different story if the focus is shifted to re-integration efforts directed towards heavily marginalised groups and the integration of refugees and immigrants into the labour market.

The Connection between Steering and Policy Content

Generally speaking, however, the labour market actors have been an important driving force behind developments in Danish labour market policy. This explains its complementary strategy – the particular Danish policy mix. The historically embedded understanding among the actors that labour market policy has both economic and welfare goals has created special conditions for its development and implementation. These conditions rest on the central role of the labour market organisations, in terms of both political consultation and implementation within the framework of administrative corporatism.

It is thus an important feature of Danish labour market policy that the institutional set-up has provided – at least until recently – a fairly undisputed setting within the framework of which policy can be developed. International trends – for example, work-first approaches – may certainly have an influence, but will always end up with a distinct Danish design in a Danish context. Duties and demands will be accompanied by opportunities to improve one's employability through skills upgrading, often due to the intervention of the trade unions (or at least out of consideration for the interests of the trade unions, in cases where they do not actively demand it). It is therefore perhaps not the policy design as such that is the key here, but rather the institutionalisation of policy implementation (with a public framework for social dialogue on labour market measures). This gives rise to new questions, both in the political debate and in research, focusing more on the institutional set-up.[4] Such an institutional focus tends to be severely underrepresented in discussions of labour market policy and the transferability of policy designs across countries (Larsen 2004, 2005).

Changes in the Danish Institutional Set-up and their Potential Consequences for Activation

Interestingly, politically initiated changes are currently under way which may point the Danish institutional set-up in a totally new direction. It is difficult to tell whether this is because the Danish right-wing government realises the importance of such reform if labour market policy is to be changed fundamentally, that is, as the result of a deliber-

---

[4] For example, based on a TLM (transitional labour markets) understanding (Schmid 1998; Schmid and Schöemann 2004) or in a 'flexicurity perspective' (Wilthagen *et al.* 2004) the question of *how to manage social risks* might best be approached in terms of the 'manager', that is, the person or organisation responsible for managing social risks (this would also involve some fundamental welfare-state considerations as regards the degree of individualisation).

ate strategy rather than merely copying elements from other countries (primarily the Netherlands), which may then have more indirect (and perhaps politically unrecognised) consequences for the special institutional set-up of Danish labour market policy. At all events, major changes are in progress which will come about mainly in the wake of the new local-authority reform (including the introduction of a 'one-stop shop system') and the beginning of the contracting out of public employment services. The Danish Parliament recently introduced a reform to create larger local authorities. In the preceding political process, labour market policy became an important issue. In order to persuade the local authorities to accept larger units, the implementation of labour market policy was used as bait: if they agree to increase in size the local authorities will be able to take over a much larger share of labour market policy tasks. The establishment of a one-stop shop system, heavily inspired by the Dutch experience, was suggested at the same time. The idea is to establish joint state and local-authority job centres and on a trial basis to launch some purely local authority-run job centres on a smaller scale. The different models are then to be evaluated prior to a final political decision.

The introduction of purely local authority-run job centres is an outright attack on the policy-making influence of labour market actors. However, the general reorganisation of the area will lead to marked changes in actors' roles. In contrast to their existing substantial proactive influence on the design of initiatives (input), the role of the labour market actors will become more reactive: their main task will be to monitor effects (output), with the possibility of imposing sanctions on job centres and local authorities (tasks would be handed over to private agents). These sanctions are connected to the government's aim of expanding the use of private agents, as envisaged by the 2002 labour market reform 'More people into employment'. Undoubtedly, this possibility of transferring tasks to private agents should also be seen in the context of ways in which the existing public implementation systems can secure a balancing of social disciplining and social integration in the implementation process (Larsen *et al.* 2001). To put it as clearly as the political rhetoric allows: private agents are expected to be able to implement the measures better and more cheaply than the public system. In particular the fear that the unemployed can get stuck in long-lasting activation measures has played an important part here. Private agents are assumed to be better at handling contact sessions, motivation and direct job provision, while at the same time avoiding long-lasting initiatives. However, it is a characteristic feature of the Danish system that trade union institutions number among these 'private agents' (indeed, they account for 1 in 4 of them).

Another important dimension of these changes is that the local authorities (though only on a trial basis to begin with) will take over responsibility for the insured unemployed. Their benefits are at present financed primarily by the state, but the system is administered by the trade unions (the unemployment funds) and the system functions as the main trade union recruitment channel. If the local authorities take over responsibility, they will have to be given a financial incentive to assume financial responsibility as well. And it is hard to imagine that the local authorities will leave it to the trade unions to administer a system for which they are ultimately responsible financially. The debate is getting under way, and several right-wing politicians have already stated that the next item on the agenda is a new joint support system. If the trade unions lose control of the administration of the support system, it is bound to lead to a profound weakening of the trade union movement. In the longer term, this may become the biggest threat to the current corporatist institutional set-up.

All in all, these significant changes in the institutional set-up may lead to a new policy, involving new types of balances. This may establish the preconditions for, and thus open up opportunities for introducing, more social disciplining and a more traditional work-first approach. The above described shift in this direction from the late 1990s into the new millennium has already resulted in less influence for the labour market actors, in relation to both 'consultations' in connection with national political decision-making processes and administrative corporatism, with diminished influence for the regional corporatist bodies (Larsen and Jorgensen 2002).

However, there is still some distance between political intentions and their realisation, and the adopted reforms have not yet been fully designed and implemented. The question now is how resistant the existing institutional corporatist system is to such attempts at fundamental change. By all accounts, the traditional Danish institutional system is under attack. Perhaps as a result of deliberate strategic political considerations, perhaps only as a by-product of copying elements (especially from the Netherlands) which were developed in a completely different context (and above all under a different welfare regime). In any case it underlines the importance of the institutional set-up alongside policy design. The political struggle does not stop with the design of the policy; determination of the role of 'manager' is every bit as important, especially in relation to its implications for the design of the content of activation policy.

The Importance of the EES
as Driver of the Activation Regime

We shall now look at the extent to which the European Employment Strategy could be said to be a driver of Danish activation policy, as the policy has been described above.[5]

The impact of the *European Employment Strategy (EES)* is a matter of much controversy, but whichever way it is analysed, its influence in Denmark has not been strong. The official Danish five-year evaluation of the EES states that

> As Danish employment policies also before 1998 were very much in line with what became the objectives of the Employment Strategy, the implementation of the Strategy has not led to any significant shift in Danish policies, [nevertheless] a number of precise targets, which were taken from or inspired by the Employment Strategy, and deadlines for the fulfilment of these targets entered Danish employment policies through the National Action Plans. (Danish National Institute of Social Research 2002, 6-7)

While Denmark has been hailed as a model country for the EES, the implementation studies that include Denmark (Langhoff-Roos 2001; Jacobson and Schmid 2001; Jacobson 2003; Madsen 2003; Rydberg and Sand Kirk 2003; Oernsholt and Vestergaard 2003) agree with the official evaluation that the impact of the EES on Danish employment policy has been slight, whether the focus is on policy contents or policy processes/learning.

One of the most direct and potentially most influential features of the EES is the recommendations to member states (issued every year since 2000). In the case of Denmark, a recommendation to reduce labour taxation has recurred constantly, while a recommendation on mainstreaming/gender segregation was dropped in 2003, and a new recommendation on encouraging more people to take up employment, especially migrant workers, has been repeated in different versions since 2002. In 2003, a recommendation on active ageing was added, and in 2004 another on 'monitoring trends in vocational training in the light of recent increases in training fees'.

Some action which could be seen as being in line with the recommendations has been taken in the area of income tax, mainstreaming/gender segregation, and integration of ethnic minority workers. However, most observers and civil servants taking part in the processes around the National Action Plan for employment have difficulties

---

[5] Where not otherwise stated, the data source in this section is Mailand (2005).

showing any causal connection between the recommendations and these initiatives.

Regarding the recommendation to reduce taxes on labour and to retain older workers, the 1999 tax reform introduced some initiatives to increase employment and reduce income tax for low-income groups, but this was not done in response to the EES (see also Danish National Institute of Social Research 2002, 20). The steps taken to reduce taxation on labour can only be described as modest, and the recommendation continued to be made. The tax reform was fully implemented in 2002.

Also related to this recommendation – but again predating it – is the Danish adjustment of the early retirement scheme in 1999. In the new scheme, the benefit period is reduced from 7 to 5 years, as a consequence of the reduction of the pension age to 65 years. Furthermore, the adjustment includes economic incentives to postpone early retirement to the age of 62 (from 60). Again, however, the impression gained from interviews with civil servants is that the recommendations did not affect the decision to reform the scheme – nor has it been possible to find other indications of this.

In the case of gender equality, in 2000 the Danish government reorganised the equal opportunity work of the PES in line with the EU mainstreaming strategy (Arbejdsmarkedsstyrelsen 2002a). This might seem to be a case of the direct impact of the EES and the recommendation on Danish employment policy, but again the action taken in Denmark predates the recommendations. The recommendation on gender mainstreaming/segregation was not repeated in 2002. Some civil servants report that this was not a consequence of the actions taken, but because Danish civil servants pointed out to the EU the existing high level of gender equality in Denmark. Other civil servants believe that references in bilateral meetings with the Commission to the PES reorganisation of equal opportunity work were decisive in the Commission's decision not to repeat the recommendation. In any case, the process indicates that the recommendations are taken seriously and not simply ignored if they do not fit government policy (see also Jacobson 2003).[6]

---

[6] It has rightly been argued that civil servants in countries where the legitimacy of EU intervention is weak might tend to underestimate the impact of the EES (Zeitlin 2005; Jacobson 2003). Nevertheless, civil servants do have in-depth information concerning political processes and are valuable sources of information. Furthermore, the study that this section builds on contains, in addition to these interviews, comparisons of recommendations and national policy programmes, including their timing.

In February 2002, Denmark received a new recommendation on integrating immigrants in the labour market. In March 2002 the newly elected right-wing government presented a plan to combine integration policy and employment policy to a greater extent, as can be seen in the initiative 'Towards a new integration policy'. The first phase of the reform (2002) included, *inter alia*, lower benefits and allowances as an incentive to take up employment, and introduced the opportunity for language schools to refer students to jobs or job training (Government of Denmark 2003, 28). However, while these initiatives might have been affected by international studies showing that the integration of immigrants is one of the weaker points of the Danish labour market, the interviewees did not think the recommendation had any impact. The timing of the recommendation and the government initiative seems to support this, as they were only one month apart.

The absence of a direct impact on Danish employment policy does not imply that the recommendations are not taken seriously by Danish governments, as repeated attempts to have Commission recommendations removed illustrates. In 2004 alone, the Danish government managed to have removed or substantially altered two of the six recommendations proposed by the Commission. Most controversial for the Danish government was the addition to the repeated recommendation on retaining older workers, which directly asked the Danish government to remove the Voluntary Early Retirement Benefit Scheme. Because this scheme has previously proved to be politically sensitive, and because the government was of the opinion that the Commission had no legal basis to interfere in specific national policy programmes, they asked the Commission to remove the addition. The Commission agreed to do so, and the addition in the final version of the recommendation was changed to 'including the removal of incentives for early retirement, where appropriate'. Furthermore, the Danish government did not find any justification for one of the other proposed recommendations, 'reverse the deterioration of basic skills', which is why they succeeded in having this recommendation removed. The other new recommendation, 'to monitor trends in vocational training in the light of recent increases in training fees, was accepted by the government.

Looking beyond the recommendations to the input/output indicators in relation to activation guidelines under the 'old' EES employability pillar, it is possible to find an area in which the EES has had a direct influence on the content of Danish employment policy. During the first years of the EES, there was a fundamental discrepancy between the Danish strategy, which tended to focus on activating the long-term unemployed, and the EES, which tended to prioritise initiatives to prevent the unemployed from becoming long-term unemployed by means of guidelines demanding activation after 6 or 12 months' unemployment. Denmark did not meet these targets, although it had been one of the countries pushing for quantitative targets in connection with the strategy. Denmark has not received official recommendations on this point, but a so-called 'second-order recommendation' to give higher priority to the prevention rather than the treatment of long-term unemployment, and to live up to the call for activation after 6 and 12 months (see also Langhoff-Ross 2001). The 'second-order recommendation' was not so much considered the problem in itself, as the fact that all other member states could read from the NAPs and elsewhere that Denmark had failed to meet one of the central employability targets.

This was something taken very seriously by the Danish government, especially former prime minister Nyrup Rasmussen. Despite scepticism among civil servants about the preventive approach, because it was perceived as a heavy burden on the PES, the introduction of the 6- and 12-month limits agreed by the European Council in autumn 1997 became hard to avoid when the prime minister reported to the Danish Parliament's European Affairs Committee that the targets would be implemented in the third phase of the labour market reform (Christensen *et al.* 2004, 100).

In contrast to many other member states, Denmark has not received any recommendations regarding policy *processes*, such as consultation procedures with labour market actors, regional and local authorities or other stakeholders. As in the case of policy contents, the interviewees did not report any impact on processes from the EES, apart from the obvious inter-ministerial coordination that takes place in connection with preparing the NAPs. There does not seem to have been any spill-over from the NAP processes to the public administration's internal coordination or their relations with external stakeholders, such as labour market actors or NGOs. The partial amalgamation of the Ministry of Labour and the Ministry of Social Affairs in the Ministry of Employment – and the accompanying partial amalgamation of 'labour market policy' and 'social policy' to become 'employment policy' – could be seen as an adaptation to a European-style employment policy (Madsen 2004), but the amalgamation had been recommended for many years by civil servants and others. Hence, domestic politics must once again be considered the most important element in this development. Furthermore, the Danish understanding of employment policy – excluding most educational, entrepreneurial and gender issues – is still much narrower than the one found at EU level, as expressed in the EES (see also Mailand 2003).

To sum up, the direct impact of the EES in Denmark seems to be very limited. There might be some indirect impact through discourses and learning processes generated by repeated interaction with representatives from the Commission and other member states. However, the lack of attention the strategy is given by national and local politico-administrative systems, as well as by the media and labour market actors, effectively limits the effects of these processes as well.

Conclusion

In Denmark, active labour market policy schemes were introduced in the 1970s, but played only a limited role during this and the following decade. Large-scale activation policy as we know it today was not developed until the 1990s. Activation policy encompasses *social disciplining*, in the form of workfare-inspired incentives such activation obligation, tougher availability assessment and shorter benefit periods, and *social integration*, in which the main goal is activation in the form of individually tailored activation and skills upgrading. Since the late 1990s, however, the balance between the two has shifted from a strong focus on social integration to greater emphasis on social disciplining.

In explaining how Danish activation policy was created and has developed, this chapter has focused primarily on the *normative foundation and justifications* and the *institutional set-up*.

Activation policy has been justified in at least four ways:

1. There is widespread political focus on *structural problems in the labour market*, where the term 'structural' refers to labour shortages in spite of continuous unemployment, usually justified on the basis of concern about macroeconomic balance problems. Two main approaches to solving these problems can be identified, supporting the strategies of social disciplining and social integration respectively.

2. From the 1980s onward *the problems of financing the welfare state* have come to be a strong focal point, and in a labour market policy context the focus is on reducing the costs of passive transfer payments.

3. A lot of attention is being paid to the *interaction between social problems and labour market attachment*, and work has increasingly come to be seen as the cure-all in relation to individuals' lack of qualifications and social problems.

4. A 'communitarian' *moral contract* between citizens and society has also helped to justify the policy. The contract could be seen as a *'quid pro quo'* deal between the unemployed and the state, where the unemployed receive unemployment benefits and assistance in improving

their employability in return for making an effort to find employment, and thus contributing to society.

However, the *institutional set-up* – especially the extensive role of the labour market actors – may have been the single most important factor. Their comparatively strong role at national and, especially, regional level has its roots in the voluntary industrial relations system, established more than a hundred years ago. Understanding this role of the labour market actors is crucial for any understanding of the peculiar Danish way of balancing economic and social considerations. The institutional set-up has thus to some extent determined the contents of the policy. Numerous measures have obtained institutional stability, among other things because the actors over time have come to count on the opposite parties' 'rationality' in terms of behaviour and experience formation. Furthermore, a historical understanding has emerged that labour market policy comprises both economic and welfare policy goals, and that there need not be a conflict between them. One of the reasons for this may be the traditions of consensus-creating institutions in the labour market.

However, substantial changes are under way in the Danish institutional set-up. These changes have so far led to a (limited) reduction in the role of the labour market actors, and to a more market-based steering, including outsourcing to new private agents and payment on the basis of the *no cure, less pay* principle. However, the not yet implemented local authority reform can be expected to increase local authority responsibility for the implementation of activation measures, the introduction of a one-stop shop system, and an even more limited and a predominantly reactive role for the labour market parties.

These changes cannot be explained solely with reference to the four normative justifications mentioned before. Furthermore, the European Employment Strategy cannot be said to have exerted any influence on the changes (just as the influence of the Strategy in Denmark is weak in general). It is difficult to tell whether the changes spring from a political awareness of the importance of changing the institutional set-up in order to change the policy fundamentally: that is, as the result of a deliberate strategy rather than by copying elements from other countries (primarily the Netherlands), which then have more indirect (and perhaps politically unrecognised) consequences for the special institutional set-up of the Danish labour market.

These significant changes in the institutional set-up may lead to a new policy being pursued, involving new types of balances. It may establish the preconditions for introducing more social disciplining. However, the changes are still some distance away from realising the political intentions, and the reforms adopted have not yet been fully designed or implemented. The question now is how resistant the existing institutional corporatist system will turn out to be faced with such attempts to change it. It thus remains to be seen whether we are witnessing a full-scale dismantling of the (proactive) role the labour market actors have previously played in Danish activation policy, or whether their role is merely changing. In the first case, Danish activation policy would change fundamentally and be a *path-shaping* process; in the second, it would be more correct to talk of a development of the existing policy, which should then be understood in terms of a *path-dependent* process.

References

Andersen, J.G., C.A. Larsen and J.B. Jensen (2003), *Marginalisering og velfærdspolitik*, Arbejdsløshed, jobchancer og trivsel, Copenhagen, Frydenlund.

Arbejdsmarkedsstyrelsen (2002), *En del af hverdagen*, Arbejdsnotat nr. 30, Koebenhavn, Arbejdsmarkedsstyrelsen.

Arbejdsministeriet (2000), *Effekter af aktiveringsindsatsen*, Koebenhavn, Arbejdsministeriet.

Carstens, A. (1999), *Aktivering – klientsamtaler og socialpolitik*, Koebenhavn, Hans Reitzels Forlag.

Christensen, P.M., A.S. Noergaard and N.C. Sidenius (2004), *Hvem Skriver Lovene? Interesseorganisationer og politiske beslutningsprocesser*, Magtudredningen, Aarhus, Aarhus Universitetsforlag.

Clasen, J. (2000), "Motives, means and opportunities: reforming unemployment compensation in the 1990s", *West European Politics* 23 (2): 89112.

Cox, R.H. (1998), "From safety net to trampoline: labour market activation in the Netherlands and Denmark", *Governance* 11 (4), pp. 397-414.

Danish National Institute of Social Research (2002), *Impact evaluation of the European Employment Strategy – Denmark. Synthesis Report*, Copenhagen, Danish Institute of Social Research.

Det Oekonomiske Råd (2002), *Dansk Oekonomi efterår 2002*, Koebenhavn, Det Oekonomiske Råd.

Esping-Andersen, G. (1990), *The Three Worlds of Welfare Capitalism*, Cambridge, Polity Press.

Gallie, D. and S. Paugam (2000), "The experience of unemployment in Europe: the debate", in D. Gaillie and S. Paugam (eds.), *Welfare Regimes and the Experience of Unemployment*, Oxford, Oxford University Press.

Government of Denmark (2003), *The Danish National Action Plan for Employment 2003*, Copenhagen, The Danish Government.

Graversen, B.K. and K. Tinggaard (2005), *Loft over ydelser*, Koebenhavn, Socialforskningsinstituttet.

Hansen, C., F. Larsen, M. Lassen and H. Joergensen (1997), *Ta' teten – i arbejdsmarkedspolitikken*, Koebenhavn, LO.

Henning, H., M. M. Juul and F. Jakobsen (2005), "Uddannelse og tilskudsjob. Prioritering på et fejlagtigt grundlag?", in V. Kold, A. Larsen, F. Larsen and J. Lind (eds.), *Flere i arbejde – status og udfordringer*, Tidsskrift for Arbejdsliv No. 2.

Jacobson, K. (2003), "Trying to reform the 'best pupil in class'? The OMC in Sweden and Denmark", draft paper prepared for the workshop "Opening the Open Method of Coordination", Florence, 4-5 July 2003.

Jacobson, K. and H. Schmid (2001), "Real integration or just formal adaptation? – On the implementation of the National Action Plans for Employment", paper for presentation at the conference of the European Sociological Association, Helsinki, 28 August-1 September 2001.

Jessop, B. (1994), "Post-Fordism and the state", in A. Amin (ed.), *Postfordism – A Reader*, Oxford, Basil Blackwell.

Joergensen, H. and F. Larsen (2003), "Aktivgoerelse af aktivering kommer ikke af sig selv – betydningen af institutionelt design for udviklingen af ledighedsindsatser", in L. Petersen and P. K. Madsen (eds.), *Drivkræfter bag arbejdsmarkedspolitikken*, Koebenhavn, SFI.

Langhoff-Ross, K. (2001), "Anderledes efter Amsterdam? – Et case-study af beskæftigelsespolitikken i Spanien og Danmark siden vedtagelsen", Speciale, Koebenhavn, Institut for Statskundskab.

Larsen, A.C. and J.G. Andersen (2004), *Magten på Borgen*, Århus, Aarhus Universitetsforlag.

Larsen, F. (2004), "Active labour market policy in Denmark as an example of transitional labour market and flexicurity arrangements. What can be learnt?" in Thomas Bredgaard and Flemming Larsen (eds.), *Employment Policy from Different Angles*, Koebenhavn, Djoef-Forlaget.

Larsen, F. (2005), "The importance of institutional regimes for active labour market policies – the case of Denmark", in *European Journal of Social Security* 6 (2) (June), pp. 137-155.

Larsen, F. and H. Joergensen (2002), "Labour market policies", in Henning Joergensen (ed), *Consensus, Cooperation and Conflict – The Policy Making Process in Denmark*, Cheltenham, Edward Elgar.

Larsen, F. and J. Stamhus (2000), "Active labour market policy in Denmark: crucial design features and problems of implementation', Institut for Oekonomi, Politik og Forvaltnings skriftserie, Aalborg Universitet.

Larsen, F., C. Hansen, H. Joergensen, M. Lassen, B. Bagge and H. Höcker (1996), *Implementering af Regional Arbejdsmarkedspolitik*, Ålborg, CARMA.

Larsen, F., N. Abildgaard, T. Bredgaard and L. Dalsgaard (2001), *Kommunal aktivering – mellem disciplinering og integrationi*, Aalborg, CARMA.

Larsen, M. and K. Langager (1998), *Arbejdsmarkedsreformen og arbejdsmarkedet – Evaluering af arbejdsmarkedsreformen III*, Koebenhavn: Socialforskningsinstituttet.

Lindsay, C. and M. Mailand (2004), "Different routes, common directions? Activation policies for young people in Denmark and the UK", *International Journal of Social Policy* 13 (3), pp. 195-207.

Madsen, P.K. (2003), "Fyrtårn eller Slæbejolle? Dansk arbejdsmarkeds- og beskæftigelsespolitik og den europæiske beskæftigelsesstrategi", in L. Petersen and P.K. Madsen (eds.), *Drivkræfter bag arbejdsmarkedspolitikken*, Koebenhavn, SFI.

Mailand, M. (2003), "The European Employment Strategy – local and regional impact in Denmark", article for the ETUI/Universidad Complutense de Madrid, seminar "The regional and local dimension of the European Employment Strategy", 17 October, Córdoba, Spain.

Mailand, M. (2005), "Implementing the revised European Employment Strategy – North, South, East, West", first working paper in the research project "Danish employment policy in a European perspective", FAOS, Department of Sociology, University of Copenhagen.

Mailand, M. and J. Due (2003), "Partsstyring i arbejdsmarkedspolitikken – perspektiver og alternativer", in L Petersen and P. K. Madsen (eds.), *Drivkræfter bag arbejdsmarkedspolitikken*, Koebenhavn, SFI.

Oernsholt, K. and T. Vestergaard (2003), "Den Åbne koordinationsmetode – en europæisk styreform baseret på deliberative processer", Speciale afleveret ved Institut for Statskundskab, Aarhus Universitet.

Peck, J. (1996), *Work-place*, New York, The Guilford Press.

Regeringen (2004), *Noget for Noget*, Koebenhavn, Regeringen.

Rydberg, M.M. and J.S. Kirk (2003), "The European Employment Strategy – an assessment of how member states' participation in the European Employment Strategy influences the development of national policy-making", Masters thesis, Institut VIII, Roskilde Universitet.

Schmid, G. (1998), "Transitional labour markets: a new European Employment Strategy", Discussion Paper FS 98-206, WZB Berlin.

Schmid, G. and K. Schömann (2004) "Managing social risks through transitional labour markets: towards a European Social Model", TLM.NET Report No. 2004-01, Amsterdam, SISWO/Institute for the Social Sciences.

Torfing, J. (1999), "Workfare with welfare: recent reforms of the Danish welfare state", *Journal of European Social Policy* 9 (1), pp. 5-28.

Torfing, J. (2000), "Towards a Schumpeterian workfare postnational regime", Working paper No. 4. CARMA, Aalborg University, Aalborg.

Torfing, J. (2004), "Det stille sporskifte i velfærdstaten – en diskusteoretisk beslutningsprocesanalyse", Magtudredning, Aarhus, Aarhus Universitet.

Wilthagen, T. (1998), "A new paradigm for labour market policy reform?", Discussion Paper FS 198-202, WZB, Berlin.

Winter, S. (2003), "Kanalrundfart eller zapning? – om kanaler og arenaer i den aktive arbejdsmarkedspolitik", in L. Petersen and P. K. Madsen (eds.), *Drivkræfter bag arbejdsmarkedspolitikken*, Koebenhavn, SFI.

Zeitlin, J. (2005), "Introduction: The open method of coordination in question", in J. Zeitlin and P. Pochet (eds.), *The Open Method of Coordination in Action: The European Employment and Social Inclusion Strategies*, Brussels, P.I.E. Peter Lang.

Activation Policy in Sweden

Eskil WADENSJÖ

Introduction: The Swedish Employment Situation

Sweden has for many years had high labour force participation and employment rates: higher than in most other European countries and higher than the targets set by the European Employment Strategy (EES). This also means that the EES employment targets have not had much influence on the Swedish debate and Swedish economic policy. At present, however, the unemployment rate in Sweden is higher than the EES target. The Swedish target in that area was set at 4% before the EES target was decided, and will probably be changed if it is reached. The unemployment rate in Sweden was below 2% in most years of the post-war period and only 1.5% in 1989 and 1990. The unemployment rate has been higher since the crisis of the early 1990s, but it is the long history of low unemployment that influences expectations.

Swedish policy has aimed at high employment for many years. The main principle of Swedish employment policy is a strong emphasis on work and a discouragement of income support. To that could be added a strong emphasis on ensuring that the labour market should function better as a *market*. The 'work' principle has strongly influenced the design of both labour market programmes and the social security system, and activation is central to the Swedish economic and social policy model.

In section 2 the labour market programmes are presented, including general programmes, those targeted at special groups and programmes financed by the European Social Fund (ESF). The ESF programmes constitute only a small share of labour market policy overall, but it is worth looking at whether they conform to traditional Swedish labour market policy or contain some new ideas. In section 3, some of the main social security programmes are presented. The development of these programmes in recent years has been in the direction of a more stringent application of the work principle. The most obvious example is the introduction of the new old age pension scheme. Section 4 describes the main directions of development of activation policy in Sweden and summarises its main characteristics. Section 5 concludes.

Labour Market Policy

Development of Active Labour Market Policy in Sweden

The OECD's regularly published comparisons of public expenditure on labour market programmes show that such expenditure in Sweden is high and more concentrated on active measures than in other countries. This emphasis on active labour market programmes is part of a long tradition.

The earliest Swedish labour market programme comprised the establishment of the first municipal employment exchanges in 1902. They were granted state support a few years later and rapidly expanded. The next programme was public relief work, marshalled against unemployment during the First World War. These works were greatly expanded in the depression of the early 1920s. Wages for these public works were set low so that no one would be tempted to stay on if another job became available. The public relief works were also used as a test of the willingness of the unemployed to work before cash support was given. The work principle was strongly emphasised.

During the 1930s the policy partially changed due to the influence of Keynes, the contemporary (though in some respects earlier) Stockholm School and the trade unions. A new form of public works was introduced in 1931, temporary job creation schemes (*beredskapsarbeten*) paid at the market rate. The Social Democratic Party which formed a government in 1932 strongly preferred this type of public works. The earlier form continued but its successor soon came to dominate and with the reorganisation of labour market policy in 1940 the old type of public works was abandoned. The number of employment exchanges increased, among other things in order to make it possible to check the willingness to accept work of those receiving unemployment insurance benefit, after this state support to the trade union unemployment insurance societies was granted from 1935 onwards. During the Second World War the municipal employment exchanges and a strong central labour market authority were established. This system was made permanent after the war.

The early post-war period was characterised by high growth and low unemployment. One problem confronting the trade union movement (LO) at the end of the 1940s was the tendency towards increased inflation and, accompanying it, political pressure on the trade unions to keep wage demands down. LO economists – with Rudolf Meidner and Gösta

Rehn as the leading figures – believed that it was unreasonable for the trade union movement to keep wages down, however. It would lead to conflicts within the organisation and weaken wage equalisation. They therefore suggested a new policy comprising the following three features: (i) a restrictive aggregate demand policy, (ii) a solidaristic wage policy (equal pay for equal work) with anticipated decreased wage differences, and (iii) an active labour market policy. The first two measures would result in tendencies towards higher unemployment compared with the then current more expansionary policy. A complementary active, selective labour market policy was therefore necessary, helping the unemployed to move to job vacancies and to move jobs to the unemployed.

This policy, the Rehn-Meidner model, won political support from the end of the 1950s. Labour market training and mobility grants were considered characteristic of the new policy. The period from the end of the 1950s until the middle of the 1960s may be seen as the high-water mark of the Rehn-Meidner model. Labour market policy expanded quickly and became generally accepted.

Developments in the 1970s differed in some respects from traditional Swedish labour market policy. Although the work principle was still dominant – in terms of both numbers and budget – the cash principle gained ground by way of changes in the income transfer systems. Another change was a shift in policy from 'employment security in the labour market' to 'job security in the enterprise'. The strong emphasis on market-strengthening measures decreased in relative terms. In the 1980s labour market policy was increasingly geared towards groups with special problems.

Labour market policy in the crisis of the 1990s differed from that of earlier recessions. First, the government waited much longer to increase the volume of labour market programmes. Second, labour market training was very much favoured compared to temporary job creation schemes at the start of the recession. In previous downturns the use of temporary job creation schemes had been the main labour market programme utilised to stabilise the business cycle. The policy changed as the crisis grew and temporary job creation schemes expanded. In 1993, however, a new form of temporary employment programme was introduced which paid lower wages (the same as unemployment benefit).

The Current Situation

Labour market policy is an integral part of Swedish economic policy. The main aims of Swedish labour market policy are to get the labour market to function better as a market and to raise the employment rate.

The work principle is central to the Swedish economic and social policy model.

Active labour market measures are the centrepiece of Swedish labour market policy, based on the employment offices. Labour market policy is implemented by the Labour Market Administration (AMV), which is organised on three levels: central, county and local. At the local level, the primary task of the employment offices is to match job seekers (unemployed or people who want to change jobs) with vacancies. For an unemployed person for whom the employment office is not able to find a job in the ordinary labour market in the short run, placement in an active measure is the preferred option. The number of programmes is large and has gradually expanded.

Active labour market policy can be divided into different parts. The demand side programmes have mainly taken the form of public sector employment programmes for the unemployed, but this has gradually shifted to subsidised employment (often with training content) in both the public and the private sector. The supply side policies have mainly comprised training programmes with vocational training in special training establishments but also non-vocational education and training in enterprises. Of lesser importance, but much discussed has been support for geographical mobility. In recent decades a large proportion of these programmes has been targeted at specific groups. Programmes for young people and for the disabled have been the most extensive.

As already mentioned, temporary jobs for the unemployed have existed as policy since the 1910s. The rules for these programmes have changed, however. Compensation was low for those employed in such programmes in their first decades but was increased in the 1930s to the market rate (or that of collective agreements). In the 1990s there was a change back to lower pay and an emphasis on a combination of work and training.

Labour market training has gradually expanded since the 1950s. In the early stages of the 1990s recession labour market training to a large extent replaced temporary job creation schemes as a counter-cyclical measure. The two main arguments for labour market training have been that it facilitates mobility from unemployment-stricken occupations and regions to those with vacancies, and that it enhances the competence of the labour force. In general the allowance is the same as compensation from unemployment insurance. For those who are not members of an unemployment insurance society, the compensation is set at a fixed, low amount. A significant number of evaluations have been made of labour market training programmes.[1] The oldest studies – which cover the 1960s, 1970s and 1980s – in many instances show positive results. However, the studies carried out in the 1990s regularly show that those taking part in a training programme lose economically compared to those (with the same characteristics and labour market situation) who do not participate. This has generally led to a more sceptical attitude towards labour market training programmes.

In July 1984 a new programme was introduced, lending support to unemployed people wanting to start their own businesses. After a trial period it became a standard programme (from July 1987). The maximum compensation period is six months, with the possibility of a six-month extension, and the compensation is the same as for people in labour market training. The measure has been given high priority and has rapidly expanded.

Swedish labour market policy emphasises active programmes, but state support for unemployment benefit societies has existed since 1935 (see section 2.1). They are closely related to the trade unions. The compensation rate was 90% of previous income up to an earnings ceiling prior to July 1993, after which it was lowered to 80%. From 1 January 1996, the compensation rate was further lowered to 75% (restored to 80% in 1998). There is a ceiling on income compensated by the system.

The Swedish labour market was less regulated by the state than those in most other European countries until the mid-1970s. The social partners (unions and employer associations) were strong and for a long time tried to regulate the labour market through collective agreements. However, in the mid-1970s several laws were introduced that regulated different aspects of the labour market. The seniority principle became law as regards the selection of whom to keep when reducing the workforce and a minimum notice period was laid down. Several of these changes gave older workers stronger employment protection.

Policies for Different Groups

A large proportion of active labour market policy is targeted towards groups with special problems. Two groups that have low employment rates are disabled people and older people. The labour market programmes for these groups are presented below.

By international comparison, Sweden has an especially strong emphasis on labour market policy programmes for the disabled (measured

---

[1] See Regnér (1997) for a study which also contains a survey of earlier studies.

in terms of the proportion of participants or costs).[2] Policies for disabled workers have a long history – the first programme started as early as 1915.[3] The first programme comprised support for disabled workers starting their own business, in most cases small shops. In the 1940s, programmes were started largely to help people who had been wounded during the Second World War. Programmes for the employment of disabled workers have gradually expanded since the 1940s.

The three main programmes now are: (i) employment in Samhall (a conglomerate of sheltered workshops); (ii) sheltered jobs in the public sector (*offentligt skyddat arbete*, OSA); and (iii) work with a wage subsidy (*lönebidrag*).

The sheltered workshops – which since 1980 have been organised as parts of one conglomerate, Samhall – are designed for workers with disabilities that make it very difficult for them to be placed in the ordinary labour market. According to its statutes, at least 40% of the disabled people employed by Samhall should have severe disabilities. In 2004 the majority of the disabled workers had physical disabilities (54%). Many stay in sheltered workshops for very long periods, despite the fact that one of the programme goals is to rehabilitate people. At present, 22,000 disabled workers are employed by Samhall. The majority are men (54%).

A special programme was introduced in 1986: sheltered work in the public sector (*offentligt skyddat arbete, OSA*). The programme is mainly intended for people with socio-medical disabilities or long-term psychological occupational handicaps. Most of those placed in this programme are men. The size of the subsidy is determined in the same way as for work with the wage subsidy programme (see below), that is, after negotiations between the employer and the employment office. In 2004 the average subsidy level was 75% of wage costs. The number of participants in OSA was 5,300 in October 2005.

Work with a wage subsidy is the labour market programme for the disabled with the most participants. As it is more integrative, it is given higher priority and is expanding compared to work in sheltered workshops (Samhall and OSA). In October 2005 more than 58,000 were in this programme (61% of those new in the programme in 2004 were men). Somatic diagnoses are the most common. The size of the subsidy

---

[2] See Bergeskog (2001), Skogman Thoursie (1999) and Wadensjö (2001 and 2002) for information on the labour market and labour market policy programmes for the disabled in Sweden.

[3] See Bergeskog (2001), Wadensjö (1984, 1984a, 2001, 2002), Wadensjö and Sjögren (2000) and Wang (2001) for more information on the structure and the development of Swedish labour market policy for disabled workers.

is determined after negotiations between the employer and the employment office. The average subsidy level was 63% in 2004. The maximum period of placement is four years but many remain in work with wage subsidies for longer periods than that. The share of older workers in that programme is still lower than in sheltered workshops: many are in the age group 40-54 years. The wage rate in the work with a wage subsidy programme follows the collective agreement for those with corresponding regular jobs. Income compensation is therefore 100%, which provides no incentive to leave the programme.

Usually mentioned alongside the above programmes are the institutes for vocational rehabilitation (*arbetslivsinriktad rehabilitering*), which are centres for extensive training and vocational guidance. The majority – but not all – of those who take part in this programme are disabled. The programme prepares workers for jobs (sheltered or otherwise) or training.

In many countries active labour market programmes are almost exclusively for other age groups than older workers. In Sweden many older workers are placed in the ordinary business cycle-related programmes.[4] Some special programmes for older workers were tested in the 1990s. Two were of the passive type – making early exit easier – and another of the traditional active labour market type. I will present the three programmes below.

In the second half of 1997 a special option for early exit was opened for the long-term unemployed who were 60 years or older, which made it possible for those with a history of being out of work for two years or more to get special compensation up to the normal retirement age of 65. The compensation was the same as that granted by unemployment insurance. It became quite popular and contributed to the reduction of open unemployment. In practice, however, this programme amounted to a one-off reduction of long-term unemployment among older workers.

Another programme of the same type guaranteed older workers compensation up to retirement if they left their job and were replaced by a long-term unemployed young person. Only a few hundred people left the labour market through this programme, however. Probably, the stringent condition regarding who was permitted to replace those leaving and the requirement that the newly employed should have tenured employment (giving them a stronger position than already employed workers with temporary contracts) made them unpopular among employers and unions alike.

---

[4] See Wadensjö (2003a) for more details.

The programme Temporary Public Sector Jobs for Older Workers started in November 1996 and quickly placed a large number of people. It was intended for long-term unemployed workers aged 55-64. The jobs were to be constructed so that they did not replace already existing jobs (and with the intention of enhancing the quality of public services). No new placements were made after 1998 so the number of people in the programme gradually fell until it was terminated at the end of 2001.

A New Labour Market Policy Programme

A special programme – the activity guarantee – was introduced in August 2000. The activity guarantee assures placement in various programmes (in most cases probably shifting over time). The programme is open to those aged 20 years and older who are looking for jobs at employment offices and have been registered as a job applicant (unemployed or in active labour market programmes) for two years or more or are at a high risk of fulfilling that criterion in the near future. The activity guarantee gives the same compensation as unemployment insurance. Persons receiving unemployment insurance benefits cannot refuse a placement under the activity guarantee without losing their right to unemployment benefits. This means that the programme follows the work-principle tradition.

A large part of those in the activity guarantee programme are older workers: as many as 37% of the 45,000 in the programme in July 2005 were 55-64 years of age. This is because older workers account for many of those registered long-term at employment offices.

The activity guarantee has not yet been evaluated. It is therefore too early to say anything about the effects of the programme on labour force participation and employment. An evaluation must study selection for the programme (what would the participants have done during the programme period if they had not participated?) and the outcome (what have they been doing since the programme period and what would they have done if they had not participated in the programme?).

ESF Programmes and their Impact on Swedish Labour Market Policy

The ESF programmes in Sweden are small compared to national policy in the same area. Therefore it is not possible to examine in terms of aggregate data whether the ESF programmes have influenced the extent of national programmes. The problem is aggravated by the fact that during the 1990s there were extremely large variations in the business cycle in Sweden, which resulted in major changes in the composition and size of labour market and educational programmes. It is not possible to look at the aggregate cost figures of the national programme in Sweden and try to draw conclusions regarding the influence of the ESF from variations in these figures.

What is feasible is to discuss the possible effects and try to say something about the likely outcome. This could be done by starting with two extreme cases. In the first, high-impact case, the programmes are just supplementary to national programmes. We get more programme activities as a result. In the second case overall policy is unchanged: the same programmes are implemented, the only difference being that financing has changed to some extent from national to EU financing. Those two extreme cases are not the most likely ones; more likely is a case in which the overall level is influenced by the ESF programmes but not to the full extent of the new programmes. However, ESF programmes could influence not only the size but also the composition of the policy mix. The emphasis on groups with special problems and on those employed by small companies could have led to a change in the composition of the people in programmes.

The financial contribution of the ESF to the total budget for labour market policy programmes in Sweden constitutes around 2% during the programme period. This means that the ESF share of labour market policy in Sweden is small. The number of participants in the ESF programmes is also small compared to the number of participants in ordinary labour market policy programmes. One intention of the ESF programmes has been to influence national policies, but it is difficult to discern national aggregate levels. The ESF programmes are too small and the business cycle-determined variations and other changes are too large.

Social Security Programmes

The social security system is a central part of the Swedish welfare state. Together with active labour market policy and the large public service sector, it constitutes what has often been called 'the Swedish model'. Coverage has been high, with residence in Sweden as the main criterion, and could be classified as a universal system. Besides a basic sum, compensation has been based on the earnings replacement principle, and the replacement rate has generally been high. There have been ceilings in the schemes, but for those with earnings higher than the ceiling, occupational insurance schemes have helped make up the shortfall. Up until the early 1990s the welfare state, defined in that way, was seen as a success by many and economic development was favourable in some respects. The unemployment rate was low and income equality was greater than in most other countries. Economic worries included a low growth rate since the early 1970s and higher inflation than that of the country's main trading partners.

Up to the early 1990s social security schemes had changed in only one direction: they gradually became more generous. However, in the late 1980s, before the economic crisis of the 1990s, the policy began to change. Intended reforms leading to even more generous systems were cancelled and a debate started on the costs of the social security system. In the early 1990s several problems in the social security system became a source of worry. The high (and increasing) take-up of sickness cash benefits, occupational injury benefits and disability pensions led to a discussion of compensation rates and eligibility rules. The slow growth rate of the economy, combined with a growing number of older people, led to worries regarding the future financing of the system and thereby its viability.

The New Swedish Old Age Pension System

The main idea behind the new pension system is to increase work incentives by making the pension system actuarially fair and so viable.[5] The system should be more of an insurance system and less a system of income redistribution. A second aim of the reform is that the pension system should guarantee a basic income for everyone in old age. This means that some redistribution should take place but it should be more visible than in the earlier system. The major change is from a defined benefit to a defined contribution system. This new defined-contribution pension system is partly a pay-as-you-go system and partly a premium reserve system, with the pay-as-you-go system as the main part. The construction of the defined-contribution pay-as-you-go system is an interesting innovation. The transition from the earlier ATP to the new system is gradual. The pensions of those who were born in 1954 or later will be completely based on the new system.

Pensions are based on the individual's earnings every year for those aged 16 years or more, including earnings after the age of 65. An amount corresponding to 18.5% of earnings will constitute the pension credits accrued during a year (the same as the fee, see below), 16% to a pay-as-you-go scheme (*inkomstpension*) and 2.5% to a premium reserve scheme (*premiepension*). In addition to earnings (including transfer payments due to unemployment, sickness, and so on), military service, care of children up to the age of four, years of study to some extent, and years on disability pension will be taken into account when calculating the pension. There is a ceiling for income which is included in the

---

[5] See Wadensjö (1999).

calculation of pension credits. The pension credits are indexed to the development of total earnings in the economy.

Each year the accumulated pension credits of those who have reached 65 years of age that year are transformed into a pension. This is done by using a partition rate, a rate that is decided anew for every cohort reaching 65. The size of the partition rate and therefore the pension depends on the expected period for which those who turn 65 will receive a pension. As the expected remaining years of life increase with each cohort, the partition rate will gradually increase, and therefore the pensions will be lower for each cohort if not counteracted by economic growth.

Secondly, there will also be a 'guarantee pension' (*garantipension*) for those with low or no earnings. For a full guarantee pension the applicant must have resided in Sweden for at least 40 years between the ages of 16 and 65. The guarantee pension is reduced if the pensioner receives an earnings-related old-age pension. The guarantee pension is reduced by 70% of what is received in the earnings related pension (but not taxed against other pensions and incomes). The pensions will be linked to a price and growth related index.

The change to actuarial pensions is intended to increase labour supply and to delay retirement. The work incentives are higher in the new scheme as it is based on earnings for all years, not only for the best 15 (as in the earlier system). The intention is that this should increase the number of years worked (earlier entry, fewer interruptions and later exit on average), and also reduce the proportion of part-time work. A number of other steps have been taken with the same intention. Previously, a reduced old age pension could be received from the age of 60, but in the new pension system 61 is the lowest age (this change took place as early as 1998). On early retirement pensioners will receive only the earnings-related pension. A guarantee pension will only be possible from the age of 65 and is calculated as if the person had retired at the age of 65. Another part of the reform of May 2001 is that mandatory retirement agreements with a stipulated age lower than 67 are forbidden. A way of combining work and retirement is a partial old age pension from the age of 61 or over (the earnings-related part). It is possible to draw a quarter, half or three quarters of an old age pension.

The Part-Time Pension System

Sweden had a subsidised part-time pension system from 1976 to around the end of the century.[6] It was part of the social security system

---

[6] See Wadensjö (1996).

and was financed by a payroll contribution. Taking up a part-time pension did not influence the old age pension (from the age of 65). There were additions to the social security part-time pensions in three of the four main collective bargaining areas (state employees, those employed by the counties and municipalities, and white-collar workers in the private sector).

From the start of the new scheme the part-time pension was an option for employees who were 60 years or older (up to the age of 65). The minimum reduction of working hours was 5 hours, the minimum remaining working hours 17 and the replacement rate 65% of earnings lost due to the reduction in hours. With a progressive income tax system the actual replacement rate was in fact higher. To qualify for a part-time pension the employer had to give his consent. The system became very popular in a short time. Many people applied and the employers were generally positive, seeing it as an opportunity to restructure and rejuvenate the work force without being forced to pay severance pay or to go through complicated negotiations with the unions.

The part-time pension changed in the 1990s, however. As part of the reform of the old age pension system the part-time pension came to an end in two stages. The formal motivation behind this was that a subsidised part-time pension was not in accordance with the general principles of the new old age pension system, namely that pensions should be based on life-time earnings.

A part-time pension system may induce some people to work part-time instead of full-time and others to work part-time instead of leaving the labour market altogether. The effect in terms of hours worked in the economy also depends on the number of hours worked before starting to work part-time (or leaving the labour market) and the number of hours worked after taking a part-time pension. The results of one study show that the total effect is an increase in the number of hours worked and that this effect is greater for women than for men. There may be other effects: the financing of the system (payroll contributions) may have an effect on labour supply, and the take-up of a part-time pension (instead of working full-time) may influence a person's health status and thereby the incidence of future take-ups of a disability pension.

The part-time pension system was quite popular. It has now been reintroduced for one important group in the labour market, state employees. It is closely modelled on the former part-time pension system. An agreement on the introduction of a similar system for those employed by the municipalities and counties has just been reached. Some private employers have also introduced part-time pension systems of their own. It should be added that there is also a part-time pension option in the new old age pension system. However, this type of part-time pension is not subsidised but leads to an actuarially reduced old age pension. Part-time pensions in the old age pension scheme have not become popular. The take-up rate is low. There are also part-time pensions in the disability pension system, the number of which has tended to increase.

The Disability Pension Scheme

The disability pension, since its start in 1913, has been part of the same system and has been calculated in the same way as the old age pension, except that earnings in the years from retirement up to the age of 65 have been estimated in pension calculations ('assumption points').[7] In 1970 it became possible to take labour market reasons into account alongside medical ones when granting a disability pension to people aged 63 or older (changed to 60 or older in 1976). In 1972 it became possible to grant a disability pension for labour market reasons only for people aged 63 or older (changed to 60 or older in 1974). In practice, this meant that people aged 63 (60 from 1974) or over who had exhausted their entitlement to unemployment compensation were disability pensioned. As the maximum period for unemployment compensation was 1 year and 9 months for people aged 55 or more, those aged 58 years and 3 months who became unemployed could in practice 'retire' (from 1974 when the minimum age for receiving such a pension was lowered from 63 to 60). This combination of payments from two income transfer systems was called a '58.3 pension'. The granting of 'unemployment' pensions was discontinued from October 1991 when the granting of new disability pensions for labour market reasons was abolished. From January 1997 the possibility of older workers getting a disability pension for combined medical and labour market reasons disappeared. Medical reasons are now the only valid criteria for granting a disability pension.

The number of newly granted disability pensions increased considerably from 2000. This was not totally unexpected as the number of cases of long-term illness had increased in the preceding years and long-term illness is often the first step to a disability pension. This increase casts some doubt on the long-term decline in the number of disability pensions but it is too early to say.

The disability pension is not part of the new scheme for old age pensions. A new system for disability pensions has been in force since 1 January 2003. The disability pension scheme is now integrated with

---

[7] See Wadensjö and Palmer (1996) for an analysis of the Swedish disability pension system.

the sickness benefit scheme instead. After a sickness benefit period of one year, monthly compensation will be paid if working capacity is expected to be reduced for at least one more year. For those on low earnings, guarantee compensation will be paid (the same as in the old age pension scheme). For others the compensation will be based on average earnings from four of the last six years (the year with the lowest and the year with the highest earnings are left out of the calculation). There is an alternative way of calculating the basis for disability compensation: the compensation is 65% of the amount calculated according to the more favourable of the two alternatives.

As already mentioned, most of those granted a disability pension start with a period on sickness benefit; in most cases an extended period. The number of people with long sickness periods has increased considerably during the last few years. This has been one of the most widely discussed issues in Sweden in recent times. Various measures have been proposed with the intention of counteracting this development, including lower replacement rates, increased experience rating for employers (the employer period has been prolonged from two to three weeks), more controls against misuse and more work rehabilitation. It is still too early to say what the outcome of the debate will be, not to mention the results of the measures that have been tried.

Trends in Activation Policy in Sweden

The above presentation of the different policy areas shows that Swedish policy has been guided by the work principle for a long time. The formulation and relative importance of that policy have changed over time. In the 1960s, 1970s and 1980s the stated policy was the work principle but several changes were made in a different direction. People were expected to work until ordinary retirement age and if unemployed were expected to return to work, in many cases after a period in an active labour market programme. In the same period, however, social security schemes were made more generous: the compensation rate increased and access to the system was made easier. The number of people leaving the labour market early increased, many of them with a disability pension. The number of people on sickness leave swelled. The costs of the welfare state increased. This led to proposals to curtail the welfare state. The first retrenchment steps as regards the welfare state were taken as early as the 1980s, but many more were taken during the crisis of the 1990s. Impetus was given to these changes by increased costs for unemployment benefits and active labour market programmes.

The changes were all intended to go in the same direction – higher employment – but the design of the changes differs between the different programmes. I will start with the changes in the social security programmes and continue with those of the labour market programmes.

The new old age pension system is very much oriented towards increasing the labour supply. The pension will be based on earnings from all years in work. An important change is that the maximum age covered by the law on employment protection has increased from 65 to 67, and that agreements on mandatory retirement below the age of 67 have became illegal.

The disability pension system was changed in different stages, from giving support also to older people with labour market problems to granting pensions only to those with longstanding medical problems. Rehabilitation has been emphasised much more for those receiving sickness benefits, as well as for those getting a disability pension.

All the changes in the design of the programmes have been intended to increase labour supply and employment. Work incentives have been enhanced and programme access has become more difficult, due to both changes in the rules and reinforcement of the role of the gatekeeper.

Changes have been made in the design of labour market programmes relevant to the activation policy debate. One important change is the lowering of compensation in active labour market programmes. Development has been from paying the going market rate to paying the same level as unemployment insurance benefits. This means that compensation has been reduced by means of two different methods. Other changes include a shortening of the period of unemployment compensation in a number of different ways, the introduction of more stringent requirements for active job search for those taking up unemployment benefits and the enhanced placement of long-term unemployed in labour market programmes (and the requirement that they accept the placement if they want to continue to receive support). Altogether this means that the welfare state now puts more emphasis on the work principle.

It is of course difficult this early on to say anything specific about the effects of the various changes in the systems, but I will give some information which may be useful. Most of the policy changes have as their main intention (or at least as one of their main intentions) an increase in labour force participation and employment among older people (60 to 64 years). Tables 1 and 2 present the development of labour force participation among men and women aged 60 to 64 in the period 1995-2004 and as a comparison the corresponding developments for those aged 55-59 and 16-64.

Table 1. Labour Force Participation among Men Aged 55-64 Years, 1995-2004 (%)

Age	1995	2000	2004
55-59	82.2	83.9	83.8
60	71.6	73.7	76.1
61	64.9	66.5	72.5
62	55.9	57.4	66.1
63	51.3	43.6	58.9
64	41.9	38.0	48.2
16-64	80.2	80.2	79.7

Source: Statistics Sweden, Labour Force Surveys.

Table 2. Labour Force Participation among Women Aged 55-64 Years, 1995-2004 (%)

Age	1995	2000	2004
55-59	77.3	79.1	79.4
60	65.7	67.1	69.9
61	59.5	58.7	67.0
62	48.6	52.1	58.0
63	37.7	35.1	49.3
64	31.2	25.2	40.7
16-64	76.1	75.5	75.7

Source: Statistics Sweden, Labour Force Surveys.

Labour force participation has been stable for those aged 55-59 and for those aged 16-64 (all of active age). On the other hand, the labour force participation rate has increased very strongly for those aged 60-64. Development is concentrated in the period from 2000 to 2004 and is very strong for those who are close to 65, the ordinary retirement age. This is in line with the aims of the policy changes.

Conclusion

Sweden has a long tradition of relying on the 'work' principle in economic and social policy. This applies to both labour market policy, which very much stresses the role of active labour market policy programmes, and social security programmes. Social security programmes in recent years have been characterised by stronger work incentives. This is especially the case for the new system of old age pensions, although the disability pension programme and labour market programmes have also been changed in the same direction. Activation is a central part of Swedish reforms. However, this is not a result of the EES targets for employment since Sweden already meets these targets by a wide margin. Swedish policy is influenced by other factors. An important one is demographic changes, particularly population ageing. Another factor is the increase in costs, especially of sickness benefits, disability pensions and (active and passive) labour market programmes.

References

Bergeskog, A. (2001), "Labour market policies, strategies and statistics for people with disabilities. A cross-national comparison", IFAU, Working paper 2001:13.

Regnér, H. (1997), "Training on the job and training for a new job: two Swedish studies", PhD thesis, Swedish Institute for Social Research, Stockholm University.

Skogman Thoursie, P. (1999), "Disability and work in Sweden", Swedish Institute for Social Research Dissertation Series 39.

Thoursie, A. and E. Wadensjö (1997), *Labour Market Studies: Sweden*, Brussels, European Commission.

Wadensjö, E. (1984), "Labour market policy towards the disabled in Sweden", Discussion paper IIM/LMP 84-4C, Berlin, Wissenschaftszentrum.

Wadensjö, E. (1984a), "Disability policy in Sweden", in R. Haveman, V. Halberstadt and R. Burkhauser, *Public Policy toward Disabled Workers*, Ithaca, Cornell University Press.

Wadensjö, E. (1996), "Gradual retirement in Sweden", in L. Delsen and G. Reday-Mulvey (eds.), *Gradual Retirement in the OECD Countries*, Gower.

Wadensjö, E. (1999), "Sweden: reform of the state pension scheme", in E. Reynaud (ed.), *Social Dialogue and Pension Reform*, Geneva, ILO.

Wadensjö, E. and E. Palmer (1996), "Curing the Dutch disease from a Swedish perspective", in L. Aarts, R. Burkhauser and P. de Jong (eds.), *Curing the Dutch Disease. An International Perspective on Disability Policy Reform*, Aldershot, Avebury.

Wadensjö, E. and G. Sjögren (2000), *Arbetslinjen för äldre i praktiken* [The work principle for older people in practice], Stockholm: Swedish Institute for Social Research and Riksdagens revisorer [the Parliamentary Auditors].

Wadensjö, E. (2001), "The employment status of disabled people in the EU. Country study: Sweden", supplement to *Employment of People with Disabilities*, Amsterdam, EIM.

Wadensjö, E. (2002), "Labour market policy for disabled people in the EU. Country study: Sweden", supplement to *Labour Market Policy for People with Disabilities*, Amsterdam, EIM.

Wadensjö, E. (2003), "Active strategies for older workers in Sweden", in M. Jepsen, D. Foden and M. Hutsebaut (eds.), *Active Strategies for Older Workers*, Brussels, ETUI.

Wang, Yu-yu Nancy (2001), "Promoting the rights to work of disabled people? A historical comparative analysis of Sweden, Great Britain and Taiwan", PhD thesis, School of Social Policy, Sociology and Social Research, University of Kent at Canterbury.

The French Activation Strategy in a Comparative Perspective

Jean-Claude BARBIER

Introduction

An already considerable body of literature has been devoted to analysing 'activation' and we have contributed to it (see References).

Yet as time passes, the imperative of defining the concept in a comparative perspective has yet to be fully achieved and the debate is still partly open: we need more reflection on how to handle 'activation', this strange object whose name has now taken a place in current European political jargon.

The comprehensive framework to which we aim to contribute will be set against the French experience. This supposes a rather detailed analysis of programmes introduced from the early 1990s onwards, in a historical perspective (without historical analysis, there is little to be understood in the unending political discourse on policies). France will be seen as a member of the continental family, although we will illustrate – in passing – the shortcomings of clustering methods in this specific instance.

Overall cross-national lessons can be drawn from the French case if one situates them in the context of the EES and raises fundamental questions concerning how to assess (and not only evaluate) the transformations presumably brought about by 'activation' in social protection systems and individuals.

How to Handle Activation? A Comparative Framework

I have argued in numerous papers in favour of a comprehensive approach, in which the concept of 'activation' applies to 'systems of social protection' as entities: in a perspective complementary to the 'restructuring of the welfare states' (Pierson 2001), I consider 'activation' as one among many dimensions of the restructuring process affecting all systems in developed countries, with varying incidence according to clusters of countries or 'welfare regimes' but also specific areas of social protection.[1] Before briefly recalling the features of various ideal-types of transformation across the developed world, it is necessary to account for the main economic reasons for the spread of such restructuring along the lines of activation. We will then proceed to explain how activation reforms can be identified across the vast domain of social protection and discuss the features of two ideal-types. Because France is commonly classified among 'continental countries', we will try and situate it generally in this regard. Although activation *discourse* is pervasive, it is obvious that institutional features of certain systems make them more prone to transformation than others. Restructuring patterns also interact with differences in values and political discourses (Schmidt 2005).

The Propagation of Flexibility: Global Constraints and Activation

All potential and actual transformations of social protection systems are constrained by the overall economic rationale of flexibilisation (Barbier and Nadel 2000, 2002). The activation of social protection is no exception in this respect. As Radaelli (2003, 7) observed in the case of the European coordination of social policies, 'open coordination is embedded in the master discourse of competitiveness'.

In the globalised economy, international monetary rules and standards profoundly affect wage competition. Containing labour costs is the overall rationale that justifies the general drive towards labour market flexibility. Moreover, in the context of the creation of the eurozone, and the adoption of the Stability and Growth Pact, EU member states are obliged to act to limit their public deficits, but also to foster 'moderation' in terms of wage increases and indirect labour costs (taxes and social contributions that finance social protection). Overall, the efforts to reduce labour costs are consistent with the containment of state expenditure, and in some cases with a reduction of social outlays. This drive is consistent with activating social protection, in terms of containing benefit expenditure and adopting sustainable funding mechanisms. However, the adaptation and restructuring of systems are not uniform across countries and across programmes (Barbier and Théret 2004). Nevertheless, in most countries – bar Scandinavia – work and employment flexibility has resulted in the concentration of the detrimental effects of flexibility on some categories of the workforce, who only have

---

[1] Overall, these various forms are consistent with Pierson's (2001) categories (re-commodification, cost containment and recalibration).

access to jobs with second-rate social protection. To that extent, activation reforms bring with them a degradation of traditional social citizenship rights won during the 1970s.

However, while social protection reforms may well increase these negative outcomes, empirical research shows that there is no universal and mechanical movement across Europe (Pierson 2001; Scharpf and Schmidt 2000). As the Danish institutional arrangements amply showed in the 1990s, strategies can reconcile highly generous welfare provision, flexibility and orthodox macroeconomic policies. However the Danish and, to a lesser extent, Swedish cases are rather exceptional in Europe. The achievement of high work flexibility in the context of the resilience of universal good quality welfare provision is still unheard of in most European countries, where work flexibility is associated with a high level of instability and insecurity of certain types of jobs, combined with patchy social coverage (Barbier 2003).

The strategic link between, on the one hand, social protection and job security, and on the other hand, flexibility of work, has prompted many analyses and proposals of changes of systems in Europe. The transitional labour market approach is among the best elaborated (Schmid and Gazier 2002). In the social democratic welfare regime, the need to institutionalise such transitional labour markets is certainly weaker than in the continental and liberal regimes for one essential reason, namely the effectiveness of the welfare system that is able to compensate for the negative aspects of increasing work flexibility. Just as the overall restructuring movement displays different aspects, it is not surprising that the styles and substance of activation strategies widely differ (Barbier and Gautié 1998; Torfing 1999; Morel 2000; Wood 2001; Goul Andersen *et al.* 2005; Jørgensen 2002; Schmid and Gazier 2002; van Berkel and Møller 2002; Serrano Pascual 2004; Barbier and Ludwig-Mayerhofer 2004). These strategies have very different consequences as regards the substance of social rights and obligations, but also the type and quality of jobs they cultivate, which can be more or less unstable or, in some countries, seen as 'precarious' (Barbier 2003). In fact, the consequences of activation reforms in a number of countries have so far been rather superficially researched.

To correctly understand what activation reforms imply in various countries, we need to define the concept of activation and to situate it in a historical perspective.

Concept and Scope of Activation

An abundant literature now shows quite convincingly that ideological and rhetorical change is going on everywhere (Serrano

Pascual 2004). This is also apparent in the context of the implementation of the open method of coordination in various areas (most notably employment, social inclusion and pensions). In the 2004 EES, before the 2005 update, this domain was mainly addressed under Guidelines 1 (active and preventive measures); 5 (active ageing); 6 (equal opportunities); and 8 (making work pay). However, in the political use of the term, activation has remained ill-defined, normative and fuzzy. 'Active policies' are only one part of activation. 'Active labour market policies'; 'workfare' (in the USA – assistance and work obligations); 'welfare to work' schemes in the UK (for the disabled, young, lone parents, and so on); '*aktivering*' in Denmark; '*insertion* programmes' in France: all these programmes more or less belong to the same type. However, other policy areas are concerned – pensions, early retirement schemes, and so on – and the activation principle may in future spread to new, more coordinated policy areas. Another important area in which activation strategies apply increasingly, at least in 'continental' and 'liberal' countries, is the reform of 'tax and benefits' systems. All these reforms are interlinked.

It is essential here to distance research from the normative notions commonly conveyed by international political discourse: agreeing on a rigorous analytical concept is all the more necessary as current programmes across Europe and America are situated within the framework of various historical legacies. For instance, with its 'Rehn-Meidner' inspiration, Sweden certainly played an important (however distant in time) role in the genesis of contemporary strategies, for the very notion of 'active policy' was invented there. In France, because of their relatively early introduction from the mid-1970s, '*insertion*' policies are also significant. Although it is certainly part of activation, 'workfare' (Lødemel and Trickey 2000) really fits only American programmes (Barbier 2005a) because of its narrow focus on assistance programmes. Moreover, taking account of historical legacies requires that we recognise that 'activation' is not a new phenomenon: for instance, in the Scandinavian countries, as well as in Germany, an important part of social policy has long been devoted to vocational training, an active policy tool *par excellence* (Barbier and Ludwig-Mayerhofer 2004). The goal of full employment was always historically deeply integrated into the welfare rationale in Denmark and Norway (Jensen and Halvorsen 2004), and it still is today, despite the different circumstances. This helps explain why the 'new activation' in the second half of the 1990s in Scandinavia appeared as a rather marginal adjustment of an already very 'activated' system of social protection with high employment rates.[2]

From this perspective, it is logical to prefer an encompassing analytical notion of 'activation', which reaches beyond the 'activation of individuals' (in the now common sense of incentivising or compelling them to seek and take jobs). 'Activation' can then be seen as a general trend, indeed compatible with a variable mix of reforms according to particular countries, in the context of a general drive towards flexibilising labour markets (see previous section). In this sense, 'activation' is new because, contrary to the past experience of many countries, it entails a new and systematic transformation of systems to make them more 'employment friendly', enhancing the various social functions of 'paid work' and labour force participation. To sum up from definitions we have proposed elsewhere (Barbier 2002a; 2004a; 2004b), 'activation' is here envisaged as the introduction (or the re-activation/reinforcement) of an explicit linkage between, on the one hand, social protection and, on the other hand, labour market participation and labour market programmes.

Hence, the domains of social protection which may potentially be 'activated' extend well beyond programmes for the assisted or the unemployed. Not being fixed for the future, the scope of activation is probably bound to be extended. Currently it applies to (i) benefit programmes (unemployment insurance and various assistance schemes for working-age groups, including disability and other family related benefits); (ii) pension systems and, most particularly, early retirement programmes; (iii) employment (or active labour market – ALM) programmes; but also, (iv) policies aimed at reforming the 'tax and benefits systems'. Such reforms may be aimed at either invigorating labour demand or at incentivising labour supply.

Ideal-Types of Activation

From the individual's point of view, these programmes are deemed to provide incentives (sometimes closely associated with compulsion and sanctions), but also, in some cases, a wide array of offers of services (for instance, counselling, job search, training); they also – at least in theory, indirectly or directly – extend individuals' choices by increasing labour demand on the conventional market (especially in the case of wage subsidies). From a system perspective, social protection is 'activated' in the sense that the delivery of services and benefits mainly

---

[2] Kvist (2002) has correctly noted that Scandinavian systems are at the same time highly de-commodified and highly commodified.

targets working-age people in some sort of 'work' activities (extending in some cases the range of 'working age'). It is also activated in the sense that funding mechanisms and the allocation of resources are designed so as to foster increased job creation.

Once a common activation trend is identified, the question remains as to whether it results in a convergence of systems, policies, programme rationales, and so on. Discussing this point is easier when one uses a three-level approach. In comparative social policy, a long tradition has stressed the similarities and commonalities of systems' evolutions (for instance, Wilensky 1975). This constitutes a first level of the discussion: overall general trends. This tradition is still active among authors who presume a unique trend towards activation and take for granted a dominant 'Anglo-Saxon' influence in the creation of new common policy paradigms. Supporters of the current reforms assess this development positively, for instance in the form of the emergence of a universal 'enabling state' (for instance, Gilbert 2002, 42-47); on the other hand, critics deplore contemporary developments which, to them, amount to a universal degradation of the welfare state in the direction of a 'workfare state' (for instance, Jessop 1993; 1996).[3]

Table 1. Ideal-Types of Activation of Social Protection

	Universalistic (social democratic)	Liberal
'Problems' activation is deemed to solve	Limits of generous universal welfare provision for the collective work ethic (incentives, collective values); budgetary costs; benefit programmes are too 'passive' in their design; labour shortages	Limits of targeted welfare provision; increase in 'passive' income support (underemployment; budgetary costs); lack of social support (voters[4]) for targeted welfare; inequality, poverty and 'worklessness'
Collective norms and values	Social citizenship as a balance between the individual and society (collective and individual rights and obligations). Social rights: universal provision	Self-reliance is prominent; the shame of 'dependency'; predominance of market solutions. Social rights are residual

---

[3] Jessop (1993) theorised the 'workfarist' nature of the present state ('Schumpeterian workfare state'). For him, such a state implies 'to subordinate social policy to the needs of labour market flexibility and/or to the constraints of international competition' (Jessop 1996, 176).

[4] The fundamental reference is the analysis by Korpi and Palme (1998).

Policy rationales/answers	Mix of market/state solutions (training + market + jobs + employment of last resort – subsidised public jobs) Close monitoring with marginal sanctions Targeted incentives	Predominance of the market: flexible mainstream jobs Activate assistance recipients by close monitoring and sanctioning Design incentives for labour market participation across the board (genders/ages/qualifications)
Programme features	Universal high quality services (inc. vocational training) Balanced delivery of the contract between society and the individual (100% achievement[5])	Enhanced short-term (targeted) services; sanctions programmed Financial incentives (generalised tax credits and make-work-pay devices)
Potential/actual outcomes (full employment, quality, flexibility, equality)	Increased labour market participation; decreasing unemployment; labour market flexibility Quality full employment (inclusive labour market); equal access to employment and income from it/ 'full' citizenship	Increased labour market participation; decreasing unemployment; labour market flexibility Persistent underemployment and inequality of access and incomes (genders, ages, qualifications) /unequal citizenship

At a second level (welfare regimes or families of systems), however, assumptions of convergence are not vindicated. Once one tries to answer the question 'convergence of what?' one must be more specific.[6] The dominant literature stresses the fact that various logics and rationales persist over time. At this level *two distinct ideal-types of activation* are easily observable (Barbier 2002a; 2004a; 2004b): they are stylised in Table 1. Finally, within clusters, significant variation is displayed at the national level (not to mention infra-national variation). A special 2004 issue of *European Societies* illustrates this persistent national diversity (Barbier and Ludwig-Mayerhofer 2004) within regimes, especially for the continental group of countries.

Liberal-type activation chiefly enhances the individual's relations to the labour market and entails both (i) the re-commodification of the system (already highly commodified in comparative terms) and

---

[5] The target of 100% achievement means that, when one is not employed, the norm is that one either gets a benefit or participates in 'activation' programmes. This is nearly the case in Denmark at the moment for the active population.

[6] For a differentiation between convergences of rules and procedures and convergence of the substantive outcomes brought about by the ongoing changes, see Börzel and Risse (2000).

(ii) efforts to reduce social expenditure (for instance, in the case of the disabled), to increase incentives ('in-work benefits') and to enhance services. Inequalities remain high, including access to quality jobs.

On the other hand, in *universalistic activation* the provision of complex services is extended to *all citizens* and the role of the market is mitigated by the role of the state. Activation entails recalibration of the previous income compensation mechanisms, in the overall context of cost containment, but the use of tax credits and subsidies plays a limited role, if any. Universal 'full' citizenship is compatible with the reform.

We have discussed the possible emergence of a third type. In fact, identifying three types of activation would nicely fit the traditional tripartition of welfare regimes (Esping-Andersen 1990). However, empirical analysis shows that such a third type is still not clearly established for continental countries (Barbier and Ludwig-Mayerhofer 2004). In section 3 we further explore this assumption using the French case, taking into account the Hartz reforms in Germany.

What Role for Quality, Preferences, Values?

Quality of 'activation' is certainly a key aspect of an evolving 'social citizenship'. Quality resides not only in the quality of services and the generosity of benefits, but also in the nature of the state's commitment to full employment. The state can intervene in creating 'employer of last resort' jobs (when the market 'fails') and also implement effective full-employment macroeconomic policies: two crucial elements indeed. In the 'universalistic' ideal-type – close to the actual Danish case – quality is probably the highest in Europe, and it is based on universal 'social citizenship' (Barbier 2005g).

A comparative assessment of actual activation strategies demonstrates the influence of differing values and norms across countries. While normative collective choices (or preferences, for economists) certainly differ between countries, they have been compatible at a general level within the common framework of the European Employment Strategy (Barbier 2002b). Our contention is that collective values should not be interpreted in terms of 'cultural' differences: in sharp contrast, value choices are embedded in specific national institutional settings and constructed over time by collective actors, who find them adequate and use them as guides for action. In their pioneering research, Maurice *et al.* (1982) clearly formulated this explanation while comparing France and Germany. Jørgensen and his colleagues have proposed a concurring explanation for the construction of 'cooperative adaptation' within Danish society (Jørgensen 2002, 237-243). We will come back to this question when dealing with the French case, indicating how far back in time one should look to understand the role of solidaristic values in that country.

Assessing the Consequences of Activation: Few Findings as yet

For many countries rigorous evaluation studies of activation are rare. Material existing in some – for instance, Denmark – shows a mixture of effects (Madsen 2005). In the Anglo-Saxon countries (the USA and the UK), apart from instant evaluations of the New Deals and TANF, it is not easy to objectify and measure impacts on activity/labour market participation (and even less on poverty and incomes). Econometric studies exist, which sometimes leads to controversy. As we will see, this is also the case in France, for the evaluation of the number of jobs supposedly created as a result of the long-term reduction in employers' social contributions. Evaluation should also encompass other aspects than labour market participation. Evaluation of strategies, with the hindsight of about 10 years of restructuring and introducing new programmes, is certainly a key point in the collective appreciation of activation at present. But standard evaluation studies[7] should certainly not be seen as the ultimate truth about what activation has changed in welfare systems; many transformations are going on which can in no way be captured by the policy tool of evaluation.

The French Case in Perspective: A Dubious Pace-setter for the Continental Group?

As one of the large members of the 'continental' family, with Spain, Italy and Germany, France has nevertheless always been difficult to locate in the cluster. In an important part of the literature, it has traditionally – and exaggeratedly – been seen as rather 'frozen' with regard to the restructuring of its social protection system (Palier 2004; Esping Andersen 1996). However, seen in the light of recent history, this picture is at least partly inadequate (Barbier and Théret 2004). With respect to activation, France is certainly not to be classified as a laggard (Barbier and Ludwig-Mayerhofer 2004; Barbier and Fargion 2004). Structural reform and flexibilisation of the French labour market have also taken place on a significant scale since the late 1980s. Unlike in Spain and Italy, remarkable developments have occurred in France combining social protection and labour market reforms. These trans-

---

[7] Evaluation can rather easily pass as research in economics, but certainly not in political science and sociology. This crucial distinction tends to be forgotten under pressure of the literature which is published by international organisations and easily downloaded from the Internet (Barbier 2005e).

formations may represent a harbinger of future evolutions towards a third, hybrid ideal-type of activation among the other members of the 'continental' family, combining German and French reforms.

In a nutshell, the French activation strategy – which today by no means appears as consistent as the universalistic and liberal approaches – is a combination of features taken from both. Indeed, the elements seem to be picked from either the liberal or the universalistic ideal-types.

(i) While activation was introduced from the late 1980s,[8] unemployment insurance and 'assistance' have recently been at the forefront of the public debate and reforms have tended to target remaining regulations leading to possible 'inactivity traps', especially for minimum income benefit recipients.

(ii) A sector of employment programmes, well established and mostly wage-based,[9] certainly amounts to significant activation (with some resemblance to Scandinavian programmes).

(iii) Large areas of social protection (social services, family and housing benefits) have so far been spared any particular linkage to work incentivising. In this respect, unlike the liberal type of activation and closer to the universalistic model, there seems to remain significant – although decreasing – room for manoeuvre for 'traditional' social policy, most notably within family policy.

(iv) A demand-side measure, the gradual reduction of employers' social contributions, has taken the leading role in activation dynamics, after it was 'embedded' in the working-time reduction process (now abandoned), along with emerging tax credits. This conjunction of reforms has thoroughly altered the traditional Bismarckian principle of the funding of social protection via social contributions.

(v) Finally, the introduction of a consistent activation strategy has yet to materialise in the domain of 'active ageing'. A more detailed (although not exhaustive) survey of particular areas of social policy would help to illustrate this situation.

Unemployment Insurance and Assistance in France

With hindsight, programmes introduced from 1975 under the banner of *insertion* could be seen as precursors to activation reforms later

---

[8] An exception is the emergence of the French innovation of *insertion*, which dates back to the mid-1970s (see below).

[9] For example, implying access to proper wages (although generally low), not assistance benefits.

implemented elsewhere, especially in Spain and Italy (Barbier 2005a). However, when they were introduced for the disabled and the young unskilled, their justification was to 'activate' these groups in a very specific sense: in deliberate contrast to any form of 'punishment' or as the only way out from presumed 'dependency', work was here promoted as a positive channel for integration into society and accessing full political citizenship. Originating in civil society initiatives, the French doctrine of *insertion* was only at a second stage appropriated by the administration, which designed fully-fledged '*insertion* policies'. In the initial solidaristic *insertion* philosophy, 'social integration' was never meant primarily in terms of constraining people to take jobs on the market. In fact, due to the particularly low rate of job creation in France at that period, many programmes entailed the opposite function of keeping people in 'welfare' rather than transferring them to work which did not exist (Barbier and Théret 2001). Although somehow watered down in recent years, this rationale can be interpreted in terms of 'Republican' values, linked to the state's obligation to act as an employer of last resort.

Throughout the 1980s and into the 2000s programmes mixing both minimum income benefits and job creation schemes have played a key role. Although a mean quantity of 400,000 to 500,000 places have been funded yearly,[10] this provision was never able to accommodate all potential candidates, thus undermining the programme's claim to 'universal solidarity'. Moreover, minimum income benefits did not feature significantly before the second half of the 1970s within a system built after the Second World War on the basis of social insurance principles. Palier (2002) has noted very aptly that 'Beveridgean outcomes' were pursued in France with 'Bismarckian instruments'. It can be argued that there are links over time between the first Republican assistance benefits introduced in the late nineteenth century and the twentieth-century system. These provided 'Republican assistance' well before the generalisation of the *sécurité sociale*.

Unlike general assistance benefits, these *minima sociaux* were introduced for categories in three stages (Barbier and Théret 2003). They included benefits for lone parents (API, *Allocation de parent isolé*, from 1976); benefits for the disabled (AAH, *Allocation d'adulte handicapé*, from 1975) and *Allocation spéciale de solidarité* (ASS) (unemployment assistance, from 1982). The RMI (*Revenu minimum d'insertion*) appeared in 1988 as a totally new benefit (a universal minimum income for all those not entitled to any of the others). Its main innova-

---

[10] The active population in France was in the range of 24 to 25.5 million in the 1990s.

tion lay in the introduction of a *'contrat d'insertion'*, defining a *'projet d'insertion'* (plan) which described the schedule of actions the benefit's recipient was supposed to undertake. Activities were in the areas of health, housing, various forms of counselling and, last but not least, employment and training: this was the 'invention' of French activation. Moreover, even today when a fresh reform is being implemented somewhat chaotically,[11] eligibility conditions have never included the obligation to actively seek work[12] or to be considered as *erwerbsfähig* [able to work], as in Germany after the Hartz IV reform.

Nevertheless, political and economic pressures have fostered reforms aiming at eliminating possible disincentive effects. This rationale presided over the reform of minimum income benefits in the late 1990s, in line with the overall influence of political 'activation' discourse but also with the political discourse of EU coordination (Barbier 2004c; 2005b). Yet AAH has never entailed problems of inactivity comparable to, for instance, disability benefits in the UK or the Netherlands. As for API, in contrast to British benefits for lone parents, it was 'activated' from the start, because it served only for the period when the children were under three years of age: presently, 40% of API recipients receive it for less than one year, and 40% of them are also active.

In contrast, for ASS, although in theory rules similar to unemployment insurance have always applied, the majority of its older recipients have tended to be exempt from active job seeking, and thus resemble early retirees. From 2002, the new conservative government introduced a reform of ASS in order to limit the duration of eligibility to two years. However, after their defeat at the regional elections in 2004, the French government scrapped the reform. It is interesting to compare this development to what happened in Germany where – despite protests and demonstrations – the Red-Green coalition stuck to the merging of the former *Sozialhilfe* and *Arbeitslosenhilfe* in the new *Arbeitslosengeld II*

---

[11] In 2004, the Raffarin government introduced new legislation for RMI recipients after a certain period of eligibility. These individuals were supposed to be transferred to a new benefit (*Revenu minimum d'activité*, RMA), which was supposed to entail enhanced employment obligations for a target of 100,000 contracts. However, the reform was met with considerable opposition from various actors and at the end of 2004, only about 500 contracts had actually been signed. The programme was subsequently completely redesigned.

[12] Indeed, successive 1988 and 1992 RMI Acts established RMI as an unconditional citizenship right. Article 2 of the RMI Act reads as follows: 'Every person residing in France whose income [...] does not reach the amount of the minimum income [...] and who is at least 25 or is in charge of one or several child(ren) [...] and who accepts participation in the activities, determined with him/her, necessary for his/her social or labour market integration, has a right to RMI' (1988, 1992 amended, Acts).

for working-age individuals after one year of traditional unemployment insurance (from 1 January 2005).[13] Value conflicts are obviously tackled differently in the two countries. In Germany the government seemed not to fear a 400,000 increase in unemployment and extended the *Erwerbsfähigkeit* rule to all assistance beneficiaries. In France, for all the talk of increasing sanctions, the government has balked, not only for fear of inflated statistics but also for fear of appearing out of tune with traditional Republican citizenship values.

As far as unemployment insurance is concerned, activation was present from the start (the 'old activation' obligation to seek work) and the 'actively seeking' clause has always been effective for the unemployed. However, in a comparative perspective, sanctions were always limited and only recently started to increase (a bill adopted in December 2004 provides for further regulations on job search obligations). In the mid-1980s, the French insurance fund innovated by providing more active support to the insured unemployed: AFR (*allocation formation reclassement*) allowed for an extension of the compensation period and additional support for training periods. Since then, the philosophy has been both to activate unemployment compensation by giving the unemployed better opportunities to improve their employability and, more marginally, to influence employers' decisions to hire the long-term unemployed.

Activation also featured strongly in the long and conflictual process of reforming unemployment insurance in 2000, when PARE – *plan d'aide au retour à l'emploi* [back-to-work support plan] – was introduced. In October 2000, employers' organisations but only three of the five French representative trade unions agreed to the reform. It was eventually implemented from July 2001 after more than a year of conflict among unions and between unions and employers' associations and the government.

Mainstream benefit, which used to decrease over time, was upgraded and remained unchanged over the total duration of entitlement.[14] This reform, which also entailed an increase in the stress on a 'back-to-work' logic, certainly looks more comparable to Scandinavian activation than to liberal 'welfare-to-work'. However, means have never been available in France at levels comparable to Scandinavia: the French system remains well short of comprehensive universal provision. The latest period of PARE implementation, now the mainstream benefit and form

---

[13] The reform is known as Hartz IV.

[14] In 2005 the mainstream duration of the benefit is 23 months (for 14 months of employment in the preceding 24).

of 'activation', has also seen a very significant increase in sanctions for the unemployed,[15] while a new reduction in benefit, laid down in December 2002 and implemented fully in 2004, was eventually partly cancelled after the conservative government lost the 2004 regional elections.

Over the same period, significant new management reforms have occurred in the public employment service (increasing outsourcing of services; possible mergers of unemployment insurance and the PES), which are still difficult to assess (Barbier 2005c).

All in all, the French picture of activation that emerges from this period is a mixture of state-led initiatives to introduce more universal coverage, under the justification of Republican solidarity and, on the other hand, an early adjustment to increasingly active compensation of the unemployed in the insurance sector, which culminated in 2001 with the introduction of PARE's 'new activation' as the standard provision for all insured unemployed. Along with the introduction of a more activation-oriented political discourse, the collapse of the reforms of social assistance (RMA, ASS) after the regional elections should be interpreted as a clear sign that the solidaristic element of French policy cannot easily be dispensed with, even by conservative governments.

Employment Programmes and the Public Employment Service

The fact that over the last 20 years France has failed to achieve full employment and has seen its unemployed population grow is well documented. Hence, governments were confronted with the 'employer of last resort' question (which dates back more or less to the French Revolution), the state being expected to provide temporary (or 'secondary market') jobs when the market has failed to deliver them. As a result – although never reaching the levels observable in Sweden and Denmark – a significant proportion of GDP has been devoted to employment expenditure (Barbier and Gautié 1998).

From the 1980s, *politiques publiques de l'emploi* gradually emerged in France as a new, significant and consistent policy area for social protection (Barbier and Théret 2003; 2004). In the first period, from the late 1980s, extensive programmes were introduced. The corresponding expenditure went from 0.9% of GDP in 1973 to more than 4.0% in

---

[15] The number of sanctions sharply increased with the introduction of PARE: in 2004/2005, there were about 35,000 to 40,000 *monthly* sanctions (*radiations*) for a total of roughly 340,000 people leaving the PES register (in 1991, when the labour market was also very depressed and the number of people leaving the register was about the same, the number of sanctions was about 50,000 *annually*.)

1995,[16] a considerable expansion, which has only slightly slowed recently. Programmes have encompassed: (i) training schemes for the unemployed; (ii) temporary subsidised employment in the public and non-profit sectors; (iii) subsidised contracts in the market sector for certain hard-to-place groups. With the exception of training programmes, almost all participants enjoyed employee status (*statut de salarié*) and, consequently, were entitled to standard social protection rights (nevertheless, there has been a clear relationship between these schemes and the emergence of a 'working poor' in France). The number of participants in the various employment programmes increased to about 10% of the active population in the late 1990s (a stock of 2.5 million in 2000, falling to 2.1 million in 2003). This figure includes a stock of about 300,000 to 500,000 places for temporary subsidised jobs in the public and non-profit sector, among which *contrats emploi solidarité* (CES) have been the mainstream contract.[17] As a result, during the period, all governments – despite obvious reluctance from the more liberal ones – have stuck to the logic of the state as an employer of last resort to a certain degree, for fear of being confronted with even higher unemployment figures and recurrent social demonstrations, like those which occurred in 1995 and 1997. The cancelling of the Raffarin government reforms implemented in 2003 is a confirmation of this fundamental feature of French-style activation.

Globally, over the period these programmes have nevertheless failed to provide hard-to-place people (and the unemployed more generally) with effective transitions to conventional market jobs. Only a minority of CES participants succeeded in gaining such access. Other forms of temporary subsidised jobs, like the *emplois jeunes*,[18] have nevertheless brought positive outcomes for participants (although net effects are controversial). Accordingly, subsidies targeted on contracts for the long-term unemployed or RMI beneficiaries in the private sector have proved

---

[16] This figure includes so-called 'passive benefits'.
[17] In 2004-2005, this contract was reformed but its basic rationale was not changed.
[18] The *emplois jeunes* (or *nouveaux services-emplois jeunes – NSEJ*) programme was one of two flagship programmes introduced by the Jospin government in 1997, along with the reduction of working time. NSEJ were 5-year temporary contracts, signed by young people under 25 in associations and in the public sector. The programme – cancelled by the Raffarin government – still had more than 100,000 participants at the end of 2004. Outside France, the rationale of the programme was largely misinterpreted (on this see Lødemel and Trickey 2000). The French regional councils, now all governed – except in Alsace – by left-wing executives, have announced a large-scale regional programme to replace the contracts. In summer 2005, the Villepin government eventually reintroduced a similar programme in the public sector, although on a much smaller scale.

effective in France. Yet, while more similar to the Scandinavian 'employer of last resort' rationale than to the liberal one in this domain, the overall French policy appears to have been only half-way implemented because of limited funding and quality. Hence, a significant proportion of employment programmes could certainly not be viewed as effective paths to activation but, as in many other countries, have acted as ways of reducing 'open unemployment'.[19] These discouraging outcomes are a constant difficulty for politicians wishing to legitimise programmes which they nevertheless continue to promote; such programmes also function as a tool for flexibilising the labour market at its margins. They also concur with the increasing prevalence of insider/outsider inequality and certainly foster the special relationship French society has built over the last twenty years with the concept of *précarité*, where the entire society is often described as 'precarious' (Barbier 2005f).

Family Benefits Unlikely Candidates for Activation

Under the liberal variety of activation, tax credits – particularly family-based tax credits – have gained a central role (Wright *et al.* 2004). None of this exists in either the universalistic model or France.

The French legacy of a large-scale family policy is well known. It encompasses a wide array of benefits, the most prominent of which have been benefits for families with two or more children, and housing benefits which have acted as effective mechanisms to alleviate poverty. This should not be equated with 'familialisation', a feature rightly supposed to be adverse to 'activation'. Indeed, the dual-earner model has prevailed in France for a long time. True, in certain cases, and very recently again, old familialistic and even natalistic features have resurfaced, clearly contradicting the mainstream policy of enhancing child care and the reconciliation of work and family life (Barbier and Théret 2004).[20] Yet, despite important persisting gender differences, the French system has long been 'de-familialised' although obviously not to an extent comparable with the Nordic countries. In contrast to Esping-Andersen's interpretation (1996), this feature clearly distinguishes France from Italy and Germany. However, French family benefits *de facto* allow many young people to remain predominantly inactive and France is among the EU countries with the lowest participation and

---

[19] It must be stressed that similar debates have developed even in the most successful countries, including Denmark (Jørgensen 2002). Germany resisted the implementation of such temporary jobs for a long time, but recently changed tack with the launch of so-called 'one-euro jobs' in the context of the Hartz reforms.

[20] This was, for instance, the case with the introduction of the *allocation parentale d'éducation* (APE).

employment rates for those aged 15-24. Universal housing benefits are also substantial for students not living with their parents and they certainly do not foster job seeking or labour market participation. Hence, the combined effect of high participation in education and family-linked benefits can be seen as directly hindering the extension of activation dynamics to the young, and to a minor extent to certain categories of mothers.

Activating the Funding of Social Protection

Another policy area for activation stands between social and tax policies. In comparative terms, the French social protection system was still dominantly funded by social contributions to the level of about 66.5% of the total bill in 2003. However, in the 1990s, indirect labour costs, it was agreed, were completely employment unfriendly, and the solution lay in reducing the social contributions paid by employers in order to foster job creation. This element of the activation strategy was deliberately implemented from the late 1980s and has resulted in a fundamental overhaul of social protection funding. The creation of a special contribution (*contribution sociale genéralisée*, CSG[21]) represented a major 'Beveridgean' innovation (Barbier and Théret 2003; 2004). In contrast to the current British tax credits, this shifting of previous employers' social contributions over to the budget is demand-oriented, aimed at fostering job creation rather than at 'incentivising' people to take jobs. Yet the French government has also introduced a tax credit, the *prime pour l'emploi*, which, although still marginal, represents an additional shift in labour market thinking. Decisive successive reforms were implemented from 1993 and 1998 (the reduction of working time or RWT). With the return of a conservative government in May 2002, the previous RWT logic has been reversed, but employers' social contributions have again been reduced. Altogether, state budget expenditure to compensate reduced contributions soared from 1993: while the aggregated outlays on unemployment insurance and traditional 'active' programmes have remained roughly unchanged, the amount spent on this compensation has multiplied almost sixfold over 7 years. The present proportion of the workforce affected by the reduction (around 60%) means that this most important feature of French activation strategy has become permanent. As a result, France emerges as very different from all the other 'continental' countries. Its originality lies in the combination of radical reform of social security funding and subsidies to labour demand, in a context of labour market flexibilisation through the introduction of atypical contracts, the latter strategy being

---

[21] CSG was invented when M. Rocard was prime minister in 1990.

introduced 'by stealth' (Barbier 2003). In Spain and Italy, only the flexibilisation element was introduced (Barbier and Fargion 2004).

As further substantiation of the intrinsic limits of the 'welfare regime' approach, within the continental cluster only France has embarked on the consistent structural transformation of its social protection, both on the funding side (the significant increase in tax-based funding and special new contributions to the state budget) and on the labour market side (reductions for employers). This has resulted in a clear strategy of 'liberalising' the system, mainly stressing the demand side of the labour market, and only marginally the supply side and individual incentives. From current evaluation studies (see later), the overall impact in terms of employment creation appears controversial. Gradually, however, the unions, political parties and employers have been at least partly convinced of the strategy of funding reforms, as linked to the reduction of labour costs and the 'solidaristic' policy of the employment schemes.

Exit or Activation for Early Retirees and Disabled People?

A last significant area of social policy susceptible to activation strategies encompasses pensions, early retirement programmes and disability benefits. In France, from the late 1970s and into the 1990s governments resorted extensively to early-exit schemes. Early retirement was particularly used to remove older and redundant workers from the labour market, their early retirement benefits being funded by the state budget. This mechanism became very palatable both to employers and to unions because it allowed for a 'socialisation' of individual consequences and allowed employers to avoid devising 'old worker'-friendly conditions of employment (Guillemard 1986). This well known prerequisite of active ageing strategies has only recently started to resurface in the public debate, although with considerable hesitation (Guillemard 2003). Resorting to such arrangements was at its highest in heavy industries and large firms in the 1980s. It then started to decrease significantly; however, new, more targeted schemes were introduced, of which only some were actually 'activated' in the sense that older workers left the labour market in exchange for the recruitment of young people. In 1994, the statistics showed a stock figure of participants in various early retirement schemes at about 210,000 people. At the same time, 284,000 older assisted unemployed were allowed to refrain from job seeking. In 2001, the corresponding figures were 204,000 and 365,000. These figures point to a persistent inability to turn away from inherited practice. Fresh initiatives were heralded in the wake of the 2003 pension reform (which increased the number of years of contributions to 40 in the public sector), but all odds are that France will prove unable to reach the targets for employment rates fixed at the EU Barcelona summit.

Features of the French System – Values and Norms in the Continental Cluster

A number of significant features tend to show France's 'continental inability' to activate its system: a structural situation characterised by the low labour market participation of the young and older workers and a clear inability so far to reform early exit from the labour market. Moreover, whatever the reforms, they have occurred against a background of low employment creation and increased labour market segmentation, with certain categories of worker particularly affected by insecurity and instability, and low quality of jobs, while the majority have retained significantly better security and social protection rights (Barbier 2003). In this respect, the 'activation' reforms of the 1980s and the 1990s have obviously not delivered on their promise of labour market integration for all. The French system has been able to limit only some of the negative consequences, with ambiguous outcomes (see the *insertion* case). The French system is also still prone to gender bias. Although labour market gaps between women and men tended to decrease in the 1990s, trapped within their supposedly 'gender-blind' Republican tradition French policy-makers began to address the gender question seriously only in the second half of the 1990s. Although the French system has been much more 'de-familialised' than Italy's, Spain's or Germany's, as individuals women in France overall enjoy lower quality social protection and lower quality provision of services related to employment. Another 'continental' feature concerns the young. In France, despite significant exceptions (the *NSEJ* programme was one in 1997-2002), the young have been eligible only for lower quality social benefits and programmes in the last 20 years. This should of course be linked to the 'familialistic' legacy. Many entitlements and benefits for which the young under the age of 25 are eligible still depend on the family policy system and are not individualised. Moreover, the young experience worse conditions than adults and older employees in terms of labour market participation and the precariousness of employment, especially the less qualified and young women.

An *inability to achieve universalism* (particularly the 'generous' universalism typical of the Scandinavian countries) is another important feature: France is certainly 'continental' in this respect. While entitlements and rights are theoretically designed as universal, *de facto* eligibility is selective: this is illustrated by minimum income benefits and, especially, RMI. This situation can be explained by many reasons:

overload of services, scarcity of resources, actual targeting mechanisms. A similar situation applies to the unequal access to places in employment or vocational training programmes. It leads to some polarisation (the opposition between better quality mainstream insurance-linked provision and lower quality assistance-linked provision, but also to the increasing emergence of a working poor stratum in French society) and labour market segmentation, along with the very high share of the French civil service in the labour force (Barbier 2005d).

Moreover – and this is probably one of the main realities which 'universalistic' analyses of 'workfare' fail to grasp – another continental feature is observable in France: like Italy, Spain and Germany it has left punitive provisions largely in the background. For all its activation discourse, France is still likely to experience only limited pressure for job seeking and the absence of a consistent *punitive* orientation. This should not only be attributed to scarce labour market opportunities and a lack of resources, but also to the enduring Republican citizenship approach. As already noted, the collapse of the Raffarin reforms in 2003-2004 confirms this. In a way, RMI is typical of this failure to 'activate' assistance along liberal lines. Its core political justifications entail the extension of the effective exercise of political participation to the polity. This 'Rousseauist' approach sharply differs from the Anglo-Saxon conception of 'rights and responsibilities' (Barbier and Théret 2003). *Insertion professionnelle* retains a positive function of political integration.[22] At least the current conservative government did not feel free to openly impose more drastic reductions. However, the Centre-right will probably try harder in the near future.

All in all, a distinct and durable type of activation has been established in France, which also borrows from British and Swedish models. As it stands so far it appears to be a hotchpotch of elements and somewhat hesitant. We have shown that, for institutional reasons, despite many similarities with France, Italy is unlikely to tread the French path in the foreseeable future (Barbier and Fargion 2004). The case of Germany is more uncertain: many of the reforms introduced in the numerous stages of the Hartz reform bear clear similarities to the French ones, probably also heading towards a hybrid of universalistic and liberal traits in the context of renewed Bismarckism with the introduction of obvious Beveridgean elements. In all the continental countries, it is obvious that internal dynamics are of greater import than outside influ-

---

[22] More generally, 'collective participation' in the definition of rights is marked by the domination of the central state, with a relatively secondary role ascribed to the social partners. Phases when unions resort to confrontation and street demonstrations are also characteristic of French politics.

ences: this important fact does not preclude the possibility of a third, hybrid type of activation emerging gradually, however. Yet whereas Denmark and the UK at the moment appear as pace-setters for activation strategies, no clear leader is likely to emerge in the continental cluster of countries.

The French Strategy: Continental Outcomes in the Context of the EES?

What Do We Know about Outcomes: Does Activation Work in France?

Typically, in France, as with the EES in general (Barbier 2005a), what is lacking is a comprehensive assessment of the effects of activation strategies. We have analysed elsewhere the absence of a rigorous evaluation of the first stages of the EES in most member states: only politicised documents have addressed this question (Barbier 2005e) and they avoid documenting causality.

It is striking that the evaluation of activation reforms seems to be dominated by a constant stream of studies conducted on the basis of mainstream economic methods and disseminated by the OECD. One frequently quoted reference is J.P. Martin (1998). Additional references include papers devoted to the question of 'making work pay' strategies (Duncan *et al.* 2003; Pearson and Scarpetta 2000). From reading this literature one might easily be led to think that programmes across countries are converging and homogenous: our findings point in the opposite direction. For instance, the very notion of a 'make work pay policy' is more often that not left vague. Duncan *et al.* (2003) skip definitions and categorise programmes in France and Denmark as if they were comparable to the EITC and the WFTC, yet empirical research shows that programmes in the two countries are completely different because they are embedded in institutional contexts completely at odds with the Anglo-Saxon environment.[23] However, many researchers seem to forget to take these evaluation studies with a pinch of salt and to contextualise them before drawing comprehensive conclusions about the reforms. Such standardised and presumably scientific conclusions drawn

---

[23] The *prime pour l'emploi* in France has remained marginal (Barbier 2003), although it is again being promoted and extended (2005). In Denmark, only across-the-board tax reductions appear in successive NAPs under the 'make work pay' item of the EES (Guideline 8). This is a good example of the effects of the EES: member states tend to translate their programmes into English in a presentational manner (Barbier 2004c).

from international mainstream economic studies should be reinterpreted in a wider framework if any significant meaning is to be extracted. The OECD's Directorate for Employment itself is beginning to understand the limits of their universalistic comparison methods.[24] Evaluation studies are certainly useful and indispensable for analysing policies, but decidedly partial.

What Can We Learn from French Activation Strategies?

The impact of the reform of unemployment insurance is mixed: before the latest reforms (from 2001) the introduction of a gradual reduction of benefit over time was paradoxically proved to be linked to a decrease in the number of those ceasing to receive unemployment benefits. The 2001 reform, for its part, has not yet been fully evaluated.

In the area of assistance benefits and temporary subsidised jobs in the public and non-profit sector, results are mixed. In the context of a highly selective labour market with low employment creation, a major proportion of beneficiaries are 'hard-to-place' and 'stuck' in a succession of either subsidised contracts or low quality market jobs and for them quality *insertion* has remained a failure. However, other, positive aspects of this form of active programme have been noted (Barbier 2003). In a number of cases, such subsidised jobs help transitions to the conventional labour market and are a source of income (albeit limited and increasing the number of the working poor); they also help beneficiaries to maintain contact with some form of employment and they express some satisfaction at that. High quality subsidised temporary jobs (the NSEJ programme is a case in point) have been successful on many counts. All these factors help to relativise decontextualised judgements such as the OECD approach in this domain.[25]

---

[24] M. Durand, deputy director of the directorate, presented a paper at a December 2004 conference in Paris organised by CEE. She states in her paper: "La mise au regard des indicateurs de performances et des indicateurs de politiques est une tâche complexe, qui ne permet pas facilement de conclure sur l'impact et l'efficacité de mesures mises en œuvre, et donc permet difficilement de tirer des enseignements définitifs en matière de prescriptions politiques" (Durand 2004, 88).

[25] J.P. Martin (1998, 21) writes that 'evaluation literature shows fairly conclusively that this measure [*direct job creation in the public sector*] has been of little success in helping unemployed people get permanent jobs in the open labour market. [...] However OECD countries continue to spend large amounts on public-sector job creation programs and the policy debate about the utility of this intervention is still alive. Temporary employment programs in the public sector can be used as a work test for unemployment benefits claimants and as a means of helping the unemployed maintain contact with the labour market, particularly in a recession when aggregate demand is depressed and vacancies scarce. But since [*these programmes*] have a low

As in most EU countries, placements of beneficiaries in the private sector are much more effective, particularly in their capacity to counter selective exclusion of the hard-to-place from available jobs. Although the French record is certainly less brilliant than, for instance, the Danish, positive results are not insignificant and, as in all EU member states, even the most successful, 'activating' assistance recipients always appears less effective (Abrahamson 2001; Jørgensen 2002).

As regards reform of social protection funding mechanisms and reducing employers' social contributions to foster labour demand, results are also mixed. The French Ministry of Finance recently published a recapitulative assessment of evaluation studies in this respect (Lacroix *et al.* 2003). In this document employment effects appear dependent on the methodology used and on the time frame within which econometric evaluation is conducted. Overall figures of job creation ascribable to the programme from 1997 vary from 210,000 to 490,000 in the 'long term' (Lacroix *et al.* 2003, 6). This has been a constant source of controversy among experts in France.

Although it is impossible to strictly establish causal links between the various sorts of activation programme and the French activation strategy as described in the present paper, it is nevertheless clear that (i) inequality and poverty rates have not been significantly affected over the period studied, although the development of a working poor within the French workforce is documented; (ii) minor targeted effects on the labour force participation of certain categories are observable; (iii) however, efforts to 'activate' older workers have not been successful.

The French case is interesting for the study of activation strategies because it clearly diverges from either the Scandinavian universalistic or the British liberal model. French features identified above easily find echoes with other reforms in countries belonging to the continental group. However, the assumption that these characteristics might eventually constitute the common elements of a 'continental' approach to activation is still somewhat far-fetched. This proves that the 'new' activation is certainly easier to implement in Beveridgean systems.

With regard to the EES influence, it is clear from its first stages (from 1997 to 2004) that the strategy has been able to accommodate all types of national activation strategies. Even from a normative point of view, very different value choices easily fit in the common framework.

Finally, the French case substantiates a clear conclusion: from the limited and rather fragmented information and research available, it is

---

marginal product, they should be short in duration and not become a disguised form of heavily subsidised permanent employment'.

very difficult to ascribe consequences and transformations to the reforms that have been implemented from the early 1990s and can be considered as pertaining to the various dimensions of activation. Moreover, universalistic analysis that contends that activation reforms – defined rigorously – have tended to downgrade the substance of 'social citizenship' in France are not vindicated by empirical research (Barbier 2005g).

References

Abrahamson, P. (2001), "L'activation des politiques sociales scandinaves: le cas du Danemark", in C. Daniel and B. Palier (eds.), *La protection sociale en Europe, le temps des réformes*, MIRE, Paris, Documentation Française, pp. 123-140.

Barbier, J.-C. (2002a), "Peut-on parler d'activation de la protection sociale en Europe?", *Revue française de sociologie* 43-2 (avril-juin), pp. 307-332.

Barbier, J.-C. (2002b), "Une Europe sociale normative et procédurale: le cas de la stratégie coordonnée pour l'emploi", *Sociétés contemporaines* 47, pp. 11-36.

Barbier, J.-C. (with A. Brygoo, F. Viguier and F. Tarquis) (2003), "Normative and regulatory frameworks influencing flexibility, security, quality and precariousness of jobs in France, Germany, Italy, Spain and the United Kingdom", ESOPE project report, Fifth Framework project, http://www.cee-recherche.fr/fr/fiches_chercheurs/texte_pdf/barbier/wp1-2FINALBarbiersynth%E8se.pdf.

Barbier, J.-C. (2004a), "Systems of social protection in Europe: two contrasted paths to activation and maybe a third", in J. Lind, H. Knudsen and H. Jørgensen (eds.), *Labour and Employment Regulation in Europe*, Brussels, P.I.E. Peter Lang, pp. 233-254.

Barbier, J.-C. (2004b), "Activation policies: a comparative perspective", in A. Serrano Pascual (ed.), *Are Activation Policies Converging in Europe? The European Employment Strategy for Young People*, Brussels, ETUI, pp. 47-84.

Barbier, J.-C. (with a contribution by N.S. Sylla) (2004c), "La stratégie européenne pour l'emploi: genèse, coordination communautaire et diversité nationale", rapport pour la DARES (Ministère du travail) (janvier), http://www.cee-recherche.fr/fr/rapports/stategie_europeenne_emploi.pdf.

Barbier, J.-C. (2005a), "The European Employment Strategy: a channel for activating social protection?", in J. Zeitlin and P. Pochet, with L. Magnusson (eds.), *The Open Method of Coordination in Action: The European Employment and Social Inclusion Strategies*, Brussels, P.I.E. Peter Lang, pp. 417-446.

Barbier, J.-C. (2005b), "Research on open methods of coordination and national social policies: what sociological theories and methods?", in T. Bredgaard and F. Larsen (eds.), *Employment Policy from Different Angles*, Copenhagen, DJØF Pub., pp. 47-74.

Barbier, J.-C. (2005c), "Embedding contractualism in national institutions: performance contracting in the French Public Employment Service", in E. Sol and M. Westerweld (eds.), *Contractualism in Public Employment Services. A*

New Form of Welfare State Governance, The Hague, Kluwer Law International, pp. 255-280.

Barbier, J.-C. (2005d), "Learning from Denmark? Reflection on the 'Danish miracle' from a French angle", in C. Buhigas Schubert and Hans Martens (eds.), *The Nordic Model: A Recipe for European Success?* (September), Brussels, European Policy Centre, pp. 94-100.

Barbier, J.-C. (2005e), "Dealing anew with cross-national comparison: when words matter", in J.-C. Barbier and M.T. Letablier (eds.), *Cross-national Comparisons: Epistemological and Methodological Issues*, Brussels, P.I.E. Peter Lang.

Barbier, J.-C. (2005f), "La précarité, une catégorie française à l'épreuve de la comparaison internationale", note critique, *Revue française de sociologie* 46-2 (avril-juin), pp. 351-371.

Barbier, J.-C. (2005g), "Citizenship and the activation of social protection: a comparative approach", in J. G. Andersen, A.-M. Guillemard, P. H. Jensen and B. Pfau-Effinger (eds.), *The New Face of Welfare. Social Policy, Marginalization and Citizenship*, COST A13 Book Series, Bristol: Policy Press, pp. 113-134.

Barbier, J.-C. and V. Fargion (2004), "Continental inconsistencies on the path to activation: consequences for social citizenship in Italy and France", *European Societies* 6 (4), pp. 437-460.

Barbier, J.-C. and J. Gautié (1998), *Les politiques de l'emploi en Europe et aux Etats-Unis*, Cahiers du CEE, Paris, PUF.

Barbier, J.-C. and W. Ludwig-Mayerhofer (eds.) (2004), "The many worlds of activation", *European Societies* 6 (4), Introduction to the special issue, pp. 423-436.

Barbier, J.-C. and H. Nadel (2000), *La flexibilité du travail et de l'emploi*, Paris: Flammarion [2002, *La flessibilità del lavoro et dell'occupazione*, introduzione di L. Castelluci e E. Pugliese, Donzelli, Roma.]

Barbier, J.-C. and B. Théret (2001), "Welfare to work or work to welfare, the French case?", in N. Gilbert and R. Van Voorhis (eds.), *Activating the Unemployed: A Comparative Appraisal of Work-oriented Policies*, Rutgers, N.J., Transaction Publishers, pp. 135-183.

Barbier, J.-C. and B. Théret (2003), "The French social protection system: path dependencies and societal coherence", in N. Gilbert and R. Van Voorhis (eds.), *Changing patterns of social protection*, New Brunswick, Transaction Publishers, pp. 119-168.

Barbier, J.-C. and B. Théret (2004), *Le nouveau système français de protection sociale*, Repères, Paris, La Découverte.

Börzel, T. and T. Risse (2000), "When Europe hits home: Europeanization and domestic change", European Integration online Papers (EIoP) 4 (15), http://eiop.or.at/eiop/texte/2000-015a.htm.

Duncan, A., M. Pearson and J.K. Scholz (2003), "Is there an emerging consensus in making work pay policies?", presentation for the conference "Political economy of policy transfer, learning and convergence", Tulane University, http://www.tulane.edu/~dnelson/PolTransConv/Duncan-Pearson-Scholz.pdf.

Durand, M. (2004), "Trois perspectives de l'OCDE sur les indicateurs et la gouvernance de l'emploi", présentation au colloque du CEE Gouvernance et expertise de l'emploi en Europe, Paris, 13-14 décembre, pp. 80-96.

Esping-Andersen, G. (1990), *The Three Worlds of Welfare Capitalism*, Cambridge, Bristol, Polity Press.

Esping-Andersen, G. (1996), *Welfare States in Transition. National Adaptations in Global Economics*, London, Sage.

Gilbert, N. (2002), *Transformation of the Welfare State. The Silent Surrender of Public Responsibility*, Oxford, Oxford University Press.

Goul Andersen, J., A.-M. Guillemard, P. H. Jensen and B. Pfau-Effinger (eds.) (2005), *The New Face of Welfare. Social Policy, Marginalization and Citizenship*, COST A13 Book Series, Bristol, Policy Press.

Guillemard, A.-M. (1986), *Le Déclin du social*, Paris, PUF.

Guillemard, A.-M. (2003), *L'Age de l'emploi*, Paris, Armand Colin.

Jensen, P. and K. Halvorsen (2004), "Activation in Scandinavian welfare policy", *European Societies* 6 (4), pp. 461-484.

Jessop, B. (1993), "Towards a Schumpeterian workfare state? Preliminary remarks on post-Fordist political economy", *Studies in Political Economy* 40, pp. 7-39.

Jessop, B. (1996), "Post-Fordism and the state", in E. Greve (ed.), *Comparative Welfare Systems. The Scandinavian Model in a Period of Change*, Basingstoke, Macmillan.

Jørgensen, H. (2002), *Consensus, Cooperation and Conflict. The Policy-making Process in Denmark*, Cheltenham, Edward Elgar.

Korpi, W. and J. Palme (1998), "The paradox of redistribution and strategies of equality: welfare state institutions, inequality, and poverty in Western countries", *American Sociological Review* 63 (5) (October), pp. 661-687.

Kvist, J. (2002), "Activating welfare states. How social policies can promote employment", in J. Clasen (ed.), *What Future for Social Security? Debates and Reforms in National and Cross-national Perspectives*, Bristol, Policy Press, pp. 197-210.

Lacroix, M.A., B. Martinot and L. Menard (2003), "Un essai de bilan économique des mesures prises depuis quinze ans pour stimuler l'emploi en France", Direction de la prévision, *Analyses économiques* 21 (décembre).

Lødemel, I. and H. Trickey (2000), *An Offer You Can't Refuse. Workfare in International Perspective*, Bristol, Policy Press.

Madsen, P.K. (2005), "The Danish road to 'flexicurity'. Where are we? And how did we get there?", in T. Bredgaard and F. Larsen (eds.), *Employment Policy from Different Angles*, Copenhagen, DJØF Pub., pp. 269-290.

Martin, J. P. (1998), "What works among active labour market policies: evidence from OECD countries' experiences", Labour market and social policy occasional papers, No. 35, Paris.

Maurice, M., F. Sellier and J.-J. Silvestre (1982), *Politique d'éducation et organisation industrielle en France et en Allemagne, essai d'analyse sociétale*, Paris, PUF.

Morel, S. (2000), *Les logiques de la réciprocité, les transformations de la relation d'assistance aux Etats-Unis et en France*, Paris, PUF.

Palier, B. (2002), *Gouverner la sécurité sociale*, Paris, PUF.

Palier, B. (2004), "Social protection reforms in Europe: strategies for a new social model", CPRN Social Architecture Papers, Research Report 37, CPRN, Ottawa.

Pearson, M. and S. Scarpetta (2000), "An overview: what do we know about policies to make work pay?", *OECD Economic Studies* 31, pp. 11-24.

Pierson, P. (ed.) (2001), *The New Politics of the Welfare State*, Oxford, Oxford University Press.

Radaelli, C.M. (2003), *The Open Method of Coordination, A New Governance Architecture for the European Union?*, SIEPS, 2003-1, Stockholm.

Scharpf, F.W. and V.A. Schmidt (eds.) (2000), *Welfare and Work in the Open Economy. From Vulnerability to Competitiveness*, Vol. I, Oxford, Oxford University Press.

Schmid, G. and B. Gazier (eds.) (2002), *The Dynamics of Full Employment*, Cheltenham, Edward Elgar.

Schmidt, V. (2005), "Institutionalism and the state", in C. Hay, D. Marsh and M. Lister (eds.), *The state: theories and issues*, Basingstoke, Palgrave.

Serrano Pascual, A. (2004), "Conclusion: towards convergence of European activation policies?", in A. Serrano Pascual (ed.), *Are Activation Policies Converging in Europe? The European Employment Strategy for Young People*, Brussels, ETUI, pp. 497-518.

Torfing, J. (1999), "Workfare with welfare: recent reforms of the Danish welfare state", *Journal of European Social Policy* 9 (1), pp. 5-28.

van Berkel, R. and I. H. Møller (2002), *Active Social Policies in the EU. Inclusion through Participation?*, Bristol, Policy Press.

Wilensky, H. (1975), *The Welfare States and Equality*, Berkeley, University of California Press.

Wood, S. (2001), "Labour market regimes under threat? Source of continuity in Germany, Britain and Sweden", in P. Pierson (ed.), *The New Politics of the Welfare State*, Oxford, OUP, pp. 368-409.

Wright, S., A. Kopac and G. Slater (2004), "Continuities with paradigm change", *European Societies* 6 (4): pp. 511-534.

The Commitment to Be Actively Available for Work and Employment Policy in Spain

Jorge ARAGÓN, Fernando ROCHA,
Ana SANTANA and Jorge TORRENTS

Introduction

The aim of the present chapter is to consider the impact of the European Employment Strategy's 'activation principle' on the design and implementation of employment policy in Spain.

In keeping with the general guidelines of the research project which generated this report, our analysis will be structured as follows.

We will begin with a general description of the institutional framework that governs the shape of Spanish employment policy and the key players involved in its design and implementation. This is particularly important in view of the highly decentralised nature of government in Spain and the involvement of private actors, in particular the social partners (that is, trade unions and employers' associations), in the development of the various actions aimed at promoting employment. The description of the institutional framework will conclude with an assessment of the positive and negative ways in which the European Employment Strategy (EES) has influenced the development of employment policy in Spain.

Section 2 will consider the new regulatory framework governing the activation of unemployed people, focusing particularly on two legislative reforms that most clearly show the way in which Spain's national legislative framework has been adapted to fit in with the European Employment Strategy.

Having established the impact of the EES on Spain's legislative framework, we will assess the way in which the activation principle has been incorporated into the employment measures contained in Spain's National Action Plans on employment (NAPs) since 1998 (section 3).

Section 4 will look at certain cultural aspects of Spanish society that go a long way towards explaining why the public employment services do not implement in practice certain formal conditions directly linked to the activation principle that are provided for both by law and as part of the actions aimed at promoting employment.

In section 5 we will move away from the employment policy perspective in order to undertake a brief analysis of certain fiscal policy measures that play an important role in the approach taken to promoting people's activation on the labour market.

Finally, we will present our key conclusions together with a short list of references containing the main sources used for this study.

The Institutional Framework of Employment Policy

This is determined by Spain's 1978 Constitution, which established a devolved state in which powers are divided between *central government*, 17 *autonomous communities*[1] and the *local authorities*, comprising 52 provinces and 8,108 municipalities. The implementation of this model over the past few decades has led to a high level of territorial and administrative decentralisation in Spain.

The Spanish Constitution stipulates that central government is solely responsible for basic labour legislation, although it may be implemented by the autonomous communities. The latter may, however, develop their own employment and economic development programmes, as long as they do not encroach on areas that are the sole preserve of central government, especially labour legislation. As for the local authorities, while they do not have any powers in the field of employment, they too may undertake various actions aimed at promoting employment and local development, once again as long as they comply with the labour legislation passed by the state. It should be pointed out at this stage that in recent years there has been a political debate concerning what is known as the 'second decentralisation', that is, the transfer of various powers – including powers in the field of employment – from the regional to the local level.

It is against this backdrop that we should understand the fact that employment policy is developed mainly at two different levels.

First, the *Ministry of Labour and Social Affairs* (*Ministerio de Trabajo y Asuntos Sociales – MTAS*) is responsible for coordinating the design of employment policy on behalf of central government. Each year, this policy is integrated into the National Action Plan on employ-

---

[1] These correspond to the regional level.

ment. The *State Public Employment Service* (*Servicio Público de Empleo Estatal – SPEE*) is a body under the auspices of the Ministry of Labour and Social Affairs and is responsible for coordinating, managing and evaluating the various employment programmes at state level.

Although SPEE received praise for its management of unemployment benefits during the 1980s and at the beginning of the 1990s, there was an intense public debate concerning its inefficient management of active employment measures. This eventually led to the ending of SPEE's monopoly in this area in 1994, which was accompanied by a certain amount of social conflict. The new regime legalised non-profit employment agencies, temporary employment agencies and latterly also *Integrated Employment Services* (*Servicios Integrados Para el Empleo – SIPES*) enabling public and private non-profit organisations to become involved in organising and coordinating active employment measures relating to the employment of job seekers and other services by signing cooperation agreements with SPEE.

At the same time, in keeping with the political principle of a devolved state, as described above, the management of active employment measures, which had hitherto been the responsibility of SPEE, began to be decentralised from 1996 onwards. As a result, all the autonomous communities apart from the Basque Country now run their own public employment service (PES), as well as managing policy with regard to training, career guidance and job placements.

These reforms have given rise to a new employment policy management model and the emergence of new public and private actors involved in its implementation. The devolution of responsibility for public employment services to the regions was not simply a political reform designed to reflect the greater role that the Constitution attributes to Spain's regional governments. It was also intended to ensure that the public bodies responsible for managing employment policy were closer to the beneficiaries of the relevant measures. The very design of the new public employment service model required *integration of government actions* in order to increase the efficiency of the measures being implemented.

However, it seems that during the time this new model has been up and running, the fact that the level of government at which employment measures are being implemented is closer to the people concerned has hitherto not led to a significant increase in the confidence of businesses in the public employment services or in the extent to which they are used by job seekers as a means of finding employment. And this is despite the improvements that are being introduced, including better information about the services they provide in the different autonomous communities.

The second goal of the reforms was the involvement of new public and private players in the development of employment policy measures that were becoming increasingly complex and diverse. The idea was that their involvement would enable the highest possible degree of specialisation and ensure that providers were as close as possible to the sources of employment. It is certainly true that ending SPEE's monopoly by allowing non-profit employment agencies to get involved in the management of job placement provision, together with the diversification of the players involved in the policies that accompany job placements – to include, among others, local councils, the social partners and partner organisations[2] – did hold out the prospect of improving the efficiency of active employment measures. However, it appears that instead of the provision of a more specialised service that is closer to its beneficiaries, what is actually happening is that measures are being implemented from a very local perspective, with little coordination with the other players involved in managing employment policy (thus risking fragmentation), as well as a pronounced lack of specialisation, resulting in an inefficient service.

The existence of partner organisations of the public employment services may indeed contribute to more effective service provision, since these organisations have a better understanding of the needs of businesses and some can offer specialised services. The involvement of these partner organisations of the public employment services will thus create added value as long as it does not result in the latter failing to perform their own functions properly. However, the creation and proliferation of parallel structures for implementing employment measures, even if these structures are tripartite in nature, may turn out to be counterproductive if it leads to resources being spread too thinly and a lack of clarity as to who is responsible for what.

Secondly, since the second half of the 1990s significant efforts to promote employment have been undertaken at regional level, although the extent of this activity has varied from one autonomous region to another in terms of both the content of policy and its implementation.

It is important to stress that this process has taken place against a background of intensive social dialogue involving the regional govern-

---

[2] That is, public and/or private bodies, depending on the regulatory framework in each autonomous community, that are involved in all or some of the functions performed by the public employment service, such as job placement, career guidance, training and integration into working life.

ments and the social partners, the upshot being that successive Regional Employment Pacts have been drawn up in all the autonomous communities.

The active involvement of the social partners in drawing up these Regional Employment Pacts has had a manifestly positive effect. This can be seen in the fact that the different measures are better tailored to the specificities of the level at which they are targeted, be it sectoral or regional, and in the way in which social cohesion has been maintained across the whole of Spain. The fact that Spain's main national trade unions and employers' associations[3] have been involved in the majority of the Regional Employment Pacts means that their goals are consistent across the regions. It is important to take into account the key role played by the *Interconfederal Agreement for Stability in Employment* that was signed in 1997 by the main national social partners, since this document served as an explicit reference point for most of the Regional Employment Pacts drawn up at the end of the 1990s. In view of the above, it is possible to claim that the social dialogue at regional level has to some extent served to promote cohesion between the different autonomous communities.

This is the general background to the question of how far *the European Employment Strategy (EES)* has influenced the shape of employment policy in Spain. Before going any further, it should be said that the National Action Plans on employment – that is, the instruments used to implement the EES – may have their limitations, but they also offer undoubted potential, whose fulfilment is largely dependent on the political will of member states to put into practice the guidelines and recommendations that are approved each year.

As far as the implementation of the EES in Spain is concerned, the annual NAPs have had a positive influence in a variety of areas, including:

1. The planning and structuring of the various programmes and actions designed to promote employment that were being run by different departments of central government.

2. National-level coordination of information on the active employment measures being implemented in the different regions, although some shortcomings continue to exist in this area.

---

[3] The trade unions involved are Comisiones Obreras and Unión General de Trabajadores, while the employers are represented by the Confederación Española de Organizaciones Empresariales and the Confederación Española de Pequeñas y Medianas Empresas.

3. Helping the public employment services to adapt to the new reality in which the management of active employment measures has been devolved to the regions.

4. The prioritisation, based on European guidelines and directives, of a number of particularly important issues, such as the much-needed development of policy in the field of equal opportunities for men and women. This has also contributed to the inclusion of these issues on the agenda of the social dialogue between the social partners.

5. The favourable development of the Regional Employment Pacts, the content of which has, on the whole, taken account of the European guidelines.

Nevertheless, from a critical perspective, there have also been a number of shortcomings:

1. The EES has, on the whole, not resulted in the development and implementation of new programmes and measures. Instead, the NAPs have simply pulled together existing actions.

2. While it is true that, since the reform of the EES, more specific long-term targets have been set with a view to complying with the Lisbon Strategy, the NAPs are nevertheless still failing to establish specific and quantified medium-term targets that would make it possible to evaluate the implementation of the actions.

3. The EU requirement to coordinate employment policy has rather ironically highlighted the current lack of coordination both at central government level (between the various ministries and departments) and between central government and the governments of the autonomous communities which, as has been explained, have considerable powers in terms of the management of employment measures.

4. The evaluation of the results of the NAPs leaves a lot to be desired. Fundamentally, this is due to the fact that, although a count is made of the measures that are easiest to quantify (for example, the actions undertaken by the public employment services with the different groups of unemployed people), there is no monitoring of the extent to which the measures contained in the Plan have been implemented or of their actual results.

As far as the last point is concerned, it should be remembered that the evaluation of employment measures in Spain takes place within a highly decentralised institutional framework in which the different levels of government – central, regional and local – develop their own evaluation systems and processes. A comparison of these systems shows up considerable differences with regard to whether evaluation processes exist and in terms of the methodology used and the system's level of development, although it is also true that significant progress has been made in recent years.[4] It should also be pointed out that evaluation studies of EES implementation in Spain carried out independently of the government are few and far between. The studies that do exist nevertheless allow a few key issues to be highlighted (Aragón and Rocha 2001; Sáez 2004):

1. The actions undertaken by both central government and the autonomous communities have a number of things in common. Overall, short-term (career guidance) measures are more prevalent, followed by training measures, while actions that directly promote employment account for the smallest number of measures.

2. The impact of employment measures on the individual target groups studied independently of each other varies significantly.

3. It is important to recognise that the ability of the public employment services to promote effective employment among the groups with the lowest level of employability is limited by the low number of job opportunities available through these services.

4. The research has highlighted the problems that exist with regard to coordination between central and regional government, particularly concerning the different methods used to gather information on the measures that have been implemented and also in terms of problems with the information flow from the regions to central government.

5. The final shortcoming is particularly significant, since it relates to the issue of governance with regard to EES implementation. Since the introduction of NAPs in 1998, there has been very little consultation of the social partners in the course of their development.[5] The social partners' involvement has largely been confined to consultation during the final phase of NAP drafting when the text presented to them is practically the final version, pending approval.[6] Likewise, there is no effective involvement of the social partners in the implementation of the measures included in the NAPs or in their monitoring and evaluation. Consequently, the trade unions and employers' associations have repeatedly called for the introduction of a stable, regular and themed working

---

[4] For example, the development of a single IT system known as the Public Employment Services Information System (Sistema de Información de los Servicios Públicos de Empleo – SISPE) that will allow real-time monitoring of the different actions in place across the whole of Spain. The system is expected to go online in 2005.

[5] This is in stark contrast to the active involvement of trade unions and employers' associations in the development of the Regional Employment Pacts drawn up by the autonomous communities.

[6] Each year since 1998, however, the social partners have put forward a series of proposals and a list of priority goals for inclusion in the NAPs.

method that would allow effective monitoring of the drafting, implementation and evaluation of the NAPs.

As for the involvement of other private players, such as organisations from the non-profit making sector, it has largely focused on the implementation of measures at local level, mostly comprising guidance, advice and training actions targeted at the social and labour market inclusion of disadvantaged groups.

In conclusion, it is important to emphasise once more that employment policy measures in Spain are currently being implemented within a complex institutional framework characterised by a high level of decentralisation and devolution of administrative responsibilities. The different levels of government all have their own initiatives running side by side, together with the initiatives promoted by the social partners in the context of social dialogue (particularly at autonomous community level).

The New Regulatory Framework for the Activation of Unemployed People

The Influence of the European Employment Strategy on Spain's National Legislative Framework

It did not take long for the influence of the recently launched Lisbon process to be seen in the structure of some of the active employment policy measures for 1998. However, rather than involving major changes, its impact at that time simply amounted to adjustments of the existing national framework to take into account the goals that had been set at European level. As such, it was not until some time later that the key legislation was modified, with reforms in two important areas being particularly significant. First, the unemployment benefit system was reformed in 2002, together with the measures aimed at improving employability. This was followed by the passing of the new Employment Act at the end of 2003. The reasons put forward for both reforms included clear references to the need to adapt to the European Employment Strategy (EES).

The Reform of Unemployment Benefit

It is clearly indicated in Act 45/2002 that both the EES and the annual Employment Guidelines have repeatedly stressed that EU member states should structure unemployment benefits in such a way that, as well as offering the necessary financial benefits to cope with unemployment, the state should also provide training and employment opportunities in order to help unemployed people find work as quickly as possible. The Act introduces two mechanisms intended to help people wishing to enter the labour market into work:

1. A commitment on the part of the unemployed person to be actively available for work. This comes into force as soon as a person starts claiming unemployment benefit and entitles the claimant to expect the public employment services (PES) to draw up the most suitable job-finding plan for them based on their professional skills and employability.

2. A new regulation defining the concept of a suitable job placement and offering unemployed people better legal safeguards in this regard. The key aspect of the new definition is that the PES can evaluate the suitability of a job placement based on an individual's personal and professional characteristics and how easy it is for them to travel to their place of work.

The New Employment Act

The goal of this new Act is to make the operation of the labour market more efficient and to improve people's prospects of finding work with a view to achieving full employment, a target that has been agreed at successive European Councils since Luxembourg. In the new Act, this translates into the public employment services offering unemployed people personalised preventive measures with special emphasis on disadvantaged groups and in keeping with the principles of equal opportunities, non-discrimination, transparency, and free, efficient and high-quality service provision. The Act also stipulates that employment policy should act as an incentive to encourage unemployed people into work by promoting active job seeking, together with geographical mobility and a readiness to do different kinds of work. The Employment Act's key innovations are in three areas:

1. The regulation of institutional coordination in order to implement the EES. Article 1 clearly states that, while following the general guidelines imposed by economic policy, employment policy shall be developed in line with the coordinated employment strategy established by the EC Treaty.

2. The regulation of active employment measures. The Act states that active services and measures to support unemployed people shall be coordinated by the public employment services in the shape of personalised job-finding plans drawn up together with each job seeker and based on their personal and professional characteristics. In return, job seekers shall, in accordance with the provisions of their personalised job-finding

plans, be required to participate in active employment measures to improve their chances of finding work.

3. Coordination between active employment measures and financial benefits for unemployed people. Unemployment protection shall comprise both financial benefits and the full range of active employment measures, and both active and passive measures should complement each other and take each other into account.

This compulsory coordination requires cooperation between the public employment services of the autonomous communities (who are responsible for managing active employment measures) and the state public employment service (responsible for monetary unemployment benefits).

The Obligation to Sign a Commitment to Be Actively Available for Work

Act 45/02 sought to strengthen the commitment of unemployed people to actively seek employment by requiring them to make a formal 'commitment to be actively available for work'. In fact, the previous unemployment benefit regulations already implied such a commitment. The classic definition of a person entitled to claim unemployment benefit according to social security legislation was already a person who 'is able to and willing to work but either loses his or her job or suffers a reduction in his or her standard working hours'. In other words, unemployment benefit is only paid to unemployed people who are willing to make themselves available for work. Under the previous regulatory framework, a claimant's willingness to work was deduced from the fact that they had registered as a job seeker and were therefore obliged to accept any suitable job placements subsequently offered to them by the employment services. However, in 2002 the legislator decided to introduce a requirement for a more explicit commitment to be available for work. Consequently, job seekers are now obliged to sign a commitment to be actively available for work in which they formally declare that they wish actively to seek employment and that they will accept appropriate job placements.

Scope of the Commitment to Be Actively Available for Work and Who It Applies to

Compared with the regulatory framework that existed prior to the 2002 reform, it should be reiterated that the commitment to be actively available for work is nothing new, except for the requirement for it to be formally written down. In other words, its intention is to get the unemployed person to make a formal declaration of their willingness to return to active employment as soon as possible. Consequently, the law assumes that an unemployed person who does not sign the commitment is not willing to work and is therefore not eligible to claim benefit. However, not all job seekers are required to sign the commitment to be actively available for work. Unemployed people who are registered with the public employment service but are not receiving any financial benefits are exempt. For this group, the mere fact that they have registered as unemployed is enough to entitle them to participate in active employment measures, since they are not claiming welfare benefits. Once they have registered as unemployed, however, these job seekers are required to participate in active employment measures in order to improve their chances of finding work.

People signing the commitment to be actively available for work are required to commit themselves to three things: (i) actively to seek employment; (ii) to accept appropriate job placements; and (iii) to participate in specific actions in order to improve their employability. The last two points will be explored briefly in the following two sections.

Compulsory Participation in Active Employment Measures

When Act 45/02 was proposed, it was with the assurance that the commitment to be actively available for work was intended to improve the employment prospects of anyone wishing to find work. It was supposedly designed in such a way that, from the moment they started claiming unemployment benefit, unemployed persons would be entitled to have the public employment services 'draw up the most suitable job-finding plan based on their professional skills and employability'. However, closer examination of the articles that comprise the Act reveals that this is far from being the case and that people signing the commitment are actually committing themselves to a complex web of obligations.

It is true that Act 45/02 establishes the requirement for job seekers to have a job-finding plan. However, it does so without offering a clear definition of what this should involve, and it lists the plan among the obligations of unemployment benefit claimants in a manner that is very far removed from the fundamental principles of job-finding plans. Normal practice would be for the development of the plan to begin with an interview for the purpose of establishing the personal and professional skills profile of the unemployed person, who would then be expected to play a major part in drawing up the plan. However, the Act intimates that it is the public employment services that will decide on the content of the job-finding plan.

Act 45/02 increased the state's discretionary powers as regards ensuring that unemployed people find work as quickly as possible. Consequently, unemployed people who are claiming unemployment benefit in one form or another do not draw up their job-finding plan jointly with the public employment service. Instead, before the plan is drawn up at all, they are obliged to sign a commitment that requires them to agree to participate in any measures that the public employment services may ask them to participate in at a later date. It would have been far better if the commitment to be actively available for work provided for the full involvement of the unemployed person in drawing up their job-finding plan, or if the unemployed person were to be shown the terms in which the public employment service intended to draw up their plan before they signed the commitment.

The more recent Employment Act also bases the preventive side of active employment measures on job-finding plans. It states that the public employment services' actions shall be brought together in the form of a personalised job-finding plan, drawn up with each job seeker and based on their professional and personal characteristics. Thereafter, all the active employment measures contained in the personalised plan become compulsory for the unemployed person, irrespective of whether they are claiming monetary welfare benefits. Once again, however, this Act fails to define the procedure for drawing up the job-finding plan or exactly how the beneficiary is to be involved in this process.

The Obligation to Accept an Appropriate Job Placement

The other main obligation contained in the commitment to be actively available for work is acceptance of any appropriate job placement offered to the unemployed person by the public employment services. Act 45/02 brought in two important changes in this respect:

(a) The criteria determining the concept of 'appropriate job placement'

The current definition of 'appropriate job placement' is based on four sets of criteria: (i) professional criteria relating to the job offered to the unemployed person; (ii) criteria regarding the location of the job that take into account the distance involved and the time needed to travel to work; (iii) the type of employment contract, working conditions and pay; and (iv) the unemployed person's individual circumstances.

As far as the professional criteria are concerned, an appropriate job placement is defined as one offering the occupation requested by the unemployed person, or their usual occupation, or any other occupation for which they are physically suited and for which they have the necessary training.

It is important to stress that the unemployed person is obliged to accept a job placement in the occupation for which they have registered with the employment services. However, the legislation makes no mention of how occupations should be prioritised if, as is often the case, the unemployed person is registered for several different occupations. As such, the Act also defines as appropriate any job placement in the unemployed person's usual occupation. The concept of a person's usual occupation was already in use before the 2002 reform, although the way in which it was interpreted by the courts had been very problematic. For example, there were cases in which an occupation in which a person had been working for more than eighteen months was deemed not to be their usual occupation, not to mention the fact that the Supreme Court found that an unemployed person's usual occupation was not the last job they had done but rather the occupation that they had held for the longest time in the past. In order to reduce this kind of problem, the Act stipulates that a job placement shall be deemed appropriate if it involves the unemployed person's most recent occupation, provided that they held that occupation for three months or longer.

The other factor that determines the appropriateness of a job placement, according to the Act, is whether the unemployed person is physically able to perform the job and has the necessary training. In other words, an unemployed person will be obliged to accept any job placement offered to them by the employment services unless they are clearly physically unable to do the job in question or they lack the required training.

While this is already a very broad definition of appropriate job placement, the Act goes several steps further in the discretionary powers that it confers upon the state. It stipulates that

> in addition to the above occupations, after a person has been claiming benefit continuously for one year, job placements in other occupations may be deemed to be appropriate if the public employment services consider the subject fit to perform them.

The next criterion is the location of the place of work. A job placement is deemed to be appropriate if the place of work is near the person's usual place of residence or within a 30 kilometre radius, unless the worker can prove that the minimum time needed to travel to and from work is greater than 25% of their working day, or that the cost of travel amounts to more than 20% of their monthly wage, or if it is impossible for the worker to find suitable accommodation near their new place of work.

As regards the type of employment contract that must be offered if a job placement is to be considered appropriate, the Act takes into account the duration of the job (that is, whether it is a permanent or temporary job), and the length of the working day (whether it is a full-time or a part-time job). Furthermore, for a job placement to be deemed appropriate, the full wage for the job being offered should be adequate to the qualification required, irrespective of the level of benefit to which the worker is entitled and even if the job in question involves community work. Pay shall under no circumstances be lower than the minimum wage once travel expenses have been deducted.

The final factor, according to the Act, that can influence whether a job placement is deemed appropriate is the requirement for the public employment services to take into account the unemployed person's professional and personal characteristics when applying the criteria described above. In addition, the following factors should also be taken into account: work/life balance, the job-finding plan that has been drawn up, the characteristics of the job being offered, the availability of transport to the place of work, and the nature of the local job market.

(b) Circumstances in which an appropriate job placement may be refused

In order to provide unemployed people with better legal safeguards, the new legislation stipulates that for a job placement to be considered appropriate the public employment services are obliged to take into account the subject's professional and personal characteristics, including their work/life balance, in so far as these affect the extent to which the job offered matches the content of the job-finding plan drawn up for the unemployed person in question.

The safeguards described above are intended to act as a significant constraint on the state's discretionary powers to deem as appropriate jobs that do not correspond to the unemployed person's usual occupation or for which the person in question has not been trained, in the case of people who have been claiming unemployment benefit continuously for one year.

Failure to Comply with the Obligations Stipulated in the Commitment to Be Actively Available for Work

Should the unemployed person fail to comply with the obligations stipulated in the commitment to be actively available for work, there are a number of penalties that may be imposed by the public employment services. The basic approach underpinning the system of offences and penalties already existed prior to the 2002 reform, although Act 45/02 did make some changes intended to provide unemployed people with greater legal safeguards. Unemployed people who fail to comply with their obligations now receive more chances to change their behaviour before the ultimate penalty of cutting off their benefit is applied. However, it should not be forgotten that, despite this, they are still being compelled to agree to undertake any activity required of them by the public employment service or to accept any job placement deemed to be appropriate.

People Claiming or Receiving Unemployment Benefit

As far as the activation of unemployed people is concerned, the law focuses mainly on people receiving unemployment benefit. Offences are classified as minor, serious or very serious: offences connected with failure to comply with the obligations contained in the commitment to be actively available for work fall into the first two categories.

In general terms, failure to comply with the obligations contained in the commitment to be actively available for work is classified as a minor offence punishable by cutting the unemployed person's benefit in accordance with the following scale:

- The first offence will lead to benefit being withdrawn for one month.
- The second offence will lead to the unemployed person losing three months' benefit.
- The third offence will lead to withdrawal of benefit for six months.
- If a fourth minor offence is committed, the unemployed person will lose their right to claim benefit.

This scale is applied only if the period between the commission of one minor offence and another is one year or less. There are two types of serious offence: (i) refusing an appropriate job placement; (ii) refusing to participate in active employment measures or to do community work. In these cases, the penalties are as follows:

- The first serious offence is punishable by withdrawal of benefit for three months.
- The second serious offence leads to withdrawal of benefit for six months.
- The third serious offence leads to the unemployed person losing their right to claim benefit.

As in the case of minor offences, these penalties apply only if the period between the commission of two successive serious offences is 365 days or less.

Job Seekers Who Are not Claiming Financial Benefits

As has already been explained, people in this group are not forced to sign a commitment to be actively available for work. However, this does not mean that they are not subject to similar obligations or to the relevant penalties for non-compliance. Thus, they are considered to have committed a minor offence if they fail to appear before the employment services when summoned or if they fail to provide written proof of their attendance at interviews for the job opportunities offered to them through the employment services. They are deemed to have committed a serious offence if they turn down an appropriate job placement or if they refuse to participate in the active employment measures offered to them through the employment services. Obviously, in the case of this group, the penalties cannot involve cutting their monthly benefit payments. Consequently, the penalty for a minor offence is the suspension of their job seeker status for one month, and three months for serious offences.

Suspension of a person's status as a job seeker means that they will not benefit from job placement actions or from the employability measures that form part of active employment measures. However, should these people find work and subsequently become unemployed again, they can then re-register with the public employment service and apply for any unemployment benefits for which they qualify.

The Contractualisation of Unemployment Benefit

On the basis of the previous points, it is not difficult to conclude that the obligations contained in the commitment to be actively available for work are nothing new and did not arise as a result of the introduction of the commitment in 2002. However, the commitment should be a useful tool insofar as it serves to integrate all the aspects of each unemployed person's search for work, acting, in the face of the increase in the state's discretionary powers, as a safeguard of the professional rights pertaining to their own personal circumstances as expressed in their personal job-finding plans. However, for this to work in practice, it is essential for the job seekers themselves to be involved in drawing up their own job-finding plans. If this is not done, then the state's discretionary powers will not be subject to adequate controls.

One issue that needs to be raised is the legal status of the obligation to sign the commitment to be actively available for work in order to be entitled to claim unemployment benefit. As has been explained above, the commitment contains a number of obligations. Under the old regime, the function of the obligations was confined to the punitive aspect so the infraction of these obligations could lead to penalties, including cutting off the unemployed person's benefit. Under the new legal model, however, signing the commitment has become a genuine legal obligation that is a prerequisite for entitlement to unemployment benefit. If the person applying for benefit fails to sign the commitment, then according to the law that person is not considered to be unemployed. This means that actively seeking work and accepting appropriate job placements have become legal requirements for anyone wishing to claim unemployment benefit.

The fact that it is a prerequisite for unemployed people to declare their commitment to comply with certain forms of behaviour indicates that a process of contractualisation of unemployment benefit is currently under way. However, signing a contract of this kind should also entitle the unemployed person to certain rights that are not detailed in the law. Put another way, the other party to the contract – namely the public employment service – should be subject to certain obligations. Thus, although it is not explicitly stated in the law, the commitment to be actively available for work should go hand in hand with the right of unemployment benefit claimants to have access to the appropriate resources needed to enable them to find work.

The requirement for unemployed people who sign the commitment to be available for more types of work means that better legal safeguards are needed. In order to provide these safeguards, the new unemployment benefit legislation has sought to redefine the concepts underlying the obligations contained in the commitment. However, it has been shown that the criteria used by the public employment service to draw up job-finding plans or to decide what constitutes an appropriate job placement are far from being precisely defined. It could even be said that they are contrary to the values expressed in the European employment guidelines, such as high-quality jobs or the promotion of functional mobility. This is because unemployed people are likely to experience frustration in terms of their expectations regarding a change in occupation or the sector in which they work if they are forced to accept any old job that the public employment service decides to offer them.

Activation in Employment Measures

Having analysed the influence of the EES on the legislative framework in Spain, this section will move on to examine its specific impact on the employment measures contained in the NAPs drawn up since 1998, focusing particularly on the measures based on the European guidelines that are most closely connected with what is known as the 'activation principle'.

However, before doing so it is necessary to provide a brief historical overview of the development of employment policy in Spain. Compared with other EU member states, employment measures in Spain began to be developed at a relatively late stage, during the 1980s. They are also rather fragmented and decentralised in nature, and during the 1990s particular emphasis was placed on promoting temporary employment as the main means of creating jobs.

A sea change came about in the direction of employment policy at the end of the 1990s as a result of various factors. The first was the impact of the *Interconfederal Agreement for Stability in Employment* that was signed in 1997[7] by the main national trade unions and employers' associations and which would later be incorporated into an item of legislation.[8] This agreement marked a major change in the direction of employment policy by moving away from the previous approach towards the fundamental principles of promoting stable employment and reducing the proportion of temporary jobs.

The year 1997 also saw the introduction of a new national system for promoting employment that involved drawing up annual programmes linked to budgetary priorities. Mention should also be made of the launch of the NAPs in 1998 and the emergence of the Regional Employment Pacts that have since been adopted by all the autonomous communities.

All of this means that an overall analysis of the various employment programmes faces the difficulty of trying to cover a very diverse and dynamic subject matter. First, the various programmes attempt to follow the different EES guidelines and the EU's specific recommendations regarding Spain's employment policy. Second, there is a combination of various initiatives promoted by central government, the autonomous communities and even the local authorities. Finally, it should not be forgotten that the beneficiaries themselves are diverse in nature and that various different approaches to promoting employment have been adopted.

Given this context, we have decided to examine eleven measures that have been included in the Spanish NAPs since 1998, in order to analyse the impact of the EES on the content of employment policy and more specifically the inclusion of elements based on the principle of activation. As can be seen from Table 1, most of the measures fall under Employment Guideline 1 (*Active and preventive measures for the unemployed and inactive*), although some also fall under Guideline 2 (*Job creation and entrepreneurship*) and Guideline 7 (*Promote the*

---

[7] That is, before the introduction of the EES.
[8] Act 63/1997 of 26 December regarding urgent measures to improve the labour market and the promotion of permanent contracts.

integration of and combat discrimination against people at a disadvantage in the labour market).[9]

As far as the characteristics of these measures are concerned, it is important to emphasise the following aspects, albeit in simplified form:

(a) The measures are aimed at two different kinds of *target group*. Five of the eleven measures in Table 1 (measures 1, 2, 5, 6, and 9) are targeted at unemployed people in general, although they do have some criteria for establishing which beneficiaries should be prioritised. These include: people who are particularly well-suited to the job being offered; job seekers with disabilities; the amount of unemployment benefit that the potential beneficiary is receiving, with preference being given to those receiving the lowest levels of protection; beneficiaries with family responsibilities (people with young persons under the age of 26 or persons with a disability in their care, or minors whom they have adopted or fostered); the age of the beneficiary; the gender of the beneficiary (women are given priority). The rest of the measures are exclusively targeted at specific groups, based on various criteria such as age, whether or not the beneficiary is claiming unemployment benefit, the region in which the beneficiary lives, or their income.

Table 1. Employment Measures in Spain

Measure	NAP guideline
1. Cooperation between public employment service and local authorities	1
2. Cooperation between public employment service and national and regional government departments, autonomous communities, universities and non-profit organisations	1
3. Temporary community work	1
4. Agricultural job creation scheme for Andalusia and Extremadura and in poorer rural areas	1
5. Career guidance for employment and assistance for self-employment (OPEA)	1
6. Occupational vocational training for unemployed people	1
7. Vocational training centres (Escuelas Taller y Casas de Oficio)	1
8. Employment workshops	1
9. Grants for experimental employment schemes	1
10. Capitalisation of unemployment benefit	1 and 7
11. Active integration benefit (*renta activa de inserción*)	1 and 2

Source: Author's own data.

---

[9] The Guidelines listed here are the revised Guidelines following the EES review in 2003.

(b) As far as their *content* is concerned, the measures can be divided into five broad groups:

1. The measures that subsidise temporary jobs for unemployed people in order to carry out community work or provide services that are in the public interest (measures 1, 2 and 3).

2. The measures that involve a range of *integrated actions* aimed at getting unemployed people into work, for example guidance, training and work experience (measures 4, 9 and 11).

3. The measures that focus on one specific aspect such as guidance or training for unemployed people (measures 5 and 6).[10]

4. The two measures that combine training and work experience. Their aim is to get unemployed people into work through a mix of training and work experience in jobs in new areas of employment (measures 7 and 8).

5. The measure known as *capitalisation of unemployment benefit* is aimed at promoting stable employment for unemployed people by paying them all or part of their unemployment benefit entitlement and/or their social security contributions subsidy as a lump sum. The idea is that the money should be used to enable them to join a workers' cooperative or a workers' limited company (that is, a PLC that has been bought out by the workforce) or to become self-employed.

Against this background, an analysis of the content of the NAPs, and more specifically a comparison of the eleven measures described above, enables a number of significant points to be made concerning the impact of the EES on Spanish employment policy.

(a) On the whole, the drafting of the NAPs in Spain has hitherto not resulted in any substantial changes in the direction and content of employment policy. Instead, as already pointed out, the various NAPs have confined themselves to coordinating and bringing together existing programmes and measures. So much so that

> indeed, we are unable to identify any significant measures that originate from the new approach to employment policy. At best, the NAPs in some years incorporated the measures resulting either from the bipartite social dialogue between trade unions and employers' associations or the tripartite dialogue including the government – but these measures were not a result of the European Employment Strategy. (Liceras 2005)

(b) The content of the NAPs has been too much skewed towards *employability* measures – that is, demand-side measures – while relatively

---

[10] In contrast to the previous group of measures, these measures do not offer a range of integrated actions, but focus instead on one aspect.

little attention has been paid to supply-side measures (measures designed to create more and better jobs).

(c) Finally, the activation element has largely taken the form of the attachment of conditions to the various measures that have been described. In other words, if an unemployed person refuses to participate in a measure that has been offered to them, this is considered to be a serious offence punishable by a variety of statutory penalties that range from a change in the administrative status of offenders who are not claiming unemployment benefit (causing them to be excluded from participating in actions offered by the public employment services) to the temporary or permanent withdrawal of unemployment benefit for those people who are claiming it.

The attachment of these conditions to the employment measures contained in the NAPs is a result of the dual aspects of contractualisation and punishment that have characterised the legislative framework for unemployment protection in Spain since Act 45/2002 was passed. As has already been pointed out,[11] these dual aspects are the most visible manifestation of the influence of the activation principle – as promoted by the EES guidelines – on labour law and social legislation in Spain.

Nevertheless, it is important to note that if we compare theory with practice, there can on the whole be seen to be a significant difference between the conditions stipulated by law and the way in which they are implemented by the public employment services. This difference cannot be explained in purely legal terms since it is largely due to various social and cultural factors that need to be analysed separately.

The Social Perception of Unemployment and Measures to Help People into Work in Spain

When analysing the social perception of the activation principle in employment policy it is necessary to take into account a number of features that distinguish Spain's socioeconomic context from that of other EU member states, since these to some extent determine the Spanish public's overall attitude towards unemployment and measures to help people into work.

The first factor is the fact that the welfare state was a long time coming in Spain and was only properly consolidated during the 1980s. Furthermore, the degree of protection afforded by social policy and the number of people it covers are currently significantly lower than in other parts of Europe, especially the Nordic countries. Secondly, active em-

---

[11] See section 3.

ployment measures containing elements of activation, such as conditionality, have been in use since the 1990s. This means that, as already pointed out, the subsequent adoption of the EES simply continued this trend rather than marking a fundamental change in approach.

The third and perhaps most significant feature is the continued existence of major imbalances in the Spanish labour market, despite the progress achieved during the past decade. These include low employment and high unemployment rates, both of which are a particular problem for women; a high proportion of temporary jobs, especially among young people; and the existence of major and persistent regional disparities with regard to employment and unemployment levels.

The result of all this is that, according to various national and international (Eurobarometer) surveys, unemployment is currently perceived by Spanish people to be the main social problem, even outranking terrorism, which is an issue that is extremely important in Spanish public opinion.

Against this backdrop, a number of particularly interesting results have been thrown up by a national survey (CIS 2001)[12] of the public's attitude towards unemployment and the inclusion of activation elements in measures designed to promote employment:

• The majority of respondents thought that the overall level of benefit available to unemployed people in Spain is low. Indeed, many people went so far as to say that they could understand why some unemployed people do casual work while claiming benefit. These responses are a reflection of the low level of protection afforded by the Spanish welfare state which, as already indicated, is much less developed than in other European countries.

• The second significant point concerns the concept of an appropriate job placement. The majority of respondents thought that people should have the right to refuse job offers that they consider inappropriate without this resulting in their unemployment benefit being cut off.

• Unemployed people are obliged to participate in the actions offered by the public employment services. It is true that the majority of respondents thought that there should be controls to prevent benefit fraud and to regulate the behaviour of unemployed people. However, when asked what they thought about entitlement to unemployment

---

[12] The survey, which studied the social conditions of unemployed people in Spain, was carried out by the Centre for Sociological Research (Centro de Investigaciones Sociológicas – CIS), which is an independent state agency attached to the Ministry of the Presidency. Despite the fact that it was carried out some years ago, its results remain relevant to the subject under discussion.

benefit being linked to participation in activation measures, a clear majority said they thought participation should be voluntary rather than compulsory.

- The final key point concerns the public's value judgements concerning unemployment benefit and the people who claim it. The results of the survey on this point are in line with the opinions expressed above: people had a positive attitude towards unemployment benefit and believed that it is wrong to *blame* people claiming unemployment benefit for their situation.

It can thus be said that, unlike in other European countries, the Spanish public is somewhat reluctant to *blame* unemployed people for their situation and is largely opposed to the imposition of conditions that can lead to unemployment benefit being reduced or cut off entirely. As already explained, this is partly due to factors such as the high level of unemployment together with the relatively low level of state benefits. However, it can also partly be put down to the inefficiency of the public employment services in helping unemployed people to find appropriate work.

It should be remembered that although the labour law and social legislation currently in force in Spain stipulate that the public employment services should have adequate staffing and resources to enable them to cater for the needs of unemployed people, in fact, as has already been pointed out,[13] this is often not the case. The problem is made worse by the lack of precisely defined criteria to be used by the public employment services in drawing up job-finding plans or defining an appropriate job placement.

In short, and by way of conclusion, it can be said that a kind of *quid pro quo* arrangement exists regarding the obligations of unemployed people and the benefits they receive from the public employment services. The overall shortcomings of the public employment services when it comes to the provision of appropriate, integrated job-finding plans and the very low job placement rates that they achieve are to some extent 'compensated' for by them not applying the conditions that are established by law and are also present in the various employment measures. In other words, the compulsory participation of unemployed people in the actions that are offered to them, if they wish to avoid the statutory penalties, is in practice more of a theoretical formality than a real requirement.

---

[13] See section 3.

Activation and Taxation

Moving away from the strict definition of employment measures, it is evident that fiscal policy measures relating to the different instruments and systems governing the money paid by individuals to the Treasury also play an important role in the approach to promoting active employment. In this context, special attention should be given to direct taxation and in particular to measures that affect people's income levels, since these measures are targeted at specific groups, as opposed to indirect taxation which is basically a tax on consumption.

The income tax (IRPF) reform introduced in Spain in 2002 further developed the 1998 reform[14] and was basically aimed at reducing taxpayers' tax bills via the following measures: increasing the income exempt from taxation in the personal and family allowances; reducing the number of income tax bands to five and reducing the lowest and highest rates on the progressive scale from 18% to 15% and from 48% to 45%, respectively; reducing the tax on capital gains generated over periods of more than one year and on savings earmarked for covering welfare needs; and tax cuts relating to the taxpayer's work situation.

The last of the above measures includes tax cuts designed to encourage over-65s to continue working beyond retirement age, incentives for unemployed people who would need to move to a different town in order to accept a job offer, and the creation of a working mothers' allowance payable for each child under the age of three.

In order to analyse fiscal policy, a wide range of issues would need to be considered. Although this is not the central purpose of this study, such an analysis would have to assess at least the following themes: the different levels of revenue generated for the Treasury by direct taxation (the main instrument of which is income tax), indirect taxation and social security contributions, and the very different effect that these forms of taxation have on income distribution; the relative levels of tax burden in relation to GDP; the extent to which the state is able to finance public spending; and the level of government spending on social welfare.

Although the abovementioned income tax reforms are not directly intended to promote the principle of activation, they nevertheless do so in some respects. As the 2002 Act itself states, the reforms tackled 'in particular the needs arising from situations such as the falling birth rate, the ageing of the population and the problems of people with disabilities, while also encouraging women to enter the labour market'.

---

[14] Act 40/1988 and Act 46/2002.

In general terms, it can be said that the abovementioned reforms are designed to lessen the tax burden and reduce the 'tax gap' between gross and net wages in order to provide an incentive for people to look for work or to stay in work once they have found a job. Although it is still too early for a comprehensive assessment, it appears that the ultimate effect of the 2002 income tax reform will be a 15% drop in revenue and a 2% increase in households' net income. However, there are two factors that significantly diminish the potential positive effects on the economy. First, the reforms fail to provide for the adjustment of tax rates in line with increases in the cost of living (so-called 'objective progressive taxation'), meaning that in the medium term, inflation will cancel out the tax cuts. Second, the greater a household's income, the greater the benefits offered by the reforms. In other words, single-parent households stand to gain less than two-parent households that are otherwise similar in terms of age and gender make-up (Castañer 2004).

Furthermore, criticism has been levelled at the new working woman's allowance of 1,200 euros for each child under the age of three up to a limit of the total amount of social security contributions paid in the tax year, which is considered to be one of the most important measures as far as promoting employment is concerned. This is because (i) it fails to cover groups such as women who are not in work, even if they are actively seeking employment, (ii) it implies that it is only women who need to achieve a work/life balance, and (iii) the limits on the allowance are regressive in relation to income levels. However, the main criticism of the policies aimed at increasing the birth rate, promoting work/life balance, supporting people with disabilities and lessening the burden on people with dependents is that such policies should not be exclusively or even predominantly implemented via income tax measures. This is because the individuals and households on the lowest incomes, who are by definition the people most in need of this type of assistance, are not in a position to benefit from measures of this type, since they are either exempt from paying income tax or their taxable income is too low for the allowances to be applicable (ECOSOC 2003 and 2004).

In short, it appears that the merits of tax reforms designed to promote employment activation are dependent on how developed the welfare state is and on the ability to provide universal public services. If these are not sufficiently developed, then tax incentives intended to encourage people to look for work or to remain in work will only affect taxpayers, leading to an individualisation of benefits that flies in the face of the welfare state model of universal public goods such as universal citizen's rights.

Conclusion

In order to analyse the incorporation of aspects of the activation principle into employment policy in Spain, it is necessary to take some of the following socioeconomic factors into account:

- The impact of the economic crisis of the 1970s in the Spanish productive structure which, among other things, was characterised by a low level of foreign trade. The crisis had a particularly negative effect on employment during the following decade: while in 1976 the employment rate in Spain was 50.2% and unemployment stood at 4.4%, by 1985 the figures had changed to 38.6% and 21.5% respectively. The current figures, for 2004, are an employment rate of 50.1% and unemployment of 10.5%.

- The relatively late emergence in Spain of the welfare state which, unlike in other European countries, only began to be developed during the 1980s when a range of policies were introduced that contributed to the establishment of universal rights in areas such as education, health, pensions, and so on.

- Finally, the fact that the employment measures that began to be developed mainly during the 1980s were fragmented and limited in nature and put particular emphasis on the promotion of temporary contracts as a means of job creation.

Against this backdrop, an analysis of the incorporation of aspects of the activation principle into employment policy in Spain since the launch of the European Employment Strategy highlights the following points:

1. Employment policy in Spain is currently implemented within the framework of the devolved structure established by the Spanish Constitution in 1978 that provides for the distribution of powers between the state, the 17 autonomous communities and the local authorities (52 provinces and 8,108 municipalities) that it created. The Constitution seeks to find a balance between the political will to promote a decentralised model that recognises the social, cultural and political diversity of the different autonomous communities and the establishment of standards that ensure equal citizen's rights and employment rights across the whole of Spain.

As far as employment is concerned, this model has mainly been implemented through the gradual transfer of responsibility for active employment measures to the autonomous communities. This process has now been completed in all the regions except the Basque Country, where central government and the regional government have not yet reached agreement on the content and scope of the transfer of powers.

Consequently, the governments of the autonomous communities have considerable freedom concerning the design and implementation of employment measures. However, it should be stressed that these measures have been developed since the second half of the 1990s against a backdrop of intensive social dialogue involving trade unions and employers, as well as the regional governments, resulting in the signing of Regional Employment Pacts in all the autonomous communities.

2. The Spanish public employment service – known as the National Institute of Employment (INEM) – which is attached to the Ministry of Labour and Social Affairs, is responsible for coordinating the different employment programmes and for managing and evaluating them at state level. In the mid-1990s, however, a two-pronged reform of its responsibilities was undertaken:

(a) INEM's monopoly on the management of active employment measures was ended in 1994, enabling non-profit employment agencies to get involved in the management of job placement provision. This was accompanied by the diversification of the players involved in the policies that accompany job placements to include, among others, local councils, the social partners and partner organisations. This was intended to improve the efficiency of active measures by promoting specialisation and ensuring that providers were as close as possible to the sources of employment.

However, a decade after this reform was introduced, not enough progress has been made towards meeting its aims. Instead, it appears that measures are being implemented from a very local perspective, with little coordination with the other players involved in managing employment policy (leading to the danger of measures becoming fragmented), as well as a pronounced lack of specialisation, resulting in an inefficient service. An attempt was made to remedy this situation with the recent 2003 Employment Act, which attaches considerable importance to the coordination of the various players involved in the design and implementation of employment measures.

(b) At the same time, the management of active employment policy measures which had hitherto been the responsibility of INEM began to be decentralised from 1996 onwards. As a result, as already pointed out, all the autonomous communities apart from the Basque Country now run their own public employment service, as well as managing policy with regard to training, career guidance and job placements.

However, it seems that in the time that this new model has been up and running, the fact that the level of government at which employment measures are being implemented is closer to the people concerned has not led to a significant increase in the number of job placements being provided by the public employment services.

In view of this, it seems reasonable to suggest that the autonomous communities' public employment services need to be strengthened, since they need to play a key role in the coordination and organisation of the various measures and of the players involved in the implementation of employment policy in their region, from the local authorities to the different bodies involved in running the programmes (for example, the growing number of non-profit organisations that are competing with each other to run programmes).

3. It did not take long for the launch of the EES as part of the Luxembourg process to be reflected in the structure of some of the active employment measures in 1998, although, rather than involving far-reaching changes, what this amounted to was nothing more than the adaptation of the existing Spanish model to the goals set at European level. It is also important to highlight the role played by the social partners (trade unions and employers' associations) who in 1997 signed a series of agreements that were essentially aimed at promoting employment and reducing the excessive proportion of temporary jobs on the Spanish labour market.

In this respect, it can be said that, in the Spanish context, the implementation of the 'activation principle' through the guidelines contained in successive National Action Plans on employment did not represent a radical shift in terms of the 'spirit' of active and passive employment policies. Instead, it was more a continuation of existing trends.

4. Nevertheless, recent years have seen reforms in two important areas. First, the 2002 reform, embodied in Act 45/2002 that introduced modifications to the General Social Security Act that constitute the current regulations governing entitlement to unemployment benefit. Secondly, Act 56/2003, a new employment act passed in 2003, replacing the previous employment act that had been in force since 1980. The new Employment Act aims to develop an integrated approach to employment policy which it defines as all the decisions taken by the state and the autonomous communities geared towards achieving full employment, promoting quality jobs, finding a qualitative and quantitative balance between labour supply and demand, cutting unemployment and providing proper protection for the unemployed.

5. The new unemployment protection regime in Spain has two features that are particularly closely associated with the 'activation principle' promoted by the EES: contractualisation and punishment.

(a)   Two legal mechanisms have been introduced to improve the employment prospects of everyone who wishes to find work. On the one hand, there is the commitment to be actively available for work. This comes into force as soon as a person starts claiming unemployment benefit and entitles the claimant to expect the public employment services to draw up the most suitable job-finding plan for them based on their professional skills and employability. On the other hand, there is a new regulation defining the concept of an appropriate job placement, the key aspect of which is that the public employment services can evaluate the suitability of a job placement based on an individual's personal and professional characteristics and how easy it is for them to travel to their place of work.

The fact that unemployed people wishing to claim unemployment benefit are required to sign the commitment to be actively available for work is an indication of the current process of contractualisation of welfare benefits. At the same time, it is true that signing up to this contractual obligation not only means that the unemployed have obligations, but it also gives them the right to the resources they need to enable them to find work made available to them by the public employment services. However, although Act 45/2002 and the Employment Act both stipulate that sufficient staffing and resources should be made available to the public employment services so that they can provide unemployed people with an appropriate service, in practice many of the key requirements are not being met.

In addition, the criteria used by the public employment services to draw up job-finding plans or to decide what constitutes an appropriate job placement are far from being precisely defined. It could even be said that they are contrary to the values expressed in the Employment Guidelines such as high-quality jobs or the promotion of functional mobility.

(b) In addition to the contractualisation aspect, the new unemployment benefit regulations also contain a punitive dimension, insofar as the law puts the requirement for the unemployed person to be available to do any job – as long as the terms of the job-finding plan drawn up by the public employment services are met – before their right to draw benefit (a right to which, incidentally, they should be entitled if they have previously paid social security contributions).

Thus, instead of recognising the right of unemployed people to have a say and be involved in determining whether an employability measure suits them or what constitutes an appropriate job placement, Spanish legislation opts to force unemployed people to accept whatever is offered them. This amounts to a rather narrow interpretation of the principles that underpin other international regulations, such as ILO Convention No. 44, that recognise unemployed people's right to refuse inappropriate measures.

The unilateral obligations imposed on the job seeker in the shape of the commitment to be actively available for work require them to follow the job-finding plan that the public employment services are supposed to draw up for them even though there is nothing that explicitly obliges the PES to provide the actions contained in the plan. However, this is not the only problem. In practice the public employment services are failing to provide unemployed people with an individual initial assessment: this means that there is in fact no job-finding plan in the sense of a package of integrated measures designed to help them find work. Instead, the best-case scenario is that the unemployed person is offered a range of indiscriminate, untailored actions, basically comprising career guidance and vocational training, provided by various private organisations that assist the public employment services with the running of the programmes.

It would be far more appropriate for the public employment services to draw up an individual job-finding plan together with each unemployed person and to be responsible for monitoring and supporting the correct implementation of the plan, irrespective of whether the concrete actions in the plan are provided by partner organisations.

In short, the process of contractualisation and the way in which it is now unemployed people who are subject to obligations have strengthened the activation elements associated with the EES, elements which were already implicit in the previous Spanish legislation on unemployment protection.

6. An analysis of the measures included in the successive NAPs adopted in Spain since 1998 yields the following observations regarding the impact of the EES on Spanish employment policy:

(a) Overall, the EES has so far not resulted in any major changes in the direction and content of employment policies in Spain. The reason for this is that successive governments have not viewed the drafting of the NAPs as an opportunity to develop new and better employment measures, seeing it instead as a bureaucratic formality that they have complied with by adapting existing programmes and measures to the annual European guidelines.

(b) As far as the content of the NAPs is concerned, too much emphasis has been put on measures that relate to the *employability* of unemployed people – that is, demand-side measures – while relatively little attention has been paid to supply-side measures aimed at creating more and better jobs.

(c) Finally, activation has basically taken the shape of attaching formal conditions to the various measures, in line with the current provisions of labour law and social legislation. As described above, if an unemployed person refuses to participate in the actions offered to him or her this is regarded as a serious or very serious offence punishable by a range of statutory penalties.

7. Notwithstanding the above, it should be noted that an analysis of the extent to which these conditions are enforced in practice by the public employment services shows that, on the whole, there is a significant gap between what the law says and the way that it is actually implemented. This gap can be attributed to two things:

(a) The first is the fact that Spanish people are acutely aware of the high level of unemployment and the relatively low level of social welfare protection. This to some extent explains the widespread rejection of discourses that seek to blame unemployed people for their situation and of the principle of making benefit entitlement dependent on the unemployed person accepting whatever job they are offered. Put another way, the Spanish public believes that unemployed people's participation in the actions offered by the public employment services should be voluntary.

(b) The second reason is that, as has already been explained, the service provided to unemployed people by the public employment services is not as effective or appropriate as it should be, both in terms of the drawing up of the job-finding plans and the provision of job placements.

Consequently, it could be said that a kind of *quid pro quo* arrangement exists regarding the obligations of unemployed people and the benefits they receive from the public employment services, meaning that, on the whole, the latter do not in practice enforce the formal conditions stipulated by the law and also by the employment measures themselves.

8. In conclusion, it is important to reiterate that the employment measures implemented in Spain in the 1980s were relatively late in appearing, limited in scope and fragmented in nature. Furthermore, they were introduced at a time when the socioeconomic context was characterised by high unemployment. Thereafter, the development towards the end of the 1990s of the activation principle on which active employment measures are based found its main expression in the commitment to be actively available for work. This commitment was already present in the previous regulatory framework, but greater emphasis has now been put on it on the one hand as a result of a process of contractualisation (the commitment now takes the shape of an explicit written document) and on the other as a result of the punitive dimension (unemployed people are now subject to penalties regulated by statute). Consequently, the EES has not led to any radical innovations in the design of active em-

ployment measures in Spain, but it has resulted in greater stress being placed on aspects connected with the 'activation principle'.

A number of criticisms can be levelled at the way in which the commitment to be actively available for work has been designed:

First, as far as participation in active employment measures is concerned, unemployed people are given a fundamentally passive role since their job-finding plan is drawn up unilaterally by the public employment services. It would thus not seem unreasonable to suggest that job seekers should be given a more prominent and active role in order to enable them to find a job that is as well suited as possible to their individual skills and needs.

Second, and in connection with the previous point, it may be said that the public authorities enjoy excessive discretionary powers when it comes to deciding whether or not the commitment to be actively available for work has been complied with. As such, if unemployed people are to be required to make themselves available for more types of work, they should be provided with greater legal safeguards.

Finally, one of the key issues is the need to improve the effectiveness of the service provided by the public employment services since the responsibility for finding work cannot be allowed to rest solely with unemployed people themselves. While there are several aspects that require attention in this respect, two are of particular importance. First, the need to improve the coordination of actions implemented at the three different administrative levels – national, regional and local – and coordination between the state and the various private organisations involved in the design and implementation of employment measures (the social partners, non-profit organisations, private companies, and so on). Second, the need for better integration of employment measures enabling more comprehensive job-finding plans to be drawn up for job seekers.

References

Aragón, J. and F. Rocha (2001), "Evaluación de los pactos y medidas de fomento del empleo en las Comunidades Autónomas: Situación y experiencias", working documents of the Fundación 1º de Mayo, No. 1/2001 (available at: http://www.1mayo.org).

Aragón, J. and F. Rocha (2003), "La dimensión territorial de las políticas de fomento del empleo en España", working documents of the Fundación 1º de Mayo, No. 3/2003 (available at: http://www.1mayo.org).

Aragón, J. and A. Santana (2005), "La estrategia europea de empleo: un proceso en construcción", in *Gaceta Sindical*, No. 5.

Aragón, J., F. Rocha and J. Torrents (2000), *Pactos y medidas de fomento del empleo en las Comunidades Autónomas*, Ministry of Labour and Social Affairs.

Aragón, J., F. Rocha and A. Fernandez (2002), "Políticas de fomento del empleo en el ámbito local", working documents of the Fundación 1º de Mayo, No. 2/2002 (available at: http://www.1mayo.org).

Castañer, J.M. et al. (2004), "Simulación sobre los hogares de la reforma del IRPF de 2003: Efectos sobre la oferta laboral, recaudatoria, distribución y bienestar", Papeles de Trabajo del Instituto de Estudios Fiscales, 10/04.

Centro de Investigaciones Sociológicas (CIS) (2001), "Encuesta sobre las condiciones sociales de los desempleados en España", II, Study No. 2,431 (October-December).

Economic and Social Council (2003), *Report on the Socioeconomic and Employment Situation in Spain 2002*, ECOSOC.

Economic and Social Council (2004), *Report on the Socioeconomic and Employment Situation in Spain 2003*, ECOSOC.

Economic and Social Council (2005), *Occupational Imbalances and Active Employment Policies*, ECOSOC.

Dahan, J., N. Duell, F. Marin and V. Singer (2003), *Renforcer la dimension locale de la stratégie européenne pour l'emploi : étude de faisabilité sur les indicateurs destinés aux niveaux régional et local et à l'économie sociale*, Final report, European Commission.

Liceras, D. (2005), "Los planes nacionales de acción para el empleo en España", in *Gaceta Sindical*, No. 5.

Saez, F. (ed.) (2004), *Evaluación de la Estrategia Europea de Empleo en las Comunidades Autónomas Españolas*, Madrid, Universidad Autónoma.

Sobrino, T. (2003), "La colocación adecuada del desempleado", in P. Gete and F. Valdes (eds.), *Nuevo Régimen Jurídico del despido y del desempleo. Análisis crítico de la Ley 45/2002, de 12 de diciembre*, Madrid, Ediciones Cinca.

Torrents, J. (2003), "El compromiso de actividad", in P. Gete and F. Valdes (eds.), *Nuevo Régimen Jurídico del despido y del desempleo. Análisis crítico de la Ley 45/2002, de 12 de diciembre*, Madrid, Ediciones Cinca.

The Activation Trend in Portuguese Social Policy
An Open Process?

Pedro HESPANHA[*]

The Portuguese Experience

The Luxembourg process is the outcome of a long journey and of a whole range of ideas. It has emerged because of a strong desire for coordinated action at the European level, but has been strongly resisted by forces and institutions deeply embedded in national cultures, institutions, and social and economic structures.

Historical differences between national welfare systems are evident. For instance, in relation to Germany, the UK, France and Scandinavia, southern European countries such as Greece, Spain and Portugal have less developed economies, more recent democratic regimes and welfare states which are either still under construction or weakly consolidated. Because these welfare states have not reached maturity, and passive social policies have been maintained at a modest level, the pressure to adopt active social policies is very low and, for that reason, these policies started to emerge only recently. Their most salient feature seems to be the reduced priority given to activation when compared to redistributive policies.

Portugal has a very progressive political constitution in the sense that it provides a wide range of social rights defining a high standard of social citizenship. However, the protection offered by existing services and systems of provision clearly falls below these standards. This problem tends to be seen in different ways according to the political orientation of the current government. However, the lack of political hegemony among leading social actors has led to the continued delay of

---

[*] This chapter has benefited greatly from the contributions of Stuart Holland, Jorge Caleiras and Teresa Oliveira, who supplied me with fruitful suggestions and valuable comments. I am also deeply indebted to Teresa Tavares for her careful revision of the manuscript.

reforms and the emergence of an electoralist discourse (eventually radical and populist) that has confused the population and has not allowed the emergence of consensus. Lacking common ground on the nature of a mixed economy, the social partners have polarised the debate on issues such as reducing social inequalities, promoting a dynamic and competitive economy, and modernising public and private institutions.

Nevertheless, the influence of EU guidelines on the expansion of active social policies and activation in Portugal is evident and widely recognised.[1] Before the implementation of the European Employment Strategy (EES) there was already a broad range of programmes aimed at increasing the employability of unemployed workers,[2] with a good platform of compensatory measures combined with a significant degree of activation (CIDES 2003, 43; Hespanha *et al.* 2002). This experience was enough to allow effective adaptation of these programmes to the European guidelines. However, the previous active labour market policies lacked strategic objectives and priorities, quantified goals and coherence.

In implementing the EES, Portugal has made successive changes in the direction of EU activation policies. A concept of preventive activation, based on the idea of a 'new start' for people on unemployment benefit, was promoted in the first version of the guidelines. This restricted concept then evolved towards a more comprehensive one, capable of including those groups most excluded from the labour market. In 1999, a new guideline was introduced in order to promote the integration of individuals with particular difficulties, such as disabled persons, ethnic minorities, immigrants and other groups. In 2001, this guideline was extended to address all forms of discrimination. After five years of implementation, the EES was substantially reformed in 2003 and oriented towards promoting social cohesion through a more inclusive labour market. An important role was accorded to activation policies in new Guidelines 1b (the long-term unemployed), 7 (persons facing particular difficulties in the labour market) and 8 (incentives for making work pay). After the Council of Nice in 2000 a new EU strategy was launched aimed at strengthening the action of member states in combating poverty and social exclusion: the EU strategy for social

---

[1] The same conclusion is expressed by an official evaluation study: 'The impact of the EES on policies has been rather strong and very clear in the case of employability and activation policies. The proximity to the spirit and the letter of the EU guidelines led to a significant increase of the programmes foreseen in the Portuguese Action Plan (PNE). This increase is very positive for the capacity to attend to very diverse situations, but generated some problems of "proliferation"' (CIDES 2003, 150).

[2] About 23, according to CIDES (2003: 128).

inclusion. Two objectives in particular stressed the importance of appropriate activation policies for the insertion of people at risk of exclusion: (i) the creation of trajectories of inclusion by mobilising training initiatives; (ii) ensuring that access to a job means an increase in income and a real opportunity for occupational insertion (Silva 2004, 6).

The Legal Basis for Activation in Portugal: Recent Trends

Before the EU influence began to make itself felt, and despite previous consistent practice, activation was an almost unknown concept in Portuguese law and political discourse. However, it now pervades the basic norms of social protection, such as the Guaranteed Minimum Income of 1996, the Protection against Unemployment Act of 1999, the Social Security Act of 2002 and the Labour Code of 2002.

Activation was included in the Portuguese legal order for the first time in 1985 through a programme aimed at allocating temporary jobs to unemployed people (*Programa Ocupacional para Desempregados*). Formally, POCs were created to 'combat demotivation and marginalisation tendencies' among the unemployed, and to aid their social integration through a 'socially useful occupation'. It was recognised that the programmes were 'targeted at neither job creation nor engagement in productive jobs in the labour market'. Job placements under this programme were restricted to public services and non-profit organisations. Participation in a POC was explicitly temporary and, at least at the beginning, had an integrative rationale. Later on this rationale shifted to more compulsory participation.

However, more than one decade passed before the creation of a clearly activation-based programme, the Guaranteed Minimum Income (GMI). GMI was introduced in 1996 under the socialist government and benefited about 3.5% of the Portuguese population. It followed the activation rule, obliging recipients to accept an insertion plan consisting predominantly of a job placement or training. The right-wing coalition government of 2002-February 2005 re-baptised this scheme Social Insertion Income (RSI), restricted entitlements (the lower age limit was raised from 18 to 25), and reinforced the mechanisms of surveillance, control and sanctioning, but the scheme survived.[3]

An important step to regulate the duties of the unemployed on benefits in terms of activation came with the Social Protection for Unemployed People Act in 1999.[4] According to this law, entitlement to

---

[3] Law No. 13/2003, 21 May.
[4] Dec-lei No.119/1999, 14 April.

any type of unemployment benefit is conditional on the following: (i) to accept: (a) a suitable job; (b) any socially necessary work; (c) a vocational training course; (d) a personal plan for employment; (ii) to be present at the Job Centre whenever summoned there; (iii) to actively seek a job; (iv) not to use fraudulent means to get benefits. The intention of activating those on benefits is very clear, but trade unions were alert to the risk that activation would become an instrument for reducing the number of beneficiaries, and the government has been very cautious in implementing the law. In 2003, the right-wing coalition prepared a revision of this law in order to make it more stringent, but it was not approved before the suspension of parliament in December 2004. One of the issues that raised particular criticism from the unions was the latitude of the concept of 'adjusted job' used by the new law to define the kind of jobs that unemployed people were obliged to accept.

Another relevant law as regards activation is the new Social Security Act of 2002, brought before Parliament by the same coalition government.[5] One of the basic principles instituted by the new law is the principle of contractualisation of insertion plans, which also applies to the social assistance subsystem.[6] Accordingly, recipients are to be engaged in and to be accountable for a personal insertion plan in order to receive a social response.

Finally, the Labour Code enacted by the right-wing coalition in 2002 was innovative in the way it combined varied, sparse and fragmentary legislation. The new Code introduced new rules on labour relations and changed the orientation of many other regulations, in three main directions: more flexible and open regulation, a reduced role for trade unions and collective bargaining, and less balanced labour relations. Changes concerned dismissals, fixed-term contracts, work duration and mobility, collective bargaining, minimum service provisions during strikes, and so on. Strong criticisms from both the trade unions and the left-wing parties in Parliament resulted in a Presidential veto of the legislation, based on the non-constitutionality of several of its provisions, and led afterwards to a re-consideration and reformulation by Parliament.

---

[5] Lei de Bases da Segurança Social: Lei No. 32/2002, 20 December. The previous law was approved in 2000, under the socialist government, with the votes of communists (Lei de Bases do Sistema de Solidariedade e Segurança Social: Lei No. 17/2000, 8 August).

[6] The insertion plans are associated with another basic principle: the principle of social inclusion. 'The principle of social inclusion is characterised by the active, preventive and individualised nature of the actions developed under the system in order to eliminate the causes of social marginalisation and social exclusion and to promote human dignity' (Art. 13).

We must recognise that both the European Employment Strategy and the later European Strategy for Inclusion have exerted a strong influence on official discourse about activation throughout this period and positively influenced the abovementioned regimes.

Portugal has enormously increased activation since the first NAP in 1998, principally in relation to Guidelines 1 to 3. According to an official report published in 1999, expenditure on active measures as a share of the total cost of employment policy had grown consistently and was then close to 50% (MTS 1999). Training, subsidised jobs, self-employment schemes and insertion programmes for Guaranteed Minimum Income earners are the main instruments now being used for activation. Preventive action against unemployment and an early-start approach to employment have been provided by two new programmes clearly inspired by Guidelines 1 and 2.[7]

The Employment Action Plan for the period 2003-2006[8] illustrates the importance given to the implementation of programmes that increase employability, with a particular focus on unemployed persons experiencing greater difficulties in gaining insertion and on employed persons at risk of losing their jobs. In this document, the government recognises that Portugal has developed activation principles in several domains of social policy: the cases of social insertion income, the accumulation of part-time work with partial unemployment benefit, unemployment benefit itself, and so on. However, it also stresses the importance of broadening these principles. Early school leavers, people with disabilities, the unemployed and inactive seeking a job, low-qualified workers and the long-term unemployed, immigrants and ethnic minorities, as well as other groups with low labour market participation (active members of single-parent families, older workers, beneficiaries of the Guaranteed Minimum Income Scheme) are to be sought out and targeted for active and preventive programmes aimed at their inclusion.

Accordingly, a strategic axis of the Plan (Axis No. 3) is an action programme to eliminate and prevent unemployment and poverty traps and to promote labour market participation by those who are most excluded or marginalised (women, older workers, people with disabilities).

In the same vein, the Portuguese Action Plan for Inclusion (2001-2003)[9] embodies all the previous basic principles, such as responsi-

---

[7] *Inserjovem*, an integral follow-up project for young people, and *Reage*, a similar project for adult unemployed.

[8] Resolução do Conselho de Ministros No. 185/2003.

[9] Resolução do Conselho de Ministros No. 91/2001.

bilisation, activation and contractualisation (Resolução 91/2001). For those identified as socially excluded, the Plan provides that they will be contacted by the local agencies of social assistance, within one year, in order to enter into a social insertion agreement, adjusted to personal circumstances and involving a large set of measures covering the areas of education and training, housing, health, social protection, basic income and access to social services. But all these measures are conditional on individual commitment to perform the actions considered necessary for successful labour market inclusion, such as Job Centre registration for those aged between 16 and 65.

Moving on to target groups, activation policies address specific categories of people and as a rule each programme defines its own clientele. Given the number of activation programmes with different priorities, it is not easy to identify target groups and to rank them in terms of priorities. Constant changes in programmes make the task more difficult.

Activation measures may be oriented to labour market inclusion or to social inclusion. There are two main strategic programmes defining employment and welfare policies and identifying target groups on the basis of this distinction: the PNE (Portuguese Action Plan for Employment) and the PNAI (Portuguese Action Plan for Insertion).

Unemployed people are one of the main categories targeted by the PNE, but several sub-categories are given different levels of priority. According to the Programme for Employment and Social Protection (PEPS 2003), which regulates incentives for job creation and geographical mobility,[10] the incentives must focus on persons in economic difficulties or with reduced access to the labour market: young people, the long-term unemployed, unemployed aged over 45, and young unemployed with higher and secondary education.[11]

According to the PNAI, all disadvantaged social groups should be activated through contractualised personal or family plans for social insertion. However, the scale and diversity of the cases led the Ministry of Social Security to establish priorities in accordance with three basic criteria: (i) accessibility of resources; (ii) vulnerability to exclusion and (iii) degree of urgency (ISSS 2004).

---

[10] DL. No. 168/2003, 20 July.
[11] It must be remembered that the priorities of PNE 1998 concentrated on the short-term unemployed due to the preventive approach adopted by Guidelines 1 and 2.

The Institutional Setting of Active Policies

The Role of the State

Compared with the relatively weak institutions of civil society, the role of the state in Portugal has been strong since the 1974 overthrow of the dictatorship by the military, with a highly regulatory role, including widespread nationalisations in 1975 (Santos 1993). Because of the concern to overcome the previous lack of institutions representing the interests of different sectors of civil society, the state has promoted and institutionalised collective agents, thereby reinforcing its own regulatory position. Paradoxically, although the relative balance of public and private power has changed since the early 1980s, the central regulatory role of the state was reinforced when Portugal joined the European Union in 1986 and adopted its wide-ranging regulations as part of the *acquis communautaire*.

In the period following the overthrown of the dictatorship in 1974, and before joining the EU, the regulatory role of the state was focussed on the institutionalisation of trade unions and workers' rights and on the construction of a public system of social protection that would respond to the expectations of the population. In regard to labour disputes, the inability of the social partners to find negotiated solutions, due to the weakness of the employers caused by the nationalisations of 1975, as well as social pressure from workers, led to their resolution by administrative means – through the mediation of the Ministry of Labour and through arbitration imposed on the parties.

During the first half of the 1980s the effects of a deep economic crisis and the need to control public expenditure imposed by the IMF led to a reorientation of state intervention in order to restore the confidence of investors and to attract new capital. Gradually, the previous pro-labour orientation in policies changed to a pro-employer orientation, favouring the emergence of an industrial bourgeoisie capable of adjusting to the new market conditions. In broad terms, these policies operated through the concession of incentives to enterprises, the re-privatisation of a large part of public enterprises, and an increased focus on flexibility in labour legislation and wage demands. However, such a change was possible only because of the closure of firms, wage arrears, redundancies, and a general rise in the unemployment rate that dramatically weakened workers' ability to put pressure on the state and reduced their resistance to the deregulatory measures demanded by employers. The creation in 1984 of the Permanent Council for Social Concertation (CPCS), composed of representatives of the government, employers and trade unions, neither substantially altered the government's room for manoeuvre nor reduced the regulatory role of the state.[12]

Trade Unions

There is a clear contrast between the views of workers and employers on the role of the state. Employers argue for the liberalisation of the labour market and demand from the state the necessary reforms to guarantee the viability of private initiative (including the flexibilisation of labour law). The trade unions try to maintain employment levels and to promote the enforcement of labour laws and the development of policies to counteract the tendency towards job insecurity.

For the CGTP, a pro-communist trade union confederation, 'unemployment is the main factor in social exclusion, and job insecurity represents the first step in that direction'.[13] The CGTP stresses that the gap between levels of employment in Portugal and those in the EU is increasing: Portuguese workers earn one quarter of the European average, their hours are much longer, social protection is inferior, there are many more work-related accidents, the level of education and training is much lower, and the information and consultation of workers in enterprises is almost non-existent (CGTP 1996a, 3).

The other trade union confederation, UGT, closer to the Socialist and Social-Democratic parties, shares the idea that job security and stability must be defended, but is more open to specific modes of temporary work and part-time work corresponding not only to the demands of firms but also to the diversity of workers' time requirements (UGT 1996, 7).

In terms of employment policies, the CGTP is opposed to job subsidies, arguing that it benefits firms, but not workers (CGTP 1996b, 21) and discriminates against workers (CGTP 1996c, 35). For the UGT, active and passive policies should complement one another, but while in the European Community active measures for the reintegration of the unemployed are favoured to the detriment of passive subsidy measures, in Portugal, given the low level of unemployment benefits, it is not possible to reduce or downgrade these measures (UGT 1996, 22). Arguing that the two policies are complementary, the UGT supports

---

[12] Several other agencies have this tripartite nature: the Instituto de Emprego e Formação Profissional (IEFP), the Observatory of Employment and Training, the National System of Certification, the Institute for Training Innovation (INOFOR) and the National Commission for Apprenticeship.

[13] Quoted from interviews made within the framework of a research project on globalisation (Hespanha and Valadas 2002).

passive employment measures whenever active measures do not produce the conditions for job creation.

The social partners were invited to support the first PNE and have been contributing to the preparation, development and follow-up of the process of implementing the EU guidelines for the PNE, while claiming a more central role in its implementation and in the evaluation of results (MTS 1998a, 66). Through an unprecedented initiative involving the social partners, a Joint Declaration attached to the PNE was supported by them in the CPCS. The terms on which each partner would be involved and the degree to which they would be responsible for the achievement of the Plan's goals were nonetheless rather unclear. In particular, the social partners expressed no view on activation policies, while recommending investment in education, training and lifelong learning.

The social partners nonetheless consented to the philosophy of the Guidelines and showed a willingness to negotiate on subjects on which they were divided (for instance, the development of lifelong learning programmes) through a tripartite work group established in 2000 for PNE follow-up. This was especially relevant in the negotiation of a set of legislative initiatives in the domain of labour and in consideration of the role to be played by the public employment service (PES) in the launching of the PNE.

While the social partners made such a strong commitment in principle to the PNE, there were significant divergences at the level of implementation. This was the case with regard to programmes aimed at upgrading employed workers' qualifications: the trade unions were highly critical of the type of intervention or involvement advocated by the employers.[14] In turn, the representatives of the employers' confederations were very critical of the recommendations on training, which they claimed did not meet the needs of firms.[15]

In effect, while there may have been an underlying consensus on the need for education and training, and a mutual recognition of the importance of knowledge, abilities and skills, the social partners had different

---

[14] 'The employers' discourse is very retrograde in relation to lifelong learning. They consider work time as only the time dedicated to production; work time dedicated to training and improving qualifications is something that does not enter into their discourse. Lifelong learning is not easy to develop with such an attitude' (Hespanha and Valadas 2002).

[15] 'We are all offering hours and hours of training, [but] the majority of the profiles needed are not met by those courses. Therefore we may be training people who in the next two years will be dismissed' (Hespanha and Valadas 2002) (Interview No. IV, 10).

interests in and perspectives on training and both prioritised their own agendas.

Within the EU, the Portuguese social partners are debating the future of the EES in the institutional forum open to their participation, namely the Employment Committee, where social partners join together with representatives of the Council, the Commission and the European Employers' Federation. In the opinion of one of the trade union confederations, dialogue between the employers' associations and the trade union confederations at the European level has never existed. On the contrary, 'the European employers' representatives (who initially appeared to be more progressive than the Portuguese employer confederations) are currently involved in a process of boycotting some of the initiatives proposed by the workers in the framework of the EES'.[16]

Local Roles

The Portuguese Action Plans also stress the need for decentralised initiatives by municipalities and other local collective agents (mostly NGOs). New instances of regional/local regulation emerged or reinforced their role associated with EES: that was the case with the Territorial Pacts for Employment, the Regional Employment Networks and the Social Network. Although some disparities resulted from the implementation of these agencies, this has not offset the efforts made to convert them into strong partnerships able to ameliorate the implementation of PNE and PNAI[17] programmes. In general, decentralisation means changing roles and responsibilities in the management of welfare state arrangements. However, in Portugal this process has so far not led to a privatisation of activation services through for-profit companies. Employment services – job centres and vocational training centres – are still in the hands of IEFP, the Institute for Employment and Professional Training, a tripartite managed body with the status of a public service.

---

[16] Hespanha and Valadas (2002): Interview I: 14.

[17] National Action Plan for Inclusion. In the case of the minimum income scheme, Local Follow-up Commissions were created at the municipal level; the Rede Social – a partnership intended to coordinate programmes for combating poverty and social exclusion – was established at the same level; and the MSE – Social Market for Employment – has been strongly associated with Networks, Pacts and Regional Employment Plans.

The Cultural and Ideological Background of Active Policies

The set of values and the cultural framework underlying activation programmes are not easy to discern. The explicit motives presented in official documents rarely coincide with underlying motives because the rhetoric of political discourse is concerned with conforming to EU praxis. Such 'political correctness' implies broad consensual arguments and exclusion of more sensitive issues. This appears clearly when we analyse the discourse of a particular social force (whether a political party, a trade union or an employers' association) in different contexts: inside or outside their 'walls', in an oral or a written form, in electoral campaigns or during parliamentary debates, and so on. Presentations of motives in legislation are carefully filtered in order to nuance strong ideological inspiration. Official documents tend to present activation as a technical rather than an ideological issue. Thus, words, whether spoken or written, cannot be taken at face value.

A deconstructivist approach has to be taken to unveil the motives beneath, behind or beyond official explanations. This approach involves a search for the history of policy programmes, comprising an intensive scrutiny of key events (political debates, compromises), social forces (ideologies, political power) and social contexts related to the process of designing and implementing the programme.

An example of one of the more controversial social policy programmes in Portugal – the Guaranteed Minimum Income Scheme (GMI) – can be used to illustrate how that approach may operate.[18]

The various political forces display strong disagreement towards the GMI based on conflicting sets of values, such as social inclusion (perceived either as combating exclusion or a subsidy for those unwilling to work), individual autonomy (either the right to find a job which is fulfilling or preventing dependency), equity (reciprocity of rights and obligations or the right to offer the going wage), individual responsibility (either as an employee or an employer) and costs (either the social costs to individuals and families of unemployment, or the costs to employers and taxpayers of offsetting it). The ideological dimensions of such differing views represent a continuum which nonetheless polarises different ideas on emancipation and regulation.[19] Emancipation equates with promotion of individual autonomy, the participation of policy

---

[18] This is also the programme in which activation has assumed its most mandatory configuration.

[19] This dual nature of social policies may be expressed in different but close terms, like 'social integration' *vs.* 'social discipline' (Larson and Mayland 2005) or 'republican solidarity' *vs.* 'rights with obligations' (Barbier 2005).

Reshaping Welfare States and Activation Regimes in Europe

takers in the design of programmes and the choice of insertion goals, and with mutual trust between state and clients. Regulation equates with promotion of responsibility, combating passivity, control of obligations, sanctioning of non-compliance and mutual distrust.

The divergences appear quite clear when we compare the views of right- and left-wing parties, employers' associations and trade unions, examine the discourse produced by those forces during electoral campaigns or parliamentary debates, and use internal documents instead of official statements.

The GMI scheme was created in 1996 when the socialists returned to government after 12 years of liberal rule.[20] Portugal was then one of the three EU member states which had not yet followed Council Recommendation 92/441 (CE 1992). The scheme was well accepted by Portuguese society and became a cornerstone of the socialist political legacy. Nevertheless, detractors insinuated that the GMI was used by the government as a political tool to reinforce clientism instead of a programme to alleviate poverty. For five years growing criticism from both the parties to the right of the socialists and conservative sectors of Portuguese society exaggerated the negative side-effects of the scheme's implementation, claiming fraud, dependency and laziness. An audit by the Court of Accounting confirming the existence of some irregularities in the first two years of the GMI has been widely used to support these general claims.

After the fall of the socialist government towards the end of 2001, the liberal (PSD) and the conservative (CDS/PP) parties, both very critical of the scheme, announced their intention to undertake profound reform in order to change its basic philosophy. Again, during the 2002 electoral campaign, the GMI scheme became one of the most controversial issues, and again the ideological differences came to the surface. The CDS/PP leader often expressed the opinion that the GMI was for people who did not want to work.[21] The new law, prepared by the governmental coalition formed by PSD and CDS/PP, was approved

---

[20] During that period, the socialist party, in opposition, proposed to the Parliament the creation of a minimum income scheme, but the proposal was rejected. The registers of the debates are crucial to grasp the main arguments used on the occasion to support or to reject the socialist proposal. The high cost of the policy and the imperatives of citizenship were the two main competing arguments.

[21] 'Once given to a 20-year-old person, the GMI, instead of stimulating him/her to work and overcome difficulties, becomes a kind of financing of laziness' (*Jornal Nova Guarda*, 28/02/2002). 'We are going to stop the abuse and fraud […] with us the GMI, such as it exists, will finish' because 'we do not want to give incentives to laziness, but to work'. Another priority was 'to give more help to those who have worked all their life' (http://www.cdsppacores.com/contents/noticias/notic30.htm).

by Parliament in 2003, but vetoed by the President and only published after some amendments introduced by Parliament.[22] The GMI scheme was rebaptised as Social Insertion Income with only minor amendments to the previous legislation.

The amendments referred to the transitory and subsidiary nature of the benefit, a more restricted set of conditions for entitlement, and heavier sanctions for non-compliance, abuse or fraud. The new regulation makes it very clear that benefits depend on the contractualisation of an insertion programme. Among a large range of possible obligations, the benefit recipient must accept being activated in a number of different ways: through a job placement or a vocational training action; an educational or apprenticeship course; an occupational programme aiming to ease labour market integration or the fulfilment of social, communitarian or environmental needs; some work within the institutions of social solidarity; self-employment initiatives.

The official explanation for the changes was very cautious, taking into account the opposition to them. As the Minister of Social Security said on presenting them to Parliament:

> It is with a constructive spirit that we are now proposing the creation of a social insertion income scheme, in order to deepen the social and family focus of the measure, and at the same time to confer greater effectiveness, more transparency and more requirements in the attribution and control of the benefit. Let me be clear: the social insertion income scheme was created not to save money, much less to save money in relation to the poor and disadvantaged. On the contrary, its philosophy and rules are oriented to spending our money better on those who are more in need.

This did not prevent considerable related rhetoric, such as: 'What the Government is proposing is not a simple change of name or an alteration of detail. It is a change in philosophy, namely in what we mean by the terms "social" and "insertion" in the name of the scheme itself, instead of a mere "unaccountable guaranteeism"' (Minister of Social Security, during the presentation of the bill to Parliament) (Diário da AR, I Serie – No. 020, 15 June 2002).

This rhetoric was echoed by other political leaders of the coalition:

> Contrary to the orientation of the previous government, which followed an assistance-oriented (in other words, a model developing assistance provisions, targeted on the uninsured unemployed, in neglect of the insured – for instance, an inappropriate level and coverage of unemployment benefits) model, the majority and the present government prefer an integrative model, where social support functions as a second line after the exhaustion of active

---

[22] Law No. 13/2003, 21 May.

integration attempts. Of course, we are not going to renounce our responsibilities in the distribution of welfare, but we prefer that those in need be encouraged to re-integrate in the world of work. (Diário da AR, Debate Parlamentar do Decreto No. 34/IX)

More explicitly, the leader of the CDS parliamentary group gave expression to the new philosophy of distrusting recipients and combating fraud.

> I remind you that the previous law was known as the 'three Fs law', meaning not only *Férias, Feriados e Faltas*,[23] but also *Falhas, Fraudes e Fraquezas*.[24] [...] I feel that it will constitute an improvement in combating fraud, as well as in control [despite the government's scarce means]. Social workers, who have the obligation to follow up cases, often complain that they are subject to coercion, that they are easily deceived and that they do not have the conditions for following up. (MP Telmo Correia, Diário da AR, Debate Parlamentar do Decreto No. 34/IX)

Left-wing parties agreed on the existence of a follow-up problem, but they associated it with the lack of human resources allocated to the scheme. However, restricting access to the scheme because of shortages was unacceptable to them. In the same vein, the then Prime Minister – now President of the EU Commission – claimed that 'in some cases it [the scheme] operated more as an incentive to idleness and laziness, not respecting the intended objective: social reintegration' (Diário da AR, Debate Parlamentar do Decreto No. 34/IX).

So far, we have stressed the importance of ideological differences – namely those of political parties – in the evaluation of political programmes. However, some ideas emerging during the debate on minimum income schemes show clearly that there are also underlying economic, social and cultural issues. The cultural differences reflect opposing views on work and leisure, rights and duties, and the relative roles of state and society.

This has to be understood in context. In the mid-1970s, at the time of the overthrow of the dictatorship, Portugal had been in stasis for 45 years. While the rest of Western Europe, except Spain, had modernised, two out of four Portuguese workers were still in agriculture. Urbanisation and the outflow of the young from rural areas was dramatic, with a construction and employment boom aided by Structural Funds equivalent to 3% of GDP, and new, though temporary, foreign direct investment. However, this process excluded the most remote and less educated sectors of the population. It also did not mean successful

---

[23] 'Vacations, holidays and absences'.
[24] 'Imperfections, frauds and failure' [of the government to do what has to be done].

adaptation by either indigenous private firms or public institutions. Hence, in the wake of Portugal's acceptance of the Maastricht debt and deficit criteria for a single currency, governments reined in public investment and expenditure. With the expectation that most of Central Europe would join the EU after the fall of the Berlin Wall, several foreign firms relocated there or, after downsizing and de-layering, went home. Portugal was increasingly at the margins of Europe. The transition both to democracy and to Europe faltered. Expectations were unfulfilled.

However, to the extent that the strong modernising trend over three decades in Portugal could not be absorbed by those unprepared for urbanisation, a predominantly rural work ethic remained. Consistent with a still widespread Catholicism, this blamed the poor for not being diligent enough in meeting their needs, stressed particularistic rather than universal values, supported individual charity and altruism rather than general welfare, and atavistically mistrusted the state. Such values collided with modern ideals of social citizenship and a welfare state. Added to them was a mix of neo-liberal ideas deifying the market and free choice, distrusting the state as welfare provider and believing that social problems will be solved as long as the economy is healthy.

Taking the notion of 'worklessness', many distinct meanings can be found across Portuguese society. In rural areas dominated by a peasant culture it would be understood first of all as a loss of (productive) time, then perhaps as a sign of bad conduct, even laziness. In these contexts, work is viewed as a decisive instrument of survival, while a special *ethics of life* postulates an intensive and wise use of work.[25] Moreover, in an economy based on reciprocity, someone who gets paid without any obligation to work or to give something in return is looked at askance, even as unacceptable. Since peasants have developed a precise moral sense of equity, any social provision that benefits those seen as less diligent or well-to-do becomes subject to criticism and a source of unrest. This is the case, for instance, with the strong objection that many people living in remote rural areas express towards the demands for free housing or other facilities coming from poor urban families.

The welfare state developed late in Portugal and has never reached levels of protection similar to those of northern EU countries. The authoritarian regime that ruled the country for nearly half a century adopted a model of social regulation adverse to the development of

---

[25] The pre-capitalist dominant classes were accused of being idle in the sense that they did not live from their own work, but from the work of those they controlled through land or capital ownership. However, the idleness of the elites was not seen as problem, only the idleness of workers.

comprehensive social policies. It staked itself, rather, on familism, a conservative ideology supported by the rural condition of a large part of the population, amplified by a deep-rooted and anti-liberal Catholicism, which permitted the maintenance of social support based on family and community solidarity and on weak expectations in relation to consumption and quality of life. It was only after the establishment of democracy in 1974 that the first systematic programmes aimed at the construction of a welfare state were developed.

The principles of social justice and equity introduced by a welfare system led to a slow but steady progression from reliance on the family to universal citizenship. During the period of democratic transition, strong and mostly urban social movements joined forces with the state with the objective of fulfilling new aspirations, in terms of housing, transportation, childcare facilities, and so on. These aspirations were legitimised by the state itself as rights sanctioned by the Constitution (Hespanha *et al.* 1997). Despite the scarcity of state support, these widespread solidarities had a fundamental role in the improvement of the living conditions of the Portuguese population. Joining the EEC in 1986 reinforced this process of building a modern system of social protection, the progress of welfare state programmes representing a real effort to extend social services and a consequence of the 'obvious need to build the legitimacy of the new democratic governments' (Laparra and Aguilar 1996, 97).

How far has this trend of expanding social citizenship and universalism changed people's minds and displaced conservatism as a distinguishing cultural feature associated with authoritarianism and Catholicism?

Recent studies on social attitudes have shown that there is widespread support among Portuguese people for welfare state policies, but opinions differ on rights and duties. One study (Cabral *et al.* 2003), using unemployment benefit and minimum income as reference policies, shows that 37% of the population consider entitlement to these policies as an unconditional right based on social justice; 47% consider them a conditional right dependent on the willingness of the beneficiaries to work in return; and only 16% believe that those policies reduce the willingness to work. This study confirms the conclusion of a previous one (Cabral 1995) that social policies are widely appreciated, although there are many criticisms of their implementation. Another finding is that opinions on social policies are influenced mostly by education and political preferences. Therefore, the negative opinion about the effect of social policies on the willingness to work increases in inverse proportion to level of education; opinions about policies as unconditional rights vary positively with levels of education; while the idea that the welfare state must get something in return from welfare programme beneficiaries seems to be stronger at both ends of the educational scale (basic and higher). The effect of political preferences on attitudes and opinions is also revealing. The idea that policies correspond to unconditional rights is clearly associated with the left, while the idea of a policy trap is associated with the right. The perception of rights as conditional seems to be stronger in the moderate left- and right-wing parties (the PS and PSD), which have governed alternately since the 1980s.[26]

In effect, conservatism in Portugal is associated with those strata of the population which are less modernised or less educated, and with right-wing parties and Catholicism. These strata tend to see welfare policies as subsidiary to individual responsibility, prefer paternalistic aid to citizenship-based solidarity, distinguish between deserving and undeserving poor, and emphasise obligations more than rights. As has been noted,

> most NGOs, trade unions and religious institutions have blamed the activation of social policies for many of the negative changes that have occurred in the labour market – precariousness, the deterioration of work quality, the aggravation of exclusion, the 'working poor' – while not taking into account other plausible determinants of the changes in Western societies, such as globalisation or the accelerated dissemination of the new information technologies. (Silva 2004)

Conservative thinking is very suspicious of redistributive policies, assuming that subsidies will inevitably lead to work phobia and dependency. For that reason, activation as a work incentive is considered an obligation: those who benefit from welfare must be prepared to give something in return.

To analyse the real impact of conservatism on activation in Portugal we must consider that activation is a rather open process in the sense that it can be appropriated by different political and ideological projects.[27] Appropriation may operate at three distinct levels and become visible in three distinct *loci*: at the level of basic principles the specific *locus* is public debate (electoral campaigns); at the level of legislation the specific *locus* is particular policy-making institutions (parliament, government); and at the level of programme implementation the specific

---

[26] Taking into account the activation trend in the EU, it is to be expected that parties with governmental experience will disseminate this perspective among their members and supporters.

[27] As Jean-Claude Barbier puts it: 'Very different value choices fit in the common framework' (Barbier 2005).

locus is administrative agencies for the management of programmes (job centres).

The introduction of the minimum income scheme shed some light on the first two levels. Little attention, however, has been paid to level three. There are many relevant aspects in the implementation process while, as has been argued, 'a great deal of the steering policy is now in the hands of "implementers"' (Hudson and Lowe 2004, 204). The opportunity to exercise discretion also risks allowing decision-makers' political, ideological and cultural biases to penetrate the scheme.

A common feature of active welfare policies is the individualised approach, that is, a method of designing the programme in such a way that it adjusts to the particular profile of the user in terms of their needs, abilities and expectations. This *intuitu personae* approach requires close contact of the provider with the user, a deep knowledge of their profile and a reasonable room to manoeuvre to design the most suitable programme. This is why providers who implement these policies are given relatively wide discretion. However, as already mentioned, discretion is the main point of access for political and ideological bias. Whatever those responsible may say, discretion is strongly influenced by norms and values which may be unconscious or unintended but nonetheless result in bureaucratic, ethical or political bias. This occurs especially when there is a lack of clear guidelines or administrative criteria for adjusting programmes to new situations, and when new evaluation procedures are not available. In these circumstances, there is a tendency for the assumptions, personal values and beliefs of professionals to dominate outcomes. A study of the minimum income scheme (Hespanha and Gomes 2001) shows that clients frequently claim that social workers decide on the basis of personal moral judgements.

Allowing for this, it cannot be said that activation programmes have been influenced by general ideological or cultural principles. However, those EU programmes which have been developed since the Lisbon Summit in 2000 are very much exposed to ideological and cultural influence by political parties, social partners and local bureaucracy. The policies for social inclusion have not lost general legitimacy, but are exposed to assault by conflicting ideologies. In this sense, it is not the legislative framework which is determinative but implementation. The recent experience of the RSI scheme made clear how easy it is to block the implementation of a programme without having to reform the law, merely by manipulating formal proceedings.

Types of Activation

Different criteria can be used for typologies of activation. Some of these may address more general problems, such as the basic philosophy underlying activation policies. Others concern more formal aspects of the design and implementation of activation programmes (Serrano Pascual 2004, 501).

Beginning with a basic criterion, based on the *degree of coercion* imposed on activated people, two main types of policies can be distinguished: first, policies under which activation is imposed on policy-takers (workfare); second, policies under which activation is merely encouraged.

The first case includes some passive policies and some active labour market policies that are conditional on individual behaviour, such as taking a job or a training course, in the context of an insertion plan.[28] Examples of these policies are unemployment benefits that may be conditional on accepting a temporary job (for example, under the occupational programme or the Enterprise Entry programme) or a training course (under *Integrar*/measure No. 1); the minimum income provision that is conditional on the formalisation of an insertion contract; and some activation schemes that may be conditional on the acceptance of a personal plan for employment by young and adult unemployed under the *Inserjovem* and *Reage* programmes.

The second case – unconditional activation policies – includes a large set of activation programmes, such as job placement in the private or public sector or in NGOs,[29] sheltered employment, incentives to employers,[30] incentives to workers,[31] training in a work con-

---

[28] This conditionality is clearly expressed in the Law on Social Security: 'The law foresees, as a condition of the granting of solidarity subsystem benefits, the assumption by the beneficiaries, when adjusted, of a contractualised commitment to insertion and its effective fulfilment' (Art. 60).

[29] 'Plano nacional de estágios' (National plan for apprenticeship, since 1997), 'Programa de Promoção do Emprego Temporário na Administração Pública' (Programme for Job Promotion in Public Administration, targeted at youngsters and LTU, since 2001).

[30] 'Majoração dos incentivos à contratação de mulheres desempregadas com mais de 45 anos' (improvement of incentives for hiring unemployed women over 45 years of age) since 1993; 'Programa Estímulo à Oferta de Emprego' (Programme for stimulating job supply) (Portaria No. 196-A/2001, 10 March).

[31] Incentives for the geographical and occupational mobility of unemployed persons (since 1987); 'Pagamento Global das Prestações de Desemprego' (Capitalisation of unemployment benefits, under the 'Regime de Prestações de Desemprego', approved in 1999); CPE (Programme for the creation of self-employment, targeted on subsidised unemployed persons, since 1994); Job Clubs (since 1993) and UNIVAS (Units

text,[32] self-employment, education and training,[33] integrated programmes,[34] and incentives to older people.[35]

Regarding entitlements, the trend in the last few years has been to increase levels of insertion (from insertion in the labour market to increased employability) and to enlarge both areas of participation (work, education, training, lifelong learning, apprenticeship, self-employment, and so on) and target groups (young people, women, older women, older employed, long-term unemployed, recently unemployed, handicapped people, and so on).

The level of 'generosity' of policies is easier to measure in the case of passive policies combining some activation schemes, because the remuneration (in the form of wages, grants or scholarships) may be related to forgone benefit. In general, the 'attractiveness' of schemes depends on the level of income supplement accorded to the benefit, although in general that supplement is kept at a modest level. For instance, in the case of the Occupational Programme for the Unemployed the pay for a new job is equivalent to unemployment benefit plus a supplement of 20% and monetary compensation for food and insurance costs.[36] In the case of training courses for the unemployed a scholarship is granted corresponding to the minimum national wage (MNW) for those seeking a new job, and a supplement of 25% of MNW for first job seekers. On top of this, there is an allowance for transportation, housing, food and insurance. But there also are other criteria.[37]

---

for the insertion of youngsters in an economic activity, since 1996); 'Programa Estímulo à Oferta de Emprego'; partial unemployment benefit for unemployed workers who have a part-time job (RPD, DL119/99).

[32] 'Programa Formação-emprego' (Programme training in a job, for the unemployed, beneficiaries of the minimum income scheme and the handicapped, since 1993); training scholarships (since 1994).

[33] 'Qualificação Inicial para Jovens' (Basic qualifications for young people with low levels of schooling under POEFDS, since 2001).

[34] 'Programmea Integrado de Combate ao Desemprego de Longa Duração' (Integrated programme to combat long-term unemployment, since 1998).

[35] 'Regime de flexibilidade das pensões de velhice' (Regime of flexible old age pensions, since 2001).

[36] The unemployment benefit (contributory) equals *grosso modo* 65% of the wage income and cannot be more than three times the minimum wage. The unemployment social benefit (means tested) equals *grosso modo* the minimum social benefit.

[37] Armindo Silva distinguishes three main categories of activation policies: (i) those based on the principle of reciprocity; (ii) those based on the concept of insertion trajectory; and (iii) those based on the 'make-work-pay' principle (Silva 2004, 9).

Degree of Individualisation

Some activation programmes, like the minimum income schemes *Inserjovem* and *Reage*, are very strict on the individualisation principle. They presuppose the negotiation with the policy-taker of a personal plan for insertion and its subsequent contractualisation. Other programmes are more universal in the sense that it is enough to belong to a pre-defined group (unemployed with low levels of schooling; women above a certain age; employed in an economic sector in crisis) in order to be entitled. The experience with the personal plans has been very fruitful since the introduction of the Guaranteed Minimum Income scheme in 1996, and has been abundantly studied. These studies have shown the difficulties of devising personal plans due to the different expectations, values and education of professionals and policy users, the amount of time and energy needed to elaborate a good plan, the costs involved in meetings and visits in order to get a reasonable knowledge of the claimant's situation, and the limited means available to meet the needs of sustainable inclusion.

The 'simplification' of the negotiation process also caused an overload of pending cases and resource constraints. The Institute for Employment and Vocational Training (IEFP) did not significantly reinforce its staff after launching the *Inserjovem* and *Reage* initiatives. An assessment study published in 2000 confirms that staff shortages and overloads were causing considerable delays in processing cases (MTS 2000, 22).

User Participation

The new approaches are likely to favour a more active role for users in the design of policies, a more diverse and flexible offer of policy instruments, a less asymmetrical power balance between policy agents and clients, and more accountability in the administration of programmes. But they also imply more discretion in actual implementation.

In broad terms, active social policies endow users with more autonomy and discretion in choosing their plans for improving employability or getting an adequate job. The personal plan for employment (PPE), under the *Inserjovem* and *Reage* programmes, is no longer simply decided and allocated by job centre professionals or counsellors, but is rather an outcome of negotiations between the client and job centre agents. Furthermore, a PPE is the result of – and is preceded by – a personalised analysis of the client's situation and environment in terms of their past employment trajectory, capacity for improving their qualifications, willingness to accept dramatic changes in life, and endowment of social capital for the purpose of making better use of labour market opportunities.

User participation in the definition of the particular activity suggested by the employment services is mandatory under those programmes which involve a negotiated individual plan (Minimum Income, *Inserjovem* and *Reage*). In other cases of activation, such as Occupational Programmes for the unemployed, there is no negotiation or other form of participation. Unconditional activation measures are heterogeneous from this point of view. Some of them consist in pre-defined activities (for example, training courses) which are not individually customised; others allow for a reasonable degree of individualisation.

The outcome is a policy mix of traditional and new forms of intervention, combining active and passive approaches; a dissonance between discourse and practice (political or legal rhetoric supporting new approaches versus local bureaucracy continuing in a traditional way); and a philosophy of empowering the weakest citizens contrasting with a presumption against those in need.

User participation is significantly dependent on the culture of the institution, the human resources available and the professionals' discretion. All these factors inhibit participation, which Portuguese law includes in the basic principles of social policies.[38]

Balance between Rights and Obligations

Throughout Europe, criticism of 'passive' welfare state policies has come from different directions (neoliberals, conservatives, the *third way*). According to Giddens, old-style social democracy presumed ever fuller implementation of social rights rather than a balance between rights and obligations, and, though he makes the claim without supporting evidence, produced very negative effects on social solidarity (Giddens 1998).

However, progress towards activation in Portugal has shown a mix rather than a balance between rights and obligations. All the major legal instruments that regulate activation in Portugal refer, in one way or another, to policy users' obligations and responsibility. This applies to the official discourse. Moreover, sanctions for non-compliance are also provided.

---

[38] The Law on Social Security defines the principle of participation as 'the involvement of the interested parties in the definition, planning and management of the system and in the follow-up and evaluation of its functioning' (Art. 19, Law 32/2002, 20 December).

It is also noticeable that some activation programmes are more compelling than others. Even among those activation programmes that are considered more coercive (see above), differences still exist in their capacity to compel users to fulfil obligations. For instance, if we compare sanctions for non-compliance with insertion plans, it is striking that while under the minimum income scheme beneficiaries lose their benefit, under *Inserjovem* and *Reage* users lose only the assistance provided by the job centre, and only for a short period. The ability to compel users to comply with activation depends on the magnitude of the benefits to which users are entitled.

Degree of Discretion

Discretion in active labour market policies relates to the room to manoeuvre that professionals enjoy in tailoring programmes to particular policy users. Sometimes the range of tools available is very large and the activation scheme very inclusive. That is the case with the minimum income policies *Inserjovem* and *Reage*, under which an individual insertion plan is a prerequisite of activation. Discretion is central to the design of the plans and for follow-up on their implementation. In other cases intervention is predefined – for example, training courses – and discretion does not apply.

Understanding the Portuguese experience also requires a more general context. Discretion is associated with regimes of authority within organisations. In a Weberian bureaucratic regime, discretion is used within certain limits imposed by the organisation's goals and guided by objective criteria justified by those goals. But other regimes of authority may coexist with a bureaucratic regime and induce some deviations in this model of discretion.[39] It may then be subject to different goals and different limits. This occurs, for instance, when a very demanding insertion plan under the minimum income scheme is used to discipline an 'undeserving' poor family or to justify an intentional subsequent withdrawal of the benefit, or when an unemployed person under the occupational programme is placed in an unsuitable job because the promoter (state service or NGO) needs low cost labour for its normal activities.[40] In contexts of resource constraints, whether or not linked to

---

[39] One of the four structural elements that Santos uses to characterise the Portuguese welfare state is precisely 'a state bureaucracy that has not internalised social rights as citizens' entitlement rather than as state benevolence' (Santos 1999, 7).

[40] In a study based on the experience of users we confirmed the existence of some distortions in the implementation and even the instrumentalisation of this programme. Often, promoting organisations use POCs to recruit cheap labour for 'normal' activities or for new activities that would be performed in any case. For

the fiscal crisis of the welfare state, discretion is expected to be used to differentiate among clients according to dominant values or subjective preconceptions, as Michael Lipsky has shown (Lipsky 1980, 114).

Quality of the Action

Nonetheless, the information available for evaluating the quality of programmes is scarce. Apart from some isolated studies on minimum income, occupational programmes and *Inserjovem* and *Reage* programmes, there has been no systematic and accurate evaluation of the quality of active labour market and activation programmes. The national training and employment agency IEFP announced the launch of a follow-up system for several programmes based on interviews with policy users, but no results have been published so far.[41] The main official source of information available is a study of the impact of EES in Portugal, published in 2003 and based on a number of different sources, which includes a volume on active labour market policies (CIDES 2003).

The conclusions of this EES study on the efficiency of activation policies refer to professional apprenticeship (*Estágios Profissionais*) as a success story. Success is measured by the high levels of insertion into the labour market of highly qualified young people and by the presumed gain in terms of high qualifications of the firms concerned. The other cases considered to be best practice are the *Inserjovem* and *Reage* programmes. Two main reasons are adduced: first, the positive effect of activation on job placement; second, the positive effect on those public employment services that adopt a more active, preventive and personalised approach (CIDES 2003, 139).

---

instance, a Health Centre recruited several unemployed women to help in the installation of a new computerised registration system. It was reported that some organisations used POC workers to replace regular workers who are on holiday.

[41] The main objective of this system of evaluation is to know, by mail inquiry, three months after the end of the action, the situation of users under programmes of employment or training, as well as users' level of satisfaction with the job and its quality, the forms of access to the job and the difficulties found in job seeking. Currently, users who participated in occupational programmes, professional apprenticeship, the FORDESQ/GESTIC programme and vocational training are under observation.

The Impact of Activation Policies

According to the CIDES study published by the Ministry of Social Security and Labour (CIDES 2003), the performance of the programmes included in the Portuguese Action Plans for Employment is rather unbalanced, but the results of those priority programmes may be considered largely satisfactory in terms of preventive action. Nonetheless, it should be noted that this positive evaluation did not take into consideration either the quality of actions or the side-effects for the regular labour market. Also, the study's conclusions recognised the context within which the implementation of the NAPs operated: in particular an international economic environment (until the middle of 2001) that was very favourable to the growth of activity and employment rates and to the reduction of unemployment rates. Therefore, it becomes difficult to say whether improvements in performance are due to active labour market policy or more generally to the business cycle.

Also, the indicators on the impact of activation policy on users are less than informative and even contradictory. Several programmes have been evaluated at different times using different methodologies. A synthetic view of the results of these evaluations would emphasise as positive outcomes the increase in the employability of users, the improvement in efficiency of the job services, the better adjustment to client needs and economic and social realities, along with some negative outcomes such as unclear goals for the programmes, heavy bureaucracy and administrative workload, difficulties in articulation among institutions or unsatisfactory follow-up of policy-users.

According to an official evaluation study,

> the implementation of this model of intervention had deep and diversified implications for the way in which the public employment services had to reorganise themselves to respond properly to the challenges posed by a new kind of intervention based on personalised attendance and better engagement with each candidate. (MTS 2000)

However, while *Inserjovem* and *Reage* were directly inspired by the EES (under its two first Guidelines), most of these programmes were created before the EES and have not been subject to significant changes since. The survey revealed that users have a very positive opinion of the process itself (elaboration of a personalised employment plan), but only 55% of respondents believe that it will help in solving their unemployment problems. The major criticisms focused on the follow-up of insertion itineraries; the adjustment of actions to individual users; and the contribution of personal plans to reducing unemployment. The view of IEFP professionals contrasts with that of users. IEFP claims that the programme led to an increase in the employability of users, although recognising that some obstacles such as work overload made follow-up difficult.

If we assess the overall success of active labour market and activation policies in promoting high-quality human resources, the answer could hardly be positive, even with limited indicators available for precise evaluation. Most of the measures appear to have no concern beyond offering an opportunity to access the labour market. Broadly speaking, the profile of users in terms of qualifications is very low. None of these programmes refer explicitly to the key Lisbon agenda aim of a knowledge-based society (KBS) or incorporate any significant component of high quality training or improvement of work conditions. Lacking investment in lifelong learning and disregarding knowledge and skills obtained from experience, the programmes do not fulfil and may even contradict the KBS demand for a high-quality workforce based on autonomy, creativity and participation (Moniz and Kováks 2001, 55).

Also, the fact that activation policies are being focussed on low-skilled and under-educated workers, who cannot refuse the activities or jobs they are offered, risks producing negative effects on the labour market. The occupational programmes, for instance, offer very precarious temporary jobs to the unemployed. In principle, job placements in the public sector and associations are available within the 'soft' areas, such as social services, environment and cultural institutions. However, these jobs often compete with regular jobs, with these institutions being allowed to recruit unemployed workers under POC instead of full-time employees. A case study on POC users concluded that the activated workers do not have the same rights as full-time employees, whether in terms of pay, entitlements, working time or working conditions. This can frustrate effective inclusion because the participants feel stigmatised or consider themselves as second class wage-earners (Hespanha and Matos 1999).

The replacement of regular workers by subsidised workers concerns the trade unions and is a central issue in their contention with current active employment policies. POCs are arguably inhibiting the creation of new jobs and trade unions support a profound reform of the programme in order to adjust it to the new social and economic contexts and also to the particular conditions of unemployed persons. An evaluation study on POCs refers to several of the above-mentioned observations and concludes with recommendations to clarify the concept of 'socially useful occupation'; to adopt a more plural legal framework in different regional contexts; to guarantee the acquisition of professional skills to reinforce longer term employability; and to make local and central administrations more accountable for policy implementation (Geoideia 1999).

Other programmes may also be contributing to a deterioration of the labour market. This occurs, for example, when people accept training opportunities but acquire skills which are not enough to access a stable job. Increasing employability involves more than merely activating someone; high-quality policies are also needed to complement customised programmes for skill extension, reinforced by on-the-job training related to that skill. Otherwise, retraining may simply recycle the unemployed, returning them to the labour market with no prospect of getting a proper job. During those years 'an accented qualitative impoverishment of the stock of unemployed people led to significant difficulties in the implementation of activation measures in populations with greater obstacles to insertion in terms of qualifications, age and availability for work' (CIDES 2003, 151). Precarious jobs not only affect their holders – those called the 'precarious periphery' by Robert Castel (LTU, youngsters looking for their first job, underqualified women, beneficiaries of minimum income in search of social insertion, among others) – but also give legitimacy and incentives to 'unstable stability' in areas where the job market is steady (Rosa 2003, 37).

Other indirect negative effects of low quality activation policies include: the creation of false expectations among activated people, institutionalising a secondary labour market for them, de-investment in passive policies and the reduction of unemployment benefit expenditure.[42]

The appropriate implementation of active policies in Portugal, therefore, has been restricted in several ways. Besides the social, cultural and political conditions that were mentioned as characterising Portuguese society (state weakness, particularistic behaviour, clientism, lack of a hegemonic project) the obstacles may be associated with the poor management of activation policies: deficiencies of organisation in public employment services (partly due to the lack of tradition in active labour market policies, partly to the shortage of human resources and logistics); the high cost of individualised programmes; mistrust of users due to earlier negative experiences (job precariousness, social marginalisation, stigma); insufficient recognition of competences and skills learned

---

[42] Paradoxically, while unemployment rates have been rising, expenditure on unemployment subsidies in the social security budget has decreased in recent years. For example, in the budget for 2005 this amount represents, in relation to the budget for 2004, an increase of only 4%, less than half of the increase of the previous year (in 2004, this amount increased by 11.8%), and less than 1/8 of the growth in 2003 (34.8%) (Rosa 2004).

informally from working life; discontinuities in programmes due to political cycles, and short-term decision-making.[43]

The Impact of the EES on Activation Policies

Activation policies in Portugal have nonetheless produced some positive outcomes in terms of (i) cooperation between departments and administrative levels; (ii) involvement of the social partners, local authorities and other entities in joint actions; and (iii) modernisation of public employment services.

The Intersectoral Approach

Activation policies directly and indirectly concerned several departments beyond those with specific competences in social affairs and employment. This move to increased interdepartmental cooperation was strengthened by the EES, with the National Action Plans becoming integrative instruments for government policies (including important contributions from departments such as Education, Economy and Finance) (MTS 1999, 8).

The integrative strategy operates at different levels. At the level of employment action, it links the fields of education, training and employment, in a way that may still be insufficient but does allow for the recognition of non-formal learning processes in the work context (MTS 1999, 36). At the level of inclusive action, it relates social protection policy to employment and training policies, thereby at least aiming to avoid labour market marginalisation which in turn leads to social exclusion. At the level of sustainable action, it brings together economic, employment and social policies with the aim of reinforcing each other.

The CIDES evaluation study points out successes in relating employment, training, social development, education and, to a lesser extent, economic policies (CIDES 2003, 151). But not all of this is due

---

[43] Since 2001 there has been a reduction in the number of programme users related to the need for a state budgetary deficit reduction. This was the case with the programmes oriented to training and employment (*Formação e Emprego*), with a reduction of 24%; the programmes oriented to the creation of jobs and firms (*Criação de Emprego e Empresas*), with a reduction of 13.8%; and other programmes oriented to employment promotion (*Outras medidas de promoção do emprego*), with a reduction of 12.3%. Numbers in SII/GMI also registered a marked decrease, and all the programmes oriented to activity development in the area of employment (*Actividades Desenvolvidas no Âmbito do Emprego*) dropped significantly, with the exception of Professional Counselling and Occupational Programmes, with a reduction of 4.7% (IEFP 2004).

to the EES. Employment and training policies have been managed by the same ministry since the 1970s, and by the same institution – the IEFP – since the 1980s. Similarly, employment policies and social policies have also benefited from being managed by the same ministry. Educational and employment policy thus already had a tradition of joint thinking and action. What is new, and appears to be an effect of the EES, is the considerable effort made to harmonise employment policy with other sectoral policies.

The Territorial Approach

A new emphasis has also been put on local and regional partnerships as an instrument for implementing and diffusing employment and training policies, adjusted to the particular conditions of each territory. Since the 1998 NAP an important role has been played by Regional Networks and Territorial Pacts for Employment. Both forms of partnership preceded the EES but gained real importance and were reinforced because of it. The Regional Plans for Employment are a product of these partnerships and were created to complement and develop the national plan at regional and local levels. Although the outcome of these regional bodies and instruments has been uneven and at times fragmented, this process of decentralisation has been positive, particularly given the earlier long tradition of state centralisation in Portugal. In the area of policies combating poverty and exclusion, a new instrument of coordination based on partnerships was also created and is being implemented at the municipality level: the Social Network.

The Organisational Approach

A series of changes in the public services for employment and training resulted from the new methodologies of intervention, in terms of both how they were organised and their role. First, they became more proactive in the sense of seeking out clients to offer them suitable programmes instead of being the front desk for clients' demands. Second, an early-start approach was taken to obtain a personal plan for labour market insertion for every registered unemployed person. Third, access to job centres and vocational training centres by clients such as minimum income recipients, drug addicts under detoxification programmes, and ex-convicts on leaving prison is now compulsory.

The implications of these changes are both profound and varied. The public employment services have had to reorganise themselves in response to the challenges of a more personalised approach, more discriminating policies and greater proximity to clients. While procedures have become complex and more demanding, a substantial increase in staff might have been expected;[44] however, as already indicated, this did not happen. For this reason, the increased workload meant reduced availability of professionally qualified staff and obstructed follow-up with clients (MTS 2000).

Activation policies have focussed on two main areas: employment and social inclusion. The *Instituto de Emprego e Formação Profissional* (IEFP) is the agency concerned with labour market activation, while the *Instituto da Segurança Social* (ISS) deals with activation for social inclusion.[45] As labour market participation is still considered by mainstream politics as the royal road to inclusion, the borderline between the two institutions is not clearly fixed and shifts in their role and influence have resulted. In this process, IEFP has gained a dominant position due to the policy priority now given to the reduction of poverty, social exclusion and inequalities, as well as to the assumption that work is a universal medicine.

No particular social group appears to have significantly influenced activation's course of development in Portugal, except perhaps the professionals (mostly social workers) involved in the implementation of social inclusion programmes, due to their strong professional ideology.

---

[44] Armindo Silva summarises the reasons for the high cost of activation policies: 'Activation policies based on the triptych integration-coordination-personalisation are very demanding in financial terms since they assume that public social services or employment services will have the human and IT resources they need to dedicate sufficient attention to the most difficult cases and those cases that need most support. The effect of such policies could thus result in an immediate increase in expenditure on active policies, which may or may not be compensated by a reduction in passive policies. This will depend on the more or less favorable conjuncture and on the degree of maturity of the social protection system. If activation policies achieve their ends and contribute to a significant reduction in structural unemployment and in social exclusion, an economy of costs is to be expected in the medium and long run' (Silva 2004, 5).

[45] 'The IEFP, as an employment policy executive body, plays a crucial role in the NAP's implementation by promoting active employment and vocational training measures and developing interventions for the achievement of the objectives described in the different NAP guidelines, namely 1, 3, 4, 5, 7 and 10' (MTS 2004, 39).

Conclusion

When we analyse the impact of the EES on the institutional setting, changes are not readily visible in the sense that no new institutions or agencies were created to develop the NAPs. The coordination body for the NAPs is also very soft in structure.[46]

There were also few changes in social protection principles when compared to the social protection practices induced by the EES (benchmarking, mainstreaming, mutual learning, management by objectives, integrated approach). Activation policies may be an exception here, but mainly because of the explicit mention of their underlying principles in the above-mentioned social security and unemployment laws.

The number of persons who have passed through the above-mentioned activation programmes and expenditure on activation show that the real impact of activation is much lower than might be expected from the declarations of policy-makers and the intentions expressed in official documents. This conclusion seems to be particularly accurate in relation to the three years after the right-wing coalition came to power. Paradoxically, it is during this period that the most coercive laws on activation were approved.[47]

This increased emphasis on activation has been beneficial in attempts to legitimate unpopular neoliberal policies, while for economic, social and political reasons – and especially costs – the compulsory side of activation has been limited. For the same reason, the experience of other countries with 'welfare-to-work' or 'make work pay' programmes has often been used, in public debates and political discourse, as an example of how to reduce costs in social expenditure. The debates on minimum income scheme reform in Parliament mentioned above are very enlightening regarding the use of activation as a political tool by right-wing parties. Now that the coalition has lost the general election and the socialist party is in power once again, we look forward to seeing how activation avoids criticisms that it is a Trojan horse of neo-liberalism.

---

[46] This body is composed of an Internal Group of the former Ministry of Social Security and Labour, an Inter-ministerial Commission, and a Social Partners' Technical Group.

[47] NAP 2004 summarises the achievements and intentions of the government: 'In 2004, in order to make work pay, some measures were implemented towards the reformulation of the benefits which appear as disincentives to work and by introducing/reinforcing criteria for granting such benefits'. In addition, activation mechanisms for unemployed workers have extended the concept of suitable employment, cut off the unemployment benefit in the case of refusal, and included provisions that promote geographical mobility (MTS 2004, 7).

References

Andreoti, Alberta *et al.* (2001), "Does a Southern European model exist?", *Journal of European Area Studies* 9 (1), pp. 43-62.

Barbier, Jean-Claude (2005), "The French activation strategy in a European comparative perspective", paper presented to the ETUI Meeting (Brussels, 7 February).

Cabral, Manuel (1995), "Equidade social, 'Estado-Providência' e sistema fiscal: atitudes e percepções da população portuguesa (1991-1994)", *Sociologia – Problemas e Práticas* 17, pp. 231-246.

Cabral, Manuel, Jorge Vala and André Freire (eds.) (2003), *Desigualdades Sociais e Percepções de Justiça*, Lisboa, ICS.

CCP (2004a), "Observações da CCP à Comunicação da Comissão 'O Futuro da Estratégia Europeia de Emprego – Uma Estratégia de pleno emprego e melhores postos de trabalho para todos' COM(2003) 6 final", http://www.ccp.pt/ CCPPortal/Default.aspx?tabid=46.

CCP (2004b), "Contributos da CCP para o PNE 2003", http://www.ccp.pt/ CCPPortal/Default.aspx?tabid=46.

CE (1992), "92/441/CEE: Recomendação do Conselho, de 24 de Junho de 1992, relativa a critérios comuns respeitantes suficientes nos sistemas de protecção social", *Jornal oficial* No. L 245 de 26/08/1992, P. 0046-0048.

CE (2001), Council Decision of 19 January 2001 on Guidelines for Member States Employment Policies for the Year 2001 (2001/63/EC) OJEC 24.1.2001.

CGTP (1996a), *Programa de Acção*, 8º Congresso, Lisboa (mimeo).

CGTP (1996b), *Relatório de Actividades*, 8º Congresso, Lisboa (mimeo).

CGTP (1996c), *Intervenções do Conselho Nacional*, 8º Congresso, Lisboa (mimeo).

CIDES (2003), *Avaliação do Impacto da Estratégia Europeia para o Emprego em Portugal. Políticas Activas e Empregabilidade*, Lisboa, DEPP/MSST.

Ferrera, Maurizio, Anton Hemerijck and Martin Rhodes (2000), *The Future of Social Europe*, Oeiras, Celta.

Geoideia (1999), *Avaliação dos Programas Ocupacionais. Síntese do relatório final*, Lisboa, IEFP.

Giddens, Anthony (1998), *The Third Way. The Renewal of Social Democracy*, Cambridge, Polity Press.

Hespanha, Pedro and Dora Gomes (2001), *Caracterização dos Perfis dos Beneficiários RMG. Famílias com Problemas de Saúde*, Estudos de Avaliação de Impactes do Rendimento Mínimo Garantido, Lisboa, Instituto para o Desenvolvimento Social.

Hespanha, Pedro and Ana Matos (1999), "From passive to active social policies. The softness of workfare policies in Portugal", *Oficina do CES*, No. 145, Coimbra, Centro de Estudos Sociais. Also in Dutch: "Van passief naar actief sociaal beleid. De zwakheid van het worfare-beleid in Portugal", *Tijjdschrift Voor Arbeid en Participatie* 21 (2/3), pp. 221-232.

Hespanha, Pedro and Carla Valadas (2002), "Globalização dos problemas sociais, globalização das políticas. O caso da estratégia europeia para o emprego", in Pedro Hespanha and Graça Carapinheiro (eds.), *Risco Social e Incerteza: Pode o Estado Social Recuar Mais?*, Porto, Afrontamento.

Hespanha, Pedro et al. (1997), "Welfare society and welfare state", in Maurice Roche and Rik van Berkel (eds.), *European Citizenship and Social Exclusion*, pp.169-183, Aldershot, Ashgate.

Hespanha, Pedro et al. (2002), "Active social policies in the EU and empirical observations from case studies into types of work", in R. van Berkel and Iver Moller (eds.), *Active Social Policies in the EU. Inclusion through Participation?*, Bristol, The Policy Press, pp. 103-136.

Hudson, John and Stuart Lowe (2004), *Understanding the Policy Process. Analysing Welfare Policy and Practice*, Bristol, The Policy Press.

IEFP (2004), *Indicadores de Actividade-Emprego* (2001-2003), Lisboa, DPL.

ISSS (2004), *Guião Operativo para o Atendimento/Acompanhamento Social. Caderno B, Contratualização para a Inserção*, Lisboa (mimeo).

Laparra, Miguel and Manuel Aguilar (1996), "Social exclusion and minimum income programmes in Spain", *Southern European Society and Politics* 1 (3), pp. 87-113.

Larsen, Flemming and Mikkel Mailand (2005), "Danish activation policy – The role of the normative foundation, the institutional set-up and other drivers", paper presented to the ETUI Meeting (Brussels, 7 February).

Lipsky, Michael (1980), *Street-Level Bureaucracy*, New York, Russell Sage.

Moniz, António B. and Ilona Kováks (eds.) (2001), *Sociedade da Informação e Emprego*, Lisboa, MTS.

MTS (1998a), *Plano Nacional de Emprego*, Lisboa.

MTS (1999), *Employment National Action Plan. Portugal*, Lisboa, DEPP.

MTS (2000), *Avaliação das Iniciativas Inserjovem e Reage. Relatório de síntese*, Lisboa, IEFP (mimeo).

MTS (2002), *Avaliação do Impacto da Estratégia Europeia para o Emprego em Portugal. Síntese do relatório final*, Lisboa.

MTS (2004), *Employment National Action Plan. Portugal*, http://europa.eu.int/comm/employment_social/employment_strategy/nap_2004/nap2004pt_en.pdf

Rosa, Eugénio (2004), "O desemprego em Portugal ultrapassou o meio milhão", http://www.sprc.pt/paginas/propostas_desemprego.html.

Rosa, M. Teresa (ed.) (2003), *Trabalho Precário. Perspectivas de Superação*, Lisboa, Observatório do Emprego e Formação Profissional.

Santos, Boaventura (ed.) (1993), *Portugal, um retrato singular*, Porto, Afrontamento.

Santos, Boaventura (1999), "The welfare state in Portugal: between conflicting globalisations", *Oficina do CES*, No. 149.

Serrano Pascual, Amparo (ed.), *Are Activation Policies Converging in Europe?*, Brussels, ETUI.

Silva, Armindo (2004), "Políticas de activação e de inclusão social no quadro da União Europeia", paper presented to the VIII Luso-Afro-Brazilian Congress of Social Sciences, Coimbra, 16-18 September (mimeo).

UGT (1996), "Um acordo económico e social para o ano 2000", Proposta da Comissão Permanente, Lisboa (mimeo).

Activation Policies and Shaping Factors in the Czech Republic[*]

Tomáš SIROVÁTKA

Introduction: Increasing Role of Activation in an Enlarged Europe

The paradigm shift from a 'passive' to an 'active' welfare state seems to be a cornerstone of reforms aimed at responding to the challenges of population ageing and global economic competition. The notion of an 'active welfare state' has been interpreted in different ways: the post-Fordist Schumpeterian workfare state represents one polar option (Jessop 1993), contrasting with the so-called social investment state (Giddens 1998). Regardless of which strategy is preferred, the ultimate and consensual objective of the 'active welfare state' is to increase labour market participation and employment. This objective is also among the Lisbon and Stockholm employment targets.

Many areas of public policy have to be addressed in order to reach these targets: the European Employment Strategy represents an attempt to coordinate them in EU countries. Among these policies, notwithstanding the broad variety of approaches to implementing the European Employment Strategy (compare Madsen and Munch-Madsen 2001), the policy of 'activation' has moved centre-stage in nearly all EU member states in recent years and a debate is under way on the convergence of activation policies (Serrano Pascual 2004). The reasons for the central role of activation policies are pragmatic: increasing economic pressures on the welfare state ('permanent austerity') imply both the need for a more economical approach to public financial resources and the need to increase employment even in those segments of the workforce in which until recently inactivity was tolerated, or which were pushed to the margins of the labour market, particularly all persons fit for work who find themselves in the position of being long-term benefit claimants (long-term unemployed).

---

[*] This paper was supported by the Grant Agency of the Czech Republic, grant No. 403/03/1007 'Social Exclusion and Social Inclusion in Czech Society'.

We will understand activation (policy) here, in line with Barbier (2004, 48), as a specific feature (characteristic) of policies rather than a specific policy tool:

> An increased and explicit *dynamic linkage* [author's emphasis] introduced into public policy between social welfare, employment and labour market programmes, which entails the critical redesigning of previous income support, assistance and social protection policies in terms of efficiency and equity, as well as the enhancing of the various social functions of paid work and labour-force participation.

This dynamic linkage is mainly produced by balancing rights and duties, harmonising social security benefit and taxation, and coordinating benefit schemes with labour market policies, with the link between social assistance and labour market policies being central (cf. Lødemel and Trickey 2001, Saraceno 2002, van Berkel and Møller 2002, Serrano Pascual 2004).

Obviously, the objective of high employment is of similar relevance in post-communist countries as it is in EU-15 member states, even more important given the permanent state of austerity generated in the process of market transformation. Besides, market transformation implicitly contains requirements of individual responsibility and self-reliance which (not only by accident) represent a central principle of activation. On the other hand, several policy trends that have emerged during the transformation period contradict activation policy or make its implementation difficult. Among other things, economic austerity was the reason why risk-absorption efforts in the Czech Republic, as in many other post-communist countries, have so far centred primarily around redistributive and compensatory tools.

Redistribution through income-tested benefits was considered to be the most effective tool for protecting vulnerable population groups against the threat of poverty and for maintaining social peace during the transition to a market economy.

Social protection systems were redesigned to a large extent as extended social safety nets with less emphasis on promoting active labour market participation.

Nonetheless, after fifteen years of transformation the 'compensatory strategies' have proved to be economically inefficient. They have failed in two respects: firstly, social expenditure is on the increase, and secondly, the labour market inclusion of vulnerable groups is inadequate and the proportion of the long-term unemployed is high.

Such a state of affairs clashes with the need to meet the EMU criteria and forces the government – irrespective of political leaning – to accept unpopular measures. These include curtailing social benefits and unemployment benefits, tightening the conditions of early retirement, and restricting human resource investment and social services. This all takes place under the umbrella of public finance reforms.

In such conditions, activation policies which were formerly not the centre of attention become quite promising: they are perceived as necessary to balance public budgets and are also supported through guidelines laid down in the European Employment Strategy. This is reflected in the National Action Plans on employment and in public employment service (PES) practice. However, activation strategies in post-communist countries are likely to be implemented in a specific form which largely depends on the corresponding ideological discourse, and economic and institutional environment.

This chapter addresses the current role and profile of activation policy in the Czech Republic and the crucial factors shaping it. First, we will focus on the core elements and aspects of existing approaches towards activation in general, and in the Czech Republic in particular, in order to position the Czech approach to activation within the framework of 'ideal types'. The factors influencing the Czech activation approach will then be analysed, including the role of EU agendas and institutions. In conclusion, we will discuss the prospects of activation policy in the Czech Republic.

Activation Policies and Labour Market/Welfare Regimes

Since the aim of activation – to integrate people fit for work into the system of paid employment in the greatest possible numbers and throughout their life cycle[1] – may be achieved with the help of a variety of social and employment policy measures, we need to situate the existing activation strategies within a broader framework of welfare state regimes. Proceeding from Esping-Andersen's (1990) traditional typology of the welfare state, four different 'unemployment welfare regimes' have been distinguished (Gallie and Paugham 2000). This distinction is based on three main criteria which are also relevant from the activation policy perspective: the extent of unemployment benefit coverage, the level and duration of income compensation and the emphasis laid on active labour market policy. *The sub-protective regime* (found in Southern European countries) provides only a small proportion of the unemployed with unemployment benefits and protects mainly those with a long and uninterrupted employment career, with the family

---

[1] Although other forms of activation, such as voluntary work and education, are important as well (van Berkel and Roche 2002).

being expected to absorb the unemployment risks of the marginal labour force. State interventions in the labour market, including active labour market policy, are little developed and rather neglected. *The liberal/ minimal regime* (typical of Anglo-Saxon countries) grants more universal but rather low unemployment benefits, set at the level of social assistance and provided for a short period of time (thus putting uncompromising pressure on the unemployed to re-enter the labour market and adjust their wage requirements). It systematically rejects any substantive intervention in market functioning; rather the unemployed should adjust their reservation wages. *The employment-centred regime* (common in continental European countries) provides the unemployed with higher benefits than both the above-mentioned models. The coverage of the unemployed, however, is far from comprehensive and entitlement to benefits derives from previous individual employment records and age, which puts certain individuals – such as women and young people – at a disadvantage, thus broadening the gap between 'insiders' and 'outsiders'. Breadwinners are expected to prevent the 'marginal labour force' – the breadwinners' family dependants – from falling into material deprivation. Therefore the system facilitates breadwinners' chances of retaining their jobs. Unlike the liberal model, this regime allows for intentional labour market regulation which selectively distributes active labour market policies: training for the core labour force and workfare-like measures (public works) for marginals fit for work. *The universal regime* (typical of Nordic countries) involves full coverage of the population with unemployment benefits and also features the highest level of compensation, though benefit duration is short. Instead, it pursues an ambitious active labour market policy which aims at eliminating long-term unemployment and accentuates 'work ethics' (benefit entitlement conditions therefore take into account the principle of merit as well as active job search and/or participation in employment programmes).

From the perspective of activation, behind these models we recognise a 'weak activation approach' in the sub-protective regime, and a 'selective activation approach' in the case of the employment-centred regime. A 'strong comprehensive activation approach' corresponds to both the liberal regime and the universal regime, although the goals, principles and methods of activation in these two regimes are very different.

The available literature on activation strategies focuses mainly on these two regimes and, comparing them, recognises two model approaches to the goal, principle and method of activation in the case of the *strong and comprehensive activation strategy*. These models have been described as the *workfare approach* versus the *insertion approach* (Morel 1998), but also as the *workfare approach* versus Nordic *produc-*

tivism (Esping-Andersen 1999); the *defensive* versus the *offensive approach* (Torfing 1999); the *labour market attachment (work-first) approach* versus the *human resource development approach* (Lødemel and Trickey 2001); the *workfare model* versus the *social inclusion model* (Nicaise 2002); the *paternalist optimists' approach ('enforced participation')* versus the *activation optimists' approach ('inclusion through participation')* (van Berkel and Møller 2002); the *liberal approach* versus the *universalistic approach* (Barbier 2004); and *passive adaptation* versus *active adaptation* (Serrano Pascual 2004). We need to understand these typologies rather as analytical tools than as reflecting existing reality, in full awareness that not only differences but also signs of their convergence have been identified in Europe (Serrano Pascual 2004; Barbier 2004).

Second, we shall distinguish between two levels of analysis which are strongly inter-linked. The first concerns goals and principles, as well as assumptions and ideologies related to activation policies and target groups and their social status. The second concerns the design of policies and measures and their implementation through the relevant institutions. When looking at activation from the perspective of goals and principles, we consider as a core distinction the choice between an emphasis on the nominal and wage flexibility of labour on the one hand, and an emphasis on functional flexibility and employability on the other. Recognition of the right to employment, understood as a citizens' right, is the focal point of this distinction (Standing 1999).

Table 1. Two Modes of Activation
(Level of Goals and Principles)

Dimensions	Workfare (liberal) approach	Social inclusion (universalistic) approach
Causes of inactivity and poverty	Individual failure, poor work ethic, lack of motivation (and skills) Institutional barriers to labour flexibility	Global competition, technological development, interplay of structural and socio-cultural factors (skills shortage, labour market segmentation, etc.)
Policy discourse	Dependency, incentives, welfare expenditure cuts Individual responsibility, citizens' duties	Social exclusion, social inclusion, social cohesion Collective responsibility, citizens' rights (and duties)
Objectives of activation	Labour market attachment, labour force flexibility (nominal and wage), activated people, 'reserve army of labour'	Social inclusion, functional labour flexibility, active people, human resource development, employability
Principles of activation strategies	Work-first, policy of enforcement, making work pay, punitive tools (more sticks than carrots)	Occupational competence (capabilities) Balanced measures: income, training, access to work, empowerment
Target groups	Long-term welfare state clients, social welfare recipients, primarily the young	Universal coverage (citizens) plus preferential treatment of the most disadvantaged
Role and status of clients	Subordination, requirement to meet conditions and duties, exposed to financial, administrative and legislative pressures	Partnership, reciprocity, clients possess rights, supposed to be responsible citizens

Source: Based on Standing (1999), van Berkel and Møller (2002), Serrano Pascual (2004) and Barbier (2004).

When focusing on policy level, we will use the four criteria identified by Serrano Pascual (2004) as follows: (i) *quality* of provision, (ii) *generosity* of employment policy expenditure, (iii) *individualisation* of programmes and (iv) *expansion/comprehensiveness* of activation strategy. We suggest several indicators for these criteria here and will attempt to characterise the most important ones in the case of the Czech mode of activation.

Table 2. Two Modes of Activation
(Level of Instruments/Policies)

Criteria	Indicators suggested	Workfare (liberal) approach	Social inclusion (universalistic) approach
1. Quality of provision (benefits, jobs, programmes)	Income support (benefits)	Weak: low and conditional benefits	Strong: high and unconditional benefits
	Access to labour market and choice	Limited range of choices	Broad range of choices
	Quality of jobs/training opportunities	Low-paid market jobs mostly	Good quality training/jobs available
2. Employment policy expenditure – generosity	Scope of ALMP expenditure – as % of GDP (per 1% of unemployment)	Low	High
	Generosity of ALMP expenditure per participant	Low	High
3. Individualisation of programmes	Emphasis on individual treatment and discretion	Medium	High
	Capacity devoted to individual treatment service	Medium	High
4. Expansion of activation and comprehensiveness	Comprehensiveness and complexity of services	Low	High
	Comprehensiveness as regards inclusion of various groups	Low, selective	High
	Variety of actors involved in policy-making	Dominance of governmental actors	Variety of actors involved in policy-making

Source: Adapted from Serrano Pascual (2004).

When analysing the Czech mode of activation we will deal directly with the level of implemented activation policies, assuming that they largely express the corresponding goals and principles. Before that we will illustrate the need for activation policies with respect to current labour market developments in the Czech Republic.

Czech Labour Market: The Need for Activation Policy

Until 1997, the unemployment rate in the Czech Republic was below 5%: however, this 'Czech miracle mirrored nothing more than the soft economic environment of 'bank socialism' and the strategy of delayed reforms adopted by the government. Following the economic slowdown in 1997-1999, restructuring processes intensified for two reasons: first, company insolvencies initiated new waves of bankruptcies; second, privatisation of the financial sector, initiated at that time, enabled foreign groups to penetrate the banking sector, increasing competitiveness requirements and standardising financial markets. This all increased pressures on the labour market.

The registered unemployment rate nearly tripled during 1996-1999, rising to more than 9%. After 1999 when the temporary economic slowdown started to recede, the Czech Republic experienced four years of economic growth of 2-3%. As economic restructuring continued, this growth was not sufficient to create more jobs than were being lost, however, since it was generated by labour productivity increases (jobless growth). Employment thus fell by nearly 3% during 1999-2003. Labour productivity in industry was growing fast (6% in 2003) due to high labour productivity in foreign-owned companies; in 2004, the latter accounted for about one third of employment and nearly half of production. Nevertheless, such partial labour productivity increases suffice neither to bridge the 50% productivity gap between the Czech Republic and the EU-15 nor to generate new employment (Sirovátka *et al.* 2003).

At the beginning of 2004, employment rates were slightly above the EU-15 and clearly above the EU-25 average: the general employment rate in the 15-64 age group was 64.7% in 2003 (the EU target stands at 67% in 2005), women's employment rate was 56.3% (the target is 57% in 2005) and the employment rate in the 55-64 age group was 42.3% (the target is 50% by 2010). This performance is not bad in terms of the Lisbon/Stockholm targets, but the employment rate is decreasing.

This negative trend of a deteriorating employment rate was mainly due to increased unemployment, which more recently has stabilised or even increased further: in 2003 it was 0.5% higher than in 2002, at 7.8% (according to the Labour Force Survey). Registered unemployment was above 9% and increased to more than 10% during 2004. However, the main labour market problem is the uneven distribution of the unemployment risk and the emerging inflexibility/stickiness of the labour market. Long-term unemployment made up 40% of registered unemployment and 50% of surveyed unemployment (LFS), the fourth highest share in the OECD in 2003 (after Slovakia, Italy and Greece). The risks of unemployment and LTU are much more uneven than in the EU-15, since ethnic minorities, disabled people and women with children are exposed to discrimination in the labour market: their unemployment rates are several times higher compared to other categories. For example, the employment impact of motherhood on women in the 20-50 age group who have children aged 0-6 years, compared to women without children, measured as an absolute difference in employment rates, is 39% in the Czech Republic. This is the highest difference in Europe, the EU-15 average being 12.2% (European Commission 2004). Similarly, young people and unskilled labour are disadvantaged much more than in other countries: for example, the specific unemployment rate of people aged 15-24 is 17.6% compared to 7% for the group aged 25-54 years and 4.4% for the group aged 55-64 years. The unemployment rate of people with lower than upper secondary education is 18.8%, but only 5.6% among those with upper secondary education and 1.8% among those with tertiary education (OECD 2004b). Such differences cannot be found in any EU-15 country, but Slovakia and Poland report similar or even higher differences, typical of transitional labour markets affected by structural change. The unemployment rate of people with disabilities reached 30% in mid-2004, while that of the Roma population is around 50% (Sirovátka et al. 2003; Sirovátka 2004).

A pattern of 'exclusive unemployment' has therefore emerged in the Czech Republic: while the general unemployment rate is around the EU average, the differences in unemployment risks are profound. This is to a large extent due to a number of structural imbalances in the labour market, above all deficient skills, discrimination and dependency traps. Labour market policies have so far not been able to respond sufficiently to such urgent imbalances in the labour market, particularly because expenditure on ALMP has been a mere 0.17-0.21% of GDP over the last five years. This is on average five times less than in the EU-15 (OECD 2003). The scope of ALMP and the capacities of the public employment offices are not sufficient to respond to the current weaknesses of the labour market. Since the beginning of the 1990s, Czech policy-makers have shown little interest in activation policies, preferring policies intended to increase labour market supply by providing opportunities for early exit and prolonging paid parental leave. On the other hand, the core of the labour force has been subjected to flexibilisation and pressures to accept any kind of market job, which was in line with the transformation strategy.

Considering the structural mismatches on the labour market (that is, overemployment, mismatch between labour demand and labour supply, skills shortages, regional disparities) which determine the extremely uneven distribution of unemployment risks, we must assume that both active labour market policies and activation policies could play a significant role in improving labour market performance. The inadequate development of active labour market policies means that the role of activation policies may be expected to increase and – as we shall show – policy-makers are becoming aware that this increase is necessary.

Activation Strategies in the Czech Republic

As already mentioned, activation is approached in the Czech Republic as a dynamic linkage between labour market participation and social protection. This linkage is shaped by both social protection schemes (unemployment and social assistance benefits, early retirement schemes, or related tax policies) and active labour market policies/measures. In EES terms, benefit/tax schemes are closely associated with Guideline 8 (Making Work Pay), while active labour market measures are linked rather to Guideline 1 (Prevention and Activation). Hence we may distinguish activation as activation through a benefit/tax package (activation stream 1) and activation through active employment policy measures (activation stream 2) (bearing in mind that the dynamic linkage between these two streams is the focal point of our analysis). We will discuss activation stream 1 first, focusing on the quality and conditionality of benefit provisions, as well as choice/access to jobs and labour market exit. Second, we will discuss activation stream 2, focusing on choice and access to active labour market measures, generosity of employment policy expenditure and scope of policies, as well as their individualisation, comprehensiveness and complexity.

Activation Stream 1: Benefit/Tax Package

Quality (Level and Duration) of Unemployment and Social Assistance Benefits

Since the early 1990s, the generosity of unemployment benefits (replacement rate and duration of benefit provision) has been considered the crucial quality influencing both system costs and work incentives for the unemployed. This is why benefits were designed in the Czech Republic as a 'residual' scheme with respect to the objectives of cost containment and providing incentives. Social effectiveness in terms of poverty alleviation has been associated rather with social assistance benefits.

Originally, the Czech system of income protection for the unemployed was inspired mostly by the continental variant: in 1990 and 1991 the replacement ratio was set at 65% of the net wage (and even 90% in the case of collective dismissals) and the duration of benefit provision was 12 months. Economic decline and the prospect of high state expenditures soon resulted, as in other post-communist countries, in a preference on the part of policy-makers for the Anglo-Saxon liberal/residual model. Some analyses show that out of all the post-communist countries this tendency was strongest in the Czech Republic (Burda 1993). In 1992, the replacement rate was reduced to 50-60% of previous net wages and the duration of benefit provision was reduced to 6 months, after which a person could only claim means-tested social assistance benefits.

A negative international trade balance led the government to adopt measures to reduce state expenditure ('austerity packages') in 1997. These 'packages' affected mostly budgetary social spending and involved cuts in a number of social benefits. Apart from other measures, the unemployment benefits replacement ratio was cut in 1998 from 60% to 50% of previous net wages (during the first three months of unemployment), from 50% to 40% (during the following three months), and from 70% to 60% (in the case of participation in labour market training). Until 1999, unemployment benefits were limited to a relatively low ceiling equalling 1.5 times the subsistence minimum for a single person. This means, for example, that the effective replacement rate of a worker on average wages was less than half their previous wage from the beginning of their unemployment.

The minority social democratic government formed after the 1998 elections proposed a number of measures to increase social benefits. In the case of unemployment benefit, it gained parliamentary agreement to raise the benefit ceiling from 1.5 to 2.5 times the subsistence minimum for a single person in 2000. At the same time, entitlement criteria were tightened for unemployed persons registering repeatedly: a minimum of 6 months of continuous employment was required between registrations. The reduced replacement ratio was not subject to further improvements, while the other restrictions introduced in 1997, such as cuts in child benefits and deceleration of benefit indexation, were only temporary (in effect only in 1998).

Even after minor improvements introduced by the new Employment Act in October 2004 in response to the minimum standards set by the ILO in Convention 102 of 1952 and later adopted by the EU (a 45% replacement rate), the replacement rate of unemployment benefit in the Czech Republic remains relatively low: 50% for the first three months and 45% for the second three months of unemployment, the ceiling being 2.5 times the minimum subsistence level, with benefits being provided for no longer than a period of 6 months. In October 2004, this was increased to 9 months but only for unemployed persons over 50 years of age and 12 months for those over 55 years of age (Zákon 435 2004).

Such a low level and short duration of unemployment benefits constitutes a strong incentive for accepting low-paid jobs, especially when a strict definition of 'suitable job' is applied which does not recognise level of qualifications or level of pay as fundamental criteria. However, we should note that the coverage of unemployment benefit entitlement is relatively low due to the high share of long-term unemployment and the short duration of benefit provision (only about 35% of the unemployed were receiving unemployment benefits in 2003).

On the other hand, about one third of the unemployed are entitled to social assistance and thus the unemployed represent nearly 75% of social assistance claimants. Social assistance in the Czech Republic guarantees a minimum subsistence amount for an unlimited period. Despite the fact that its level has been frozen (in fact, it has not increased since 2001), the replacement rate is still quite acceptable for low-wage earners. This is not only due to the low level of wages but also due to the high ratio of the subsistence minimum to the Eurostat relative poverty line. In the case of working age households, this ratio is higher in the Czech Republic than in any of the EU-15 countries except Sweden (see Table 3).

Table 3. Net Disposable Income of Households on Social Assistance Benefits as a Proportion of the Relative Poverty Line, 2001

	Working age		Elderly	
	couple	lone parent	couple	single
Czech Republic	86	93	86	76
Germany	58	77	58	71
Netherlands	96	85	117	109
Portugal	58	58	58	44
Sweden	88	95	116	108
United Kingdom	76	84	108	115

Source: Cantillon *et al.* (2004, 25), own calculations for the Czech Republic.

Activation through Making Work Pay

The problem of incentives has been in the focus of policy-makers' attention in the Czech Republic since the early 1990s. While the right-wing government froze the level of the minimum wage in the first half of the 1990s, it was politically unacceptable for the social democratic government which came to power in 1998 to reduce the replacement rates of social assistance benefits too much. It rather preferred to increase minimum wages in order to improve work incentives for low-wage earners. Between January 1998 and January 2003 the level of the minimum wage as a proportion of the average wage increased from 23% to 37% through a number of regular minimum wage adjustments. On the other hand, the subsistence minimum has not been increased since 2001 and lags behind both the average and minimum wages. Since the level of wages in the secondary sector is still low because of low labour productivity, the level of social benefit entitlements of low-wage earners seems to be high when compared to the other European countries, mainly in the case of complete families with children (see Table 4).

Table 4. Net Replacement Rates for Four Types of Households and Average for Two Income Levels (Average Wage and Two Thirds of Average Wage) Long-Term Benefit Recipients after 5 Years of Unemployment, 2002

	Single person	Couple, no children	Couple, 2 children	Single, 2 children	Overall average
Czech Rep.	**39**	**62**	**81**	**68**	**63**
Germany	72	75	77	85	77
Hungary	32	32	40	39	36
Netherlands	45	66	75	69	77
Portugal	56	63	66	66	63
Spain	46	48	57	54	51
Sweden	67	83	89	67	77
UK	54	67	75	65	65

Source: OECD (2004a).

The relatively high level of social assistance (although far from generous given increasing housing costs and its declining proportion of average wages) may be surprising given the poor unemployment insurance benefits which were re-designed in a manner resembling the liberal regime. Czech policy-makers' awareness of the history of egalitarianism and narrow income distribution in Czech society explains their interest in alleviating potential threats of poverty in the name of the 'social acceptability' of economic reforms.

The problem of incentives was addressed in the new Employment Act of October 2004 which enables people to work part-time without loss of unemployment benefit entitlement if their earnings do not exceed half the minimum wage. Unfortunately, this positive incentive does not affect long-term unemployed persons on social assistance who are entitled to earnings up to the subsistence minimum level anyway. This is why the proposal of the new Social assistance act which is soon to be debated in the Parliament includes another positive incentive for the long-term unemployed (social assistance claimants), namely disregards on low earnings (only 70% of earnings below the subsistence minimum would be taken into account when deciding on social assistance benefit entitlements).

A taxation structure which is not favourable for job creation remains a serious problem: while income tax is below the EU average in the Czech Republic, social and health insurance contributions are among the highest in Europe. In total they represent a mammoth 47.5% of wages, the major part (35%) being paid by the employers. Hence total tax on labour costs in the case of low-wage earners is 43%, the third highest rate in the EU, after Belgium and Sweden (European Commission 2004). The high labour tax burden, for low-paid workers in particular, has been criticised by the European Commission but so far no proposal has been submitted to decrease it.

Access to Benefits and Jobs: Conditionality and Choice

Access to unemployment and social assistance benefits has been conditional since 1991 on claimants' willingness to accept a 'suitable job'. A strict definition of suitable job has been applied that disregards level of qualifications as a fundamental criterion. Another precondition of entitlement is cooperation with the employment office: this condition is defined in a rather general manner and is understood to comprise an obligation to keep the agreed schedule of meetings at the employment office, to meet and negotiate with employers according to employment office recommendations and not to reject 'suitable' job offers. On the other hand, the obligation to participate in programmes has not been clearly defined in legislation, and public employment service officials have not been consistent in applying the above-mentioned conditions, despite the high degree of discretion formally granted to them. Inadequate personnel capacities at employment offices, as well as the organisational division between employment offices (which are subordinated to the Ministry of Labour and Social Affairs) and social assistance offices (which are subordinated to local authorities) make individual case management difficult. In a situation in which labour market training opportunities or subsidised jobs are scarce and only low-paid jobs at a level close to the minimum wage are available for the most disadvantaged unemployed, about 10% of unemployment-register outflows were due to sanctions on the unemployed: the unemployed lose their benefit entitlements and cannot renew them until at least three months have passed.

The new Employment act, in force since October 2004 (Zákon 435/2004) includes several new activation elements: above all, it emphasises the duties and obligations of the unemployed. First, access to unemployment benefits has been restricted for young people: while secondary school studies were formerly recognised as a substitute for an employment record for the purpose of unemployment benefit entitlement, this is no longer the case. Thus secondary school and college graduates are no longer entitled to unemployment benefits. Second, the strictness of the requirement of job search and programme participation has increased significantly: the concept of a 'suitable job' is now stricter than before, neglecting not only level of qualifications but to some degree also the situation of the family. Third, temporary jobs lasting for more than 3 months are considered 'suitable' (including public works), as are all jobs lasting for more than 80% of standard working time. Lastly, refusal to participate in labour market training programmes or refusal to undergo a medical examination may lead to a person's exclusion from labour office registers and a loss of benefit entitlements, as may failure to comply with duties outlined in the individual action plan. We should note that the individual action plan for the first time represents some sort of balance between rights and duties. However, it is only provided for a select group of the unemployed (young people under 25): they are given the right to contract individual services – but also subjected to the obligation to follow the activities contracted. There are two reasons why the IAP offer is only guaranteed for this group: first, it is in line with the trend of preferential treatment and overrepresentation of young people in active employment policies in the Czech Republic, largely influenced by the fear that lasting inactivity might spoil young people's motivation to work and work habits, and lead to social pathology; second, given the inadequate personnel of employment offices, which prevents more extensive application of a more individualised approach, young people seem to be more adaptable than the long-term unemployed and vulnerable groups like unskilled, elderly or disabled people, ethnic minorities, alcoholics, and so on.

Choice of Early Exit

Since the beginning of the 1990s early exit has been easily available: it has been possible to retire 2 years before reaching the retirement age in the case of unemployment lasting for more than 6 months, with only a temporary pension reduction until the advent of regular retirement age (a penalty of 1% of the pension for every 3 months of early exit). Another option was to retire 3 years before the retirement age, with a pension reduction of 0.6% for every 3 months of early exit.

Strong levelling tendencies in favour of low-income households are also apparent in the pension benefit system. First, the Pension Act of 1995 introduced a new pension formula: the pension is composed of a basic flat component, which is about 20% of the average pension, plus an earnings-related component, amounting to 1.5% of the calculation base for each working year. Significantly, the calculation base only equals full earnings up to the level of half the average wage, while between half the average wage and the average wage only 30% of earnings are taken into consideration, while in the case of income above that only 10% is taken into consideration. Rabušic (2004) shows that the replacement rate of net pensions in relation to gross wages was 47% for average net earnings in 2002, but 77% for earnings at half the average wage and only 27% for earnings amounting to two average wages (the proportion of the net wage is about 7-10% higher: pensions are not subject to taxation). Therefore low-wage earners preferred early exit to unemployment benefits or low-paid employment and that is why between 1996 and 2002 the number of early pensioners increased dramatically, from almost zero to about 15% of the total number of pensioners.

In mid 2001 the government increased the penalty for early exit from 0.6% to 0.9% for every three months of early exit, and from 1% to 1.3% in the case of a temporary reduction of pension (early exit for unemployment reasons). In 2004, the option of early exit for unemployment reasons with only a temporary pension reduction was cancelled. The stricter sanctions on early exit implemented in 2001 influenced early exit rates: between 1996 and 2001, when unemployment was on the increase, the total number of early pensioners rose from 7,000 to 200,000 (that is, about 4% of the labour force). In 2002 the number of early pensioners increased by only 10,000, while the previous year it had increased by 33,000 (MLSA 2003). However, because unemployment benefits are so low, early exit remains a preferred strategy for redundant elderly low-skilled workers whose choice in the open labour market is limited to low-paid secondary jobs or social assistance (minimum subsistence level). Thus the general trend of increasing numbers of early pensioners has not been reversed.

To sum up, the activation strategies introduced in the benefits package in the Czech Republic represent a continuation of the strategy of weak and selective work-first activation: weak unemployment benefit entitlements are combined with fairly acceptable social assistance. The compulsion to take low-paid jobs is theoretically strong but its application on the ground is not systematic.

Activation elements have recently been implemented in benefit schemes, in the form of penalising early exit, increasing the minimum wage and some minor earnings disregards for unemployed people who accept temporary low-paid jobs. Most importantly, however, the conditionality of benefits has been increased, meaning that temporary jobs and labour market training are required for benefit entitlement. The right to activation in the form of individual treatment has also been granted (selectively).

Activation Stream 2: Labour Market Policy Measures

Facing an unemployment shock at the beginning of the 1990s, the government instead of boosting the labour supply fought the growing unemployment by pursuing a strategy of labour market exclusion (Offe 1985), encouraging early retirement and prolonging parental leave. In contrast, 'active' welfare state measures – particularly active labour market policies – lagged far behind EU-15 countries (cf. Cazes and Nešporová 2003), owing to insufficient resources and staff for their implementation. These circumstances also make implementation of strategies aiming to coordinate activation measures in several fields of public policy quite complicated.

The policy of delayed restructuring and tolerance of overemployment in the first half of the 1990s was associated with a low emphasis on active labour market policy measures. During 1996-2000, when unemployment was increasing, the scope of ALMPs increased as well, though it remained quite limited and even decreased in 2002 and 2003, despite the fact that unemployment was growing (see Table 5).

Table 5. Unemployment, Vacancies and Active Labour Market Policies

	1995	1996	1997	1998	1999	2000	2001	2002	2003
Registered unemployment rate (end of year)	2.9	3.5	5.2	7.5	9.4	8.8	8.9	9.8	10.3
Number of unemployed per vacancy	1.7	2.2	4.3	10.3	13.9	8.8	8.9	12.8	13.5
Ratio of ALMP participants to total number of unemployed (%)	36.0	17.1	11.3	12.0	13.7	20.3	19.0	14.5	15.8
Ratio of labour market training participants to total number of unemployed (%)	8.8	6.5	4.3	4.2	4.7	7.3	7.6	7.0	8.0

Source: MSLA, own calculations.

Generosity of ALMP Expenditure

As we can see in Table 6, active labour market expenditure is much higher in the EU countries with a similar level of unemployment to the Czech Republic. The same applies to the number of participants. Still, inadequate expenditure is the main problem because it determines not only the low numbers of ALMP participants but also the inadequate quality of measures and the personnel inadequacies of the public employment service. Also, only low-cost activation is available. For example, with increasing emphasis on activation, short-term motivation programmes were implemented and enlarged during 2003-2004. Rarely are these followed by a job offer or skill-related training/job experience improving employability. This problem also impedes the strategy of employment offices and makes them focus their efforts on this part of the unemployed, who might in any case be efficiently activated without much effort or cost.

**Table 6. Labour Market Policy Measures:
Expenditure and Participants in 2002
(Czech Republic Compared with Selected Countries)**

Country (LFS standard unemployment rate)	CZ (7.3)		HUN (5.6)		SPAIN (11.4)		SWE (4.9)		UK (5.1)	
Expenditure + participants	E	P	E	P	E	P	E	P	E	P
Administration	0.07	–	0.12	–	0.09	–	0.37	–	0.16	–
Vocational training	0.02	0.70	0.06	1.17	0.22	15.27	0.29	2.50	0.03	0.31
Youth measures	0.02	0.15	–	–	0.05	–	0.02	0.61	0.13	0.94
Subsidised jobs	0.02	0.20	0.08	0.66	0.26	4.47	0.17	1.70	0.02	–
Self-employment	0.01	0.06	0.01	0.22	0.05	0.12	0.04	0.25	–	–
Public works	0.03	0.32	0.25	5.82	0.08	1.10	–	–	0.01	–
Sheltered workshops	0.01	–	–	–	0.03	0.25	0.27	0.99	0.02	0.17
ALMP total	0.17	1.43	0.51	7.88	0.85	21.21	1.40	6.05	0.38	n.d.

Note: E = expenditure as % of GDP; P = participants of ALMP measures as % of labour force.
Source: OECD (2003).

Access to the Labour Market, Choice and Quality of Job/Training Offers

Not only is the scope of labour market policies in the Czech Republic limited, but they are also insufficient to support activation goals due to their failure to respond to the needs of vulnerable groups (Sirovátka *et al.* 2003; Sirovátka *et al.* 2004).

Considering the high proportion of long-term unemployed affected by various disadvantages, the targeting of measures to marginalised groups in the labour market seems poor. The least represented category of unemployed in labour market training programmes is the unskilled (targeting index[2] equals 0.42). The position of disabled persons is nearly the same (targeting index of 0.44). Elderly workers are also underrepresented. This means that while about 7% of the unemployed participate annually in labour market training programmes, among disadvantaged groups – such as the unskilled, the disabled, the elderly and the very long-term unemployed (for over 24 months) – it is only about 3%.

Good-quality labour market training programmes for the unskilled or for people with obsolete skills which would enable their successful integration in the labour market are lacking. Typically, labour market training programmes aim at people who already have some skills and need only supplementary training: people with at least upper secondary education participate three times more often in labour market training than those less educated. The low level of unemployment benefits during training (60% of previous wage) makes long-term unemployed persons unwilling to participate in more demanding and long-lasting training programmes, as do the poor prospects of getting a job after the programme's completion.

Young people, mainly school graduates, constitute the focus of active labour market policy measures. With about 8,400 young people participating in vocational training programmes and about 8,000 work-experience jobs created for this category of the unemployed, an activation rate of over 30% was reached in 2003, double the average. As already mentioned, activation measures implemented in the form of individual counselling aim mainly at this group, including individual action plans which cannot be implemented for the long-term unemployed owing to the limited personnel capacity of employment offices.

Summing up, activation strategies are only insufficiently backed by active labour market policy measures. This means that simple job-search support in the form of mediation and counselling prevails. Such an approach may be effective for those with sufficient human and social capital. In contrast, low-cost measures, insufficiently tailored to their needs, limited in scope and poorly targeted do not enable the long-term unemployed to integrate effectively in the labour market.

---

[2] Defined as the ratio between the share of programme participants from a specific category of the unemployed and the share of the same category in the total number of the unemployed (the average being 1.00).

Emphasis on Individualisation, Complexity and Comprehensiveness of Services

In 2003, in line with Guideline 1 of the European Employment Strategy, employment offices started to experiment with Individual Employment Plans. The new Employment Act (in effect since October 2004) established a duty for employment offices to offer an Individual Action Plan to unemployed persons below 25 years of age. The job mediation capacities of employment offices have thus concentrated explicitly on young people. The main reason for limiting the programme to this group was pragmatic: the workload of employment office counsellors/mediators is between 250-500 persons, which does not enable them to provide high numbers of the unemployed with individualised services. Most experts from employment offices estimate that the workload has to be reduced to 150-200 clients per mediator/counsellor in order to achieve an acceptable standard of service. Such a workload would allow at least two 20-30 minute appointments a month with each applicant. However, employment offices do not function under such conditions.

Owing to the limited staff capacity, IAP implementation is based on the principle of voluntary participation, and the programme – owing to the self-selection of clients – targets applicants with a sufficient degree of motivation to secure effective cooperation with the PES. The number of IAP contractors who receive 'individualised services' is not very high (about 10-15% of the relevant cohort of young unemployed). Besides, the individualised approach often seems to resemble the 'formal' one as the activities contracted in the individual action plans do not diverge from standard job-mediation practices. Such formalised practice is mostly necessitated by the limited personal and professional capacities of employment offices. Similarly, experimenting with IAPs in 2003 showed that the number of unemployed who participate in active labour market policy measures did not increase due to IAPs, given the limited capacity of ALMP.

Czech activation policies may be considered selective and not particularly complex in service provision. Economic and legislative incentives are of course aimed at the unemployed in general, and at social assistance claimants in particular. More recently, efforts to enhance incentives targeted at social assistance claimants have evidently been increasing. On the other hand, the range and complexity of services delivered to the most marginalised groups in the labour market remains quite limited: the capacity of individual counselling for vulnerable groups is insufficient and labour market measures are mostly low-cost, simple and do not respond effectively to the complex character of their disadvantages. These measures are selective in favour of younger and skilled people as far as training is concerned. The same applies to mediation and counselling services delivered through individual action plans.

Institutional Setting and Coordination of Activation Policies

The institutional framework of labour market and activation policies in the Czech Republic is characterised by the dominance of state administrative (governmental) bodies (the Ministry of Labour and Social Affairs, public employment service, employment offices), while the role of other collective actors, including social partners, regional and local authorities, NGOs and private agencies is minor. Coordination of the initiatives taken by both 'primary actors' (the state administrative bodies) and 'secondary actors' is weak; action taken by public administrative bodies at different levels is not coordinated consistently either (Sirovátka et al. 2003).

At the central/national level, the Ministry of Labour and Social Affairs (MLSA) and the public employment service are fully responsible for the design and implementation of the National Action Plan (NAP) on employment, labour market policy measures and the unemployment compensation scheme. Only recently (in 2003) was an inter-ministerial body (Council for the NAP) established to improve coordination of the preparation of this core programme document and to ensure participation of different ministries and non-governmental bodies in the process. At the central level, all crucial legislation and programme documents are discussed by the tripartite Council of Economic and Social Agreement, which is, however, only a consultative board whose recommendations are often ignored by the government. Nonetheless, this tripartite board provides a channel for the trade unions to comment on the NAP, the Employment Act and the Labour Code. They emphasise particularly the inadequate level of unemployment benefits, the limited scope of active labour market policy and, besides trying to improve these core conditions of employment policy, recommend measures contributing to job creation as investment stimuli. In summary, they tend to advocate the interests of 'insiders', which are associated with economic development, job creation and short-term unemployment spells.

At the regional level, regional public authorities were established (14 boards) in line with the public administration reforms implemented since 2000. Among other things, they are entrusted with developing the 'regional development concept'. Nevertheless, this programme document is not effectively coordinated with employment policies outlined in the NAP because their preparation is in the hands of different ministries.

Since 2003, selected local employment offices in the new 'regions' have been appointed as coordinators within the PES structure. They do not have a specific budget at their disposal, nor are their decisions binding on local employment offices. Nevertheless, they are responsible for coordination and assisting local employment offices on methodological issues, as well as in the management of EURES activities and ESF projects. The coordination of action taken by regional public authorities, regional PES and other actors, such as regional trade unions and employers, is facilitated by newly established consultative Boards of Human Resource Development. Given the unclear competences of regional bodies and their lack of experience in policy coordination, their influence on activation policies seems negligible at the moment.

At the local level, local employment offices (77) play the central role in policy-making, being entrusted with a high level of policy-making authority (on the other hand, their activities are dependent on finance and personnel determined by the Ministry). Since the early 1990s, advisory boards (which consist of representatives of local PES, local authorities, social partner organisations, key employers, NGOs, universities, and so on) have operated as consultative bodies, but their role is negligible. The role of local authorities in designing employment policy has traditionally been weak: they engage mainly in the implementation of public works, typically in the countryside. Their local social assistance departments function to a large extent independently of local employment offices (they are not interested in implementing activation measures as the government guarantees full repayment of local social assistance budgets). The activation approach is thus difficult to apply consistently.

The new activation measures mentioned in previous sections have in recent years been implemented solely on the initiative of the Ministry of Labour and Social Affairs, in particular the public employment service, which was to a large extent inspired by the European Employment Strategy guidelines. The trade unions at local/enterprise level have neither undertaken any direct action nor explicitly suggested any activation initiative in recent years. However, during the transformation process, the social partners (employers and trade unions) at enterprise level were in some cases engaged – especially in regions undergoing the most intensive restructuring – in preparing outplacement programmes for redundant employees (based on counselling and re-training).[3]

Several NGOs offer activation measures for the most disadvantaged groups (disabled people, ethnic minorities, young people) in the form of

---

[3] Such initiatives were supported by the Phare-Palmiff scheme.

counselling, guidance, assisted job mediation, job experience programmes, vocational training, job creation in the private and public sectors, and self-employment, with a substantial contribution from the Phare-Palmiff scheme (or, since 2004, ESF programmes). However, we should note that such initiatives are increasingly dependent on non-governmental funding and thus the scope of implemented measures is rather modest considering the needs of disadvantaged groups.

Since the early 1990s, private agencies have been allowed to provide job mediation (they have traditionally concentrated on the hiring of candidates for managerial and professional positions or on temporary jobs) and they also often provide labour market training financed from employment office budgets (outsourcing). In recent years these agencies have been greatly involved in providing motivational programmes and individual diagnostics for the unemployed. Under the new Employment Act, they are now allowed to provide agency (temporary) work.

The coordination of actors and activities in the field of activation is still unsatisfactory and the role of non-governmental bodies is minor. Nevertheless, both are improving. In the coming years, these trends might improve conditions, favouring a significant expansion of activation measures.

Czech Mode of Activation Summarised

The Czech Republic has adopted a *weak activation approach* which shares a number of features of the *liberal/work-first model*: the scope and generosity of active employment measures is exceptionally low and their quality, complexity and comprehensiveness extremely poor. Furthermore, we can identify a certain conservative tendency in their application consisting in a high degree of selectivity of active labour market policies and strong segmentation of the measures provided. At the level of implementation, various forms of rationing described by Lipsky (1980) have been identified which affect both the quantity and quality of service. Thus the divisive impact of labour market segmentation is being reinforced.

However, the Czech activation approach is inconsistent in the application of the weak and selective variant of the liberal work-first approach in three respects:

1. The quality of income compensation – the replacement rate of social assistance benefits – is much better (especially for low-income earners) than in many countries in Western Europe.

2. The conditionality of benefit provision is not adequately emphasised.

3. The individual approach is not applied systematically due to the inadequate personnel and professional capacities of the public employment service.

Regardless of the fact that the new Employment Act lays down stricter conditions on access to benefits, as well as sanctions, several months after its implementation MLSA statistics show no evidence of any increase in the number of unemployed persons sanctioned.

The above-mentioned combination of highly inconsistent strategies (the liberal work-first approach contrasting with 'acceptable' replacement rates of social assistance benefits, selective activation measures failing to target the most disadvantaged groups and implementation deficiencies) is probably the least effective variant of the activation approach. Under such circumstances, it is a logical option for the most disadvantaged groups in the labour market to claim benefits, given that their employment prospects are mostly tied to low-paid jobs.

The Factors Shaping the Czech Mode of Activation

How did it happen that the liberal/work-first mode of activation policy has been applied in the Czech Republic, but in a weak, selective and inconsistent form? We can identify three sets of influencing factors. Among the internal factors, the cultural and ideological framework, combined with the economic and institutional context (including other social policies), was important. External factors have also played a role: the influence of the EU agenda on some aspects of policy formation has been obvious recently.

Cultural and Ideological Framework of Activation

In general, the post-communist countries have seen a paradigm shift in relation to the welfare state since the beginning of the 1990s, labelled by Ferge (1997) the 'individualisation of the social'. The profile of social policy has been reformulated from a 'premature welfare state' into a 'smaller welfare state': the dominant goal is now to redesign social policy as a social safety net protecting the population against poverty and unemployment, while aiming 'at the truly needy' and at 'educating the citizens to self-responsibility', while at the same time containing costs (compare Barr 1994; Standing 1996). Regardless of whether social policy was really consistent with this residual model – or rather opportunistic – in the Czech case, the (neo)liberal rhetoric dominated policy discourse and was adopted by the mass media, significantly influencing not only the legislative process but also the approach of public administrative staff to unemployment and social assistance benefit claimants. 'Deeply-rooted habits inherited from the communist past' on the part of people who claim unemployment benefits and social assistance, as well as their reliance on the state, were declared to be a decisive cause of unemployment and poverty. These circumstances are probably the main reason why the Czech public, politicians and public administration were, especially at the beginning of the 1990s, so strongly inclined to support the liberal/work-first approach to activation.

In 1991, 54% of Czechs believed that people themselves were to blame for their poverty; their condition was caused by laziness and a lack of will power; only 17% believed that social injustice was to blame. The percentages changed during the 1990s but the rank order remained the same (see Table 7).

Table 7. Potential Causes of Poverty in Czech Society, 1991 and 1999

	1991	1999
Why are there people living in poverty in the Czech Republic? There are four possible causes: Which of them do you find most important?	% of respondents	% of respondents
They have had bad luck.	12%	15%
They are lazy and lack will power.	54%	42%
There is injustice in our society.	17%	19%
Poverty is an unavoidable part of progress.	22%	18%

Source: European Values Study, Czech Republic 1991, 1999

When van Oorschot and Halman (2000, 13) compared the distribution of answers to this question in various European countries, as well as countries overseas (data from European Values Study 1990), they were surprised to find that Czechs were the most likely to blame the poor themselves for their dire straits. By the same token, the share of respondents attributing the existence of poverty to social injustice was several times lower in comparison with other countries in Europe. This pattern was confirmed by data from 1999 (see Table 7).

In the second half of the 1990s, the growth in unemployment, particularly long-term unemployment, along with the booming grey economy, did not significantly change the pattern of opinion, as we can see from Table 7, but rather led to the formulation of an assumption commonly shared in the professional discourse of public employment service personnel about a relatively significant proportion of 'artificial unemployment': employment office personnel estimate that about a third of the unemployed come into this category.

This hypothesis continues to be echoed in the mass media and shared by the public. Even in mid-1999 when unemployment stood at 8-9%, 54% of respondents in the Czech Republic agreed that unemployed people often or very often misused unemployment benefits. Also, 54% stated that unemployed people often or very often had illegal jobs, while 49% said that unemployed people were often or very often passive in searching for a job (Sirovátka 2002, 338).

Given this public conviction, it is not surprising that no strong political consensus on developing active labour market policies in line with European standards has ever been achieved in the Czech Republic, regardless of the political profile of the government.

The questioning of the legitimacy of active labour market policies and the preference for imposing negative sanctions on the unemployed is largely due to policy-makers' (and the public's) assumption that large numbers of the unemployed are working illegally and/or misusing social benefits. Therefore the scope, quality, targeting and professional standards of active labour market policy measures lag far behind EU countries in consequence of insufficient funding and staff shortages. The 'human resource development' strategy has not been adopted as a key element of activation either. Preference has been given rather to policies based on imposing economic pressure on the unemployed and social assistance claimants to make them seek work and accept any job offer (nominal flexibilisation or the 'work-first' approach).

Economic and Institutional Context

At least three contextual circumstances have supported the prevalence of the 'work-first' strategy in the Czech Republic: (i) the low level of unemployment which lasted until the second half of the 1990s; (ii) the continuing importance of the shadow economy (and its overlap with registered unemployment), and (iii) a lack of resources for activation policies.

Until 1997, the soft economic conditions of 'bank socialism' were responsible for persistent overemployment and for the fact that unemployment did not exceed 5%. Neither the structural changes in the labour market nor the objective disadvantages of the labour force were considered a serious problem by politicians or the mass media. On the other hand, from the very outset of the transition attention was paid to the issue of work incentives in the formal labour market, for several reasons. Incentives were not strong, given the low level of wages, especially in the secondary labour market. On the other hand, there were significant opportunities in the informal economy (also owing to the failure of the public administration to effectively eliminate them): if we take into consideration all possible methods of estimating the scope of the shadow economy, we may assume that it fluctuated between 10% and 15% in recent years, which is less than in other post-communist countries but still more than in the older EU countries.[4]

Overall, social policy development has to some extent been contradicting liberal rhetoric which since the early 1990s has been promising to improve incentives. Governments have instead been pragmatic (and to some degree even opportunistic) in seeking to provide low-income groups with a sufficient level of compensation to protect them against poverty. While the social insurance system, universal benefits and most social services have been reduced, the level of social assistance benefits was set at a relatively high replacement rate and a range of other income-tested benefits for low-income households has been implemented (child benefits and supplementary social benefits were effectively targeted on low-income households). The system thus set unemployment traps for low-income households (see Table 4). These changes were perceived as inappropriate by the middle classes (Sirovátka 2002) and, together with the public assumption of unemployed persons' frequent participation in the shadow economy, legitimated the preference for the 'work-first' model of activation.

Also, the reluctance of government to provide the public employment service with appropriate capacities hindered their professional ability to make a proper use of their considerable discretion on the ground when dealing with the unemployed, in terms of applying a greater degree of conditionality and putting pressure on the unemployed to boost their activity. The Social Democratic government which came to power in 1998 for two terms of office had little impact on the approach to activation policies, as public activation discourse did not change at all. The only deviation from the existing policy path was a modified approach to minimum wage increases: the government adopted a policy of making work pay rather than one of cutting social assistance benefits because cuts in benefits did not correspond well with the Social Democrats' election programme.

---

[4] The Czech Statistical Office's estimate of undeclared work based on a composed method was 9.7% of GDP in 1993, 10.1% in 1997 and 8.1% in 2000 (Ondruš in Fassmann 2003, 50). Gutman's monetary method was used by Fassmann (2003, 70) who arrived at the estimate of 6.1% in 1992, 11.7% in 1996, 18.1% in 1998, 19.7% in 2000 and 15.9% in 2002. Strecková *et al.* (1999) presented an estimate by 123 officials from labour offices, tax offices and the municipalities' small business licensing offices. While 29% of respondents estimated the share of undeclared work as below 15% of GDP, 55% of them estimated it as above 15% of GDP, while 20% of respondents estimated it as above 20% of GDP.

Another crucial contextual factor influencing the approach to activation is the increasing constraints on the budget. In 1997-1999, the economic slowdown strongly affected the budget and led to the adoption of 'austerity packages' (this pattern was repeated due to the floods in 2002). Since 2003, public finance reform has been under way, aimed mainly at expenditure cuts and a reduction of the public debt from 6% of GDP to about 3% within three or four years. It is symptomatic that whenever it has faced economic constraints, the government has sought savings in active labour market policy expenditure. Finally, a decision was made in 2003 to stabilise the public finances by cutting social insurance contributions to the employment fund from 3.6% of wages to 1.6% and transferring the money thus saved to the deficient pension insurance budget.

Owing to these cuts, the development of active labour market policies still lags behind EU standards, despite the implementation of National Action Plans since 1998. Although ALMP expenditure increased due to increasing unemployment, it remains relatively low in international comparison, with a growing emphasis on low-cost measures (for example, when motivational courses for the long-term unemployed were implemented).

The inadequate personnel and professional capacities of employment offices and social assistance offices, as well as poorly developed coordination and partnerships with other bodies and institutions, not only make a human resource development strategy based on an individual approach difficult but also represent a barrier to efficient application of the work-first strategy.

The Role of the European Union

The ambiguous and contradictory consequences of the EU accession process for social policy in post-communist countries have been discussed elsewhere (for example, Guillén and Palier 2004). Some authors have portrayed these consequences as a tension between the Copenhagen criteria and the Lisbon strategy (Potůček 2004). In the case of the Czech Republic, the contradiction can be seen between directives of programme policy documents that promote European employment strategy targets (that is, full employment, labour productivity and social inclusion) and are based in principle on the human development approach, supplemented by other policies, on the one hand, and the Copenhagen monetary criteria imposed on public expenditure which are to be fulfilled by the new member states in order for them to be allowed to participate in European monetary union, on the other.

With regard to programme documents, the Czech Republic has resolved this contradiction by finding a way to cope effectively with the EC recommendations (specifically with the objectives and guidelines of the European Employment Strategy), that is, by presenting the European Commission with the right rhetorical gestures. This does not seem difficult because the programme documents in the field of social and employment policy are not very demanding; goals may be defined at a relatively general level and existing policies may be re-organised according to the obligatory structure of NAP guidelines. No sanctions are linked to a failure to adequately meet the vaguely specified targets.

Thus while the programme documents declare a policy which corresponds to some degree with the human resource development approach, the actual policy steps seem to be guided by slightly different priorities that are more in line with the existing policy path preferring weak and selective activation and dominated by elements of the work-first approach.

The attempts to rebalance the public finances in a low-productivity economy bring, among other things, restrictions on human resource investment because cuts in expenditure on mandatory transfers are politically unfeasible. On top of that, while the external EMU criteria have to be met, compensation policies targeted at 'the deserving' and at larger population groups (like pensioners and working families with children) are still given political priority.

In the Czech Republic, not only were the possibilities of improving human development policies undermined in 2003 when the active labour market budget was affected by cuts in contributions allocated to the employment fund, but similarly the personnel capacities of the public employment service were frozen in December 2003 when the government rejected a proposal from the Ministry of Labour and Social Affairs to increase PES staff by about 450 (nearly 10%) in order to meet the requirements of an increased emphasis on activation.

Nevertheless, in addition to the impact of the pragmatic approach to reconciling the tension between the social/employment policy programme documents – as suggested and required by the European Commission – on the one hand, and the Copenhagen EMU criteria on the other, we may identify other influential mechanisms that have emerged from the new methods of EU governance. These mechanisms are related to 'policy-goal transparency', 'actor mobilisation', 'know-how transfer' and 'institutional learning' and initiate the process of a silent evolution towards EU targets and policies. In this way, EU forms of governance have contributed substantially to cultivating and professionalising policy-making in the Czech Republic, even in the field of activation policies. At least, activation issues have entered the debate between the Ministry of Labour and Social Affairs and other ministerial bodies through the National Action Plan, and understanding of the need to adopt a broad and coordinated approach has improved. The problems of the labour market have been identified and formulated better, and the corresponding goals have been set at least at the general level. This transparency and problem awareness, as well as the mobilisation of the actors concerned, do contribute to a more comprehensive approach. The changing approach has manifested itself in the adoption of a new institutional measure, which is the establishment of an inter-ministerial commission for the preparation of NAP 2004-2006.

In the near future, the possibility of applying for support from the ESF may also play a crucial role. It might help to substantially expand the scope of activation measures, especially in the area of human resource development: it is estimated that resources available for active labour market policy measures may grow by 50% during 2004-2006 owing to the ESF. At the same time, it facilitates mobilisation of local partners, owing to the influence of EU methods of governance. Not only were new regional offices established within the framework of the public administration reform initiated in 2001, but also regional employment offices in 2003 (although as yet endowed with only limited competencies). Also, non-governmental actors should be given many more opportunities to participate in policies. The establishment of new implementation structures, participation of new actors, access to new resources and the application of new governance and management methods associated with the administration of ESF projects may substantially improve the public administration's capacities.

Finally, institutional activation and learning are also crucial aspects of EU influence. The adoption of specific implementation methods will contribute indirectly to the process of institutional learning. For example, in the Czech Republic, the implementation of IAPs, although not adequately backed in terms of personnel and financing, has contributed to the identification and development of new methods of approaching the unemployed. Specifically, the public employment services have implemented – on the basis of individual action plans – new methods of working with the unemployed: individual diagnostics and profiling, assisted mediation, motivational programmes, and agency work. They also learned to involve NGOs in the process of job mediation and other forms of intervention. We are witnessing rapidly improving professional capacities as young people – particularly university graduates in social sciences – enter the public employment services and other bodies participating in activation, such as NGOs and private agencies.

Conclusion

The need in the Czech Republic for strong activation policies and their systematic implementation is obvious. This is indicated by a high share of long-term unemployment and extremely unevenly distributed unemployment risks, which are associated with a lack of human capital and work incentives. Since the beginning of the 1990s, the Czech Republic has unfortunately followed the path of weak activation, characterised by a number of features of the liberal/work-first model. The scope of active employment measures is exceptionally narrow and they are poorly targeted and lacking in quality, complexity and comprehensiveness. Simple job-search support in the form of mediation and counselling, supplemented by sanctioning, is the dominant measure. Unemployment benefit entitlements are poor and the definition of a suitable job is strict. At the same time, certain conservative features can be identified in this approach which consists in a high degree of selectivity of active labour market policies and strong segmentation of available measures, with measures concerning human resource development being targeted at the better-endowed part of the labour force.

On the other hand, the Czech activation approach is in several respects inconsistent even with the weak and selective variant of the liberal work-first approach: the replacement rate for social assistance claimants is more generous than in many countries in Western Europe. The conditionality of benefit provision is not systematically applied in practice due to the inadequate personnel and professional capacities of the public employment service. The above-described combination of inconsistent strategies is not effective with regard to activation and meets neither the need for human resource development nor the need to increase administrative pressure on the unemployed and work incentives.

We have identified three interlinked sets of factors which shape the Czech mode of activation: the cultural and ideological framework, the economic and institutional context and the EU policy agendas.

In the Czech Republic, both the policy discourse and public opinion show an extreme inclination towards (neo)liberal policies – including the work-first activation approach – in comparison with other European countries. A number of other circumstances also favour this approach: unemployment remained low until the second half of the 1990s, while the scope of the shadow economy, overlapping with registered unemployment, has long been above the EU average. On top of that, the resources allocated to activation policies have been scarce due to a lack of political consensus and the government's preference for covering mandatory transfer payments.

The EU accession process has generated tensions between the European Employment Strategy targets and the Lisbon strategy guidelines promoting a human development approach on the one hand, and the Copenhagen monetary criteria imposed on public expenditure which have to be met by the new member states on the other. At the moment, preference is given to EMU, as manifested by public finance reform and cuts in the public budget. These cuts affect labour market policies in the first place and block further advancement of the human development approach.

On the other hand, we have identified other influential mechanisms that have emerged from EU methods of governance in relation to goal transparency, actor mobilisation and institutional learning, and at the same time new opportunities to develop policies with the support of the ESF. These conditions have launched a process of continuous evolution towards a more comprehensive strategy which may change the weak liberal (but inconsistent) activation approach that has prevailed so far. The process of continuous change incited by EU methods of governance is being further reinforced by a generational change and increasing professionalism on the part of the public administration and others participating in activation policies.

References

Barbier, J.-C. (2004), "Activation policies: a comparative perspective", in A. Serrano Pascual (ed.), *Are Activation Policies Converging in Europe? The European Employment Strategy for Young People*, Brussels, ETUI, pp. 47-84.

Barr, Nicolas (ed.) (1994), *Labour Markets and Social Policy in Central and Eastern Europe. The Transition and beyond*, New York, Oxford University Press.

Burda, Michael (1993), "Unemployment, labour markets and structural change in Eastern Europe", *Economic Policy* 16 (April), pp. 101-138.

Cantillon, B., N. van Mechelen, I. Marx and K. van den Bosch (2004), *The Evolution of Minimum Income Protection in 15 European Countries 1992-2001*, paper presented at the meeting of the International Sociological Association, Research Committee 19 on Poverty and the Welfare State, 2-4 September, Paris.

Cazes, S. and A. Nesporova (2003), *Labour Markets in Transition. Balancing Flexibility and Security in Central and Eastern Europe*, Geneva, ILO.

Esping-Andersen, G. (1990), *The Three Worlds of Welfare Capitalism*, Oxford, Oxford University Press.

European Commission (2004), *Indicators for Monitoring the Employment Guidelines 2004-2005*, Compendium, Second Version, EC, DG Employment and Social Affairs (update 22/9/2004).

Fassmann, M. (2003), *Stínová ekonomika II* [Shadow economy II], Praha, ČMKOS and Sondy.

Ferge, Zs. (1997), "The changed welfare paradigm: the individualization of the social", *Social Policy and Administration* 31 (1) (March), pp. 20-44.

Gallie, D. and S. Paugam (eds.) (2000), *Welfare Regimes and the Experience of Unemployment in Europe*, Oxford, Oxford University Press.

Giddens, A. (1998), *The Third Way: The Renewal of Social Democracy*, Cambridge, Polity Press.

Guillén, A. and B. Palier (2004), "Introduction: does Europe matter? Accession to EU and social policy developments in recent and new member states", *Journal of European Social Policy* 14 (3), pp. 203-210. Special issue "EU Enlargement, Europeanization and Social Policy" (August 2004).

Jessop, R. (1993), "Towards a Schumpeterian workfare state? Preliminary remarks on post-Fordist political economy", *Studies in Political Economy* 40, pp. 7-39.

Lipsky, M. (1980), *Street Level Bureaucracy. Dilemmas of the Individual in Public Services*, New York, Russell Sage Foundation.

Lødemel, I. and H. Trickey (eds.) (2001), *An Offer You Can't Refuse. Workfare in International Perspective*, Bristol, The Policy Press.

Madsen, P.K. and P. Munch-Madsen (2001), "European employment policy and national policy regimes", in D.G. Mayes, J. Berghman and R. Salais (eds.), *Social Exclusion and European Policy*, Cheltenham, Edward Elgar, pp. 255-276.

MLSA (MPSV) – Ministry of Labour and Social Affairs Czech Republic (2003), *Basic Indicators on Employment and Social Security in the Czech Republic*, Prague, MPSV.

Morel, S. (1998), "American workfare versus French insertion policies in application of Common's theoretical framework", paper presented at the Annual Research Conference of the Association for Public Policy and Management, New York, 29-31 October.

OECD (2003), *Employment Outlook*, Paris, OECD.

OECD (2004), *Benefits and Wages. OECD Indicators*, Paris, OECD.

Offe, C. (1985), *Disorganised Capitalism*, Cambridge, Polity Press.

Potůček, M. (2004), "Accession and social policy: the case of the Czech Republic", *Journal of European Social Policy* 14 (3), pp. 203-210. Special issue "EU Enlargement, Europeanization and Social Policy" (August 2004).

Rabušic, L. (2004), "Why are they all so eager to retire? (On the transition to retirement in the Czech Republic)", *Czech Sociological Review* 40 (3), pp. 319-342.

Saraceno, C. (ed.) (2002), *Social Assistance Dynamics in Europe. National and Local Poverty Regimes*, Bristol, The Policy Press.

Serrano Pascual, A. (2004), "Conclusion: towards convergence of European activation policies?" in A. Serrano Pascual (ed.), *Are Activation Policies Converging in Europe? The European Employment Strategy for Young People*, Brussels, ETUI, pp. 497-518.

Serrano Pascual, A. (ed.) (2004), *Are Activation Policies Converging in Europe? The European employment strategy for young people*, Brussels, ETUI.

Sirovátka, T. (2002), "Opinions of Czechs about the welfare state", *Czech Sociological Review* 38 (3), pp. 327-344.

Sirovátka, T. (ed.) (2004), *Sociální exkluze a sociální inkluze menšín a marginalizovaných skupin* [Social exclusion and social inclusion of minority and marginalised groups], Brno, Masarykova univerzita.

Sirovátka, T. *et al.* (2003), "Problémy trhu práce a politiky zaměstnanosti" [The problems of labour market and employment policy, Czech Republic], Výzkumná zpráva (research report), Brno, Masarykova univerzita. (www.mpsv.cz)

Sirovátka, T., M. Horáková, V. Kulhavý and M. Rákoczyová (2004), "Efektivnost opatření aktivní politiky zaměstnanosti v roce 2003" [Effectiveness of active labour market policy in 2003], Výzkumná zpráva (research report), Praha/Brno: Výzkumný ústav práce a sociálních věcí [Research Institute of Labour and Social Affairs] (www.vupsv.cz)

Standing, G. (1996), "Social protection in Central and Eastern Europe: a tale of slipping anchors and torn safety nets", in G. Esping-Andersen (ed.), *Welfare States in Transition*, London/New York, Sage, pp. 225-255.

Standing, G. (1999), *Global Labour Flexibility. Seeking Distributive Justice*, Basingstoke: Macmillan. New York, St. Martin's Press.

Strecková, Y. *et al.* (1999), *Institucionální možnosti minimalizace vlivu stínové ekonomiky na trh práce ČR.* [Institutional possibilities to minimise the influence of the shadow economy on the labour market in the Czech Republic), Závěrečná zpráva (final research report), Grant MPSV ČR: GK MPSV 01-36/98, Brno: Masarykova univerzita, Ekonomicko-správní fakulta.

Torfing, J. (1999), "Workfare with welfare: recent reforms in Danish welfare state", *Journal of European Social Policy* 9 (1), pp. 5-28.

van Berkel, R. and I.H. Møller (2002), "The concept of activation", in R. van Berkel, and I.H. Møller (eds.), *Active Social Policies in the EU. Inclusion through Participation?*, Bristol, The Policy Press, pp. 15-44.

van Berkel, R. and M. Roche (2002), "Activation policies as reflexive social policies", in R. van Berkel, and I.H. Møller (eds.), *Active Social Policies in the EU. Inclusion through Participation?*, Bristol, The Policy Press, pp. 197-224.

van Oorschot, W. and L. Halman (2000), "Blame or fate, individual or social? An international comparison of popular explanations of poverty', *European Societies* 2 (1), pp. 1-28.

Zákon č. 435/2004 o zaměstnanosti [Employment Act No. 435/2004].

Activation Regimes in Europe: A Clustering Exercise

Amparo SERRANO PASCUAL

Introduction

The country chapters show that the activation-based intervention paradigm is being adopted by several European countries. Barbier demonstrates in this book that this process has resulted in major reforms to the social welfare system, while other authors (Vielle, Pochet and Cassiers 2005) trace its impact on the Welfare State model being promoted. Nevertheless, endorsement of this interpretative framework does not necessarily mean that it will lead to common outcomes. A wide range of policies are labelled with recourse to the same interpretative framework and a *pluralistic approach to implementation* could serve just as well to empower as to weaken workers'/citizens' position in society.

Institutional settings and in particular power relationships among different groups in society (employers/employees, political representatives/civil society, women/men, left-wing/right-wing parties, women's movements), as well as prevailing work values and standards all have an important role. Activation *regimes* play a central role in defining the instruments to be used in national activation strategies to regulate the behaviour of job seekers. In each country, we encounter a specific balance between rights and duties, obligations and responsibilities and the services provided in return. Policies differ in terms of the extent to which measures are compulsory, penalty mechanisms, the degree of coercion exercised upon claimants and the types of option on offer (quality of job offered, relationship to the life path and so on).

Activation Regimes: An Interdisciplinary Approach

The "regime" concept can be useful for analysing the different implementations of activation policies. We have understood the term to refer to the hegemonic mode of governance in a given community, comprising not only all the institutions regulating how power is exercised by the different social actors, but also all the values that legitimate these institutions and provide a community with social cohesion and a sense of purpose. *Institutions* are taken to mean not only social actors with political power, but also all the historical standards regulating and legitimating the way power is exercised and shared. We have used the term *activation regimes* to stress the social regulation methods of the activation policies adopted by a given community. Activation regimes are the outcome of the fragile balance of power between the different actors involved in the design and implementation of these activation policies and of all the hegemonic regulatory and cognitive benchmarks that shape a community's understanding of the social exclusion problem.

While the Esping Andersen typology could serve as a starting point for classifying the various activation regimes that have emerged in different countries in response to the most urgent social problems, we also need to be sensitive to intracluster differences. Esping Andersen's intention was to provide a classification of welfare regimes, not employment or activation policies.[1] However, the semantic field of the activation concept as used in this study goes beyond the strict meaning associated with employment policies, as it also includes the Welfare State's intervention and reproduction logic and principles. Activation policies are paradigmatic and illustrative of major social changes in the principles governing the functioning of the Welfare State and consequently Esping Andersen's classification criteria may be at least partially relevant to our study.

Esping Andersen's classification identified criteria for a comparative analysis of the different forms of socialisation of solidarity, providing us with a better understanding of the differences between countries as far as their social achievements and responses are concerned. This much quoted and much criticised seminal work has been extremely valuable in enabling different scenarios to be analysed, thereby avoiding deterministic interpretations of the role played by the demands of industry and market laws in the institutionalisation (or lack of it) of solidarity.[2]

---

[1] For a summary of some of the activation policy classifications that have been undertaken, see Sirovátkain this book, Barbier (2006), Lodemel and Trickey (2000).

[2] This pioneering work made it possible to identify the factors influencing the wide range of social responses to the institutionalisation process of industrialised societies, for example the regulatory configurations that define the problem (individual vulnerability vis-à-vis the market, the fact that everyone does not start on an equal footing, inequalities in the way social welfare is implemented) and consequently also the goals of State intervention (equality for all citizens, workers' rights, preventing poverty, guaranteeing incomes, protection against market forces, etc.) and who is responsible for solving it (the Welfare State, the market, the family, social partners, profes-

The problem of having such a typology is that it may result in an analytical trap which forces us to see more similarities and differences than there actually are.[3] We have a selection of countries that should help to avoid this analytical trap: two Nordic countries (Sweden and Denmark), two southern European countries (Portugal and Spain), an "atypical case" (the Netherlands), a continental European country (France), a new EU member state (Czech Republic) and an Anglo-Saxon country (UK). Furthermore, the problem with Esping Andersen's typology is that countries are classified according to criteria which, by definition, give high scores to Nordic countries in comparison with other countries that are placed in a less favourable position.

This typology has been challenged by a number of studies, for various different reasons.[4] Alternative typologies have been proposed based, for example, on the predominant social security financing model (e.g. Bonoli 1997), the Welfare State's approach to the family (e.g. Lewis 1992, Siaroff 1994), or the level of development and nature of the Welfare State (Leibfried 1993), to name but a few. Furthermore, as discussed in the introduction, recent Welfare State reforms have resulted in a degree of institutional hybridisation, forcing a partial reassessment of Esping Andersen's classification.

Although some aspects of this classification may be debateable, we nevertheless believe that the criteria the author identified are important for obtaining a good understanding of the extent and nature of the changes in the welfare intervention model, even if these criteria are not always explicit. They also enable an interdisciplinary perspective that looks at the role of both social and psychosocial factors, such as the prevailing regulatory values and benchmarks in a given community and socio-political aspects, such as institutional development and the modes of governance regulating the balance of power among the various social actors.

---

sional groups); the role of the prevailing institutions and historical agreements between the political actors and the social classes in a given country (corporatist, mercantilist, family-based); the political and economic situation and the prevailing industrial model.

[3] That is also the problem with concepts. Once a concept has been created, it forces to see reality in a structured way, creating *ad hoc* differences and similarities in what is a more complex reality.

[4] For example, they question the fact that the analysis is based exclusively on paid work and the relationship between the State and the market (Lewis 1992), dispute the inclusion of some countries in certain categories (Ferrera 1996), argue that insufficient attention is paid to care provision strategies and gender role division (Mósesdóttir 2000; Pfau-Effinger 2005) and criticise the failure to take into account the role played by gender concepts and divisions (Walby 2001), etc.

The provisional typology proposed in this chapter is nothing more than an incomplete first attempt at outlining a classification, since to do full justice to such an ambitious task would require a much more detailed analysis. Nonetheless, we hope that it will at least serve as a proposal, albeit one that may need to be revised, for the important task of classifying the wide range of social welfare model reforms throughout Europe. There are two key factors that enable us to distinguish between different activation regimes:

Governance structures and institutional setting: Several authors (Larsen and Mailand in this book, Jorgensen, 2002) have drawn attention to the importance of the role played by the institutions and actors representing civil society in the priority setting process and the historically institutionalised agreements between them (*consensus, conflict, cooperation, competitiveness*). Van Berkel (in this book) comes at the issue from another angle by stressing the importance of the activation of institutions in this paradigm shift. In many countries, the adoption of the activation paradigm has been accompanied by administrative and management reforms (privatisation, marketisation, competition, decentralisation). This involves a transformation of the way the roles and responsibilities concerning the running of the Welfare State are shared among actors at different geographical levels (national/supranational/regional/local), social actors (social partners, civil society), economic actors (public/private) and administrative actors (education, social, economic and finance departments).

Hegemonic regulatory assumptions: This is an aspect that has received little attention in the various comparative studies of the dissemination of specific "styles" of adapting the activation paradigm. The regulatory assumptions regarding the meaning of work, who is responsible for social exclusion, the meaning of citizenship and the duties of job seekers act as cultural frames that not only influence policy design, but also serve as a regulatory justification/foundation for these policies (Boltanski and Chiapello 2002). For example, a culture's prevailing understanding of the nature of the individual (as either competent and responsible or dependent and passive) will have a significant influence on the kind of welfare policies considered to be reasonable and legitimate by society. In addition, a community's values and standards concerning work and worklessness will influence the social representation of these policies.[5] As well as contributing to the social legitimation of

---

[5] A predominantly moralistic concept of unemployment may favour a brand of activation policy designed to discourage dependency and promote responsibility; a political understanding of unemployment linked to the affirmation of national identity and the viability of the Welfare State, may result in a form of activation that fo-

the activation model, these regulatory and cultural assumptions also influence the specific way it is interpreted. Indeed, given the individualised nature of the interventions in the activation paradigm and the fact that the local professionals and actors who implement these policies have greater discretion to tailor them to their clients' specific needs, skills and expectations, these standards and values may also be influencing these professionals' personal opinions, as pointed out by Hespanha in this book.

Governance Structures and Institutional Setting

The modes of governance that have been arrived at in the past regulate power relationships among the different social actors and affect how strong the position of the unemployed is. One of the public actors that have had the greatest influence not only on the regulation of activation policies, but also on income distribution and on the power status of the unemployed is social partners. In the current context of social welfare system reforms, the countries where trade union involvement is more institutionalised and where there is a strong tradition of consensual governance setting have managed to preserve a degree of balance between institutional pressure to encourage people to work and the protection of social rights. Trade union involvement has limited the extent to which activation policies could be used as a strategy for promoting cheaper and more insecure labour. As demonstrated by Larsen and Mailand in the chapter on Denmark in this book,[6] trade unions have defended the social contract between the State and its citizens, enabling a degree of balance to be achieved between economic and social considerations in the welfare reform process. In countries with strong social partners, such as Denmark and Sweden, social welfare system reforms have had to be accompanied by compensatory measures that benefit human capital. A key element of the cultural identity of countries like Denmark is their skill at consensus building and their confidence in their ability to do so (Jorgensen 2002), resulting in strong social and institutional pressure for this state of affairs to be maintained. Given a favour-

---

cuses on national citizenship; an economic concept of unemployment may lead to activation instruments designed to promote adaptation to new economic challenges, either through investment in human resources or through coercive strategies aimed at ensuring the availability of an army of reserve workers.

[6] These authors show how, during the adoption of the activation paradigm, any concessions involving a weakening of certain acquired rights (e.g. restrictions on access to unemployment benefit, reduction in the period of benefits, etc.) have had to be compensated for by the strengthening of other rights (e.g. provision of suitable jobs, investment in training, or initiatives geared towards developing individual skills).

able balance of power, this is something that acts in favour of the protection of citizens' rights, but when the balance of power shifts, it can become a problem.[7]

Sweden has managed to maintain extensive social rights despite an explicit emphasis on citizens' duties. Consequently, since the 1970s, there has been a balance between the work principle (active policies) and the cash principle (passive policies). These two countries and the Netherlands are examples of highly developed social models with a strong Welfare State and a correspondingly high level of investment in social policies, the labour market and social welfare. These models are designed to provide universal access to social welfare.

Recent pressures in these countries, particularly in the Netherlands, have contributed to a shift in the traditional balance between rights and obligations, with greater emphasis being placed on the regulation of duties. Since the 1990s, there have been a number of significant changes that explain the increasingly punitive approach of activation policies, accompanied by far-reaching reforms of the pensions system and of disability and early retirement benefits. Van Berkel's contribution to this book describes how this situation has come about as a result of a gradual weakening of the social partners' position and their replacement by actors from the world of business, resulting in a dramatic transformation of intervention logic and principles. The social security administration has been gradually commandeering control from the trade unions, causing their role to become marginalised. A shift in the political perception of the trade unions' purpose has been a major contributor to this weakening of their position. According to one increasingly popular interpretation of the Dutch economic crisis in the 1990s (the "Dutch disease"), the predominant corporatist regulation system (of industrial insurance boards organised in each sector) is more a part of the problem[8] than the solution. The perceived failure of the previous model has led to a far-reaching review of the principles of the Dutch welfare model (Visser and Hemerijck 1997). This is in contrast to the situation in Denmark and Sweden, where, at least until recently, the corporatist culture and its strong consensus building capacities have continued to be favourably represented. As a result, the corporatist system is perceived

---

[7] Mailand (2005) describes how the new liberal government is garnering the support of social partners for labour market reform (more people in employment) despite initial scepticism from the trade unions.

[8] The strong involvement of social partners in the administration of the Disability Benefit is considered to be the chief cause of the problem ("they misused and abused"), leading to the privatisation of Dutch sickness benefits (cf. van Berkel in this book).

as a success story and indeed as the key to achieving an optimal combination of economic growth and social prosperity ("Swedish model"/ "Danish model").

Another explanation[9] that has been proposed for the different scale of welfare retrenchment in the Netherlands and Denmark, particularly in the 1990s, and despite various efforts made by the governments of both countries, is the political consensus between the different parties in the Dutch government. Green Pedersen (1999) suggests that certain political constellations facilitate the implementation of controversial and unpopular policies, such as major Welfare State reforms, by making it easier to use "blame avoidance" strategies. According to this author, such far-reaching reforms of the social welfare system have been possible in the Netherlands because of the broad political consensus on economic policy among Dutch political parties. This has prevented the issue from becoming politicised and construed in a negative light, so that public opinion on these aspects has been depolarised. The author argues that in Denmark, on the other hand, the Social Democrats' opposition in the 1990s explains why it was so hard to implement unpopular reforms of the social welfare model in that decade, due to the effective pressure brought to bear by the opposition parties.

However, since the end of the 1990s, the Danish social welfare system has in fact been reformed, largely as a result of a shift in the balance of power in Denmark's institutional system. The corporatist system is being undermined and unemployment benefit management, which had previously been the main channel for recruiting trade union members, is being transferred to local actors (see Larsen and Mailand in this book). The spread of principles derived from the new public management approach, the growing regionalisation of policies and the increasing contractualisation of public employment services are all altering the established balance between rights and duties and at least partly undermining the provision and regulation of social rights. As a result, opportunities for the unemployed to undergo training have been scaled back significantly, with greater emphasis being placed on guidance. In addition, a particular type of policy designed to get people into work more quickly has been heavily promoted and employment services have been partially privatised (Mailan 2005). Larsen and Mailan suggest that the new right-wing Danish government's political interest on the Dutch model may in fact be specifically targeted at undermining the trade

---

[9] Del Pino (2005) presents an interesting discussion on the various factors influencing the extent of welfare reforms in different countries.

unions' political position so that they are able to pursue policies that are more in line with their liberal political ideas.[10]

In the other countries in this study, the extent to which the social partners have been able to act as a counterbalance has been somewhat more limited, although they do have considerable ability to mobilise public opinion in Spain and France and to a lesser degree also in Portugal. Despite very low levels of trade union membership and the absence of any real tradition of social partnership, the trade unions have been very successful at organising protests in these countries, resulting in major strikes, demonstrations and public statements of opposition to the development of active policies. This has had a substantial influence on the evolution of social policy (Guillén et al. 2002; del Pino 2005; Aragón et al. in this book). In Spain's case, the involvement of civil society has been regarded as an essential part of social modernisation. However, in Spain, as in Portugal, the fact that this involvement was institutionalised during the transition to democracy, at a time of high unemployment, has largely neutralised civil society's ability to oppose the labour market deregulation measures promoted by successive Spanish governments, particularly in the early stages of the transition. This moderate approach changed in the 1990s, when these institutions came to play an important role in the design of social policy. Indeed, the trade unions are less likely to back government policy than in countries such as Denmark and Sweden. In Spain, for example, the trade unions called a general strike in 2002, in opposition to controversial legislation aimed at reforming the unemployment benefit system, forcing the government to back down on the most polemical measures. The political decentralisation process has not led to a reduction in trade union participation. Instead it has actually strengthened it in some cases, resulting in a growing number of regional pacts (see Aragón et al. in this book).

As far as the UK and the Czech Republic are concerned, the weakness of the trade unions has led to an imbalance in the relationship between the State and benefit recipients.

In addition to the social partners, we are witnessing the gradual emergence of new actors who have an influence on the regulation of these policies. This is happening as a result of a dual process of decen-

---

[10] This appears to be quite a sound argument if we consider that the integration of new public management principles in the delivery of activation policies has had very disappointing results as far as efficiency and effectiveness are concerned (see van Berkel in this book and Struyven and Steurs 2005). This might lead us to surmise that the reason for adopting this strategy is not simply the pursuit of greater financial efficiency.

tralisation, on the one hand, and contractualisation of public policies, on the other. Significant decentralisation is occurring in Spain, the UK, Denmark, the Netherlands and Portugal and this has often been accompanied by the involvement of private actors, particularly in the case of the Netherlands.[11] Consequently, various different actors have become involved in controlling and managing employment policy. In fact this shift has often gone hand in hand with a proliferation of different players, resulting in a complex network of interactions between public and private actors. There is an increasing trend for key duties to be delegated to private actors and in some cases the local authorities, who are responsible for running the social welfare system, are offered incentives to cut welfare spending (performance-based funding system), thereby encouraging the adoption of a commercial approach[12] (see van Berkel in this book). This privatisation process is geared towards improving effectiveness (through greater specialisation and proximity to the source of the problem) and efficiency (cheaper interventions). The adoption of these commercial criteria has resulted in this kind of intervention being governed by quantitative rather than qualitative considerations. At the same time, the intended improvement in the quality of the interventions and how well they cater to individual needs has not always been achieved.

In the UK, two opposing trends are currently in evidence. On the one hand, local and regional authorities are gaining greater budgetary powers, enabling them to choose to contract service provision out to private actors. But, on the other, the "Training and Enterprise Councils", which are predominantly run by the private sector, are being replaced by "Learning and Skills Councils", which include representatives of social partners, although their involvement in the implementation of activation policies is strictly peripheral.

In France and Spain, major organisational reforms of public employment services are also being undertaken (involving increased outsourcing of services). In Spain, as in the UK, these reforms have also been accompanied by a significant degree of decentralisation at both the regional and local level and by a proliferation of public and private actors, creating a complex intervention network. However, the efficiency of this set-up is limited, owing to the lack of co-ordination and specialisation (see Aragón *et al.* in this book). Nevertheless, the high

---

[11] Private actors are also involved in France and Spain, but in this case they are mostly private non-profit making organisations.

[12] In the 1990s, activation was focused not only on the clients but also on the institutions involved in the administration and implementation of social security. The adoption of approaches based on New Public Management and New Governance was encouraged.

level of decentralisation has served to promote innovation and to disseminate innovative ideas across all regions (Guillén *et al.* 2002). Furthermore, the active involvement of the trade unions in the Regional Employment Pacts appears to have had a positive effect (by maintaining social cohesion across the whole of Spain).

Like Spain, Portugal became industrialised later than the other countries in the study and the Catholic Church still retains considerable influence. Another factor shared with Spain is the period of dictatorship that weakened civil society significantly. As Hespanha indicates in this book, this uneven balance of power was accentuated by the rise in unemployment, a factor that undermined potential opposition to the deregulation measures called for by employers. Despite their scepticism of activation policies, the trade unions have been unable to prevent the loss of social rights that these policies contributed to. Although a significant degree of decentralisation has been promoted, this has not resulted in privatisation of the public employment services. Compared with Spain, where there is a highly decentralised political system, Portugal is a centralised republic. Another major difference between Spain and Portugal is that the former was governed by a centre-left party for fourteen consecutive years, something that favoured the development of welfare policy, whereas in Portugal there was a greater alternation between left-wing and right-wing governments (Ballester 2005). The Portuguese social welfare system was late to develop, like Spain's and the Czech Republic's, and it has never afforded the level of protection found in other European countries. Consequently, it can be said that these three countries share the trend towards transformation from a "premature Welfare State" to a "smaller Welfare State" highlighted by Sirovátkain the chapter on the Czech Republic. The State continues to play a major role in both Portugal and the Czech Republic. Although the trade unions are not very powerful, social dialogue has consolidated considerably in recent years, accompanied by the spread of major regional networks for the promotion of employment. Both countries, therefore, have a very strong State, causing other collective actors (social partners, regional and local actors and private actors) to have little more than a peripheral role, although their involvement is on the increase.

One significant institutional trend shared by many countries is the merging of the Benefits Agency and Employment Service into a "working age agency" and/or the merging of the Employment Ministry with the Ministry for Social Affairs. In some cases this is accompanied by the tendency to centralise activation policies aimed at people covered by social security and those targeted at people claiming welfare benefit into a single organisation. This demonstrates the increasingly widespread assumption that paid work is the only route to social integration.

Regulatory and Ideological Factors

Only a few studies (van Oorschot and Halman 2000; Aust and Arriba 2004; Larsen 2005; Pfau-Effinger 2005) offer a comparative analysis that takes into account the role played by regulatory benchmarks and cultural values in the justification and direction of employment and welfare policies. Nevertheless, regulatory values have a fundamental influence on the way that the meaning of reality is construed (and indeed questioned) and on the terms used to define the "social question". Furthermore, these hegemonic values may be used as a strategic resource by civil society and social movements in the process of symbolic negotiation of social models. Consequently, cultural assumptions about the meaning of work and citizenship comprise an important source of social support for certain welfare policies.

Van Oorschot (2000) stresses the fact that social judgements of the "deservingness" of the unemployed and socially excluded people play an important role in the social legitimation of the Welfare State. He identifies five major criteria influencing judgements about deservingness: control (i.e. the social perception of how much control the unemployed have over their predicament and therefore how responsible they are for their situation), need (evidence and extent of their need), identity (whether or not they belong to the group, social skills), attitude (submissiveness and diligence) and reciprocity (evidence of the fairness of the "contractual" exchange of social obligations and individual duties). As can be seen in the country chapters, deservingness is a key issue as far as the adoption of the activation paradigm is concerned, since it underpins the direction being taken by Welfare State reforms in various European countries and in particular those where the social reforms are based on neoliberal political ideas. Factors connected with control ("work for those who can, welfare for those who cannot"), need ("means testing" of benefit recipients), the attitude of the unemployed (identification of "good unemployed people": judgements regarding the motivation and attitude of the unemployed play a key role in local actors' decisions as to whether or not to continue paying them benefits) and reciprocity (consolidation of the contractual nature of welfare benefits – formal statement of both parties' duties and obligations, in order to strengthen this reciprocity element) have all acquired a central role in the direction taken by the activation measures implemented in the United Kingdom. They have also gradually come to the fore in the other European countries, particularly in the Czech Republic and Portugal.

Authors such as Larsen (2005) suggest that the specific characteristics of a given country's welfare regime could actually have the effect of promoting certain attitudes towards policies concerning poverty and unemployment, by increasing the influence of certain questions in the shaping of the public debate. The institutional setting of a country's welfare regime (for example the eligibility criteria for claimants, the degree of generosity, the type of job opportunities and the social divide between people who are out of work and those who are in work) may steer the social debate towards issues such as control, need, identity and reciprocity, causing *deservingness* to become a key issue as regards the direction of these policies. Larsen shows how under liberal regimes (characterised by selective social policies, the social perception that there are plenty of jobs available, a high level of individualism which promotes the opinion that people are able to control their own situation and a pronounced differentiation between the employed and the unemployed), the unemployed are directly questioned as to whether or not they meet the deservingness criteria and this can lead to public support for a given social policy being rather more precarious (Larsen 2005). In contrast, in countries where the proportion of client/beneficiaries is higher, such as Sweden, Denmark or the Netherlands, there is also a higher level of public backing for social welfare policies (del Pino 2005). At the same time, the debate surrounding deservingness is less of an issue in countries with a Bismarckian regime like France and Spain, where the social security system is financed by social security contributions paid by employers and employees. This is because this kind of regime promotes a greater "feeling of entitlement" (Green Pedersen 1999) than in countries with a Beveridgean welfare regime that is financed mainly through taxation (see Aragón *et al.* in this book).

In addition to the question of whether or not deservingness or the social judgements concerning it are a key issue, another important aspect relates to the prevailing social representations of poverty and unemployment. Van Oorschot and Halman (2000) carried out an interesting comparative study of the hegemonic explanations of poverty, based on the European Values Survey. They distinguish between the preponderant view in the Czech Republic that attributes poverty to personal characteristics (48%) and the perception in other countries, such as those included in this study, based on a predominantly social explanation where poverty is considered to be the result of social injustice. In the first case, the people affected seem to be responsible and to blame for their predicament, while in the second they are seen as victims of social injustice. The Danes, and to a lesser extent the Swedes, provide an exception to this view, since their prevailing explanation of poverty is the "social fate explanation" (i.e. uncontrollable social factors). This may serve to explain the importance that these countries place on successful adaptation to new economic demands (resulting from globalisation and a tougher competitive environment), factors that they take as a given. However, while countries like Denmark and Sweden achieve this adaptation through training, guidance and promoting mobility, countries such as France and Spain have opted for a more defensive response to these challenges, based on reducing labour costs by cutting employer contributions or partially subsidising wages.

While there is a social rather than an individual explanation in the countries covered by this study (with the exception of the Czech Republic), the importance of individualistic explanations of unemployment and poverty is greater in the UK than in the rest of the group (Feather 1982). At the other end of the scale, the countries that record the lowest proportion of people who blame the poor for their predicament include the Netherlands, Sweden, Denmark and France. Van Oorschot and Halman (2000) conclude that, although there is no direct correlation between the prevailing explanations of poverty and a country's welfare regime, it can nevertheless be said that "in countries where the social causes of poverty dominate people's views, there is a combination of high social security spending and tax-based financing... While in countries where the idea prevails that poverty results from the actions of certain actors, instead of from fate, there is a combination of low spending and contribution-based financing [...]" (p. 20).

It is, therefore, possible to distinguish between two views: the one where a moral understanding of the problem predominates, as witnessed mainly in the Czech Republic, but also in the UK and to a lesser extent in Portugal and the more socio-political understanding shared by countries such as France and Spain. In Denmark and Sweden, on the other hand, it could be said that the prevailing representation of the problem is more socioeconomic than socio-political.

Sirovátka(in this book) offers a detailed analysis of the way disincentives to claiming unemployment benefit are promoted in the Czech Republic, highlighting how the modernisation process in that country has partly been founded on a rejection of the previous nanny State regime that favoured passive attitudes and State dependency. This explains the limited nature of government spending to combat unemployment. By contrast, there has been a comparatively generous level of spending on social welfare programmes aimed at tackling poverty, something that can be at least partly attributed to the policy of promoting equality handed down from the previous regime. These two different attitudes towards welfare benefits and people on social security seek to protect the population against the risk of poverty and also to educate citizens to become more self-reliant (see Sirovátkain this book). One contributor to this situation may be the second factor identified by van Oorschot (scepticism regarding the existence of proof that people are really in need), owing to the high underground economy percentage. One might expect the continued high unemployment rates to favour a social view of the problem. However, it is generally assumed that there is "artificial unemployment" due to the extent of the black economy.

This has resulted in the moral perception that the unemployed deserve censure, since they are supposedly abusing society's collective solidarity either by working illegally or by being too passive to find work. In 1991, 54% of the Czechs believed that poor people are responsible for their own predicament and that poverty is due to laziness and a lack of determination. As a result, there is a tendency to redefine unemployment as an issue that is not really a social problem and to suspect that unemployed people are probably up to no good. This in turn means that there is no real political consensus regarding the need to promote active policies, but rather to penalise passive ones.[13] Against this background, it is no surprise that Czech policy focuses on interventions targeted at increasing the motivation of the unemployed through financial pressure and flexibilisation of the labour market.

This hegemony of neoliberal principles also characterises the State intervention system in the UK. Lindsay (in this book) shows how UK policy is targeted at encouraging people to take responsibility for solving their own problems. Unemployment and poverty are explained by individual factors, such as Mead's arguments on the "culture of poverty" and passivity, or by those that stress the negative consequences of unemployment for the unemployed in terms of demotivation and personal decline. These are accompanied by neoclassical economic interpretations suggesting that the longer a person remains in a state of dependency, the more their skills will deteriorate and the more they will get out of the habit of working and lose touch with the world of work. All these attitudes explain why the dominant understanding of the causes of unemployment focuses on a lack of incentives to work (Duman 2005) and why the UK government's interventions have concentrated on the unemployed's motivation and attitude. Another contributory factor to this state of affairs is the fundamental importance placed on having a job. The UK shares a belief with the Nordic countries in the key role of work as a means of achieving economic and social welfare, a

---

[13] Gilens (1999) shows in a study of the United States that many US citizens oppose social welfare not so much because they are against State intervention or social welfare policies as such, but rather because they have a negative perception of the recipients of public support.

view that is also supported by the British labour and trade union movement.

While the Dutch scenario is similar to the UK in gradually placing more emphasis on "deservingness", arguments in favour of maintaining a relatively generous Welfare State also play a significant role. As indicated above, unlike the prevailing view in the Nordic countries, where a high level of welfare spending is compatible with strong economic growth, in the Netherlands it is predominantly thought that one thing is incompatible with the other. The debate concerning the negative effects of the Welfare State (the Dutch disease) has led to its development being regarded as responsible for promoting economic inactivity and unemployment and this in turn has had an impact on people's support for its expansion (Cox 2001). The increasing use of disability benefits as a means of getting older workers to give up their jobs during times of high unemployment and the growing spread of a "crisis mentality" have been used to justify a string of reforms and budget cutbacks since the 1980s. Therefore, the main problem has become the high inactive population and this has resulted in the need to encourage labour market participation as a key issue in the debate on welfare reform. Social partners have come to be seen as part of the Dutch disease and commercial principles have been applied to the management of social services, while the privatisation of public services has been promoted. The justification of these major reforms rests on the twin arguments of cutting public spending while at the same time improving the operational efficiency of the public employment services so that they are better equipped to combat inactivity and unemployment (see van Berkel in this book).

In Denmark, the major changes in the principles of welfare intervention that have occurred since the 1990s are the result of a hybrid approach to the problem. The political debate is becoming increasingly focused on factors that constitute a threat to the work ethic (demotivation and reluctance to make oneself available for work as possible consequences of long-term unemployment) and on the concurrent problems of a labour shortage in some sectors together with high unemployment (structural problems in the labour market).[14] Consequently, a

---

[14] In the 1990s, Denmark experienced an unusual situation where major structural unemployment coexisted with job vacancies in some sectors. This resulted in inadequate training being identified as the source of the problem, leading to substantial investment in education measures. The main problem was considered to be the inefficient functioning of the labour market owing to the lack of people with the required skills. However, since the new liberal government came to power, this investment in human resources training has been scaled back in favour of a greater emphasis on getting people into work as quickly as possible.

dual approach has been adopted to tackle the problem. On the one hand, a more coercive approach has become increasingly popular, on the basis that "passive" support could constitute a threat to the work ethic, a theme that was at the centre of the political debate in the 1990s (Andersen 2001). On the other, a training-based approach has also been favoured in the belief that education and training are the "magic wand" that will solve the structural crisis. As such, there has been broad agreement that activation has the twin effect of promoting motivation and training (Barbier *et al.* 2006). Until the beginning of 2000, training was the main measure targeted at social security beneficiaries and also, albeit to a lesser extent, at welfare benefit recipients. Since then, however, there has been an unfavourable shift in the balance of power as already described above. This has caused the understanding of the problem in terms of a lack of training to be displaced by another that focuses on a lack of motivation, with greater emphasis being placed on the punitive aspects of interventions. These reforms of the Danish model were based on a number of evaluation studies that adopted an economics-based approach and encouraged greater attention to be paid to labour market attachment aspects. They were also influenced by the adoption of a moralistic approach to the problem that stressed the reciprocal nature of the interplay between rights and duties (Larsen and Mailand, in this book).

As a result, as suggested by Lind and Moller (2004), the tendency towards a reinforcement of work-related standards and morals has played a key role in the development of the Danish social welfare system. Various authors (Christensen 2001; Lindsay in this book) have pointed out that viewing work as both a right and a duty is in keeping with the traditional values of the labour movement in countries as diverse as Denmark, Sweden and the UK. However, this interpretation has changed over the course of time. Christensen (2001) describes how in Denmark, the labour movement's strategy was initially based on the political and legal consolidation of labour rights. Later, during the Golden Age of the Danish system, it moved towards a socio-liberal approach focused on the right to labour, before entering a final phase, in the period when the moral aspects of work came to the fore, when it came to be based on the duty to work. The fact that the Danish labour movement has taken on board the regulatory approach that establishes work as a central value may at least partly explain why, in contrast to the southern European countries, the recent increase in activation measures has not really been regarded as a major problem.

This work concept has also been a key value in the Swedish model, indeed the idea of work as a duty has always been present in Swedish policy. However, the Swedes have managed to maintain a relatively successful balance between training provision for job seekers and pressure to find work. Training has constituted the main activation measure, since it is regarded as a means of promoting occupational and geographical mobility. As in Denmark and the Netherlands, the severe recession in the 1990s led to the introduction of major reforms geared towards improving the efficiency of active measures, but so far this has not led to any significant reduction in training or other forms of investment in human capital. Nevertheless, the increased use of disability benefits has turned the debate towards the eligibility rules, in view of the growing concern that Sweden shares with the Dutch and the Danes with regard to the financing of the Welfare State.

In Sweden, Denmark and the Netherlands, the expansion of the Welfare State took place in a period of strong economic growth, reinforcing people's positive attitude towards social welfare spending. This contrasts with the situation in countries like Spain, Portugal and the Czech Republic, where the expansion of the Welfare State occurred at times of political transition and economic crisis, a fact that has significantly impeded the development of social welfare in these countries. This was accentuated by the fact that organisations such as the OECD promoted an understanding of the problem that suggested that the job creation problems experienced by these countries were due to the excessive protection and regulation of their labour markets (describing them as "rigid" labour markets). As a result, the view became widespread that social intervention (or social regulation) is supposedly incompatible with economic development. Indeed, the main labour market policy in Spain has focused on interventions geared towards labour market (de)regulation in order to promote temporary jobs for disadvantaged groups. This is the reason why the insecurity of the labour market is just as big a problem in Spain as unemployment or economic inactivity.

In France, the values of republican citizenship have played an important role in the development of the social welfare system. Barbier (in this book) describes how these values have promoted a social concept of unemployment and citizenship that opposes a more coercive approach to employment policies. Until the end of the 1990s, citizenship involved not only a purely economic dimension but also a political one (collective participation in defining rights), as can be seen from examples such as the welfare programme and the guaranteed minimum income (*Revenu minimum d'insertion*). These programmes have been reformed to include a more punitive approach since the new conservative government came to power. However, as in Spain, the reforms met with significant public opposition.

Liberalism, in the broadest sense of the word (i.e. recognition of civil and social rights) and the consolidation of individual rights *vis-à-vis* the State played a key role in the early development of the Welfare State in France, the Nordic countries, the UK and the Netherlands. However, this was not the case in Spain, Portugal and the Czech Republic, where there were authoritarian political regimes until only recently. Nonetheless, the way that these philosophical principles were implemented in practice differed greatly from country to country, ranging from a rather more abstract concept of freedom and rights (the right to resistance, security, etc.) to the more specific freedoms that characterise the Anglo-Saxon countries. Jefferys (2005) points out the tension that has existed over the past 200 years between two differing views of freedom: on the one hand, the view that inspired the American Revolution, where freedom is seen as the right to own and use one's own property and, on the other, the view that underpinned the French Revolution, where freedom is regarded as the ability to associate with others in the pursuit of collective goals (i.e. the social contract) (Jefferys 2005). Therefore, while some countries have concentrated on the principle of private ownership (including the idea of being one's own master), others have adopted a more political focus of citizenship.

In contrast to these liberal roots and the different social welfare systems that they have resulted in, the countries with authoritarian regimes experienced a more paternalistic and minimalist attitude to social welfare. Consequently, when these countries began to modernise, people rejected authoritarianism and were rather suspicious of the role of the State which many people identified with the denial of individual rights rather than their promotion. This may perhaps explain the widespread scepticism of State protectionism in countries such as the Czech Republic and Portugal.

In Spain, as in France, people are opposed to the increased use of punitive measures and coercion and are more tolerant of the possibility of benefit fraud than the Czechs and Portuguese. There is widespread rejection of the idea that the unemployed are to blame for their own situation (owing to cultural factors and also to the high unemployment rate, low level of welfare benefits and the poor quality of the available jobs) and this explains why it is considered perfectly legitimate to reject a job offer and why people favour voluntary rather than compulsory participation in active employment measures. In Spain, as in Sweden, it is widely believed that there is little that excluded people can do to escape their predicament (World Value System 1995-997: Larsen 2005). This, together with the low level of protection provided by the Welfare State, explains Spanish society's strong opposition to government plans to restrict access to welfare benefits. This public opposition to the increased use of coercion in activation measures is having significant social consequences that go beyond mere protests or demonstrations. As Aragón et al. explain in this book, local actors enjoy a high degree of discretion with regard to the specific approach adopted in implementing interventions and the influence of the social standards described above means that in practice punitive measures are rarely enforced. Furthermore, in Spain (and probably also in Portugal and the Czech Republic) the principles of democratisation and modernisation have been core values in the development of the Welfare State, since modernisation is something that has been associated with political development. As a result, EU membership has had a significant influence on national identity (since it is associated with social modernisation and economic development) and the goal of achieving the levels of social welfare available in other European countries has been one of the main drivers of the Welfare State's development. In Spanish society, cutbacks in social services are therefore viewed as a backward step for society and democracy.

Another factor that may be influencing the strong public opposition to social welfare reforms is the fact that employment policies are often negatively perceived by Spanish society. Compared to other sectors such as healthcare and education, the field of employment policy has often provided an opportunity for rights to be curtailed (deregulation of the labour market, promotion of temporary contracts). This has resulted in public opinion being very sceptical about so-called employment measures, in contrast to the strong public support for so-called *passive* measures that provide income support.

In Portugal, regulatory unemployment models vary considerably and are to some extent similar to those in the Czech Republic. Conservative rural attitudes and a strong emphasis on the family continue to be prevalent in a large proportion of the population, resulting in a widespread work ethic that blames poor people for failing to have the foresight to meet their own needs. This attitude is also characterised by the proliferation of individual values as opposed to universal ones, an emphasis on individual charity rather than on a collective approach to social welfare and consequently a deep suspicion of the State (see Hespanha in this book). This explains why, despite the insignificant scale of the problem, there has been a great deal of alarmism in Portuguese society concerning the issue of benefit fraud (Moreno et al. 2003). These attitudes have combined with a mixture of neoliberal ideas promoting the myth of the market and stress the importance of economic aspects over social ones. Therefore, although Portuguese society supports social welfare measures, 47% of Portuguese citizens believe that entitlement to welfare benefits should be dependent on the beneficiary's attitude.

Activation Regimes: A Provisional Classification

The psychosocial and socio-institutional factors described above have resulted in very different kinds of activation policies. In order to identify different activation regimes, in other words different ways of organising the policies and actors that deal with the problems of social exclusion and economic activity, we believe that it is important to stress two aspects. The first relates to the prevailing modes of *managing individuals* that are based on different ontological conceptions. The second has to do with the contents and reciprocity of the 'contract' between the unemployed and the State (*quid pro quo*) and the specific (im)balance of power between the two.

Modes of Managing Individuals

As far as the *first* aspect is concerned, i.e. the way in which the behaviour and attitudes of the unemployed are regulated, there are a number of different scenarios. These span the two extremes of, on the one hand, a mode characterised by *moral-therapeutic management* of individuals' behaviour and, on the other, a mode of intervention based on *matching* workers' skills and labour costs to the new economic circumstances. Both modes seek to legitimise themselves by drawing on the concept of 'autonomy', but their underlying interpretation of what is meant by autonomy is different, since they are based on differing understandings of human nature. These two approaches match the dichotomy that Crespo and Serrano (2005, forthcoming) have identified in the activation model promoted by EU institutions. This model is characterised firstly by an ontological concept that defines the individual as ethically autonomous but psychologically dependent and secondly by a view of individuals as politically autonomous but economically dependent. We believe that these two views of the nature of the individual are not mutually exclusive and that both are to some extent present in the majority of activation models found in each country, although one or the other will predominate depending on the one in question.

Moral-Therapeutic Management of the Behaviour of Welfare Recipients

This first type of intervention assumes that individuals are *passive* by nature and that it is therefore necessary to force them to fulfil the moral duty of all individuals to take responsibility for their own lives. This paternalistic view considers individuals to be incapable of managing their own personal development and career path. In some countries, this approach is especially characteristic of interventions targeted at certain social groups viewed with suspicion, for example the young, socially excluded people, groups that are particularly at risk of exclusion, etc. Within this overall view, two main interpretations can be distinguished. The *first* understanding of the problem defines the behaviour of unemployed or inactive people as the consequence of a rational decision that they have chosen to take, suggesting that they do not wish to work (or it is not worth their while) "for logical and rational reasons". The *second* interpretation is that their behaviour is due to personality failings rather than to a rational decision.

The *first* interpretation rests on an anthropological understanding of individuals as beings motivated by instrumental goals, with an "innate" tendency to be idle. This intrinsically moralistic interpretation of unemployment and economic inactivity establishes a connection with human nature. The behaviour of the unemployed with regard to the labour market is taken to be the result of a rational financial calculation, meaning that it may often turn out to be rational and logical to stop working, albeit morally reprehensible.

One of the trends that have emerged in interventions based on this understanding of the problem is the selection and identification of "good" unemployed people. The initial requirement for the unemployed to attend meetings with public employment services in person is now increasingly accompanied by the requirement for them to provide an explicit indication that they are "honest" about their desire to find work (for example, the requirement to sign a formal, legally binding agreement stating that the welfare recipient is actively seeking work) (this is the fourth deservingness criterion identified by van Oorschot 2000). This kind of intervention therefore pursues the twin goals of selecting "good unemployed people" (those who demonstrate that they are actively seeking employment) and helping them into work as quickly as possible.

This approach has steered the political debate towards a redefinition of what is understood to constitute a "suitable job". The debate surrounding the redefinition of the conditions that make a job "suitable" for a benefit recipient has been extended to include *terms of responsibility* in the event of an offence, such as refusal to accept a job offer. The result is that recipients are subject to constant assessment and their attitude to work is judged on an ongoing basis. The purpose of this monitoring of beneficiaries' behaviour is to evaluate whether or not they deserve to receive assistance. As such, this kind of activation policy is designed to influence personal motivation, offer incentives that may serve to coerce people's will and influence individuals' behaviour with regard to the labour market (to '*make work pay*').

The *second* variant of the moral-therapeutic intervention model is based on the assumption that the unemployed suffer from certain failings. According to this view, the role of the Welfare State is to help individuals to "free themselves from themselves" and avoid the *snares* or *traps* that they could *irrationally* fall into, leading them into a life of poverty and dependency.[15] Activation thus constitutes a means of enabling individuals to take control of their own lives. Difficulty in finding work is put down to "personality" problems and interventions are therefore targeted at improving self-esteem, career guidance, CV writing skills, teaching people how to "sell themselves" on the labour market, self-knowledge, job search skills, etc.[16] While the first interpretation is based on an ontological state where individuals' innate idleness leads them to take a "rational" decision not to work, based on a financial calculation ("the individual *doesn't want to* work or *it is not worth his while*"), the second interpretation holds that the individual is not *able* to work owing to his (personality) failings. Consequently, the first scenario sees the question as a moral issue (i.e. it is a case of reminding people that all citizens have a duty to contribute to society through their own labour and of reaffirming the law of reciprocity), while the second scenario treats the problem as a therapeutic issue.[17]

This kind of activation measure could be seen as a means of *disciplining* people with a view to producing individuals who meet the new demands of industry by promoting habit-forming practices. This disciplinary approach is accompanied by *normalisation practices* that involve separating out the people who are unemployable based on an overall rule of thumb (employability). In this respect, it is customary for job seekers to be divided into categories[18] in order to evaluate how hard it will be for them to find work and to "diagnose" the correct treatment for them. In other words, they are evaluated in terms of how employable they are in order to establish a classification based on their ability to manage their own personal development. Specific interventions are then

---

[15] Although it is customary to analyse the two concepts of "making work pay" and "unemployment traps/snares" together, we consider them to belong to two different symbolic orders.

[16] For an excellent analysis of how these processes function in everyday practice in the bodies responsible for implementing these policies, see Darmon *et al.* 2004.

[17] For an interesting examination of medicalised therapeutic interventions in the US welfare system, see Schram (2000).

[18] This practice of evaluating and categorising groups of unemployed people based on how hard it is likely to be for them to find a job reinforces the perception of excluded people as a separate group to "employable" people and thus has an indirect influence on the appraisal of an individual's deservingness as established by van Oorschot (Larsen 2005).

proposed on the basis of this classification. This approach does not punish behaviour and personal failings so much as individual attitudes and lack of willingness. The most important thing is not so much the substance of the offence itself as how far this offence is indicative of some personal maladjustment or lack of willingness. Consequently, this type of measure does not focus so much on punishment as on treatment, i.e. on trying to cure people of their negative attitudes towards employment or lack of willingness to look for work. This debate is ongoing in a number of different countries and is characterised by three processes: the search for the cause of the offence, the apportioning of causality and ultimately the judgement that a person has achieved "normality".

As such, many measures are geared towards *monitoring and checking up on* job seekers in order to establish their attitude (as opposed to their behaviour) to employment. The aim of this monitoring is to "cure" them rather than to control and punish them. It is assumed that the problem is due to individual failings that are therefore treatable, sometimes "therapeutically" (Schram 2000).

Individuals become "clients" who are required to share the responsibility for finding work by a contract that governs the terms of social reciprocity.[19] According to Hamzaoui (2003), the idea of a contract is replacing the previous regulatory instruments (such as laws) with the aim of encouraging the negotiation of rules. This contract, however, presupposes equality between the parties to it. It assumes that they are willing participants in the process who are able to exercise their right to state their own case and that there is an even balance of power between the parties. As such, it represents a social technology that allows individuals greater autonomy, while at the same time subjecting them to greater pressure, with 'autonomy' becoming a byword for self-discipline. This type of policy re-establishes the value of work as a means of self-discipline and as the cure for all ills, whether they be ills that afflict the individual or society as a whole.

The activation model adopted by countries like the UK and the Czech Republic (and to a lesser extent Portugal) is characterised by the first moralistic explanation of unemployment that regards passivity as a voluntary state resulting from a rational financial calculation to the effect that it is not 'worth the unemployed person's while to work'. This favours an attitude that blames the unemployed for their own predicament and therefore legitimates greater use of coercive measures. The

---

[19] This is the underlying approach of the European employment guidelines that identify the need to draw up a personalised activation plan with the unemployed person in order to take account of their specific circumstances.

second interpretation, found in the Netherlands and to a lesser extent also in Denmark, sees passivity as the consequence of involuntary factors (personality failings, lack of motivation, etc.), favouring more disciplinary and therapeutic interventions geared towards normalising the behaviour and regulating the will of individuals (i.e. helping them to escape the unemployment "trap"). Interventions of this type tend to be delegated to "activation professionals" who develop therapeutic measures aimed at treating each individual's problems in order to encourage them to enter the labour market.

Matching Up Workers to Market Demands: Adaptive Skills Management

A second approach views people as *autonomous* individuals who nonetheless require certain resources (training in some cases and work experience in others) in order for them to make use of their autonomy. According to this second model, the role of the Welfare State is to provide the conditions for producing individuals who match the new requirements of industry. Consequently, interventions based on this model are designed either to provide people with the education and individual skills needed in order to manage their career path (personal training) or to match labour costs to the new requirements of industry (by cutting employer contributions or subsidising the employment of certain groups) in order to incentivise the recruitment of particular groups of people. Unlike the first approach described above, this type of intervention is not so much aimed at managing behaviour and attitudes as at matching labour supply and demand. The goal is not so much to force unemployed people into work but rather to maximise their potential skills and make sure that they are able to meet the new demands of industry. There are two different approaches that are based on this model: a more proactive approach, found in Sweden and to a lesser extent in Denmark, that focuses on developing individual skills (through training, mobility, guidance, etc.) and a more defensive approach found in Spain and France, which is designed chiefly to reduce labour costs. Both seek to improve the functioning of the labour market.

Nevertheless, this kind of model also rests on a number of analytically very debatable assumptions such as the naturalisation of the existing economic conditions and the assumptions that the problem is due to people's inability to adapt to new market demands, that all the jobs in the labour market are good and that autonomy and self-reliance are solely determined by the individual. However, this model is completely inappropriate in countries, regions or industries where the majority of jobs are low-skilled and insecure, or where there simply are no jobs at all. Furthermore, this approach may serve to expand and legitimate the secondary labour market. In addition, it begs the question of how an individual is supposed to act autonomously if we assume the individual's ontological condition to be one of interdependence rather than independence.

Indicators for this first aspect of managing individuals include:
- means of regulating the behaviour of unemployment benefit claimants: benefit sanctions, limiting income replacement, reducing the period of entitlement, conditionality of welfare benefits, less generous unemployment benefit, stricter benefit regime;
- introduction of tax benefit reforms;
- definition of a "suitable job";
- comprehensiveness or extension of these measures to all economically inactive people;
- attitude towards the client (role of the individual in defining his job-finding plan; top-down approach);
- client supervision;
- marketisation of services;
- degree of discretion/formalisation in the role of the State.

A New Social Contract: The Balance of the Quid Pro Quo

The *second* factor influencing the type of activation model relates to the specific content of the social contract between the State and the unemployed person, in other words the (im)balance between rights and duties or the balance of the *quid pro quo*. In this context, the first approach focuses more on the duties of welfare recipients than on the Welfare State's obligations. This approach characterises the UK model that aims to increase unemployed people's duties as far as their commitment to finding work is concerned, while at the same time promoting incentive-based State interventions (see Lindsay in this book). However, the demands placed on job seekers in this intervention model far outweigh any rights they may acquire (in terms of the quality of the job-finding process, the kind of job that is available, the level of government investment in individual job-finding plans, etc.). Despite the fact that they may have been involved in negotiating a given job offer, job seekers are nevertheless expected to accept jobs almost unconditionally. In this instance, the service (*quo*) provided by the State does not match the demands placed on the job seeker (*quid*).

The second places a more equal emphasis on both the community's obligations *vis-à-vis* the individual (*quo*) and the individual's duties (*quid*). The social contract is thus more balanced, since, although it places significant demands on the job seeker, it also has high expectations of the State's interventions. This approach is found in Sweden, the Netherlands and Denmark and to a lesser extent also in France, since the French retain a strong republican tradition of social commitment despite the major reforms of their social welfare system (see Barbier in this book). This model, where individual rights and duties are given equal weight, incorporates elements of responsibility-based communitarism. The reciprocity standard underpins much of the relationship between the individual and society and the community is seen as having an important role in empowering individuals and building shared values, in particular the value of work. Nevertheless, this approach remains fragmented and individualised in so far as it considers the social contract to be the only thing that binds individuals together.

The third approach, found in Spain, Portugal and the Czech Republic, is also characterised by a balance in the social contract between the community and the individual citizen (*quid pro quo*). However, this balance is based on the lowest common denominator. Therefore, although no great expectations and pressures are placed on job seekers, the level of government spending on social welfare is correspondingly low.

Indicators for this second aspect (i.e. the balance of the social contract) include:

- extent of entitlement (coverage of income replacement, comprehensiveness, generosity, etc.);
- government spending on social welfare;
- degree of individualisation in the approach towards clients;
- participation of the benefit recipient in the activation process;
- the range of defined options for participation;
- type and quality of the options on offer (getting people into work as quickly as possible or vocational training for job seekers);
- link with labour market segmentation.

Based on the above criteria, it is possible to identify five activation regimes that are shown in the following table:

Trade-offs \ Modes of managing the individual	Moral-therapeutic regulation of behaviour	Matching regulation
Quid / quo (focusing on regulation of the obligations and duties of benefit recipients)	Economic springboard regime	
Quid= quo (based on provision of rights and regulation of obligations)	Civic contractualism regime	Autonomous citizens regime
Quid= quo (limited rights and obligations)	Minimalist disciplinary regime	Fragmented provision regime

Analytically speaking, the activation regimes described above are *ideal types* and do not therefore claim to represent all the different national settings in their pure form. Instead they seek to identify certain typical trends in the modes of political and regulatory governance of activation regimes. The following section takes a closer look at what each of these activation regimes involves.

Economic Springboard Regime

This type of regime is characterised by the heavy emphasis placed on ensuring that citizens fulfil the duties in their contract with the community, in particular their duty to achieve financial independence so that the community no longer has to provide for them. This is accompanied by a responsibility-based understanding of unemployment where the State has the dual role of helping the unemployed to find work as quickly as possible and reaffirming work as the norm for all citizens. While this kind of regime favours limited intervention overall, existing interventions are targeted at the moral qualities of job seekers, aiming to change their individual attitudes and predispositions.

This is the approach followed in the *United Kingdom*, where the main emphasis is on coercive aspects (stronger conditionality and compulsion, poor quality of the jobs on offer) and inductive aspects (lowering the tax burden for low-paid workers so that working is "worth their while"). It seeks to ensure that benefit recipients fulfil their civic duty to find work and despite the provision of tailored services by personal advisers hinting at a more therapeutic kind of intervention, the lack of funding for this type of measure makes successful implementation impossible. The gateway period is intended to enable a trust-based relationship to be built between the adviser and the client (intensive job search activity, confidence-building, counselling and advice) (see Lindsay in this book). However, this approach is hindered by the low level of public spending per client in the programme and its focus on "soft" skills and on getting clients into work as quickly as possible. The interventions are fundamentally geared towards reminding benefit recipients of what the "norm" is and as such they contain strongly moralistic elements. This intervention approach is not restricted to welfare benefit access and is tending to spread to the other areas of social policy, including tax reforms (working tax credit) designed to make work pay by offering people incentives to work. Therefore, as well as compulsion in some cases, the aim is also to demonstrate to people that "working is worth their while", thereby helping dependent people to fulfil their moral duties.

Civic Contractualism Regime

What this regime shares with the one above is a strong emphasis on ensuring that citizens fulfil their duties. But it differs in that citizens also enjoy extensive social rights guaranteed by a strongly interventionist Welfare State. Interventions still place great emphasis on individual responsibility, but in this case the underlying understanding is of the individual as someone who needs to be "accompanied" in order to ensure that they can manage their personal development successfully. This type of regime is therefore characterised by delegation of employment services to "intervention professionals" who aim to develop interventions tailored to individual circumstances and designed to strengthen the beneficiary's personality.

The contract is a key feature of this regime and forms the basis of a new mode of social regulation that often arises from the perception that previous modes of regulation have failed. Contractualism thus comes to be seen as a means of rewriting the social contract with citizens. In this context, we are using the term "contractualism" to refer to the growing use of the metaphor of the "contract" as a key instrument for regulating relations with the public (Mosley and Sol 2005). There are two sides to this concept, both of which aim to reform the mechanisms of social regulation. On the one hand, it involves a new approach to public policy management designed to achieve quality and efficiency improvements (contractual relationships between the organisations involved, accompanied by a more market-oriented approach). On the other, it involves an approach to managing individuals' behaviour that seeks to reaffirm the reciprocity standard and the values of the community, particularly the value of work, thereby promoting "accountability". A significant part of the employment actions are based on an individual action plan drawn up together with the job seeker. At the same time, it is argued that the use of public service contracts for services that were previously provided exclusively by the State is a means of making these services more professional. As a result, commercial considerations take on a fundamental role (Sol and Westerveld 2005). In both cases, contractualisation is regarded not just as an individual necessity (in order to promote the social inclusion of the individual), but also as a collective necessity in order to ensure the continued viability of high levels of social welfare spending (maintaining the Welfare State is seen as something that affirms the collective identity). Consequently, appropriate and effective participation in the labour market is viewed as a civic duty.[20]

This type of model is found in the Netherlands, where commercial factors are a prime consideration in the operation of implementation organisations. Particular emphasis is placed on the activation of institutions, for example through results-based funding aimed at cutting costs and improving services (see van Berkel in this book). Struyven and Steurs (2005) show how the Dutch approach seeks to create the conditions "to enable the market to play" (p. 225) and it is characterised by a tendency to replace entitlement (automatic right to benefit) with a contract (emphasis on rights and obligations). The increased involvement of multiple actors has been aimed at achieving more professional interventions with welfare recipients, who are now treated as "clients". Service providers are expected to find a solution tailored to their clients' personal circumstances and employment prospects. The pressures to which these "intervention professionals" are subjected under the terms of their outsourcing agreements with the public authorities mean that their role is not confined to helping job seekers find work, but also includes therapeutic interventions intended to "normalise" their situation.

Two trends have been witnessed in the case of the Netherlands. On the one hand, since the 1980s there has been a series of reforms promoting incentives geared towards influencing the behaviour of the unemployed, including: tighter checks on people's willingness to accept job offers and surveillance of the behaviour of the unemployed, reduction in the unemployment benefit claim period, lowering wage replacement levels of social insurance, tightening eligibility criteria, broadening the

---

[20] In this context "civic" is taken to mean compliance with a range of standards imposed by the community in order to exercise one's citizenship fully. It therefore involves a code of morals or virtues for citizens.

"suitable job" concept,[21] extending instruments designed to get people into work as quickly as possible (quick and short-term job placements), stipulation of tougher obligations for the unemployed and specification of penalties. On the other, while spending on active measures was below the European average between 1986 and 1991, it rose above the European average between 1991 and 1995, although it has recently been cut back again,[22] despite a rise in unemployment. As a result, despite an increase in coercion, there has been substantial spending on "individual treatment" of the problem, pointing to a more therapeutic type of intervention. An empirical study carried out by Darmon et al. (2004) shows how the funding conditions imposed by government institutions on contract service providers encourage them to normalise clients and use the "institutional" way of defining the problem in their dealings with them (telling them that they should blame themselves), promoting self-control and encouraging acceptance of any working conditions.

The outsourcing of social services, the emphasis placed on market forces in the implementation of measures and the use of performance incentives as a means of regulation are all having significant repercussions on the quality of interventions (see van Berkel in this book). The Dutch government continues to invest substantial amounts of money, but its interventions are geared towards medical-coercive actions aimed at socialising clients and teaching them to accept work as a norm. Having said that, the Dutch have still managed to strike a better balance than the British between the introduction of stricter standards and obligations and the extent of welfare spending on the integration of the individuals in question.

At the same time, the legitimacy of inactive situations is being redefined, resulting in a large percentage of social security claimants being considered to be "normally" unemployed. Consequently, the target group for this type of policy has been widened to include not only the young and the long-term unemployed, but also the disabled and single parents who are dependent on social welfare. There has been a redefinition of the status of various categories of social security claimants and of the legitimacy of people's claim to welfare benefits on the grounds of

---

[21] Since 2003, the "suitable job" concept has been replaced by a "generally accepted job". As a result, welfare recipients, and in particular the long-term unemployed, are now required to accept any job offer made to them, irrespective of their qualifications or previous work experience. In other words, they are obliged to accept any kind of work at all.

[22] There are widespread references in the Dutch press to the concept of '*bezuiniging*' (cutbacks) in relation to the government's recent public policy decisions. Although there has only been a small rise in unemployment, it appears that there is a profound sense of crisis in Dutch society.

age, disability, childcare and widowhood. It seems that the problem is increasingly being evaluated and diagnosed on the basis of an understanding of "inactivity" in terms of individual psychosocial competences (personality failings) as opposed to physical or social problems (inability to work because of one's role as a carer, one's age, illness, etc.).

The situation in Denmark could be said to fall somewhere between the civic contractualism regime and the autonomous citizens regime, although it has tended to follow the Dutch model increasingly closely, particularly since 2001. While on the one hand greater use of coercion is being promoted in order to increase motivation (reduction in training measures, tighter access conditions, more emphasis on guidance and personal skills, abolition of some leave schemes), the Danish are nevertheless continuing to make substantial investments in human capital (individual tailoring of measures and upgrading of skills, involvement of the unemployed in drawing up their job-finding plans). The "moral contract" between the State and society is acquiring a key role, with particular emphasis on the "negotiated" contractual nature of rights and duties. While the level of public spending remains high, the approach varies depending on the social group targeted by the intervention (immigrants and social welfare recipients are subject to more disciplinary measures), a trend that breaks with Denmark's universal welfare tradition.

In any event, it is clear that recent years have seen the inclusion of punitive elements designed to change individual behaviour, coerce people's will or influence their attitudes. The trend is towards a combination of vocational training measures (job training, education, jobs on special terms, etc.) with measures that place more emphasis on "soft skills" (motivation, job-readiness of participants) (Mailand 2005). In addition to the decline in social partners' influence on activation policies, the change in the government's political philosophy since the new liberal government came to power and the gradual increase in the role of market forces resulting from outsourcing activation measures to private enterprises, a key role in this process has also been played by the widening of the principles of activation to cover all excluded people, including people whose problems are not simply a question of difficulty in finding work (e.g. people with mental problems, alcoholics, etc.) (Mailand 2005). This has resulted in the spread of a psychological-therapeutic approach towards job seekers.[23]

---

[23] Firstly, the active measures targeted at unemployed people covered by social security and those who are not covered by social security were brought together under a single Ministry in 2001. Secondly, an aggressive approach to activation (that strengthens the coercive and punitive elements which promote employment as the only way

Autonomous Citizens Regime

This regime is typified by its focus on both individual and collective responsibility with a view to achieving self-determination. The fundamental principle underlying this strategy is the desire to ensure the continued viability of the prevailing welfare model which enjoys a high level of public support. While the job-finding process is still contractualised, in this case the contracts contain a significant degree of reciprocity and many things are left to the individual's discretion. The main focus is on a training-based approach resulting in the predominance of measures geared towards investment in the workforce.

This model is characteristic of Sweden, where high public spending combines with investment in long term employability measures. Activation and the work ethic have been core values of the Swedish welfare system since the beginning of the 20th century. The active measures have traditionally focused on both demand-side interventions (public sector programmes that subsequently shifted to subsidised employment in the private and public sector, temporary jobs, support for business start-ups, wage subsidies for disabled workers) and supply-side interventions (training programmes, education and efforts to influence unemployed people's willingness to work) (see Wadensjö in this book). However, as in Denmark, there has been a substantial decline in the level of benefits and major reforms have been implemented in some parts of the welfare regime. As a result, there has been a gradual increase in the importance attached to supply-side policies (training and motivation of job seekers).

France is positioned somewhere between this regime and the fragmented provision one. The French case is a hybrid one (Barbier *et al* 2006) incorporating aspects of different types of policy depending on the measure's target group. Although public spending on employment policies is lower than in the Scandinavian countries, it has still been significant and has focused mainly on training (training schemes, temporary subsidised employment in the non-profit sector and in the market sector, government as employer of last resort), despite the fact that measures designed to reduce labour costs are becoming increasingly popular (e.g. cutting employer contributions). This "defensive" strategy of subsidised employment, aimed at encouraging labour integration by reducing labour costs, does not have an influence on productivity.

---

of combating the problems associated with exclusion) that was initially used only with young people, has now spread to include unemployed people not covered by social security, immigrants and ultimately all unemployed people.

However, it does appear to have led to a fall in unemployment among low-skilled workers (Cahuc and Zylberberg 2005).

Another aspect that testifies to the important role of the State is the high level of investment in direct job creation schemes that accounted for 41.9% of all spending on active measures in 2003 (Eurostat, June 2005). Furthermore, the French approach to integration, in particular as far as welfare benefit recipients are concerned, aims to promote full access to political, as well as economic citizenship, although a lack of funding has meant that universal access has not been achieved (see Barbier in this book). In the case of the guaranteed minimum income (*Revenu minimum d'insertion* – RMI), the intervention was targeted at various areas (health, housing, counselling, employment and training), but as in the case of the Netherlands, greater weight has been attached to the economic aspects of citizenship since 2004. The RMI is due to be replaced by the new minimum activity income (*Revenu minimu d'activité* – RMA), which places greater emphasis on the economic aspects of this particular welfare intervention. While on the one hand there is therefore a growing emphasis on the economic aspects of citizenship rather than on political or social ones, on the other, France, like Spain, is adopting a less punitive approach to tackling the problem. This is due not only to a partial lack of resources, but also to the French republican tradition and understanding of citizenship. As in the Danish model, penalties vary depending on the programme in question. Penalties are rarely applied to unemployment benefit recipients, but this contrasts with the significant penalties contained in the recent PARE programme. As in Spain, employment policies have tended to be seen as an instrument for improving the how the labour market operates and in some cases this has led indirectly to low-paid jobs and a rise in the number of working poor.

The complex range of different measures in France is intended to promote complementary interventions targeting both the supply side (training) and the demand side (job creation and reducing labour costs). These measures form a marked contrast with the moral-therapeutic approach to intervention in some of the other countries described above.

Fragmented Provision Regime

Spain, Portugal and the Czech Republic cannot be said to have a coherent strategy for disciplining or emancipating individuals, since the low level of spending on employment measures has made it impossible to implement such strategies. Nevertheless, there are certain trends that explain why these countries are classified under different regimes.

Spain belongs to the fragmented provision regime, which is characterised by differences in the approach to and extent of different welfare interventions. Moreno et al. (2003) describe the segmented nature of safety nets in Spain. On the one hand, welfare measures concerning the risk of unemployment and the fight against poverty are very underdeveloped, as are personalised services (the social welfare system is rudimentary and limited, making it similar to the minimalist regime found in countries with a liberal tradition). On the other, universalistic principles are widespread in the pensions, education and public healthcare systems. The decentralised nature of active policy management means that the nature and quality of welfare measures and social interventions varies considerably from one region to another. Furthermore, the criteria for unemployment benefit entitlement draw on various levels and regimes. Finally, there is insufficient co-ordination of the multitude of actors at different geographical, social and economic levels. Consequently, the extremely ineffective administration of these measures is the result of a lack of co-ordination combined with inadequate funding (see Aragón et al. in this book).

Spain's employment policy approach is based mainly on measures designed to promote economic competitiveness (i.e. keeping labour costs in check through offering incentives to work and cutting employer contributions and to a lesser extent through vocational training). As in France, the intervention approach is increasingly focusing on the reduction of employers' social security contributions. In Spain, this is accompanied by ever greater contractualisation of employment measures. The unemployment benefit reforms of 2002 and 2003 introduced a more personalised intervention approach (individual job-finding plans) together with a new definition of a "suitable job" based on a person's personal and professional circumstances and how easy it is for them to travel to and from work. This more individualised approach is intended to promote a positive attitude to work (increasing the unemployed person's involvement in the search for employment) through a personal job-finding plan negotiated with the job seeker. However, a lack of financial and human resources has hindered its effectiveness. Inadequate resources and the top-down approach typical of the implementation of these interventions have meant that plans focus more on job seekers' duties than on regulating the reciprocity of rights and duties between the individual and the community (they are required to look for work, to accept suitable jobs, to take part in specific actions to improve their employability) (see Aragón et al. in this book). While they are presented as a right at a rhetorical level, the plans are in fact an asymmetrical contract that can be used by the public authorities as a disciplinary tool. As such, they increase the discretion available to the public authorities to force people to accept a suitable job. In practice, however, the prevailing structural understanding of poverty shared by Spanish society and the social actors (i.e. an unfair distribution of welfare) (van Oorschot and Halman 2000) means that this scope for coercion is rarely used (see Aragón et al. in this book). There is strong public support in Spain for State Welfare provision and Spanish political culture considers it to be the State's and the family's obligation to help all citizens (del Pino 2005). Del Pino describes how there is a great deal of consensus in Spanish society as far as welfare measures are concerned and major public opposition to any proposed cutbacks. Public spending in this area is also perceived to be insufficient. As a result of these social and cultural factors, the conditionality and greater duties required of welfare recipients by law are in fact rarely enforced in practice.

This is, therefore, a situation where there are not only few obligations, due to welfare reasons, but where economic and political factors mean that rights and State Welfare benefits are limited, although the extent of State intervention varies from one part of the public sector to another.

Minimalist Disciplinary Regime

This regime is characterised by the limited extent of State welfare intervention to protect or support people who are excluded from the labour market and other socially at-risk groups. However, although it is limited, it nevertheless contains a significant disciplinary dimension. The fact that this limited State intervention is geared towards getting inactive people into work can be put down to the weakness of the social actors that represent civil society and the public's highly sceptical attitude towards the unemployed. The approach is therefore based on minimalist interventions designed to ensure that individuals fulfil their duties as citizens. However, the fact that the Welfare State guarantees only limited rights means that by the same token only limited pressure can be brought to bear on citizens. While none of the countries in this study are truly representative of this regime, Portugal and the Czech Republic come closest to this ideal type.

Portugal falls somewhere between this and the fragmented provision regime. The Portuguese case promotes a mix of rights and obligations as opposed to a balance between the two. Hespanha (in this book) describes how the extremely modest scope of redistributive policies has meant that there has been very little pressure to adopt active policies. The limited implementation of active policies can be put down to a number of factors: the low level of welfare protection for the unemployed covered by social security, institutional weakness, bureaucracy and institutional culture, the lack of any tradition of active policies and the lack of human and logistical resources. On the other hand, as in the Czech Republic, anti-poverty programmes are fairly well developed. Public spending has concentrated on the poorest people in society, resulting in a much more developed social welfare system than in Spain.

Although a personalised approach is being promoted, as in Spain, implementation of this type of measure has been severely hindered by a lack of human resources. The individualised approach involves more complex procedures, but staffing levels have not been increased in order to ensure successful implementation. Furthermore, the strongly sceptical attitude of some parts of Portuguese society with regard to these measures has resulted in a major trend towards strengthening fraud control mechanisms and disciplinary measures.

There has been an increase in the use of mechanisms for monitoring, controlling and punishing beneficiaries; beneficiaries' duties are more tightly regulated and the jobs that people find are low-paid ones in the secondary labour market, resulting in high job turnover. This has led to the institutionalisation of a category of "second-class" wage earners and has fuelled the development of a secondary labour market (see Hespanha in this book). At the same time, more individualised measures are being promoted and the areas of participation are being expanded (work, education, training, etc.), as are the target groups (young people, women, aged employed, etc.). As in France and Denmark, the quality of the measures is heavily dependent on the type of programme. Unlike most others, the *Inserjovem* and *Reage* programmes offer beneficiaries more scope to choose the scheme best suited to improving their employability or to find a suitable job.

The Czech Republic is positioned somewhere between the minimalist disciplinary regime and the economic springboard regime. Sirovátka (in this book) describes how this regime has evolved from a continental system to a minimalist liberal regime typified by the low level and limited duration of unemployment benefit. The Czech case shares a number of features with the springboard regime: job seeker training initiatives are few and far between, particular emphasis is placed on the beneficiary's duties and obligations to search for work, pressure is put on people to accept low-paid jobs, a stricter definition of a suitable job has been adopted (which fails to take account of a person's family situation, skills level, or the duration of the job being offered) and the quality of income compensation and interventions is very poor. An individualised understanding of poverty prevails in Czech society, where poor and unemployed people are blamed for their own predicament. As a result, people tend to be sceptical about developing the social welfare system because of the possibility of benefit fraud.

Nevertheless, as in the case of the fragmented provision regime, these coercive principles are not enforced systematically owing to a lack of resources and the ineffectiveness of public employment services. Furthermore, there are big differences depending on the target group. High quality measures with individual action plans are available for young people who are considered to be more adaptable and more in need of motivation. Meanwhile, the measures aimed at the most excluded groups contain more punitive elements and place greater emphasis on getting people into work as quickly as possible. The approach can also be said to be hybrid, since, on the one hand, only a small proportion of the unemployed has access to this kind of measure, while on the other, social welfare provision is considerably more developed and the Czech Republic actually has one of the lowest poverty levels in Europe. Many people are able to claim social welfare benefits for an unlimited period of time and although payments are low, they are adequate.

Consequently, it can be said that this regime makes substantial investments in certain social groups (i.e. the poorest people in society and the young, in order to prevent them from developing a weak work ethic). However, spending on other groups can be described as minimalist, since provision for these groups is either non-existent or of very poor quality. Where substantial investments are made, more emphasis is placed on the beneficiary's duties, as in the civic contractualism regime and disciplinary measures also play an important part in this type of approach.

One of the boxes in the activation regimes table presented above is empty. This is because a social contract that emphasises the social duties of an unemployed or inactive person is incompatible with interventions designed to match the workforce (qualifications, labour costs) to market requirements. In some cases, this is because the match with market requirements is achieved through job seeker training initiatives requiring high levels of welfare spending. In other cases, it is because the matching process focuses on the cost of labour rather than on the workforce's behaviour or attitudes.

Conclusions

The spread of the activation paradigm has had major repercussions, not only for welfare interventions aimed at combating unemployment and economic inactivity, but also for the political regulation of the *social question* and citizenship. According to Jensen and Pfau-Effinger (2005)

[...] the new discourse pertaining to activation is not merely a discourse about rebalancing the relationship between rights and obligations; rather, it contributes to the formulation of new civic virtues – a new role for the citizen – with its accompanying expectations for appropriate behaviour. Thus, new discourses call for a reinterpretation of the role of individuals as citizens (p. 4).

We have seen how citizenship is being redefined in contractual terms and how greater emphasis is being placed on its economic aspects. The moral justification for this shift is based on ethical demands for people to manage their own lives.

The activation paradigm has resulted in a variety of different activation policies in the EU member states. While there are various reasons for this diversity, we have focused on two: the prevailing regulatory benchmarks shaping the representation of unemployment or social exclusion and the social actors considered to be responsible for solving the problem; and the power relationships and (im)balance of power between the various social actors (governance structures). The more individualised interpretations of unemployment steer the public debate towards an intervention style that focuses on correcting personal failings (i.e. moral or personality failings), favouring more coercive and/or therapeutic interventions. Meanwhile, representations that view unemployment as a consequence of economic changes or social factors tend to result in interventions designed to promote training or match the cost of labour to the requirements of the labour market. At the same time, the (im)balance of power between the various social actors and institutions governs how strong (or weak) the position of the unemployed is and shapes the terms of the social contract, i.e. the obligations of the State with regard to the most vulnerable individuals in society and the duties of these people *vis-à-vis* the community.

We have identified a number of prototype activation regimes based on these criteria. In drawing up our classification, the results of activation policies were not our primary consideration (e.g. the activity rate, the proportion of various groups in employment, equality, the number of women in work, etc.). In addition to the methodological difficulties implicit in such an approach (Prieto 2004; Barbier *et al* 2006), it also fails to take into account the different starting points of the various countries. We have therefore concentrated on analysing the principles and trends of the different activation models and on examining their political and ideological modes of regulation (regimes).

One factor shared by these different modes of regulatory and political regulation of activation models is the transformation of the established relationship between work, taxation and social welfare in industrialised societies. The institutionalised relationship between these three factors enabled industrialised societies to consolidate an ethos of modernity characterised by "sovereign" individuals.[24] The recent changes in this relationship do not actually constitute a threat to this regulatory principle of modernity. Instead, the spread of the activation intervention paradigm may be seen as a "radicalisation of modernity" (Giddens 1990) aimed at resolving the contradiction that characterises our post-industrial society. On the one hand, the heteronomy and vulnerability of workers and job seekers is more evident than ever before, especially since the widespread acceptance of the fatalistic discourse of economic globalisation. On the other, there is greater emphasis on the regulatory reaffirmation of ideological demands for individual self-management, whereby individuals are expected to be responsible for their own fate. Perhaps the spread of different forms of the activation paradigm should be understood in this context. The risk is that this paradigm will replace political regulation of the market with moral regulation of behaviour. If this happens, there will be a variety of consequences for citizenship, depending on the activation regime in question.

References

Aust, A. and A. Arriba (2004), "Policy reforms and discourses in social assistance in 1990s: Towards "activation"?, *Unidad de Políticas Comparadas. Working Paper* 04-11.

Ballester, R. (2005), "European Employment Strategy and Spanish labour market policies", Working Papers. Department of Economics. University of Girona, No. 14, pp. 1-31.

Barbier, J.C., N. Samba Sylla and A. Eydoux (2006), *Analyse comparative de l'activation de la protection sociale en France, Grande Bretagne, Allemagne et Danemark, dans le cadre des lignes directrices de la stratégie européenne pour l'emploi*, Research report to the DARES.

Bonoli, G. (1997), "Classifying welfare states: a two dimension approach", *Journal of Social Policy* 26 (3), pp. 351-372.

van Berkel, R. (2000), "Activation in the Netherlands. The increasing hybridisation of policies", *Tijdschrift voor Arbeid en Participatie*, Vol. 21, No. 2/3, pp. 195-217.

---

[24] In modernity, the "individual" is construed as a "sovereign individual", as opposed to a subject of some higher authority (the monarchy, religious or mythical authorities, etc.). Social welfare is guaranteed politically through the institutionalisation of solidarity. Instead of being understood to constitute a state of submission and dependency (as suggested by the activation discourse), it has been interpreted as an essential condition for individuals to exercise their sovereignty (by freeing them from dependency on the market).

Cahuc, P. and A. Zylberberg (2005), "L'impact des réductions de cotisations sociales", *Cahiers francais*, No. 327, pp. 18-22.

Carrasco, C., Alabart, A., Mayordom, M. y Montagut, T. (1997), "Mujeres, trabajos y políticas sociales: una aproximación al caso español", Instituto de la Mujer, Serie Estudios, No. 51, Madrid.

Christensen, E. (2001), "The rhetoric of rights and obligations in Workfare and citizens' income. Paradigms/Discourses in Denmark in a labour history perspective", *Borgerlonsvevaegelsen* (available at: http://www.borgerloen.dk/ kronik/ art053.htm.

Cox, R.H. (2001), "The social construction of an imperative. Why welfare reform happened in Denmark and the Netherlands but not in Germany", *World Politics*, 53, pp. 463-498.

Crespo, E. and Serrano, A. (2005), "De paradoxen van het actieve subject in het discours van de Europese Unie instituties", *Tijdschrift voor arbeid en participatie* 26; 2/3, pp. 111-135. Also in: "I paradossi dell'attivazione nel discorso istituzionale europeo", *La rivista delle Politiche Sociali*, No. 1, pp. 19-47.

Crespo Suárez, E. and Serrano Pascual, A. (forthcoming), "Political production of individualised subjects in the paradoxical discourse of the EU institutions", in R. van Berkel and B. Valkenburg, *Making It Personal. Individualising Activation Services in the EU*, Bristol, Policy Press.

Darmon, I., D. Demazière, C. Frade and I. Haas. (2004), "Formés et formateurs face à la 'double contrainte' des programmes de formation à l'employabilité des chômeurs de longue durée", *Formation emploi*, No. 85, janvier-mars, 2004, pp. 57-75 (also in *Cuadernos de Relaciones Laborales* 2006).

del Pino, E. (2005), "La reforma del Estado de Bienestar Bismarckiano: Instituciones político-económicas, opinión pública y estilo de la reforma de la protección por desempleo en Francia y España", Unidad de Políticas Comparadas (CSIC), Working Paper 05-12. October 2005.

Duman, A. (2005), "Unemployment compensation in Sweden, Germany and the United Kingdom: is there a tendency towards marketisation?, Paper for the ESPANet young researchers workshop.

Ferrera, M. (1996), "The "Southern Model" of Welfare in Social Europe", *Journal of European Social Policy*, 6:1, pp. 17-37.

Gallie, D., and S. Paugam (2000) (eds), *Welfare regimes and the experience of unemployment in Europe*, Oxford, Oxford University Press, 412 p.

Giddens, A. (1990), *Las consecuencias de la modernidad*, Alianza editorial.

Gilens, M. (1999), *Why Americans Hate Welfare: Race, Media and the Politics of Antipoverty Policy*, Chicago, University of Chicago Press.

Goul Andersen, J., A. Guillemard, P. Jensen and B. Pfau-Effinger (2005), *The Changing Face of Welfare. Consequences and Outcomes from a Citizenship Perspective*, Bristol, Policy Press.

Green-Pedersen, C. (1999), "Welfare state retrenchment in Denmark and the Netherlands 1982-99. The role of party competition and party consensus", Paper for the 11th SASE conference, Madison, Wisconsin, 8-11 July 1999.

Guillén, A. and S. Alvarez (2004), "The EU's impact on the Spanish welfare state: the role of cognitive Europeanisation", *Journal of European Social Policy*, Vol. 14(3), pp. 285-299.

Guillén, A., S. Alvarez, and P. Adâo e Silva (2002), "European union membership and social policy. The Spanish and Portuguese experiences", Center for European Studies, Working Papers, Harvard University, No. 85.

Hall, P.A. (1993), "Policy paradigms, social learning and the state; the case of economic policy-making in Britain", *Comparative Politics*, Vol. 25, No. 3, pp. 275-296.

Hamzaoui, M. (2003), "La politique sociale différenciée et territorialisée : activation ou ébranlement du social?", Le minimalisme social au service du marché ou la déconstruction des politiques sociales et leurs effets: analyses et comparaisons internationales, *Cahiers de sociologie et d'économie régionale*, No. 4, pp. 11-27.

Jefferys, S. (2005), Contribution to the round table, changing resources, changing employment? RESORE conference employees' resources and social rights – May 11th 2005 Brussels.

Jensen, P.H. and B. Pfau-Effinger (2005), "Active citizenship: the new face of welfare", in J. Goul Andersen, A. Guillemard, P. Jensen and B. Pfau-Effinger (eds.), *The Changing Face of Welfare. Consequences and Outcomes from a Citizenship Perspective*, Bristol, Policy Press.

Jorgensen, H. (2002), *Consensus, Cooperation and Conflict. The Policy Making Process in Denmark*, Cornwall, Edward Elgar.

Larsen, C. A. (2005), "How welfare regimes influence judgement of deservingness and public support for welfare policy", Paper presented at the International Sociological Association RC19 conference in Chicago on Re-theorizing welfare States: Restructuring States, Restructuring Analysis, September 2005.

Leibfried, S. (1993), "Towards a European Welfare State?", in C. Jones (ed.), *New Perspectives on the Welfare State in Europe*, Routledge, pp. 133-156.

Lewis, J. (1992), "Gender and the development of welfare regimes", *Journal of European Social Policy* 2(3), pp. 159-173.

Lind, J. and I. Moller (2004), "The Danish experience of labour market policy and activation of the unemployed", in A. Serrano Pascual (2004) (ed.), *Are Activation Policies Converging in Europe?*, Brussels, ETUI, pp. 163-197.

Lodemel, I. and H. Trickey (2000) (eds.), *An Offer you Can't Refuse: Workfare in International Perspective*, Bristol, The Policy Press.

Mailand, M. (2005), *Implementing the Revised European Employment Strategy North, South, East and West*, First working paper of the research project: Danish employment policy in a European perspective. Available at http://www.sociology.ku.dk/faos/fnotat58.doc.

Melis, A. (2005), "Dépenses consacrés aux politiques du marché du travail 1998-2003", *Statistiques en bref, Population et conditions sociales*, thème 17/2005.

Moreno, L., M. Matsaganis, M. Ferrera, and L. Capucha (2003), "¿Existe una malla de seguridad en la Europa del Sur? La lucha contra la pobreza en España, Grecia, Italia y Portugal", Unidad de Políticas Comparadas (CSIC), Documento de Trabajo 03-17.

Mósesdóttir, L. (2000), *The Interplay between Gender, Markets and the State in Sweden, Germany and the United States*, Aldershot, Ashgate.

Mosley, H. and E. Sol (2005), "Contractualism in employment services: a socio-economic perspective", in E. Sol and M. Westerveld (2005) (eds.), *Contractualism in Employment Services. A New Form of Welfare State Governance*, The Hague, Kluwer Law, pp. 1-21.

van Oorschot, W. (2000), "Who should get what and why? On deservingness criteria and the conditionality of solidarity among the public", *Policy and Politics*, Vol. 28, No. 1, pp. 33-48.

van Oorschot, W. and L. Halman (2000), "Blame or fate, individual or social? An international comparison of popular explanations of poverty", *European Societies* 2(1), pp. 1-28.

Pfau-Effinger, B. (2005), "Cultural change and the restructuring of European welfare states – the case of care policies", Paper for the ESPAnet conference 2005, University of Fribourg, Switzerland, 22-24 September.

Prieto, C. (1994), "Mercado de Trabajo y condiciones de empleo: comparabilidad societal y poder social de negociación", *Cuadernos de Relaciones Laborales*, No. 5.

Schram, S. (2000), "The medicalisation of welfare", *Social Text* 62, Vol. 18, No. 1, pp. 81-107.

Siaroff A. (1994), "Work, Welfare and Gender Equality: a New Typology", in D. Sainsbury (ed.), *Gendering Welfare-State*, London, Sage.

Sol, E. and M. Westerveld (2005), *Contractualism in Employment Services. A New Form of Welfare State Governance*, The Hague, Kluwer Law.

Vielle, P., Ph Pochet and I. Cassiers (2005), *L'État social actif vers un changement de paradigme?*, Brussels, P.I.E. Peter Lang.

Visser, J. and A. Hemerijck (1997), *A Dutch Miracle: Job Growth, Welfare Reform and Corporatism in the Netherlands*, Amsterdam, Amsterdam University Press.

Walby, S. (2001), "From gendered welfare state to gender regimes: National differences, convergence or re-structuring?", Paper presented to Gender and Society group, Stockholm University, January 2001.

Notes on Contributors

Jorge Aragón Medina is Economist and Director of the 1st May Foundation, a research institute on labour relations, employment and social policies. He is a member of the Economic and Social Council of Spain and author of publications on macroeconomics, the labour market, employment and collective bargaining.

Jean-Claude Barbier is senior CNRS (Centre national de la recherche scientifique) researcher at Matisse (UMR Centre d'économie de la Sorbonne) in the University Paris 1 (Panthéon Sorbonne). His research interests include comparative research about the social protection systems and epistemological and methodological issues of the very practice of comparison. His recent publications include: *La flessibilità del lavoro et dell'occupazione*, Donzelli, Roma (2003); *Le nouveau système français de protection sociale*, La Découverte, Repères, Paris (2004); *Social Policies: Epistemological and Methodological Issues in Cross National Comparison*, Brussels: P.I.E. Peter Lang (2005).

Rik van Berkel is a Researcher and Lecturer at the Department of Interdisciplinary Social Science, Utrecht University. His research interests include unemployment, (comparative) social and activation policies and public governance. His publications include *Active Social Policies in the EU. Inclusion through Participation?* (with I. Hornemann Møller ed.), Bristol, Policy Press 2002; "The marketisation of activation services: a modern panacea?", *Journal of European Social Policy*, 15/4 (together with P. van der Aa 2005).

Pedro Hespanha is Professor at the Faculty of Economics of the University of Coimbra. His main research is on the area of Social Policies. He participated as main researcher in several national and EU research projects and research networks, dealing with active social policies, social exclusion and poverty, employment and unemployment experiences and strategies. He is the scientific coordinator of the Social Development Observatory at the University of Aveiro. Some of his publications are *Entre o Estado e o Mercado, Risco Social e Incerteza: Pode o Estado Social Recuar Mais?* and *A Transformação da Família e a Regressão da Sociedade-Providência*.

Flemming Larsen is associate professor at the Centre for Labour Market Research. Department of Economics, Politics, and Public Administration, Aalborg University. His main topics of research are labour market policies, flexicurity, etc. Some of his most recent publications are (with Thomas Bredgaard): "Employment policy from different angles", Djoef-Forlaget, 2005; (with Thomas Bredgaard and Per Kongshoj Madsen): "Opportunities and challenges for flexicurity – The Danish example", in *Transfer, European Review of Labour and Research*, Vol. 12, No. 1, Spring 2006.

Colin Lindsay is a Research Fellow at the Employment Research Institute, Napier University, Edinburgh, UK. He has published research on a range of issues including: unemployment and job seeking; labour market policies; social networks and social exclusion; the digital divide; and the concept of employability. His current research focuses on modes of governance in activation and regeneration policy.

Mikkel Mailand has been attached to the FAOS since 1996. His research interests are employment policy, industrial relations in Eastern and Central Europe, social partnerships, neo-corporatism and network theory. Among his publications are contributions to the anthologies "Denmark – Status quo or a more self-assured state?" (Bergham Books, 2001) and "Partsstyring i arbejdsmarkedspolitikken – perspektiver og alternativer" (SFI, 2003), as well as the journal articles "Different routes, common directions? Activation policies for young people in Denmark and the UK", *International Journal of Social Welfare*, 2004, and "Social dialogue in Central and Eastern Europe – Present state and future development", *European Journal of Industrial Relations*, 2004.

Lars Magnusson is Vice-rector of Uppsala University and Professor and Chair in Economic History at the same university. He is the Chairman of SALTSA and has published a number of works dealing with the political economy of Europe, the social dimension of Europe and the European Employment Strategy. He is also the author of *An Economic History of Sweden* (2000) and *Mercantilism. The Shaping of an Economic Language* (1994). He is a regular visitor at the European University Institute in Florence and is currently engaged in a project (together with Professor Bo Stråth) on the prospects for a social Europe.

Fernando Rocha Sánchez is a Sociologist and Senior Researcher at 1st May Foundation. He is an author of publications on employment policies, collective bargaining and corporate social responsibility.

Ana Isabel Santana Alonso is a Sociologist and Research Officer in the Employment Department of the Trade Union Confederation of Comisiones Obreras (www.ccoo.es). She is a member of the European Social Dialogue Committee and author of publications on employment, the labour market, gender equality, training/lifelong learning and immigration.

Notes on Contributors

Amparo Serrano Pascual, a PhD in sociology, is a Researcher and Lecturer at the Complutense University in Madrid (Faculty of Political Sciences and Sociology). Her main research interests are comparative employment, social and activation policies; the deconstruction of EU discourses, the political production of individuals in the European Employment Strategy, the knowledge society and the 'new social contract'. Some of her most recent publications are (ed.) *Activation Policies in International Perspective*, Brussels: ETUI (2004), and, with M. Jepsen (eds.), *Unwrapping the European Social Model*, Bristol, The Policy Press (2006).

Tomáš Sirovátka is a Professor of social policy and social work at the Masaryk University (Faculty of Social Studies) in Brno, Czech Republic. His research focuses on social and labour market policies, work-family balance, social exclusion and social inclusion. He has contributed to such journals as *Czech Sociological Review*, *Prague Economic Papers*, *Polish Sociological Review*, *Journal of Marriage and the Family*, *Journal of Comparative Policy Analysis*, *Social Policy and Administration*. He has also edited several books in Czech on Czech social and labour market policy and contributed to some books in English (e.g. Towsend, P., Gordon D. (eds.), *New Policies to Defeat an Old Enemy*, Bristol, The Policy Press, 2002).

Jorge Torrents is a Lecturer in Labour and Social Security Law at the Complutense University of Madrid since 1994, having previously been a researcher for the Spanish Education Ministry (1990-1994). His main research interests are working conditions, collective bargaining, worker representation and European social policy.

Eskil Wadensjö is a Professor of labour economics at the Swedish Institute for Social Research, Stockholm University. In his research he has covered different aspects of labour economics, labour market policy and social policy. Currently his research is mainly focused on immigration and the situation of immigrants and different aspects of social and occupational insurance systems.

"Work & Society"

The series "Work & Society" analyses the development of employment and social policies, as well as the strategies of the different social actors, both at national and European levels. It puts forward a multi-disciplinary approach – political, sociological, economic, legal and historical – in a bid for dialogue and complementarity.
The series is not confined to the social field *stricto sensu*, but also aims to illustrate the indirect social impacts of economic and monetary policies. It endeavours to clarify social developments, from a comparative and a historical perspective, thus portraying the process of convergence and divergence in the diverse national societal contexts. The manner in which European integration impacts on employment and social policies constitutes the backbone of the analyses.

Series Editor: Philippe POCHET, Director of the Observatoire
Social Européen (Brussels) and Digest Editor
of the Journal of European Social Policy.

Recent Titles

No.54 – *Reshaping Welfare States and Activation Regimes in Europe*, Amparo SERRANO PASCUAL & Lars MAGNUSSON (eds.), SALTSA, 2007, 319 p., ISBN 978-90-5201-048-9.

No.53 – *Shaping Pay in Europe. A Stakeholder Approach*, Conny Herbert ANTONI, Xavier BAETEN, Ben EMANS, Mari KIRA (eds.), forthcoming.

No.52 – *Les relations sociales dans les petites entreprises. Une comparaison France, Suède, Allemagne*, Christian DUFOUR, Adelheid HEGE, Sofia MURHEM, Wolfgang RUDOLPH, Wolfram WASSERMANN (eds.), SALTSA, 2006, 243 p., ISBN 90-5201-323-3.

No.51 – *Politiques sociales/Social Policies. Enjeux méthodologiques et épistémologiques des comparaisons internationales Epistemological and Methodological Issues in Cross-National Comparison*, Deuxième tirage/Second Printing, Jean-Claude BARBIER & Marie-Thérèse LETABLIER (eds.), 2006, 295 p., ISBN 90-5201-294-6.

No.50 – *The Ethics of Workplace Privacy*, Sven Ove HANSSON & Elin PALM (eds.), SALTSA, 2005, 186 p., ISBN 90-5201-293-8.

No.49 – *The Open Method of Co-ordination in Action. The European Employment and Social Inclusion Strategies*, Jonathan ZEITLIN & Philippe POCHET (eds.) with Lars MAGNUSSON, SALTSA/Observatoire social européen, 2005, 511 p., ISBN 90-5201-280-6.

N° 48 – *Le Moment Delors. Les syndicats au cœur de l'Europe sociale*, Claude DIDRY & Arnaud MIAS, 2005, 349 p., ISBN 90-5201-274-1.

No.47 – *A European Social Citizenship? Preconditions for Future Policies from a Historical Perspective*, Lars MAGNUSSON & Bo STRÅTH (eds.), SALTSA, 2004, 361 p., ISBN 90-5201-269-5.

No.46 – *Restructuring Representation. The Merger Process and Trade Union Structural Development in Ten Countries*, Jeremy WADDINGTON (ed.), 2004, 414 p., ISBN 90-5201-253-9.

No.45 – *Labour and Employment Regulation in Europe*, Jens LIND, Herman KNUDSEN & Henning JØRGENSEN (eds.), SALTSA, 2004, 408 p., ISBN 90-5201-246-6.

N° 44 – *L'État social actif. Vers un changement de paradigme ?* (provisional title), Pascale VIELLE, Isabelle CASSIERS & Philippe POCHET (dir.), 2006, 355 p., ISBN 90-5201-227-X.

No.43 – *Wage and Welfare. New Perspectives on Employment and Social Rights in Europe*, Bernadette CLASQUIN, Nathalie MONCEL, Mark HARVEY & Bernard FRIOT (eds.), 2004, 206 p., ISBN 90-5201-214-8.

No.42 – *Job Insecurity and Union Membership. European Unions in the Wake of Flexible Production*, M. SVERKE, J. HELLGREN, K. NÄSWELL, A. CHIRUMBOLO, H. DE WITTE & S. GOSLINGA (eds.), SALTSA, 2004, 202 p., ISBN 90-5201-202-4.

N° 41 – *L'aide au conditionnel. La contrepartie dans les mesures envers les personnes sans emploi en Europe et en Amérique du Nord*, Pascale DUFOUR, Gérard BOISMENU & Alain NOËL, 2003, en coéd. avec les PUM, 248 p., ISBN 90-5201-198-2.

N° 40 – *Protection sociale et fédéralisme*, Bruno THÉRET, 2002, en coéd. avec les PUM, 495 p., ISBN 90-5201-107-9.

No.39 – *The Impact of EU Law on Health Care Systems*, Martin MCKEE, Elias MOSSIALOS & Rita BAETEN (eds.), 2002, 314 p., ISBN 90-5201-106-0.

No.38 – *EU Law and the Social Character of Health Care*, Elias MOSSIALOS & Martin MCKEE, 2002, 259 p., ISBN 90-5201-110-9.

No.37 – *Wage Policy in the Eurozone*, Philippe POCHET (ed.), Observatoire social européen, 2002, 286 p., ISBN 90-5201-101-X.

N° 36 – *Politique salariale dans la zone euro*, Philippe POCHET (dir.), Observatoire social européen, 2002, 308 p., ISBN 90-5201-100-1.

No.35 – *Regulating Health and Safety Management in the European Union. A Study of the Dynamics of Change*, David WALTERS (ed.), SALTSA, 2002, 346 p., ISBN 90-5201-998-3.

No.34 – *Building Social Europe through the Open Method of Co-ordination*, Caroline DE LA PORTE & Philippe POCHET (eds.), SALTSA/Observatoire social européen, 2002, 311 p., ISBN 90-5201-984-3.

P.I.E. Peter Lang – The website

Discover the general website of the Peter Lang publishing group:

www.peterlang.com